Heartbeat of Struggle

Critical American Studies Series

George Lipsitz, University of California–Santa Cruz, Series Editor

Heartbeat of Struggle

The Revolutionary Life
of Yuri Kochiyama

DIANE C. FUJINO

Critical American Studies

University of Minnesota Press
Minneapolis • London

All royalties from this book will be donated to the Yuri Kochiyama Fund for Political Prisoners to forward the cause closest to Yuri's heart. We are grateful to Yuri for allowing us to honor her with the establishment of this fund and create this opportunity to support political prisoners; her initial reluctance to include her own name in the title of the fund reflects her humility and commitment to the collective. Those prisoners with critical consciousness and activist practices who seek support from this modest fund, and those who would like to contribute to it, may write to the Yuri Kochiyama Fund for Political Prisoners, P.O. Box 80145, Goleta, CA 93118.

Photographs in this book are courtesy of Yuri Kochiyama, unless credited otherwise.

Published by the University of Minnesota Press
111 Third Avenue South, Suite 290
Minneapolis, MN 55401-2520
http://www.upress.umn.edu

Library of Congress Cataloging-in-Publication Data

Fujino, Diane Carol.
  Heartbeat of struggle : the revolutionary life of Yuri Kochiyama / Diane C. Fujino.
    p.   cm. — (Critical American studies series)
  Includes bibliographical references and index.
  ISBN 0-8166-4592-2 (alk. paper) — ISBN 0-8166-4593-0 (pb : alk. paper)
  1. Kochiyama, Yuri. 2. Japanese Americans—California—Biography. 3. Japanese Americans—New York—Biography. 4. Japanese Americans—Evacuation and relocation, 1942–1945. 5. Asian Americans—Civil rights. 6. Civil rights movements—United States—History—20th century. I. Title. II. Series.
  E184.J3F8335 2005
  979.4'004956'0092—dc22

                                                                              2004026943

Printed in the United States of America on acid-free paper

The University of Minnesota is an equal-opportunity educator and employer.

12 11 10 09 08 07   10 9 8 7 6 5 4 3 2

For my parents, May and the late Yasuo Fujino, and my grandparents, who created a community out of the shackles of the concentration camps.

For Richard Williams and the other political prisoners, who embody the sacrifice and determination of struggle.

For Matef and my other comrades, for practicing the spirit of liberation.

For Kano and Seku and the future generations, for giving us life and hope and a reason to carry on.

Contents

Acknowledgments

The Japanese character for *people* is represented by two leaning strokes mutually supporting one another. If either stroke were missing, the other would collapse.

From the start, this project was a collective effort. First and foremost, I owe a debt of gratitude to Yuri Kochiyama, without whose cooperation this book would not have been possible and without whose lifework this book would not have been necessary. Working with Yuri has been a tremendous honor and responsibility. She has graciously given her time, emotional energy, political and intellectual investment, and archival resources to this project, despite the multitude of nonstop demands on her. Along the way, I learned much from Yuri. I learned about the hidden history of the revolutionary movements and of my own Japanese American community, and I met many activists and expanded my political work. But the most important lesson I gained from Yuri is how to treat people: I was inspired by how she radiates a genuine love for people and exhibits humility, compassion, and generosity in all she does. Yuri has helped me to enhance my own humanity, and for that I am truly grateful.

Yuri's family has been most generous in allowing me to make public their mother/sister/aunt/grandmother's life and part of their own as well. Audee Kochiyama-Holman, Eddie Kochiyama, Jimmy Kochiyama, Tommy Kochiyama, Peter Nakahara, Elizabeth Nakahara, and Akemi Kochiyama-Sardinha granted interviews, offered thoughtful and critical advice, and provided photographs and materials. I especially thank Audee for graciously responding to my many inquiries.

Writing this book facilitated my entry into the lives and homes of many of Yuri's friends and comrades. That I was, time and time again, met with extraordinary hospitality was often a reflection of the respect and love these individuals have for Yuri. I thank those who granted interviews, provided archival materials and photographs, and offered astute comments and critiques: Muhammad Ahmed (Max Stanford), Bolanile Akinwole, Bibi Angola, Richard Aoki, A. Peter Bailey, Norma (Benedetti) Brutti, Marilyn Buck, James Campbell, Bill Epton, Linda Evans, Herman Ferguson, Dollie Fukawa, Mani Gilyard, Nan (Carlson) Grimm, Genevieve Hall-Duncan, Vivian (Martinez) Hardy, Fred Ho, Kazu Iijima, Leslie Inaba-Wong, Kei Ishikawa, Corky Lee, Steve Louie, Wayne and Gloria Lum, Mae Mallory, Monica Miya (Miwako Oana), David Monkawa, Greg Morozumi, Nick Nagatani, Mo Nishida, Ahmed Obafemi, Glenn Omatsu, Dylcia Pagan, Betty Robinson, Sumi (Seo) Seki, Mutulu Shakur, Nyisha Shakur, Victor Shibata, Laura Whitehorn, Steve Yip, and Yuriko (Endo) Yoshihara.

Several of my colleagues provided close readings and offered keen insights that greatly enhanced this manuscript. My deep appreciation goes to Sucheng Chan, who in her usual manner gave honest, direct, and razor-sharp, line-by-line feedback to several chapters, despite constraints on her own time and health. I thank Yolanda Broyles-González, Jon Cruz, Douglas Daniels, Nancy Henley, George Lipsitz, Don Nakanishi, Paul Spickard, and David Takeuchi for their reading of various chapters. The feedback from two anonymous reviewers was exceptionally incisive, and the intellectual discussions with and fine editing of Matef Harmachis improved each page of this manuscript.

The research assistance of Caroline Choi and Sue Park was invaluable to the completion of this project. Special thanks also go to others who shared their labor and resources: Tiffany Arroyo Tabin, Sally Foxen, May Fujino, Brian Hayashi, Masumi Hayashi, Glen Kitayama, Rosa Kurshan-Emmer, Helene Lee, David Li, Patricia Fenwick Miller, Venus Nasri, Arlene Phillips, Cecilia Sapp, Alison Satake, Renee Tajima-Peña, Tofi Tana, and Emily Woo-Yamasaki. Archivists Marjorie Lee of the UCLA Asian American Studies Center, Debbie Henderson and Toshiko McCallum of the Japanese American National Museum, Gary Johnson and Gary Colmenar of the University of California–Santa Barbara's Davidson Library, and staff of the University of California at Berkeley's Bancroft Library provided precious materials.

Book-length projects require funding and leave time. I am particularly grateful to the Japanese American redress activists, whose struggles won a vindication for the wrongful incarceration of thousands of Japanese Americans during World War II and a public education fund for teaching and research, of which I was a recipient through the Civil Liberties Public Education Fund. The American public, through taxes and other resources, also helped fund this project through grants and fellowships from the University of California, Santa Barbara (Academic Senate, Faculty Career Development Award, Regents' Junior Faculty Fellowship, Interdisciplinary Humanities Center, and the Institute for Social, Behavioral, and Economic Research).

It has been a joy working with the enthusiastic and highly professional staff at the University of Minnesota Press. I wish I could thank each by name, but I would be remiss not to recognize the wonderful work of humanities editor Richard Morrison and managing editor Laura Westlund. This book would not have been possible without the support of George Lipsitz. I am grateful to be a beneficiary of his intellectual and political generosity.

My deepest love and respect go to Matef Harmachis, who not only is the biggest enthusiast of this biography but who also provided concrete work on the book and in our home that enabled me to complete this project, despite its many disruptions to our lives. To our beloved sons, Kano and Seku Fujino-Harmachis, who daily remind us of the miracle of life and the reason to struggle forward. And to the Creator of the Universe, who blesses us richly, though not of our own accord, and who made smooth every crooked path in the process of completing this book. There are others, too numerous to name, but whose lives give me strength and inspiration to carry on, including those who provide such loving care to our children, my extended families, my friends and students, and the many activists working for a better world. All these varied people greatly improved the book; any errors are mine alone. It is my hope that this book will capture the spirit and vision of Yuri Kochiyama, and in doing so inspire others to transform their characters and to participate in the collective struggle for justice, as Yuri has done for me and for so many others.

Family Tree of Yuri Kochiyama

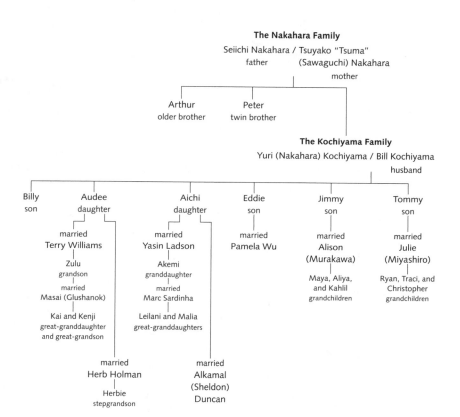

The Nakahara Family

Seiichi Nakahara /   Tsuyako "Tsuma"
father   (Sawaguchi) Nakahara
                         mother

Arthur   Peter
older brother   twin brother

The Kochiyama Family

Yuri (Nakahara) Kochiyama / Bill Kochiyama
                           husband

Billy   Audee   Aichi   Eddie   Jimmy   Tommy
son   daughter   daughter   son   son   son

               married   married   married   married   married
               Terry Williams   Yasin Ladson   Pamela Wu   Alison   Julie
                                                               (Murakawa)   (Miyashiro)
               Zulu   Akemi
               grandson   granddaughter   Maya, Aliya,   Ryan, Traci, and
                                                               and Kahlil   Christopher
               married   married   grandchildren grandchildren
               Masai (Glushanok) Marc Sardinha

               Kai and Kenji   Leilani and Malia
               great-granddaughter great-granddaughters
               and great-grandson

               married   married
               Herb Holman   Alkamal
                                (Sheldon)
               Herbie   Duncan
               stepgrandson

Introduction

Change

On Sunday, December 7, 1941, as bombs fell on Pearl Harbor, Yuri Kochiyama's tranquil and idyllic life changed overnight. This young woman, born Mary Yuriko Nakahara, had just returned from church around 11 a.m. when:

> Not ten minutes after I came home, three tall White men came to our house, showing their FBI cards and asking for Mr. Seiichi Nakahara. I told them, "He's sleeping in the back room. He just came home from the hospital yesterday." They pushed their way right in, went to the back and told Pop to put on his bathrobe and slippers. They whisked him right out. The whole thing took only a couple of minutes and I didn't have a chance to ask anything, not even "Where are you taking him?"[1]

Earlier that morning, as she did each week, the twenty-year-old Sunday school teacher had driven to the Presbyterian church near her home in San Pedro, a port town in south Los Angeles. But that morning, Yuri sensed something was odd. She saw soldiers in uniforms hitchhiking to Fort MacArthur, the nearby military base. One of the soldiers, a high school friend, told her that Japan was bombing Pearl Harbor. She could hardly believe her ears. Although she did not know where Pearl Harbor was located, she understood the implications: America was at war, and Japan was the enemy. At church, Yuri recounted: "The class I had was made up of twelve- and thirteen-year-old junior high school girls, who were a very lively bunch. But as soon as I walked into the church, I could feel the difference. It was something I had never felt before. . . . It was a kind of pall. The superintendent dismissed us early from class and we all crowded into the assembly hall, where he asked if the students were aware that a territory of the United States was being bombed." For Yuri, the only Japanese American among the teachers, the situation was fraught with racial overtones: "I think what happened at that point was that, for the first time, they realized I was Japanese. Before, maybe they just thought of me as an American of Asian extraction. Beyond that it didn't matter to them what I was. Then, all of a sudden, they realized I was part of an enemy country." Afterward, as they did each Sunday, the kids from her class, eight to ten of them, piled into Yuri's car and she took each one home.[2]

Yuri's life was to change in more ways than she could have imagined on that somber drive home from church. After the FBI arrested her father, Yuri, the only one home at the time, rushed to call her mother, who was down the street at her relatives' home. "Mom came running home. She started calling people like my father's lawyer. My aunt [Kondo no obasan], my father's sister, also started calling people. We didn't know anything for a few days," recounted Yuri. It was a frightening and disconcerting time, made more difficult because Mr. Nakahara, it seemed to them, had been singled out for arrest. But unknown to Yuri's family, the FBI and police had arrested numerous Japanese American fisherfolk, produce distributors, farmers, influential businessmen, Shinto and Buddhist priests, Japanese language school teachers, and consular officials, among others. More than seven hundred Japanese Americans, mostly immigrant men, were apprehended within the first twenty-four hours of the Pearl Harbor bombing and thirteen hundred within the first forty-eight hours. By March 1942, some three thousand Japanese Americans had been arrested.[3]

Japanese American community leaders or those with connections to Japan were arrested, even though high-ranking officials in the military and the Justice Department, as well as President Roosevelt, had access to governmental and military reports that the Japanese in the United States posed no threat to national security. Concealed from the public, the FBI and the Office of Naval Intelligence had carried out surveillance on the Japanese American community since at least the early 1930s, a decade before the bombing of Pearl Harbor. In addition, as war with Japan appeared imminent, Curtis Munson of the

State Department and Kenneth Ringle of Naval Intelligence conducted separate investigations into the loyalty of Japanese Americans. These investigations, carried out in the fall of 1941, found no evidence of espionage, sabotage, or fifth-column activity on the part of any Japanese American. In fact, they found the Issei (immigrant or first generation) and Nisei (U.S.-born children, the second generation) to be overwhelmingly loyal to the United States. Yet the arrest and imprisonment of a few thousand Japanese Americans took place immediately following the bombing of Pearl Harbor. Those detained were never charged with any criminal or subversive activities. Nonetheless, the arrests signaled their guilt to the non-Japanese community and suspicions arose among neighbors that these men were spies for Japan.[4]

In a time of patriotic zeal, it was hard for the Nakaharas to contest the widespread rumors that Mr. Nakahara was an enemy spy. Yuri recalled: "The fact that Pop was taken in made it look like he had done something wrong. He was taken in even before they took in all the Japanese fishermen. He was the only Japanese arrested in San Pedro proper. The Japanese community was shocked that even a middle-class Japanese American, living on the White side of town, was suspect. The White people were shocked because we had been friends for so long. They may have thought, 'They're subversive when we thought they were American as apple pie.' And our family was shocked that Pop had been taken. My father's arrest seemed to signify his guilt, and people's attitude toward us changed."[5]

It was not until years later that the family came to understand the reasons for his arrest. Yuri, as well as her brother Peter, relayed that the U.S. government feared that Mr. Nakahara would assist the Japanese military in navigating the Pacific waters because of his interactions with the captains and officers of Japanese naval and merchant ships such as the *Nippon Yusen Kaisha, Osaka Shosen Kaisha,* and *Kawasaki Kisen Kaisha.* Through his small business, he supplied fish and other marine products, rice, canned goods, and produce to Japanese ships that docked in San Pedro harbor, and he entertained Japanese ship officials in his home and at the golf course. That he also sold fish products to U.S. naval ships seemed to bypass the investigative eyes of the FBI. When Mr. Nakahara extended his professional and social networks by taking Japanese naval officers golfing, "the U.S. government feared he was showing them military installations along the roadside; but these installations didn't even exist at the time," said Yuri. Peter Nakahara added that the FBI was suspicious of an intercepted telegram sent to his father from Kichisaburo Nomura, then the Japanese ambassador to the United States and one of the principal peace envoys to this country in the days preceding Pearl Harbor. En route to Washington, D.C., to try to improve U.S.–Japan relations, Nomura had wanted to see his childhood friend. But when urgent business precluded this visit, Nomura sent a telegram mentioning how he regretted they would not enjoy his favorite *sanma* together. The FBI became alarmed that *sanma* was a Japanese code word when, in fact, it was a type of fish that Mr. Nakahara sold. In addition, a decorative piece in the Nakaharas' yard—an extension of Mr. Nakahara's creative design of a cactus garden and fishpond—aroused the suspicions of the police. Yuri recalled: "Pop built this ornamental, wooden lattice that was displayed in the front of our house. On the top of this artwork was a steeple that I guess could be mistaken for a radio antenna. A few times, the police station called implying that this beautiful artwork that my father had built was being used to signal the Japanese military. This was ridiculous."[6]

The FBI records—at least the material not withheld or blacked out—support the general premise of Yuri's and Peter's explanations for their father's arrest, but add a slightly different twist. Following the arrest of Itaru Tachibana, a language officer with the Japanese Imperial Navy, on espionage charges in June 1941, the intelligence agencies found among Tachibana's effects Seiichi Nakahara's name listed on the membership records of Nippon Kaigun Kyokai (the Japanese Navy Association). According to the FBI, Mr. Nakahara explained that he had not joined the organization but that it had made him a member when, upon being solicited, he made a donation to help Japanese navy men and their families. This donation was made some five years before the United States entered World War II. The U.S. government interpreted Issei support of Japan's war effort as evidence of disloyalty. But in light of years of legal discrimination against Japanese immigrants—including being denied naturalized citizenship, banned from purchasing land, and excluded from immigrating to the United States—it is not surprising, observed historian Yuji Ichioka, that many Issei no longer saw a future for themselves in America and turned to support Japan, the country of their birth and citizenship. To equate support of Japan's war efforts—all before the bombing of Pearl Harbor—with sabotage or espionage was a grave error. In addition, some twenty years earlier, Mr. Nakahara had been a leader of the Central Japanese Association of Southern California and the Japanese Association of San Pedro, both affiliated with the Japanese Associations that emerged as the key political organization of Japanese immigrants. Although the Japanese Associations formed in the early 1900s to improve goodwill between Japan and the United States during a period of growing anti-Japanese hostility, the Office of Naval Intelligence listed the Japanese Associations among those organizations most actively involved in subversive activity. This charge was without substantiation. In fact, the Japanese government had little faith that the Japanese immigrants or their children could be trusted. Nonetheless, Mr. Nakahara's affiliations with Japan aroused the suspicions of the FBI and won him a place on the bureau's list of allegedly "known dangerous" Japanese Americans to be picked up in the event of a national emergency.[7]

Like other Japanese Americans whose husbands and fathers were detained, the Nakaharas did not know why Mr. Nakahara was arrested, where he was taken, for how long he would be detained, or when they would get to see him. But in time, with the help of the family lawyer, Mrs. Nakahara found out her husband had been taken to the federal penitentiary on Terminal Island and she began visiting frequently. The family had the added concern of Mr. Nakahara's health problems. Yuri recounted:

Mom was so worried. Pop had just come back from having ulcer surgery; he was really thin. I know Mom talked to the lawyer about getting Pop into a hospital where he could receive proper medical treatment. That's all she worked for in those first days. She must have sent telegrams to everybody from the city council to the president, but it took a couple of weeks to get a response. Finally, my father was taken out of prison and put in the hospital in San Pedro; it was the same ward where they placed seamen who had come back from the Pacific. My father's bed was the only one in the ward that had a sheet around it with a sign: "Prisoner of War." Naturally, we were concerned for Pop's safety and afraid the merchant marines might beat him up. So

Mom begged the hospital to move Pop into a separate room, which they did some time later.[8]

The first time Yuri was allowed to visit her father was five weeks later, on January 13, 1942. But "by then his mind seemed delirious," she recalled. It turned out to be a disturbing and difficult visit. She had gone with her twin brother, Peter, who proudly donned his new U.S. army uniform. "As soon as Pop saw Pete, he didn't think it was his son. He just saw the uniform and thought he was a guard who had come to question him. Pop just quivered," Yuri said. Peter explained that his father said, in Japanese, "You are not my son. You came here to interrogate me." He then addressed his daughter: "When he saw me, Pop asked, 'Who beat you up?' Nothing had happened to me, no one had even touched me. His mind was hallucinating. Maybe they were telling him that your family's been beaten up; maybe they interrogated him harshly; we didn't know what." Frightened by their father's state, Yuri and Peter quickly ended their visit.[9]

The only other time Yuri saw her father was when he was sent home the following week. By then, he was close to dying. Yuri recalled: "When he came home, he couldn't talk at all. He only made guttural sounds. There was no way to communicate with him." The next day, on January 21, 1942, Seiichi Nakahara died in his home.[10]

The effort to uncover the cause(s) of Mr. Nakahara's death has led to various speculations but no definitive answers. Yuri believes that her father, still weak following surgery, died as a result of inadequate medical care during his imprisonment. Elizabeth Nakahara, Peter's daughter, learned from her father that Mr. Nakahara suffered from diabetes, in addition to ulcers and respiratory problems. It is her understanding that the prison authorities refused to administer his diabetes medication, despite Mrs. Nakahara's appeals. A delirious state caused by untreated diabetes could account for Mr. Nakahara's bizarre behavior during his children's visit. Peter Nakahara explained that his cousin, Teek Kondo, believed that Mr. Nakahara had been physically abused. Yet the Nakaharas' family doctor, who had conducted a postmortem examination, did not find any evidence of physical injury. Whether or not physical abuse occurred, Teek Kondo told Peter that Mr. Nakahara endured psychological torture—the authorities would awaken him in the middle of the night, put him under glaring lights, and interrogate him—which could account for his deteriorated physical and psychological health. The death certificate listed "duodenal ulcer" and "hypertrophic cirrhosis of liver" as the immediate cause of death. Although cirrhosis of the liver raises the question of alcoholism, there are other causes for this illness, and there is no indication that Mr. Nakahara had a drinking problem. The FBI files simply state that Mr. Nakahara died in the family home of natural causes. Whatever those causes, it is reasonable to suggest that the conditions of his imprisonment accelerated his death at the relatively young age of fifty-four.[11]

How did Yuri, then age twenty, respond to the loss of her father under what appeared to be preventable circumstances? What is most striking is her lack of response. In the seven months of recordings in her camp diary, which she began three months after her father's death, on the day her family departed for the Santa Anita Assembly Center, Yuri referred to her father only once, on the six-month anniversary of his death. Her comments on July 21, 1942, contained here in full, are sparse and reveal little of her emotions or thoughts: "Pop's birthday. Also his 'farewell' day. Doesn't seem possible that six months could have sped so fast. Just six months ago, after suffering both physically and mentally, death relieved him of pains and hurts, yet. . . . well, perhaps it was for the best. But—guess mom will never forget what hell he went through in the last month of his life." One wonders what Yuri wanted to say following "yet." Did she doubt the official explanation for her father's death? Did she harbor resentment against the U.S. government? Or did the external and internal pressure to demonstrate patriotism, at a time when U.S. society distrusted the loyalty of Japanese Americans, override any possible questioning of the government's actions? Did she choose to suppress any negative feelings because the thought of challenging the government's account caused too much inner turmoil or because she feared the government might read her diary? Perhaps it was easier to focus on how her mother felt, no matter how superficially, than to confront her own ambiguous, perhaps even angry and frightening, feelings. Yuri appears to have coped with her father's death—as well as the traumatic events surrounding the incarceration of West Coast Japanese Americans—by remaining optimistic, even Pollyannaish, and by keeping so busy that any upsetting and contradictory feelings would not surface.[12]

A Biographical Sketch

Today, Yuri Kochiyama is regarded as one of the most prominent Asian American activists to emerge in the 1960s. But at the time of her father's death, she was apolitical, provincial, naive, and ultrapatriotic. In the 1930s, this highly assimilated and popular youth participated in a whirlwind of community service activities, including being an avid sports enthusiast and local journalist, an adviser to multiple preteen girls' clubs, the first girl elected as a student body officer at her high school, and a dedicated Sunday school teacher. But these activities occurred in an apolitical context. Yuri's color-blind worldview did not yet reflect a sophisticated understanding of how social conditions were affected by race, class, gender, or immigration status, even as her life was shaped by these factors. She barely recognized discrimination in her father's arrest and her family's subsequent incarceration.

World War II inaugurated Yuri's racial awakening. For the first time, she began to perceive race discrimination when organizations asked her to leave and the police accused her of spying for Japan. Race and place combined to transform her worldview. Inside the all-Japanese concentration camps, she began to listen to the stories of other internees—stories of hardship, racism, resentment, and anger. These testimonies, along with the undeniable differential treatment of Japanese Americans, triggered Yuri's awareness of race discrimination and other social problems. By contrast to her previous service work, during and after World War II, her activities took on a racial focus. From inside the Jerome, Arkansas, concentration camp, she organized an expansive letter-writing campaign to some three thousand Japanese American soldiers. And in New York, she and her husband, Bill Kochiyama, organized a group to provide recreational and housing services to Japanese and Chinese American soldiers en route to the Korean war front.

Still, her newly acquired racialized worldview did not lead to political protest. As she articulates, "It didn't make me political because I didn't understand the politics of why these things happened."[13] But by following newspaper accounts of the Civil Rights Movement and inviting local political speakers to her family's weekly open houses, she slowly developed an oppositional political consciousness. It was only in 1960, when her family moved from midtown Manhattan to Harlem, with its predominantly Black population, that her oppositional consciousness turned into political protest.[14] She began participating in the Civil Rights Movement encircling her in Harlem, working to improve education for inner-city children, including her own six. She also joined in demonstrations protesting the racially discriminatory hiring practices of construction crews building the Downstate Medical Center, a protest organized by the Congress of Racial Equality (CORE).

As a result of courtroom hearings for Yuri and several hundred others arrested for using their bodies to block the entry of construction trucks at the CORE demonstrations, she met the person who would revolutionize her life—Malcolm X. Despite her initial disagreement with Malcolm over his "harsh stance on integration" and her appeal for the "togetherness of all people," expressed in her first letter to Malcolm, there followed a fairly rapid transformation in Yuri's political ideology and practice. At Malcolm's invitation, she began attending his weekly Organization of Afro-American Unity Liberation School, where speakers and readings introduced her to the history of colonialism in Africa, the political economy of slavery, and contemporary manifestations of institutionalized racism. She previously viewed race discrimination as an aberration in a society committed to the "liberty and justice for all" promised in the Pledge of Allegiance. Such irregularities could be eradicated through reforms to the system. But the Liberation School challenged the reformist, integrationist, and nonviolent beliefs contained within her civil rights ideology. As she questioned the possibility of gaining equality and liberation in a system built on racism, she began to fathom an entirely different system—one that was not only antiracist but also anticapitalist.

By the time of Malcolm's assassination in 1965, a mere sixteen months after their introduction, there is evidence of Yuri's politics embracing the eclectic radicalism and revolutionary nationalism represented by Malcolm X. By the late 1960s, Yuri was involved with the Republic of New Africa, known for its ultimate nationalist and controversial position advocating a separate Black nation in the U.S. South. As the FBI intensified its repression of Black militants and arrested many of her comrades and friends, Yuri began what would become her most steadfast area of struggle—support for political prisoners. As she had done with the Nisei soldiers a quarter century earlier, Yuri felt the internal pressure, almost an obsession, to stay up until the wee hours of the night writing letters to prisoners, writing articles for Movement publications, and organizing events to defend political prisoners. She maintained detailed, up-to-date records such that she became a major resource of information on political prisoners. She also became situated as one of the first persons prisoners called when released. And with her large political and social networks, she created a wide support base for political prisoners. Yuri has a profound respect for those willing to risk their own lives to forward political struggle. "Political prisoners . . . are the heartbeat of struggle," she has proclaimed. "[They] were the most vocal and visible community activists. They were the most dedicated. They educated and politicized their communities. They are leaders. . . . They are the symbols of resistance and courage. We honor them by remembering them, that their deeds live on."[15] Yet, it was Yuri whom many regard as that "heartbeat of struggle"—pumping life and energy into the Movement and sustaining the struggle, especially at times when it seemed to be dying.

When the Asian American Movement began to emerge in the late 1960s, Yuri was not only one of its earliest participants but also one of its foremost political mentors. The predominantly youthful and budding activists sought out Yuri to provide Movement history, key grassroots contacts, and inspiration to their activist work. She was particularly renowned for her connections with Malcolm X and the radical Black Power Movement and her abilities to connect Black and Asian issues and social movements. She also became known for her hospitality, her warmth and friendliness, her incredible memory for people and interest in others, and her ability to tell interesting, compelling, and hilarious stories about political happenings. In the late 1960s and early 1970s, she was especially involved in opposing the war in Vietnam as an imperialist conquest, supporting struggles for ethnic studies, condemning nuclear proliferation, especially in light of U.S. atomic bombings of Hiroshima and Nagasaki, and in the 1980s, struggling for Japanese American redress and reparations.

Despite a debilitating stroke in the late 1990s, Yuri remains an energetic, fervent fighter for justice and liberty for all. She is a fierce antiwar activist in the post–September 11, 2001, environment. She continues to struggle for Asian and Black liberation, among a great many other issues. And her top priority continues to be building support for political prisoners. After seven decades of community service and four decades of political activism, Yuri is regarded as one of the most influential and consistent U.S. political activists.

One as Loved and Claimed as Yuri

"Movement activists increasingly lost the ability to relate to one another in human terms," laments Charles Payne, in his study of civil rights organizing in Mississippi.[16] By contrast, Yuri Kochiyama's emphasis on the interests, feelings, and concerns of the individual, even as she worked to collectively and militantly contest institutionalized racism and state power for more than forty years, provides a powerful contrast to Payne's concerns. When debating political ideas or tactics at meetings, Yuri takes care to phrase her opinions so as not to offend or alienate others. In addition to strategizing about legal options for politicized prisoner David Wong, Yuri reminds the group to send cards for Wong's upcoming birthday.[17] Following the assassination of Malcolm X, Yuri's most influential political mentor, she reached out to his family in both personal and political ways. To this day, Malcolm's oldest child, Attallah Shabazz, refers to Yuri as an aunt, and while in New York City for her mother's funeral in 1997, Shabazz made several phone calls to Yuri.

The qualities that endear Yuri to others also heighten the tensions involved in writing a biography about one as loved and claimed as Yuri Kochiyama. That Yuri is loved is apparent—she has a knack for making people feel special; for remembering the backgrounds, interests, and names of those she recently met; and for working with intense drive and commitment in service to others for more than seventy years. Since her youth in San Pedro, in the 1920s, people saw her as someone extraordinary, as someone in whose honor decades later childhood friends felt compelled to organize not one, but three, reunions. *Claimed,* by contrast, is an odd choice of word to describe a person. But as I spoke with many people, those close to her as well as those who had never met her, I detected a desire in them for Yuri to represent their dreams and aspirations, to fit the political ideologies and practices imaged in their own minds. Childhood friends claim her warmth, friendliness, and deep community service commitments. Civil rights activists claim her liberal political allegiances. Revolutionaries claim her radical beliefs and militant stances. Like the *Rashomon* effect depicted in Akira Kurosawa's film, people see skewed visions of Yuri's personality and commitments.

That so many different views of Yuri exist stems, in part, from her tendency to listen attentively to others and to refrain from inserting her own opinions. Many think Yuri agrees with them, even when she opposes their views or winces at the arrogance of their remarks. But in private conversations, Yuri has strongly asserted her own oppositional beliefs. Among those who know her well, "stubborn" is a common descriptor.

As a result of the diversity of claims on Yuri's story, many expectations have been placed on *Heartbeat of Struggle*. There are at least six major sources of these claims. First, Yuri's friends and family want her humanness and interpersonal style to be conveyed. They do not want her to become the object of intellectual inquiry but rather for her personality, quirks, and humanity to be highlighted. In reviewing a draft of an article I had written about Yuri, a close friend of hers reproached me for failing to represent adequately the specialness, the liveliness, and the enormity of character contained within his admiration of Yuri.

Second, Yuri's comrades want to ensure that her political ideologies and practices are correctly represented. But even as Yuri identifies as a revolutionary nationalist, her politics are complex, containing revolutionary and reformist, nationalist and internationalist, and separatist and integrationist elements. It seems common for people to see only one or two sides of her politics, in part because that is what Yuri conveys to them and in part because their own desires shape their interpretation of her.

Third, Yuri's children have particular claims on how they wanted their mother's story portrayed to a public readership. In general, I found her family to be generous, cooperative, and forthright about their views of Yuri and about problems in the family. Still, there were times when, as they saw in print information they had verbalized to me, they wanted a different framing of the story or wanted the material excluded altogether. One of Yuri's children was reluctant to be interviewed, and his gut instinct not to participate was reinforced when some of the material on past family conflict reopened old wounds. Moreover, Yuri and several of her children have sharply conflicting views on how Yuri's political involvement affected the family. It is understandably difficult for family members to have their story made public, especially when one is as candid as Yuri in disclosing her private life.

Fourth, young people, including Asian American youth, are hungrily searching for role models, particularly in a community devoid of public political (s)heroes. Yuri fits the bill. Her credentials as an activist not only demonstrate a long-standing and principled commitment to justice, but her work for Black and Latino liberation provides a paradigm for antiracist organizing that resists gains made at another group's expense and thereby subverts the model minority image.[18] In addition, her warmth, friendliness, humility, and interest in others' lives make those with whom she interacts feel affirmed, even special. While this biography offers a sympathetic portrayal of Yuri, there is also an effort to demythologize, for example, her relationship with Malcolm X and to refrain from shero worship in order to show the complexity of struggles and decisions and the triumphs and the failures facing activists.

Fifth and significantly, Yuri has her own investments in this biography. While she has a remarkable ability not to impose her desires on this book, giving the author the self-determination to carve out her own interpretations, it is also understandable that Yuri is concerned about how her life is portrayed in a very public and more or less permanent medium. It was particularly difficult for her to hear criticism of her parenting, even as she was able to tolerate public criticism of her political practice.

Finally, academic claims diverged from those of the previous types. In contrast to the criticism of not being subjective enough in praising Yuri's accomplishments, academic reviewers seek a more objective work with greater attention to context and interpretation.

From the beginning, these varied and at times competing claims made it clear that this biography would not fulfill everyone's expectations and longings. It is my hope that others will write about various aspects of Yuri's life and help round out the inevitable biases contained in any one book. Already, there is a documentary on her life, a biography published in Japan, and her own recently released memoirs.[19] In constructing Yuri's biography, there were certain objectives that I strove to achieve. I always envisioned *Heartbeat of Struggle* as a *political* biography, one that focused on Yuri's political life, the development of political consciousness, the struggles and joys contained in her activism, and the significance of her political contributions. But given the ways that public and private lives are mutually constitutive, I would be remiss were I to exclude a discussion of her family and personal life. While I could have written more extensively on Yuri's private life, I consciously chose to focus on elements of her family background that illuminated her political work.[20]

It was important to me to keep Yuri as a person with her own interests and styles, with agency and consciousness in the forefront of my analysis. I did not want her reduced to an object of inquiry, of my probing, and of my interpretations and contextualization. To accomplish this, I had to wrestle with finding a balance between the relative emphasis placed on Yuri's voice and on my own as author. My initial plan was to write this book as an oral history narrative; my role was to facilitate the writing of Yuri's story in her own words. As I began the work, however, I encountered several problems with this approach. Writing in the first person placed an unfair burden on Yuri to explain the histories of the social movements in which she worked. Yet, she made it clear that her priority lay with the day-to-day activities involved in creating social change, even as her life is part of social movement history. It was my job to piece together, contextualize, analyze, and research her life, but relegating my ideas to the endnotes and to introductory and concluding chapters created a disjointed and awkward manuscript. In addition, while Yuri provided wonderfully descriptive material, there was a need to interpret her narrative and her work. Telling the story in Yuri's humble words, for example, rendered it impossible to discuss the significance of her activism. Assessing the accuracy of her statements against archival materials, secondary sources, the memories of others, and her earlier writings and speeches enhanced the credibility of the book. As I saw problems with treating this story as a first-person narrative and as I learned that Yuri's own story would be published in her memoirs, I decided to approach this book as a more traditional third-person biography.

Methodological Considerations: Creating Yuri's Story

Despite the biographical framework, I wanted this book to reflect my belief, as a feminist-humanist scholar, in people's abilities to understand their own lives and in the importance of individuals from marginalized groups giving voice to their own experiences.[21] Oral history as a means for centering the experiences of the disenfranchised, of empowering those who have been marginalized by the traditional writers of history, provided a particularly useful methodology.[22] Historian Gary Okihiro observed: "Oral history is not only a tool or method for recovering history; it also is a theory of history which maintains that the common folk and the dispossessed have a history and that this history must be written."[23] Certainly, the history of resistance, especially resistance by Asian American women, has been ignored and overshadowed by the emphasis placed on the privileged as well as by the way the model minority image, which emerged in the mid-1960s during a period of intense political struggle, functions to promote nonresistance as a pathway to upward mobility.[24]

Part of the richness of this book comes from Yuri giving her consent and cooperation to the project. In fact, *Heartbeat of Struggle* is based on the most extensive set of interviews conducted with Yuri by any U.S. activist, scholar, writer, or cultural worker. From December 1995 to March 1998, I spent five weeklong visits with Yuri. All the interviews were conducted in her home in Harlem, except for one week when Yuri was speaking in Santa Barbara, California, during which time I interviewed her in my home. I stayed at Yuri's home each visit, save the first trip, which enabled me to participate in her daily activities, to observe her habits and interpersonal interactions, and to accompany her to numerous Movement events, as well as to help with her work.

Staying in Yuri's home simultaneously facilitated and hindered the interview process. I gathered a tremendous amount of information through observation, noticing how Yuri conducted her life, seeing the huge number of phone calls and requests she received on a daily basis, discerning the subtle ways she was able to ask for help, and observing how much more rigid and less animated she was during our formal, tape-recorded interview sessions. I also discovered, however, that my constant presence made it easy to postpone the interviews, which took a lower priority for Yuri than her activism. This was particularly evident the first time I stayed at her home, which occurred in 1997, a few months after her stroke. She was adjusting to physical limitations, had frequent doctor's appointments, and fatigued easily. She was annoyed by the slow pace at which she had to work and was understandably preoccupied with attending to her Movement activities. Still, I became frustrated at the limited number of interview hours in which we engaged. Thereafter, I learned to set a schedule with Yuri before traveling to New York, and the interview process proceeded much more smoothly. During one trip she generously spent every day being interviewed by me, although other people had extensively interviewed her during the preceding three weeks and even during my visit. Needless to say, she was sick and tired of talking about her life.

I am grateful to Yuri for the amount of time she has spent telling me stories about herself and the social movements in which her life is embedded, totaling thirty-four hours of recorded interviews, in addition to hundreds of hours of informal conversations and interactions in person and by telephone during and after my trips to New York. The oral history interviews and participant observations have enabled me to insert Yuri's own words, including some rather lengthy quotations, into the text. Even as I interpret her motivations, choices, and actions, I have tried to convey Yuri's interpretations of her life and to juxtapose the divergent views of others or of myself as author, when relevant.

It was also my responsibility as biographer to conduct the necessary research to augment and assess Yuri's remembrances. I conducted formal interviews with thirty-seven people (all four of her living children, her sole surviving sibling, a niece, and thirty-one friends or political associates), some in person and some by telephone, for a total of more than sixty-five hours of recorded interviews. This was in addition to countless hours of informal conversations with numerous others. Most of these audiotaped interviews—and all of my interviews with Yuri—were transcribed. For the ones that were not transcribed verbatim, I relied on my extensive notes taken during our interviews and transcribed the specific sections needed for the book. As well as providing information by which I could verify Yuri's narrative, these interviews filled gaps in my understanding of her life, especially in those areas she chose not to discuss in detail.

I also obtained primary sources, including Yuri's World War II diary, War Relocation Authority records on those incarcerated in U.S. concentration camps, the Kochiyama family's annual newsletters, FBI files, newspaper articles, a complete set of Yuri's class notes at the Organization of Afro-American Unity Liberation School, scores of her speeches, and a complete set of *Asian Americans for Action* newsletters and other original social movement documents. These primary source materials facilitated my understanding of Yuri's views, and others' views of her, at specific points in time, with greater independence from the teleological reinterpretations of events that tend to occur over time. I also conducted an extensive search for secondary sources to assist my contextualization of Yuri's experiences. Some sources were readily available, such as materials on the Japanese American incarceration during World War II. But others were obscure and difficult to locate, such as Imari Obadele's books and pamphlets on the Republic of New Africa. In many cases, our activist networks, in addition to valuable library resources, proved useful in locating materials.

While *Heartbeat of Struggle* represents, to my knowledge, the first U.S. biography of an Asian American woman activist, the biographical genre seemingly contradicts Yuri's life philosophy. In dedicating herself to justice and equality, Yuri believes it takes masses of people to create social change. Neither she nor I believe in constructing a "cult of personality," that is, putting the individual, no matter how charismatic, above the collective struggle. Preeminent intellectual and activist Noam Chomsky, who deeply deplores the biographical genre, told his biographer: "I'm not happy with the personalized framework. Things happen in the world because of the efforts of dedicated and courageous people whose names no one has heard, and who disappear from history. I can give talks and write because of their organizing efforts, to which I'm able to contribute in my own way."[25]

Yet, it is precisely the personalized framework that allows for an exploration of the dialectical relationship between social movements and the individuals who compose the collective. Many social movement scholars have argued convincingly for the need to reinsert social psychological and biographical dimensions of protest.[26] While I chose not to explicitly frame Yuri's story within social movement theory, this study of a longtime political activist contributes to the understanding of the ways political opportunities and available resources facilitate activism, the ways activists cognitively frame their causes and activities, the development of political consciousness, the role of collective identity in social movements, and individual motivations for collective action, among other issues. In short, Yuri's life and work, as seen in *Heartbeat of Struggle,* are positioned in conversation with resource mobilization, political process, framing, and new social movement theories.[27]

Despite their individual analysis, biographies provide material to complicate and nuance the study not only of social movements but of history itself. By documenting Yuri's involvement in antiracist, anti-imperialist movements, *Heartbeat of Struggle* contributes to the collective understanding of how modern ideas about race are rearticulated over time, particularly through political contestation. In their classic book on racial formation, Michael Omi and Howard Winant view "race as an unstable and 'decentered' complex of social meanings constantly being transformed by political struggle." Just as "the black movement redefined the meaning of racial identity, and consequently of race itself, in American society," Yuri's political work helped transform ideas about race in the U.S. context. In particular, her practice and cognitive framing of racial issues were part of the larger social movements that produced paradigmatic shifts in the sociological study of race. Political protest activities helped propel race thinking from ethnicity theories, with their focus on identity and assimilation, to class- and nation-based theories that emphasize power relations and the need for structural transformation of oppressive systems, namely, capitalism, imperialism, and racism. In turn, the changing social context shaped Yuri's racial and political consciousness, and moved her from political apathy to awareness to activism. By connecting Yuri's life to the stories of Japanese Americans and of Third World social movements, *Heartbeat of Struggle* becomes the narrative and analysis of the collective as well as the individual.[28]

A Note on Terminology

The selection of vocabulary to refer to ethnic and racial groups is a complex and contested enterprise. While a variety of terms is used to signify people of African descent living in the United States, I chose the term *Black people*. *People* is appended because, in my mind, the harsh objectification and subordination of this group require that we set their humanity in our consciousness. *Black* was selected, despite my objections to linking a people with a color rather than a land base, because it is the word Yuri most frequently uses and it is also the least ideologically polarizing term. The word *Black* has historical roots in the revolutionary and Black Power movements of the 1960s and was used to affirm a militant racial identity by inverting its negative connotations. The terms *New African, African,* and *African American* are associated with distinct ideological positions on the Black nation question; namely, that of a Black nation in the U.S. South, of Africa as the land base for Africans worldwide, and of Black people working toward liberation as part of the U.S. working class, respectively. Although Yuri advocates the first position, I believe the content of this book should reflect her overarching opposition to polarization. Thus, the selection of the term *Black people.*[29]

In a much less controversial position, *Asian American* is used throughout this book to refer to people of Asian descent living in the United States. The term has political roots, emerging from the Asian American Movement in the late 1960s, and is strongly preferred by activists and Asian American studies scholars to the older, more objectifying term *Oriental.* The term *Japanese American* is used to denote that Japanese in the United States have a history and culture distinct from White Americans, other Asian Americans, and people in Japan. At the same time, I use *Japanese American* synonymously with Japanese and Asian American synonymously with Asian, given the transnational flow of people, ideas, cultures, resources, and capital across nation-state borders. Here context provides cues about the group, most often those living in the United States, to which I am referring. Finally, I use the Japanese-language generational terms—Issei, Nisei, and Sansei—because U.S. labor practices and U.S. and Japanese migration policies created distinct generations of Japanese Americans, each with its own cultural patterns. The Japanese word *Nikkei* is also used interchangeably with *Japanese American.*

When discussing social movements, I frequently use the vernacular term "the Movement." Certainly, one can problematize the use of such an all-encompassing, homogenizing term. But in conveying Yuri's story, I chose to align with the wide usage of this phrase to refer to multifaceted and nonspecific social movements in a manner that reflects her colloquial language. Again, the context provides cues about the particular social movement being discussed.[30]

Finally, the choice to refer to the subject of this biography by her first name came about when, in reference to a draft of an article I had written, one of her comrades remarked that using her last name was so distancing and aloof—precisely the opposite persona of Yuri, who radiates warmth, closeness, and a preference for nonhierarchical relations. It is my hope that *Heartbeat of Struggle* conveys the vitality and values of its subject in both content and form, although the written word cannot do justice to someone as complex, contradictory, compassionate, and committed as Yuri Kochiyama.

1

A Color-Blind Patriot
in Prewar America

The FBI's intrusion into Yuri's family's life did not end with Mr. Nakahara's death. Yuri recounted: "As soon as the FBI heard the report of his death, we got a phone call from them and were told that anyone who came to the funeral service would be under surveillance. The Japanese people came in from Los Angeles, twenty miles away despite a five-mile travel ban. And some of the fishing folks who were still left in Terminal Island and the farmers from the San Pedro hills came, too. Even our Caucasian neighbors attended. And sure enough, the FBI was right there in front of the funeral parlor." The Nakaharas, who considered themselves the paragon of American patriotism, were shocked to discover years later that the FBI had been watching their family for, as Yuri asserts, more than two decades. This was in addition to the daily FBI visits since Mr. Nakahara's arrest:

> Starting the day after they took my father, the FBI were in my house every single day searching through every closet and drawer, going through books, notebooks, papers, and personal letters, especially from servicemen. I had been writing to my White friends in the army because so many hometown guys I knew had immediately volunteered. Years later, I found out that the FBI had sent letters to each of the army friends I had written to, requesting that they stop corresponding with me because my family was suspect. [At the time,] I never knew why many didn't write back. After the war was over, they told me the FBI sent them a letter that my father and family were suspect and warned them not to communicate with me.[1]

The Nakahara family not only had to cope with Mr. Nakahara's condition, harassment from the FBI, and isolation from neighbors and friends, they also experienced the uncertainty, fears, and trauma that virtually every Japanese American underwent after the bombing of Pearl Harbor. Initially, the newspapers urged the public not to jump to conclusions about Japanese Americans. However, as Yuri often states, "There is a saying that 'the first casualty of war is truth.'" The highest U.S. military officials were soon broadcasting misinformation about subversive activities by Japanese Americans. Throughout the first half of 1942, until Japanese Americans were removed to concentration camps, stories about the alleged national security threat of Japanese Americans filled newspapers and the airwaves. The *Los Angeles Times* ran the following headlines from December 8, 1941, through late February 1942: "Jap Boat Flashes Messages Ashore," "Enemy Planes Sighted over California Coast," "Two Japs with Maps and Alien Literature Seized," "Caps on Japanese Tomato Plants Point to Air Base," and "Japs Plan Attack in April." Although the articles were mainly about fabricated events, it was hard for Japanese Americans to defend themselves against the onslaught by virtually every sector of U.S. society. As the press fanned the flames of racism, animosity toward Japanese Americans grew. Yuri has described the situation in numerous speeches:

> Japanese Americans began losing jobs, feeling unwanted in schools, facing hostility in their neighborhoods, undergoing surveillance wherever they went. Bank accounts were frozen by federal orders and many Japanese-owned businesses folded. Some stores would not sell provisions or provide services to Japanese. Japanese language schools were closed. FBI roundups were everyday occurrences. Civic, business, professional, and religious leaders were taken to jail for interrogation. There was a five-mile travel ban and an 8 p.m. curfew—imposed only on the Japanese, not the Germans or Italians.[2]

Strong agitation against Japanese Americans came from the American Legion and the Native Sons of the Golden West, primarily for racist reasons, and from agribusiness groups, who saw Japanese American farmers as economic competitors. Almost every church and civil rights group, including the national American Civil Liberties

Union, was silent. Radical groups like the Communist Party likewise turned their backs on Japanese Americans, though a few progressive and radical organizations opposed the forced removal. To their credit, the American Friends Service Committee (a Quaker organization) and the Socialist Party denounced the forced dislocation, and some non-Japanese individuals provided friendship and material assistance to the Issei and their families. The lack of organized support for Japanese Americans, in conjunction with the governmental, military, media, business, and public attacks on Japanese Americans, created conditions of isolation for the numerically small population of Japanese Americans. It was this climate, molded in an era before the Civil Rights Movement created a mass consciousness of resistance, that made it difficult for Japanese Americans to collectively protest their incarceration.[3]

Racism and wartime hysteria were taking their toll on the Japanese American community. Families were losing material goods, psychologically and physically distressed, and uncertain about their future. Yuri's family, in addition to coping with Mr. Nakahara's imprisonment and death, had to deal with administering the family business. Yuri's older brother, Art, had the responsibility of maintaining the business, making sure employees were paid, and then closing the market after the banks froze their accounts. In the meantime, Peter returned from UC Berkeley. Yuri recalled: "The Japanese were asked to leave the campus. But even getting home was an ordeal because the ticket agents at the bus and train stations refused to sell him a ticket. We just told him to come home any way he could. Years later I found out that a White San Pedro school friend drove him all the way from Berkeley to San Pedro."[4]

As soon as he returned, Peter abided by what he considered his patriotic duty, even during a period of great difficulty for his own family: "I tried to volunteer for the Marine Corps, but they refused to take me. I then volunteered for the navy, but they also refused to take me. Finally, the army said they'd take me under the draft, providing I had my mother's consent since I was under twenty-one. . . . When I asked my mother if she would consent, she said, 'Yes, if that's what you want to do.' But she was concerned that she would never see me again. She thought I would get killed in the army, and she looked very sad." Art also tried to enlist but was declined for health reasons. Some may wonder why the army accepted Peter when his father was in prison as, according to the FBI, a "known dangerous" immigrant. Yuri reasoned: "It seems the decision depended on the local army board, and because we had lived in San Pedro for so long, they trusted our family. The local draft board saw Pete as a Japanese American and not as the enemy."[5]

In contrast to her previously idyllic life, Yuri began encountering anti-Japanese incidents on a daily basis. She noticed, for example, that Peter, like most Nisei soldiers, was treated differently from White GIs: "When Pete was leaving San Pedro for training in Wyoming, I went with him to the train station. I'll never forget it. He was in uniform and so gung ho about being in the American army. I had just said good-bye to him and was turning to go out of the station when this White guy came up to me and said, 'Damn, how could they let him in? Was that a member of your family?' I was wondering why he asked. Then he said, 'Isn't he a Jap? Aren't you a Jap? They shouldn't let anyone like that in the American army.'" Even friends and neighbors treated Japanese Americans differently. "Being friendly to the Japanese was considered unpatriotic and carried the stigma of being labeled 'Jap lovers,'" observed Yuri. "So many Americans shied away from their longtime Japanese friends and neighbors." Some abruptly ended long-standing friendships. Others, knowing the Japanese Americans would soon be leaving, took advantage of the situation and bought Japanese belongings—china, furniture, large appliances, even agricultural land—at abusively low prices.[6]

In early 1942, most of the organizations for which Yuri volunteered as an adult counselor requested her resignation. "Even the YWCA asked me to leave, which surprised me because the Y was a Christian outfit," she recounted. "They said: 'I'm sorry, but there have been complaints when they found out you're of Japanese background and that your father's been taken in. This is the Y and we have many meetings. The military and wives of military meet here. So I'm sorry you have to leave.' And here I was teaching first aid there." When Yuri drove youth to the beach for summer camp, she was told, "If there's one complaint, if one mother feels ill at ease under your counseling, you'll have to leave." During this period, Yuri was invited to serve on the planning committee for a San Pedro High School alumni gathering:

The committee was very nice, one of the few groups that didn't say, "People may not trust you because you're Japanese." But I remember this one incident with the police. The war had just begun. I was sitting at the Hamburger Hut in midtown San Pedro, which was a hangout for many high school students and alumni. The Alumni Committee had made nice posters, in all different colors, to announce an upcoming dinner-dance fundraiser. I had gone there to see if they would display the posters to advertise the event. I remember saying "hi" to a lot of the people there and asking if I could put up the posters. All of a sudden, two police officers came in and demanded, "What are you doing?" I said, "Oh, these are high school alumni posters." They said, "Wait a minute. She could be signaling to her people. We're taking the posters and you're reporting to the police station." I was shocked and scared and didn't know what to do. All the students eating there were surprised too. Though I knew many of them, no one said: "She's okay, I know her" or "She writes for the paper." There was absolute silence. Only one person spoke out on my behalf—and he was a total stranger. The tall short-order cook told the police, "I don't see anything wrong with what she's doing. It's just a poster. What are you getting excited about?" I never got his name nor had the opportunity to thank him. But, it meant a lot to have someone supporting me at a time like that.

The police insisted on taking me down to the station. Since I had my own car, I asked to drive separately. They took the posters, but allowed me to meet them at the station. I was so scared. I didn't want to call home and upset my brother or my mother. I figured Art would probably say, "Why do you do these crazy things at a time like now? You're only going to make it worse for us." And Mom was having a hard enough time with Pop being taken away and the FBI coming every day and looking through every drawer. I had a lot of friends who I thought I could turn to. Yet every time I went to one of their homes, I just couldn't go up and ring the doorbell and ask for help. I didn't want to bother them, and I was afraid they might begin to question the things I did. So I ended up going to the police station by myself. But the sergeant who looked at the posters said, "There's nothing wrong with these posters. I've seen them all over town. So why are you bringing her here?" The sergeant at the desk made the two lieutenants who brought me in feel like they did something stupid. The sergeant gave me the posters and told me to go home. I was really shaken up, but I never told my family.[7]

The degree to which Yuri felt isolated, with no one to turn to for support or guidance, is striking. That there were tensions between Yuri and her brother Art is evident in this passage (and discussed later in the chapter). She also wanted to protect her family, and perhaps her Nisei friends, from further problems and was not sure how much she could trust her White friends. These experiences with race discrimination were particularly disturbing for one who had minimized differential treatment based on race. In part because of her apolitical and color-blind worldview, Yuri tended to internalize the problem, feeling as if there was something wrong with her or her community. It is also instructive to observe how she interpreted these encounters with race discrimination. At the time, these events did not immediately change her worldview. She merely incorporated them into her daily experiences in a manner concordant with Japanese cultural values: Yuri saw no option other than to *gaman* (endure) because there's nothing that can be done, *shikataganai*. These experiences, however, planted seeds that activated a gradual process in Yuri of developing a racialized understanding of the world.

To understand how disconcerting it was for Yuri to incorporate race into her color-blind worldview, it is informative to look at her life prior to World War II. Yuri was born in 1921 in a location that she describes with affection: "San Pedro was a small, homey, friendly port town in Southern California. I loved this town. It was exactly what I wanted a hometown to be." She lived comfortably with her mother, father, older brother, Art, and twin brother, Peter, in a custom-designed house on the corner of Eleventh and Meyler streets. "No non-Whites could live above Meyler," Yuri said, alluding to the widespread residential segregation during that time. "Later, other Japanese moved in above that line. But when I was growing up, there were very few Japanese in my neighborhood, except for my uncle and aunt's family, the Kondos, who lived just down the block."[8]

In the 1920s and 1930s, Yuri barely noticed race differences. "To me, at the time, it didn't seem like anything unusual for Japanese to be living in a mostly White neighborhood." Yuri appeared to be more Americanized than most Nisei. But her assimilation came at the expense of her cultural identity. *Banana*—yellow on the outside, white on the inside—is the derogatory term she used, years later, to describe her ethnic identity in her youth. In retrospect, Yuri noticed that the Nisei growing up in San Pedro, like herself, seemed more ashamed of their Japanese ancestry compared to the Nisei growing up in the more insulated, majority-Japanese fishing village of Terminal Island, across the bay from San Pedro:

> Niseis on the San Pedro side did not seem as proud of or as aware of our heritage. But, more so, it could also have been because we did not wish to emphasize our ethnicity in a society where a wee overdose of Japanese culture may have been thought to be too foreign to the larger society. Somehow, I think we negated or denied our Japaneseness to be on the safe side. I felt Americans liked us in San Pedro because we acted so American, exactly what Americans wanted us to be. We wanted so much to be accepted by America. This was even before the war. I am glad there was a Terminal Island where the Japanese people were not afraid to express their Japanese pride. I hope some Niseis from both Terminal Island and the Palos Verdes Hills will write openly about their years of growing up prior to World War II and after.

Monica Miya (then Miwako Oana), a San Pedro Nisei, observed: "Looking back, a lot of us Niseis grew up in a really divided world because we wanted to be American much more so than today. Since stories like Alex Haley's *Roots* came out, people became much more conscious and proud of their ethnic background. The Civil Rights Movement made a world of difference. But when we were growing up before World War II, we wanted to be American."[9]

Yuri and her friends, Japanese and White alike, believed that San Pedro was a place free from prejudice where all were accepted and could succeed. Indeed, the San Pedro High School yearbook of Yuri's graduating year, 1939, shows that, unlike most high schools, the Japanese American students were integrated into school activities.

Many participated in organized sports, student government, band and cheerleading, academic honor societies, and various clubs; they were not simply relegated to the Japanese Club. In elementary school as well, Yuri and her brothers participated actively in extracurricular activities, where, for example, Peter served as sixth-grade class president and Yuri as vice president. Nonetheless, racial boundaries existed. While interracial friendships were common, Nisei rarely ventured into romantic relationships with their White peers. Residential segregation and job discrimination were also customary, institutionalized forms of racism. But the youthful age and apolitical stance of Yuri and her friends made it difficult for them to understand racism in forms other than name-calling and interpersonal mistreatment. Plus, Yuri's family's economic status enabled them to live in the White part of town, her gender role rendered job discrimination less salient, and her own popularity protected her from individual-level racism. It is not surprising then that as she grew up, Yuri was not aware of racism. She was, in her own words, naive.[10]

Yuri's naïveté also blinded her to racial tensions on the political front: "I was very provincial, and thus ignorant of the serious issues in the country and around the world. I was hardly aware that World War II was just around the corner." Yet other Nisei youth in the 1930s were more politically astute. In her autobiography, Monica Sone wrote: "International matters took a turn for the worse when Japan's army suddenly thrust into Shanghai. . . . The editorial sections of newspapers and magazines were plastered with cartoons of hideous-looking Japanese. . . . When stories about the Japanese Army on the other side of the Pacific appeared in the newspapers, people stared suspiciously at us on the streets. I felt their resentment in a hundred ways. . . . 'Sorry, we don't want any Japs around here.'"[11]

That few Japanese American families lived in San Pedro proper diminished their threat to the White power structure. And that the Nakaharas were Christian and their neighbors were also immigrants, including many Italians and Slovenians, further reduced cultural differences and potential animosity between the Nakaharas and the local White community, at least prior to World War II. Because of these factors, mainstream activities as well as friendships with Whites were accessible to Yuri and her brothers. Predictably enough, Yuri developed an ideology of color blindness, or the belief that racism does not function structurally to subordinate racialized groups. To Yuri back then, anyone in the United States, even those with disadvantages, could "make it" through hard work and perseverance. Conversely, a lack of hard work and determination—and not institutionalized racism in hiring, access to education, and so forth—would account for an individual's "failure" to assimilate. While Yuri rejects such ideology today, this belief system offered a certain appeal to a young Nisei woman in the 1930s as well as to many individuals, Whites and people of color alike, today. In order to maintain a color-blind ideology—and the hope that the American dream of "equality and justice for all" applied to her—Yuri had to minimize or deny the incidents of racial discrimination against her and her family. This color-blind worldview, her middle-class status, and her mother's liberal child-rearing practices helped develop in Yuri a confidence in her abilities as well as a boldness—almost an expectation that she would be accepted—atypical in Nisei women. The only problem was that, as she regularly faced racialized job discrimination and with the advent of World War II, it became harder and harder for Yuri to reconcile her color-blind worldview with her reality.[12]

Yuri's father, Seiichi Nakahara, was born on July 21, 1887, in Iwate Prefecture in north-central Japan. Her mother, Tsuyako Sawaguchi, was born on April 19, 1894, in Fukushima Prefecture, also in north-central Japan. Yuri does not recall many details of her parents' background. However, her cousin, Teek Kondo, and his mother, Mary Tama Kondo, wrote a short article for a family photo album explaining the Nakahara history:

Seiichi . . . was the youngest of eight children born to Masanao Nakahara, a retired samurai, and Koto Yasumi, daughter of a samurai scholar and physician. . . . Seiichi came to America in 1907 hoping to make his fortunes and return [to Japan] and live a life of ease. When Seiichi arrived in America, he first worked picking oranges at an orchard outside of Los Angeles. Later he worked in a fish cannery on Terminal Island. Then, with his brother-in-law, Mr. Toyama, he opened a fish market in downtown Los Angeles. From there, I assume, he started The Pacific Coast Fish Company and wholesale fish business in San Pedro.

This business was a great success and enabled him to return to Japan to seek a wife.[13]

Mr. Nakahara returned to Japan in 1917 to marry his future wife. Theirs was an arranged union, as was customary in Japan at the time. Tsuyako Sawaguchi taught English at the high school where Seiichi Nakahara's father was principal. She presumably came from an affluent family because she graduated from college at a time when advanced educational opportunities were closed to most Japanese women. Although her class position enabled her to evade gender barriers to education, her life was constrained by patriarchal norms in many other ways. In terms of her legal status, the 1908 Gentlemen's Agreement effectively meant that she and all Japanese women could enter the United States only in relation to a man—as his wife, daughter, or mother. In addition, the immigration authorities mistakenly registered her as "Tsuma," meaning "wife" in Japanese. This name, which stuck with her throughout her life, symbolized the dependent status of women in both Japanese and American societies. Here, as there, she would fulfill the prescribed role of a "good wife." Yuri's parents entered the United States together on January 30, 1918.[14]

The Nakaharas' first child, Arthur Masao, was born on December 23, 1918. Two and a half years later, twins, Mary Yuriko and Peter Minoru, were born on May 19, 1921. That Yuri has the same birth date as Black militant leader Malcolm X (1925) and Vietnamese revolutionary Ho Chi Minh (1890) holds symbolic meaning for her later work as a radical activist. Growing up, Yuri had assumed she was born in a hospital like her White peers—a belief consistent with her minimization of racial differences. But her mother informed her: "No hospital allowed the Japanese to deliver their babies there. Tanaka-san delivered you and all the other Japanese children in the area." Not uncommon among Nisei, Yuri and her brothers went by their American first names. It was not until 1969, as a result of a tranformed political and cultural identity, that Yuri began using her Japanese name.[15]

The Nakaharas' immigration history was fairly typical of the Issei, except that most came from rural areas in southwestern Japan. The Issei men, mostly single and young, immigrated in large numbers between 1885 and 1908, when the Gentlemen's Agreement closed immigration to Japanese laborers. Like most, Yuri's father initially worked menial jobs. Those who rose out of the laborer ranks usually established small service-sector businesses within the Japanese American community. Yuri's mother became part of the flow of Japanese women migrating to America between 1908, after a loophole in the Gentlemen's Agreement opened up immigration to women, and 1920, when anti-Japanese hostilities in the United States compelled the Japanese Foreign Ministry to cease issuing passports to picture brides. As a result of this narrow window of opportunity for women's immigration, most Nisei were born between 1910 and 1940, with the majority born between 1918 and 1922. The births of all three Nakahara children fit this pattern.[16]

In contrast to the Nakaharas' typical immigration pattern, their socioeconomic status was unusually high among the Issei. In California, Mr. Nakahara made considerable money through his small business, enough to build a custom-designed house in a White neighborhood and to cover travel expenses for at least four trips to Japan. The first trip was to marry and return with his wife. Because only a few Issei men could afford the expense or time to travel to Japan to meet their wives, most Issei wives came as picture brides, traveling across the seas to meet their future husbands after their families arranged the marriage through the exchange of photographs and background information. The Nakaharas also traveled to Japan for lengthy stays on two separate occasions when Yuri was young and at least once more after she completed high school. Also, while economic necessity required many Japanese American wives and children to work in the family business, the Nakaharas' financial situation made it possible not to rely on family labor. Yuri and her brothers had few, if any, responsibilities at the family's fish market. Neither did Mrs. Nakahara, though she had an occasional, part-time job teaching Japanese to Nisei youth.[17]

Along with his economic success, Mr. Nakahara held social prestige within the Japanese American community. While he served as the head of the San Pedro Japanese Association and the Central Japanese Association of Southern California in the early 1920s, most of his influence came through his connection with prominent people in Japan. He was a childhood friend of Kichisaburo Nomura, who served as the Japanese ambassador to the United States until the bombing of Pearl

Harbor. On behalf of the Japanese emperor, the emperor's brother Prince Chichibu decorated Mr. Nakahara during his 1937 visit to Los Angeles. Mr. Nakahara also had developed professional and social relationships with the captains and other officers of the large Japanese merchant, passenger, and naval ships to whom he supplied provisions from his fish market. While Mr. Nakahara's activities—chauffeuring the ship captains to golf courses and serving them dinner in his home—could be interpreted as the services of a servant, the relationship appeared to be egalitarian. Mr. Nakahara was being a good host, entertaining his guests while they were abroad. Yuri's childhood friends remember Mr. and Mrs. Nakahara, not in any subservient role, but as a stately and elegant couple who entertained VIPs. In turn, these officers reciprocated services to show their gratitude and fulfill their debt of obligation in accordance with Japanese customs. Monica Miya (Miwako Oana), whose father worked as a bookkeeper for Mr. Nakahara's business, recounted: "*Nakahara no ojisan* [a Japanese term of respect and closeness, literally meaning Uncle Nakahara] had a wide circle of contacts with businesspeople who came over on these big ocean liners. . . . These were beautiful ships like the *Titanic* that we don't have today. They transported passengers. . . . When my mother took me and my brother to Japan, we were going third class. . . . But somebody found out that we were connected with Mr. Nakahara and they put us in first class." When the 1932 Olympics were held in Los Angeles, the Nakaharas entertained some of the Olympians from Japan who competed on the athletic field a block away from their home.[18]

The Nakaharas' socioeconomic status enabled Yuri to have a comfortable and carefree childhood. She remembered playing in the neighborhood with her brothers, cousins, and friends: "My cousin, Teek [Kondo], about twenty at that time, was a neighborhood leader who organized art shows, paddle tennis tournaments, kite-flying contests, and nationality parties, where teenagers brought their own ethnic food to share. These nationality parties were held in our backyard, where the boys built a clubhouse." In elementary school, Yuri exchanged secret notes with her friend Nan (Carlson) Grimm, who recalled: "We started writing each other little notes in a vacant lot. We'd dig a hole and we'd write the notes in lemon juice and if you held them over a flame, you could read it. This was intriguing. We'd always tell one another, 'Hey, I left you something, I left you a note.' It was child's play. It was great fun." As a young teenager, Yuri, who was known as Mary, continued her secret note writing, this time with Vivian (Martinez) Hardy, who said: "We had a little secret thing. There was a gym and Mary and I found a little loose rock . . . and we said we'd hide our little notes. We were the silliest kids. Every day I'd look and sure enough there'd be a little letter from her. And I'd write her a letter. It was always about boys. She always had two or three boys that she had crushes on. We wrote silly stuff . . . 'Oh, I saw so-and-so. I wonder if he'll ever notice me.'" Like other teenage girls, Yuri spent long periods talking to friends. Monica Miya relayed: "We'd always walk back and forth between our homes. We'd get so busy talking that she'd start walking me back. Then I'd say, 'I'll walk back with you a ways,' and we'd walk back and stand on the corner and talk some more. What did we talk about? It must have been things we wanted to do when we grew up and we also went through our girlish crushes."[19]

In addition, Yuri and her friend Vivian played tennis together a couple of times a week. And in the summer, they went swimming in the ocean just about every day. Vivian (Martinez) Hardy remembered their fun:

> We'd go out before daybreak. There was skinny Mary and skinny Vivian out there swimming. She was what you'd call my swimming buddy. . . . If I got in trouble, got cramps, there's not one doubt in my mind that Mary would give her life to save me and I for her. We would go out past the breakwater at Cabrillo Beach and start swimming. Neither of us had any lessons, didn't even have a swimming cap. And we'd start swimming along the breakwater all the way to Long Beach. And we'd swim out past the buoys. We were just side-by-side, laughing and batting around like the idiots we were. . . . Then we saw in the paper they're having the county one-mile race. She and I had never been in a race. We didn't even know how far we could go. All we know is we're not bad swimmers, me doing everything wrong, but strong as an ox. . . . She dives in and waits for me. The other swimmers are all over the place. And we're off . . . And we're coming down to the last stretch and by that time the water was cold and a lot of people dropped out. . . . And I look

to see Mary and there's one swimmer ahead of us. She was the lifesaver's wife who could swim. We didn't know what we were doing. And I looked and we're down neck and neck. . . . The lifesaver's wife won the gold medal. Little Mary got the silver and little Vivian comin' right behind on her tail—I could have pinched her behind—I got the bronze. We were just excited.[20]

Yuri was also able to enjoy such a carefree childhood in large part because she had few domestic responsibilities. Her parents had a typical Issei marriage, characterized by a patriarchal structure, though not completely governed by it. From a Western feminist analysis, the Nakaharas' middle-class status reinforced the traditional gendered division of labor in the nuclear family, with the husband as breadwinner and wife as homemaker. Issei marital roles were also shaped by the husband's location within his family of origin. Anthropologist Sylvia Yanagisako observed that compared to husbands who were "successor sons" (the son, often the oldest, who inherited the family wealth), Issei marriages were less patriarchal when husbands were "nonsuccessor sons," as was the case with Mr. Nakahara. It is possible that being married to a nonsuccessor son and being well educated helped offset, to a degree anyway, the pressures for a traditional marriage dictated by their class. Mrs. Nakahara's habit of smoking, which embarrassed Yuri because of its unladylike appearance, is one such example. Nonetheless, Yuri's parents' relationship was largely bound in traditional patriarchal and cultural structures.[21]

It was not unusual for an Issei man to serve as master of the household, someone who gave orders but contributed little, if any, toward its maintenance. Peter recalled his father being "a little bit stern," albeit a "very nice person" and a "good father." This matches the observations of Monica Miya: "I think Mary was rather in awe of her father. I got the feeling that Mr. Nakahara wasn't a tyrant, but if he said something there was no question. I'm sure that he was the dominant voice in the house." Consistent with her prescribed gender role, Mrs. Nakahara's life was devoted to husband and children. Her days were filled with vacuuming, cleaning, scrubbing the kitchen floor, polishing furniture, gardening, cooking, and hand-washing laundry (although they had an old-fashioned washing machine). She also sewed the family's clothes and chauffeured her husband and her children to their many activities. Yuri recalled: "[Mom] drove my girlfriends and me to all the high school games, and waited in the car to take us home. She had gotten used to waiting because she also drove my father around when he was not well. She'd bring her Japanese women's magazines and read while she waited." The consistency with which Mrs. Nakahara attended to her housework, and the fact that such work was seen as her responsibility, made it easy for family members to overlook her efforts. "Sadly, I was never very appreciative of all Mom did for me," remarked Yuri.[22]

The degree to which Yuri's parents did not socialize their only daughter into a prescribed female gender role is striking. Some of Yuri's friends indicated that, like Yuri, they had very few household responsibilities. Their mothers single-handedly cared for the home and family so that the daughters had time to study. But further questioning revealed that these teenage girls did the dishes nightly, in addition to a few other chores. Others had tremendous household responsibilities—cleaning the house, doing laundry, washing dishes, and cooking—particularly those whose mother figures worked outside the home or had ailing health. Despite differences in the amount of work done, most Issei mothers had their daughters assist them with cooking and cleaning tasks, as did the vast majority of White American mothers in the 1930s. While this eased the mothers' workload, the significance lay in training daughters for their future roles under patriarchal structures as "good wives." Moreover, within the Japanese household, individual interests were often subordinated to that of the family. So by both gendered and cultural prescriptives, one would predict that Yuri, as the only daughter, would have contributed substantially to maintaining the family household. But she barely did any housework.[23]

In fact, her brother Peter remembered doing more chores than his sister: "Mary did very little housework, whereas I, from a young age, helped my mother clean the house, do the dishes, scrub the kitchen floor, vacuum, and when we had guests, I was the one who waited on them. Mary and Art were never around. I don't recall them ever helping in the kitchen or serving my father's guests. Maybe my sister helped me once in a while, but she often would leave the house." While there is agreement that Art did little housework—his status as the eldest son and his chronic asthma seem to have excused his participation—Yuri has a different memory about her relative contribution. She admits that she rarely did chores, but to her recollection, neither did Peter. She recalled helping with the dishes occasionally and, along with her brothers, serving her father's guests and "lining up and bowing, to *ojini* or *irashaimasen*. . . . That seemed to be the only things I did. I was spoiled because Mom did so much," recounted Yuri. However, it seems plausible that Peter did more housework than Yuri, as friends also recalled. Because Yuri was frequently away from home, Peter may have helped his mother in ways that Yuri was not aware.[24]

One would have expected an Issei mother to have pressured her only daughter to fulfill a traditional gender role. But neither Yuri nor Peter recall their mother ever chastising Yuri for neglecting household chores. Rather, as Peter said: "I don't know if my mother liked it, but she just accepted it. She was kind and generous to everybody. She was very understanding and very sympathetic to Yuri and she really was an excellent mother. I can't recall her ever yelling at Yuri." Yuri agreed: "My mother never asked me to do more around the house. She gave me a lot of freedom." It appears that, in contrast to her traditional marital role, Mrs. Nakahara had a liberal, perhaps even lenient, parenting style and gave her children considerable autonomy to pursue their own interests. "Mom was very open and broad-minded, and I could discuss anything with her. I had never heard her put down anyone. Her thinking and assessments were also very understanding and even sensitive. She was never pompous; rather she was humble and kindly. I felt lucky to have a mom like her," observed Yuri. Friends noted Mrs. Nakahara's support of her children's activities, even having a pal-like relationship with Yuri. By contrast, most Nisei girls were more constrained by prescribed gender roles. "Being an only daughter, my mother kept me close to her. Therefore, I did not participate in after-school socializing with other students," noted Yuriko (Endo) Yoshihara.[25]

Three main images of Mrs. Nakahara emerge based on the memories of Peter, Yuri, and several of Yuri's friends. First, Mrs. Nakahara was seen as an elegant, sophisticated, gentle, and soft-spoken woman. She dressed beautifully, kept an immaculate home, entertained distinguished guests, and was the wife of a refined gentleman. Second, Mrs. Nakahara was seen as a woman devoted to her family and home, a dutiful mother and wife, kind and generous to those around her.

She spent her time cooking, cleaning, doing laundry by hand, sewing clothes for her children, and transporting her husband and children to their varied activities. She was a gracious hostess to her husband's business associates and to her children's friends. Third, she was viewed as liberated and modern. She was college educated, spoke English, and had learned to drive—tasks that few Issei women had accomplished. Although the images of being liberated and subservient seem contradictory, the two also coincide. Mrs. Nakahara was seen as modern because she could drive a car, but this skill was used mainly in service to her husband and children. She was also seen as sophisticated and stately, but these qualities enhanced her ability to entertain her husband's business associates. In short, Mrs. Nakahara fit the image, under patriarchy, of an idealized middle-class woman.[26]

It is not clear how Mrs. Nakahara, a college-educated woman who had a professional teaching career in Japan, felt about spending her time in America catering to her husband and children. When she traveled to Japan for more than a year when Yuri was young, was she trying to escape confining gender roles and gain support from her family of origin? Or, like many Issei women raised under the patriarchal and duty-bound Japanese culture, did she find satisfaction in performing her familial obligations? Women often did not see themselves merely as maids to their families, but enjoyed the ideological trappings of the nuclear family, particularly the respect gained through being "good wives" and "good mothers." They also frequently had a degree of power in the household. While there were a variety of ways conjugal power was distributed in Issei marriages—including ones where parents controlled the household, where husbands dominated, and where husbands and wives jointly made decisions—it was most common, Sylvia Yanagisako found, for husbands to control the family finances and to some extent the social activities, for the wife to control the housekeeping, and for both to make decisions about the children. While Mr. Nakahara played the dominant role in the family, Mrs. Nakahara also exerted control over aspects of family life, most likely the housekeeping and children's schooling, activities, and upbringing. Given the influence Mrs. Nakahara had on her children, the social and economic prestige she gained through her marriage, and the possible contentment derived from fulfilling her familial obligations, it is understandable that Peter could state: "I really don't recall that my mother ever complained about doing the housework. I think she felt that it was the duty of a wife to act in such a manner as to satisfy the husband."[27]

While Mrs. Nakahara had a liberal parenting style, there is some indication that she also wanted her daughter to be more ladylike, more traditional, and more domesticated. This is not surprising given Mrs. Nakahara's own embodiment of a feminized role as well as her focus on appearance. Perhaps Mrs. Nakahara made gentle comments to her daughter to encourage her to be a more obedient daughter. If she did, the messages may have been so subtle that neither Yuri nor Peter understood them. Or, as is more likely the case, even if Yuri understood the implicit meaning, she did what she thought was important, which was to help those in need. Whereas Mrs. Nakahara and so many other Issei and Nisei women attended to their own families, Yuri saw her duty bound to serving the larger human family.[28]

Yuri's twin brother also seemed quite tolerant of his sister's activities and her limited household contributions. Although it was highly unusual for a son to do more housework than a daughter in a Japanese American or any American family in the 1930s, it seems that Peter accepted his role without protest: "I didn't even think about it. I didn't mind doing the housework. I got along very well with my mother. I felt close to her and I just wanted to help her." This also gave Peter a special role within the family. Art gained attention as the firstborn son in a traditional Japanese household and as the child with special health needs. Yuri gained attention through her many activities and friends. And Peter came to feel close to his parents, particularly his mother, by helping her in the home and by, according to him, being the child who spent the most time with his parents: "As a youngster, I recall going to the [American] movie theater with my father and mother. I was the only one who went with them. Both Yuri and Art didn't go, but I remember going."[29]

"My twin brother and I were very close," recounted Yuri. "Being in the same grade, we walked to school together until Pete got a bike. Then I rode on the crossbar of his bike. In junior high, I got my own bike and Pete taught me how to ride it. Once I learned, I was off. I really became crazy about riding bikes." Still, Yuri and Peter spent little time together and had separate circles of friends, though they were in the same class. When Yuri's friends came over to the house or were given rides by Mrs. Nakahara, they do not remember Peter being around. Several of Yuri's friends recall Peter being quiet, mellow, and seemingly tolerant of the fervent pace of Yuri's activities.[30]

Yuri's limited contribution to maintaining the household, however, was a source of conflict with her older brother, Art. As children, Art and Yuri were constantly bickering. According to Yuri:

> Art and I fought every moment. When I was in high school, if Art and I were walking on the same side of the street, one of us would cross the street to avoid little sibling spats. When he'd bring his friends over to study together, I was like a little pest, interested in Art's friends, because they were three years older than Pete's. Art hated that. He would always say, "When my friends come over, don't show your face. They came to see me, not you. Just get out." But, of course, I would always be peeking and pestering around. We grew up always at odds.

Peter attributed the arguments between his siblings to "Mary [being] so different and Art [being] just such a typical Nisei . . . a traditional Japanese." Because the structure of a traditional Japanese family meted out privileges based on gender and age, it was to Art's advantage, as the firstborn son, to reinforce this hierarchy. Art pressured Yuri to stay within her prescribed gender and cultural roles. "Whatever Mary wanted to do, Art would tell their mother, 'Don't let her do that. Why does she have to do that?'" recalled Monica Miya. Yuri's admiration of athletes, when Art's chronic health problems limited his participation in sports, may have further antagonized their relationship. Yuri noted: "I guess my values were topsy-turvy. I used to put athletes on a pedestal and Art couldn't go out, except for tennis. Pete went out for football and all that. Later, I came to see how much more I admired Art because although he couldn't go out for basketball, football, track, yet he supported sports like nobody."[31]

Mr. Nakahara might have also chastised Yuri for not attending to the family. Peter recounted: "My father was never mean to Mary, but he thought she was a little nutty. I can't blame him. . . . He became very angry because Mary was doing so much to help other people. . . . He thought she should stay at home and help more around the house. And he and Mary got into arguments about this." Yuri's memory differs: "Pop never reprimanded me. He gave us our freedom. If anything, I had more arguments with my mom. I remember telling her I didn't want to play the piano. . . . My brothers never complained, but I always seemed to be doing so and Mom used to say to me, 'You always *monku monku* [complain].'. . . But I don't remember any arguments with Pop." In contrast to the constant presence of her mother, Mr. Nakahara's work—at the fish market and entertaining Japanese ship officers—marked his relationship to the home. Perhaps because of his absence, Yuri cherished the time spent with her father. Yuri recalled that before she became involved in tennis, bike riding, and other activities in junior high school: "I loved to caddie for him, though the golf bag was so big and heavy. It was a special time being with Pop. He was not very talkative, but I felt comfortable with him. I used to look forward to coming home from school, quickly changing clothes, getting in the car, and driving off to a nearby golf course at White's Point in San Pedro." Mr. Nakahara also played cards with his children after dinner, while Mrs. Nakahara continued to do housework. Moreover, Mr. Nakahara's chronic respiratory problems, which required at least one trip to a tuberculosis sanatorium, meant that he received special treatment above his role as head of household. "I can't remember a time when he wasn't sick. So Mom made sure that we weren't too rambunctious in the house," said Yuri.[32]

The theme of physical illness ran in Yuri's family, with Mr. Nakahara and Art having chronic respiratory problems. In response to chronic illness, parents often become overprotective. Perhaps this added to Mr. Nakahara's concerns about Yuri's extensive activities. The healthy children in a family can also end up vying for their parents' attention, which is often disproportionately given to the sick child. This could explain Peter's willingness to help his mother with housework. But more likely, Mrs. Nakahara did so much for each of her children that none of them felt neglected. Also, chronic illness can leave family members feeling paranoid about their own health. If Yuri did, she likely denied or minimized these fears by keeping herself occupied—a common coping mechanism throughout her life. In any case, based on Yuri's memories, the time spent with her father was filled with fun and relaxed interactions.

One wonders, however, if Yuri remembers her relationship with her father in a more favorable light than actually existed, especially given his sudden death. Constructing a positive memory would be particularly important if she felt that she had disappointed her father by falling short of his expectations for a good Nisei daughter or if she harbored any guilt for having let the FBI into the house. That Yuri has some regrets is evident in this statement:

> When one looks back on one's life and sees how much has been omitted, how options closed certain doors, I do feel remorseful. I was always busy with one thing or another, whether covering a tennis match or softball game, working with children or teaching first aid to teenagers, or leading a story hour group for Mexican children at the Homer Toberman Settlement House; I did very little in the house for my family. I can't relive those youthful years, where I did just what I was interested in and not for the family.[33]

Not only did Yuri spend little time at home, she also disclosed little about her family or her inner thoughts, even to her closest friends. "Mary never revealed anything about herself, her family, or her emotions," observed Nan (Carlson) Grimm, who used to share secret notes with Yuri in elementary school. "We talked about everything but our personal lives," remarked Vivian (Martinez) Hardy, who in her teenage years exchanged daily letters with Yuri in addition to spending hours playing tennis and swimming with her. Yuri's focus was more outward. Not only did she spend her time on activities outside the home, she also felt more comfortable hearing about other people's problems, participating in numerous activities, or discussing light material rather than sharing intimate feelings.[34]

Even as Yuri rebelled against a traditional gender role, she did so in the absence of any conscious feminist beliefs. That Yuri's actions were not ideologically motivated helps explain her aspirations for a traditional marriage. Still, her upbringing may have created in her a flexible worldview, with less rigid notions of what is considered appropriate behavior for Nisei women. Today, Yuri holds contradictory attitudes toward women's roles—at once conservative and liberatory—but her actions are more revealing than her words. Regardless of Yuri's values, she behaves in ways that have liberated her from narrow gender and cultural constraints within her own marriage and in her outspoken protest against injustice.[35]

From a young age, Yuri exhibited an unusual concern for the well-being of others. Whether it was reaching out to shyer people, telling stories to poor children of color, giving moral support to local athletes, or serving as a counselor to preteen girls, she was constantly working to help other people, primarily in a quiet, understated manner. As early as the third grade, Yuri displayed sensitivity to those marginalized by circumstance. Eight-year-old Nan (Carlson) Grimm had just moved to San Pedro to be with her grandmother after living in foster homes for most of her life. It was her first day at a new school in a new city. She felt the anxiety and loneliness of not knowing anyone and assumed that she would spend lunchtime alone. But to her surprise, another student approached her, inquiring if she would like to join her for lunch. Nan and Yuri soon became good friends; at least Yuri became Nan's closest friend. Seventy years later, Nan has not forgotten Yuri's kindness during a difficult period in her life. Rather than focusing on her own popularity or self-interests, Nan noticed, Yuri tended to reach out to "the shyer people, those sitting in the corner."[36]

Because of her service to others, her thoughtfulness, and her humility, people were drawn to Yuri. Yuriko (Endo) Yoshihara recalled that when students from various elementary schools came together at the only junior high school in San Pedro, "Mary was immediately the most popular person in school. . . . Never did I ever see Mary focus on herself—she seemed to always be interested in other people, especially those in trouble." Classmate Norma (Benedetti) Brutti exclaimed: "Mary was like an icon. She was so outgoing, one of the most popular students. I'm not exaggerating when I say she could have won any office she ran for. . . . She never sought accolades . . . but rather embodied everything good." Sumi (Seo) Seki recounted: "Mary was the sweetheart of San Pedro. . . . She was so popular. I remember one day when I was in high school—Mary was already out of school—it seemed like there was a fight. There's a bunch of kids all gathered around someone in a circle. I looked and I see a little girl in between all those kids. It was Mary. They all had their hand out, saying 'Mary, Mary,' they all wanted to shake her hand. Everybody talked of her, 'Do you know Mary?' I had heard about her, but didn't actually know her. But they'd say, 'She's so nice. She does this and she does that. She just knows everybody.' Because of her friendliness and warmth toward people, they all wanted to shake her hand."[37]

Some friends and family members recall that Yuri consciously promoted the concepts of fairness and equality. Peter Nakahara observed: "Mary certainly was different from other Nisei children, different even from *hakujins* [White people]. She was always sticking up for minorities and defending people who were oppressed. She always wanted to help the poor." Nan (Carlson) Grimm remembered back to the fourth or fifth grade, at a time when she and Yuri were close friends at church and school:

> It was around Easter time and Mary said we should do something for some of the poor people here. She was always so concerned about other people. She said we should make some candy and take it to them at Easter. So we did. We rolled up powdered sugar with some canned milk and made little round rolls of this and then we put a walnut on top. We had a little wagon and we went up and down the street of this poorer section of San Pedro and gave this candy away. I remember I was a little bit embarrassed that one of the children who took the candy was one of our classmates. But it didn't seem to bother Mary too much, she just went on her little way.[38]

Nan, who herself had grown up poor, noted, "My sister and I probably could have been receiving some of that candy we gave out." By contrast, Yuri grew up solidly middle-class. But to Yuri, the high-tone style, social status, and wealth of her parents were to be shunned. Remembering back to their elementary school days, Nan said: "Mary didn't like me telling her how beautiful her home was. She saw it as ostentatious and it embarrassed her. She didn't like to believe that she had more than others." Yuriko (Endo) Yoshihara recounted: "Mary decided that she wanted to experience working for someone. So she got a job as a maid to a woman. . . . One day, the woman offered to take Mary home after work. Mary had the woman let her off away from her home. She didn't want the woman to see where she lived. This is typically Mary—she didn't want to embarrass the woman— that the maid lived in a much nicer home than the employer." Yuri's twin brother similarly remarked: "We lived quite a distance from our high school and our mother drove us to school. She drove us in a very nice car. I don't remember what kind, but it was an expensive car. But Mary was ashamed to be seen in such a car. She would get out three or four blocks from school and walk the rest of the way. I didn't care, so I stayed in the car. . . . Mary also would refuse to ride in my father's car because it was so fancy. I think he had a Packard. It was a big car, and she wouldn't even get in the car." But Yuri countered this story, insisting that carsickness, not any self-consciousness, explained her refusal.[39]

Yuri is adamant that as a child and youth, "what I did had nothing to do with equality. I wasn't political at all." Although she did question why some people were poor and others rich, she was not consciously fighting for justice in any political sense, observed several of her friends. It seems that, in her youth, humanitarian concerns and a need to be active—more than any philosophical contemplation—motivated her service to others. What is remarkable is the degree to which she transformed her concerns into action. Vivian (Martinez) Hardy questioned whether Yuri was driven by traits of mania, which could help to explain her tremendous energy and her obsessive need to stay busy. Norma (Benedetti) Brutti observed that Yuri was "hyper," "had a ton of energy," and "never stood still." This image of Yuri, like a hummingbird darting here and there, full of energy, has remained with her throughout her life. Virtually all her friends and family were at a loss to explain the motivation for Yuri's expansive activities; their final conclusion: "She was just born that way." As Monica Miya put it, "I guess some people are just born with a crusading spirit."[40]

While seemingly true, there were other influences on Yuri's community service activities. Her parents demonstrated a concern for the community, although nowhere near the level of Yuri's involvement. Mrs. Nakahara participated in the Parent-Teachers Association (PTA) at her children's school. Mr. Nakahara was active in the Japanese Associations in Southern California, at least in the early 1920s. That neither Yuri nor Peter remembered their parents' community service activities—except their hospitality to the Japanese ship captains, which was more of a social or professional activity—suggests that their parents' community participation was limited. Nonetheless, it is possible that her parents', especially Mr. Nakahara's, activities and views helped shape Yuri's beliefs.[41]

The Japanese Association of America, formed in 1908, and its affiliates became the key political organization of Japanese immigrants. While the various Japanese Associations acted as an overseas arm of the Japanese government—processing papers, registering marriages, births, and deaths, and so forth—the organizations also served to defend Japanese Americans against the growing anti-Japanese movement. When Mr. Nakahara served as its director in 1923, the Central Japanese Association of Southern California had already struggled to protest racist legal discrimination when, for example, California's 1913 and 1920 Alien Land Laws barred "aliens ineligible for citizenship" from purchasing land and the 1921 California state legislature regulated private foreign language schools. Under Mr. Nakahara's directorship, the Central Japanese Association of Southern California passed resolutions to appeal the 1922 U.S. Supreme Court ruling denying Japanese immigrants the right to naturalized citizenship, to demand equal rights and privileges for Japanese residing in California, and to work against anti-Japanese propaganda. Although it appears that Mr. Nakahara's community activities slowed down after the mid-1920s, perhaps owing to the onset of asthma and tuberculosis, it is possible that his views on racial equality had an effect on Yuri.[42]

Another influence was the Christian church. Although the majority of Japanese in the United States were Buddhists, as in Japan, Yuri's parents attended the Japanese Episcopal St. Mary's Church in Los Angeles, headed by Rev. John Yamazaki. That Mr. and Mrs. Nakahara were Christians is not entirely unexpected, however, because Japanese American Christians, compared to Buddhists, tended to be from urban, educated, and higher socioeconomic backgrounds. What was unusual is that from a young age, Yuri attended church on her own. She first went to the nearby Christian Science church, and later, to the Presbyterian church, which she preferred. As early as ninth grade, Yuri had wanted to be a Sunday school teacher. And in 1939, right after graduating from high school, she began teaching Sunday school to a small group of sixth graders, following a three-week Bible training workshop.[43]

It is not clear to Yuri why she started going to church, why she attended on her own, or what kept her interested. But in a letter written in May 1944, when she was preparing to leave the Jerome, Arkansas, concentration camp where she had taught Bible studies, Yuri explained to her Sunday school class what religion meant to her:

> Junior high and high school . . . It was then, that certain values of life were taking hold of me. I can't quite explain "how" but I will say, it wasn't just church that touched me. It wasn't any

one significant organization or person. It was everybody and every experience. Yet, as I think back, of one thing I am sure: it was through God. He permitted me to meet so many of you and experience so many situations, because he wanted me to understand Life. This may all sound crazy, but please do not misunderstand me. I am certainly not a "religious" fanatic, in the sense that many think of religion. In fact, I am far from it. To me, religion is something one "actually" believes in. Then one's only religion is his conscience.[44]

Yuri's approach to religion was humanitarian, rather than theological. She pulled from the Bible lessons about how to treat people and how to become a better person and was much less interested in scriptural doctrine about promoting Christian-specific tenets for salvation. The Bible passages she remembered were those that focus on ethical teachings or provided inspiration: "I used to memorize passages from the Bible. I especially liked the Beatitudes, the twenty-third psalm, Paul's message about love, and the Ten Commandments. I think a lot of those ideals become a part of one's life." These passages emphasize caring about humanity based on unselfish love, treating people with respect and compassion, leveling inequalities, and finding comfort in God, particularly in difficult times. These passages, as well as those promoting service to others and release to the oppressed, laid the foundation for Yuri's community service.[45]

Not surprisingly, Yuri disliked the aspects of Christianity that clashed with her humanitarian ideals: "I only knew about the Christian religion, but in the Bible, I didn't like the part, 'I, the Lord thy God am a jealous God, inflicting iniquity onto the third and fourth generation of them that hate me, and showing mercy unto the thousands of them that love me and keep my commandments.' I'm not sure if those were the exact words, but the words upset me. God didn't seem any different from ordinary human beings if he had the same failings and weaknesses, being jealous and wishing to hurt those who did not adhere to his teachings. Why wasn't he more understanding?" Moreover, while she believed in a spiritual Creator, hers was a nondenominational, interfaith God. Had she been raised in a Buddhist family or in a Japanese American community, she likely would have attended a Buddhist temple. Years later, Yuri embraced Islam for several years through the influence of Malcolm X. Her nondenominational views reflected her condemnation of any type of chauvinism, including religious sectarianism: "When I became older and learned of the many religions throughout the world, I was disappointed that all the religions or the people who were committed to them had the same frailty: they thought their religion was the best and the only religion. The chauvinism and intolerance seemed to weaken religion. I thought religions should have similar ingredients where there would be no need to quibble over minor differences."[46]

Yuri also gained inspiration from poetry and quotations with similar humanitarian messages. "Thinking of people's need for religion," Yuri commented, "this brings to mind a couple of quotes on religion: From Ben Franklin—'If men are so wicked with religion, what would they be without it?' From [Charles Caleb] Colton—'Men will wrangle for religion; write for it; fight for it; die for it; anything, but live for it.'" Perhaps the most influential message Yuri heard came from a teacher at a Los Angeles Presbyterian church: "It's more important what you teach a child to love than what you teach a child to know." To sum up her humanitarian view of religion, Yuri quoted from Thomas Fuller: "A good life is the only religion."[47]

Even though Yuri has not attended any religious institution for most of her activist life, her early years in the Christian church cannot be dismissed. She was an active participant in the church, she encouraged her friends to go with her, and she taught Sunday school during her teens and twenties, until the 1950s, when an active family life and other activities took precedence over church. Most significantly, her early Christian experience laid the foundation for her ethical humanitarianism, which, I contend, is at the core of her community service and political activism to this day.[48]

Many of Yuri's interests and activities—poetry, sports, community service—have reflected this ethical humanitarianism. Yuri discovered a love for inspirational poetry in junior high school, one that has followed her throughout life. She was surprised to discover decades later that one of her favorite poems, Rudyard Kipling's "If," was one Malcolm X carried in his pocket, a gift given to him by his sister, Ella Collins. Yuri even drew encouragement from poems considered sappy by today's standards, like this one that she included in her 1942 scrapbook:

> *For it isn't by money that you measure a town*
> *or the miles its borders extend.*
> *For the best things you gather whatever the town*
> *are contentment, enjoyment, and friends.*

Yuri's favorite poet, Edgar A. Guest, was well known to her contemporaries during the 1920s and 1930s. She eagerly pored through his poems by checking out one book after another from the library. From these poems, Yuri was reminded to treat others kindly, to grow as a Christian, and to persevere during adversity.[49]

Reflecting on her youthful love for inspirational poetry, Yuri commented, "Back then, I was far from being developed, and my mind's eye had not yet begun to focus on the real world of racism, stigmatizing, marginalizing, hypocrisy, poverty, and imperialism." As her understanding of systemic oppression expanded, her poetry repertoire grew to include "the writers of the Harlem Renaissance, the sizzling '60s outlaw poets, and the current new crop of the '90s." Yet to this day, Yuri continues to find inspiration in the poetry of her youth.[50]

As a youth, Yuri was involved in numerous community and extracurricular activities. She was an avid sports fan, a journalist, a tennis player, a counselor to numerous preteen girls' clubs, an officer in her high school's student government, and a Sunday school teacher. Perhaps the activity Yuri was most passionate about was sports—as a spectator, participant, and journalist. In the absence of professional sports in 1930s Los Angeles, she, like many in San Pedro, were fervent fans of high school athletics. Yuri's hometown pride was intertwined with her love of sports:

> San Pedro, I felt, was one of the greatest little sports towns anywhere in the USA. It was not just the athletes that made San Pedro outstanding, but the fans. Never have I heard where the sport fans generated such interest in high school sports as has been done in San Pedro. One could be thirty, fifty, seventy, or even ninety years old, and be attending the games—football, baseball, basketball, track, any of the major sports, and even some of the minor sports like gymnastics, swimming, tennis, girls' sports. San Pedro High School sports galvanized our hometown.

Yuri commented that her older brother was such a devout SPHS fan that when he passed away in 1995, his wife had him dressed in his black-and-gold SPHS booster jacket in the casket.[51]

"I could relate to sports because I learned about teamwork and about sharing and that was exciting to me," explained Yuri. It appears that cooperation and humility, rather than competition, were Yuri's mottoes as a sports writer for the high school and community newspapers. At a 1989 reunion in Yuri's honor, a classmate told the audience, albeit in patronizing language: "[There] was our little Mary Nakahara, a busy human dynamo, taking those countless thousands of pictures . . . diligent, modest, always smiling, and this, Mary, I discovered, is your charm, your manner, your unassuming naturalness." That unpretentiousness was reflected in her refusal to take the team bus to cover sporting events. Instead, she rode her bicycle, trimmed in the school colors, as far away as Santa Monica and Gardena. Even as a member of the high school tennis team, she was so self-effacing that she hated to win, recalled classmate Mickey Panovich: "You've heard of the thrill of victory and the agony of defeat? . . . Well, she had it backward. To her, it was the agony of victory and the thrill of defeat."[52]

But humility does not necessarily translate to meekness. At age sixteen, Yuri had the boldness to ask whether she could write sports articles for the community newspaper. She recounted:

> I wrote a note to Joe Goss, the sports editor of the *San Pedro News-Pilot:* "We have some of the best tennis players here in San Pedro. For a little town we have five players in national ranking, and tennis hardly gets any coverage. I know I'm only sixteen but would you take a chance?" He said, "Cover this event and send in your story and I'll see." I didn't get paid or anything, but he let me do tennis, then gymnastics. I even did boxing, which was exciting. He said if you want to cover B and C games, you can. He covered varsity and college.[53]

"The biggest event I covered was the Davis Cup," recalled Yuri, relaying how the sports editor asked her to interview the sixteen-year-old star of the Philippine Davis Cup team. Felicimo Ampo was the youngest Davis cup player at that time. Goss gave Yuri two tickets to the tennis match so that she could bring a friend. After the match,

Yuri and her friend, Vivian (Martinez) Hardy, waited for the Filipino players to come out and Yuri asked Ampo, "Can we go to the country club to have something to drink and interview you?" Ampo agreed and brought a male friend. Yuri noted: "I never had a drink in my life before then. I wouldn't have known how to order a drink, but my girlfriend, who was three years older, said, 'Don't worry, I'll order the drinks.' Vivian ordered the most common drink, not too strong, something like a gin fizz. It was sort of funny because we didn't know what to say. We were giggling and laughing and carrying on like kids anyway. But he was only sixteen. He was so nice to go with us."[54]

Yuri was the first girl at SPHS to receive a varsity letter jacket for sports. And two decades later, in 1958, her San Pedro friends organized a reunion picnic in her honor at which they presented her with the "Sportsman's Prayer," an appeal to good sportsmanship. Yuri had consistently written newspaper articles on sporting events, especially the minor sports that people often neglected. She had also sent morale-boosting notes and poems to athletes before each game and after particularly difficult matches. Her friends recalled that Yuri had the ability to remember everybody's name and to be a special friend to all. While Yuri remains a sports enthusiast to this day, her passion for athletics has waned with the expansion of the corporate sports industry: "Sports has become big business with money, huge bucks in the millions, that control the sports arena. My interest in sports has sorely dwindled. Of course, I still watch Michael Jordan and the rest, but not with the zeal I once held for the San Pedro Pirates in the Marine League."[55]

Yuri also was actively involved in a multitude of other community service activities. She became the first girl to hold a student government position at San Pedro High School, where she served as student body vice president. By contrast, Nisei generally did not participate in student politics; the racial and economic barriers were too strong except where Nisei comprised a substantial population, which was not the case in San Pedro. After completing junior college, Yuri worked as an adult counselor or leader for numerous junior high–age, multiracial girls' groups, including the YWCA Girl Reserves, the Girl Scouts, and the Blue Birds. And she read stories to the children at the Homer Toberman Settlement House, improvising to keep their attention. She enjoyed working with the youth so much that she had her Sunday school class over for slumber parties on weekends, noting, "My mom was really patient and generous with the kids sleeping all over our living room and dining room. She was a terrific cook and often made simple meals for them." Hearing Yuri talk about her activities as a youth, one gets the impression that her involvement in her students' lives was spontaneous, that she had them over simply because it was fun. But Yuri conscientiously chose to play an active role in her students' lives. In a two-page creed that she wrote at age eighteen, she explained:

> What I teach, I want them, as well as myself, to apply in our daily living. I will never think that the 2-1/2 hours on Sunday mornings is sufficient in giving my time to God as a Sunday School teacher. I must understand the girls by being with them, playing with them; singing with them; studying with them; laughing with them; and even crying with them. I will take the girls on recreation trips, such as to the beach, park and shows . . . and have class parties and get-togethers. . . . I will watch them at school, attend their assemblies, sport contests and dances, and take an active interest in all that they partake.[56]

This standard of involvement that Yuri established was lofty, yet she worked to live by it.

In struggling to live in two cultural worlds, many Nisei have expressed what W. E. B. Du Bois termed "double-consciousness": "this sense of always looking at one's self through the eyes of others, of measuring one's soul by the tape of a world that looks on in amused contempt and pity. One ever feels his twoness,—an American, a Negro; two souls, two thoughts, two unreconciled strivings; two warring ideals in one dark body, whose dogged strength alone keeps it from being torn asunder." Nisei author Monica Sone wrote: "*Nihon Gakko* [Japanese school] was so different from grammar school I found myself switching my personality back and forth daily like a chameleon. At Bailey Gatzert School I was a jumping, screaming, roustabout Yankee, but at the stroke of three when the school bell rang and doors burst open everywhere, spewing out pupils like jelly beans from a broken bag, I suddenly became a modest, faltering, earnest little Japanese girl with a small, timid voice." A Nisei woman told Mei Nakano: "It's a wonder we aren't all schizos. Our parents were always telling us to be 'good Japanese.' Then they'd turn right around and tell us to be 'good Americans.'" Yuri too felt this double consciousness: "I grew up like many other Nisei. Inside the home we were very Japanese, but outside we were 'red, white, and blue' Americans."[57]

While Yuri lived in her "red, white, and blue" world, she also attended Japanese language school, as did most Nisei. Most Japanese American communities had established one or more Japanese language schools by the mid-1920s. The Japanese schools taught reading, writing, and grammar as well as history, geography, and culture. Some children attended Japanese school every day after regular school, while others attended only on Saturdays. Parents viewed Japanese school as a critical institution for inculcating Japanese culture in their children, but the younger generation often regarded *Nihon Gakko* as a time to socialize with other Nisei. Through attending Japanese school and communicating in Japanese at home, a few Nisei became completely fluent in the language of their parents. But most understood only simple conversational Japanese and spoke even less. Yuri fell into the latter category.[58]

Yuri and Peter started *Nihon Gakko* in junior high school, which was much later than most; Art apparently was excused from attending because of his asthma. Like many other Nisei, Yuri attended reluctantly:

> The first Japanese school I went to was way out in the country in a cantaloupe patch in Lomita, just over the San Pedro Hills. We students gave the teacher a hard time because we weren't interested in learning Japanese. There were times we'd run away, have rock fights in a quarry, and then walk back over the San Pedro Hills. We did things that were difficult for the teacher, a sweet woman who came from Japan where students show respect for their teachers. Here, we didn't even think about how difficult it was for the teacher and the hardship of that little school. As a Nisei, I had no appreciation for what the school or the Japanese community was trying to do: to imbue us with some knowledge of the language and culture of our ancestors.[59]

Later on, Yuri and Peter attended Compton Japanese School, which local Nisei considered the best Japanese language school in Southern California. Yuri's indifference toward *Nihon Gakko* was exacerbated by the fact that she and another friend, June Toguri, were much older than the other students: "When the entire school had to participate in the *gakugeikai,* an annual program performed before the parents, we were both reluctant butterflies and flowers, always feeling ill at ease with these roles for youngsters." More than language skills, what Yuri gained from *Nihon Gakko* was an exposure to Nisei culture. Until her junior high years, there were few Japanese Americans outside of family in Yuri's life. But by starting Japanese school and knowing Japanese Americans at school for the first time—Nisei from Terminal Island, Palos Verdes, and San Pedro came together to attend the only junior high school in town—Yuri began interacting with other Nisei. She recounted: "I must say that I'm glad I went to Japanese school because I met Niseis from Compton, Gardena, and Los Angeles. Fumi Kato became one of my closest friends. I also became close to June Toguri, whose older sister, Iva Toguri, became widely known as Tokyo Rose during World War II." Yet it is likely that these new experiences also presented a challenge to her racial self-concept. She was a "red, white, and blue" American, who relied on a color-blind worldview, who "wanted so much to be accepted by America." But as her world incorporated more Japanese Americans, she gradually began to develop an awareness of her own ethnic identity.[60]

Yuri's dating patterns reinforced her assimilationist attitude. In general, the Nisei had mixed experiences with participating in interracial high school activities and friendships; some participated freely with Whites while others faced race discrimination. But almost all hit the boundary of racial tolerance when it came to forming intimate relationships where, noted Mei Nakano, "social segregation outside of school remained in force for even the most popular and active [Nisei]." Most went to dances, football games, and the movies only with other Nisei. This was the experience of most Nisei in San Pedro, including Yuri's brothers and close friends. That few Japanese-White romantic relationships existed is a reflection of both legal and cultural prescriptions. Until 1948, California state law banned interracial marriages with Whites, and both Japanese and White parents favored coethnic unions. Nonetheless, the majority of Yuri's dating partners were White, although she did attend a school dance with a Nisei and another with a Mexican: "I didn't really date that much in high school; just went to school activities or to the movies and I didn't have a boyfriend before [my husband] Bill. Because San Pedro's mostly White, that's who I went out with. I have to say all the White guys I went out with were really nice; even their parents were wonderful to me and I felt as if I was accepted."[61]

How did Yuri's parents feel about her interracial dating? Yuri observed: "My mom was really open-minded; she didn't care what color the guy was. Other gals my age said they never met an Issei mother like that; they couldn't even go out." Predictably enough, her mother's racial tolerance diminished as the level of intimacy increased. "But Mom did worry about who I would marry. I think she was afraid I'd marry a White guy. She'd say it's up to you who you marry, but Pop and I hope you meet a nice Japanese guy. When she met Bill, I think she hoped he was the one. She could then tell her friends, 'My daughter's going with a nice Nisei boy.'" Peter offered a different motivation for their mother's tolerant behavior: "My parents knew that Yuri was a very strong-willed person and that they couldn't stop her from doing what she wanted to do. My mother did not object [to Yuri's interracial dating]. While my father may not have looked favorably upon her going out with non-Japanese, I don't recall that he ever complained to her not to do so. I don't think that it would have done any good anyway."[62]

To Yuri, marriage and family superseded any educational or occupational goals: "I just wanted to finish school, get a job, meet the right guy, get married, and have a family. I didn't have any ambitions for a career." Among Nisei women, Yuri's educational attainment was typical. She graduated with an associate of arts degree from Compton Junior College in June 1941, where she majored in journalism and English and minored in art. The proportion of Nisei, both male and female, completing high school exceeded the U.S. average by a significant margin. Although it was less common for Nisei females to complete even one year of college, a number of Nisei women went on to earn bachelor's degrees.[63]

After graduating from junior college, Yuri experienced what may well be her first acknowledged encounter with race discrimination: "Back then Japanese could not find jobs except in Japan Town and China Town. It seemed impossible to get an ordinary job in town. Even when I finished junior college, I was one of the only Japanese Americans who was working in San Pedro proper and I heard it was the first time that a five-and-dime store hired a Japanese. Woolworth hired me where three other five-and-dime stores wouldn't even let me make out an application." While Yuri's job at a mainstream American business may have bolstered her assimilationist views, she also acknowledged, "They hired me, but only as a fill-in for summer vacations, Christmas, Easter, and Saturdays. Par for the course, for all Japanese were either working for a vegetable stand or doing domestic work." Yuri is correct in noting how unusual it was for a Nisei like herself to be working outside the Japanese American community in a job other than farming or domestic service. Race discrimination prevented the vast majority of Nisei, even the college educated, from obtaining employment commensurate with their education or that of their White peers. One Issei man in Monica Sone's autobiography exclaimed: "How many sons of ours with a beautiful bachelor's degree are accepted into American life? Name me one young man who is now working in an American firm on equal terms with his white colleagues. Our Nisei engineers push lawn mowers. Men with degrees in chemistry and physics do research in the fruit stands of the public market. And they all rot away inside." While the majority of Nisei aspired to professional or business careers, racism closed those doors to most. Instead, many Nisei became economically dependent upon Issei small businesses. As for Nisei women in Los Angeles in 1940, the greatest number worked as clerical or sales workers—primarily within the Issei economy—followed by nonfarm laborers and domestic servants.[64]

Yuri soon discovered that, when it came to low-paid, exploitative labor, she did not even have to look for work: "I'd be riding my bicycle and some White woman, a wife of a naval officer, would ride by and say, 'Do you want a job?' When you're young, you want any type of job. I had no skills, not even to clean house, but I'd say, 'Yes, I can do this and that.' It was lightweight cleaning. They'd ask, 'Have you taken care of infants?' I'd say, 'No, but I can learn.' Everything was 'I can learn. I can't cook, but I can learn,' and they would take me." With this type of discrimination affecting middle-class Japanese Americans, Yuri noted, in retrospect, the greater hardships on those with lower incomes: "How different it must have been on Terminal Island or the San Pedro Hills, where most of the Japanese lived. Young people there did not have time for extracurricular activities. They worked."[65] These experiences with job discrimination began bit by bit to challenge Yuri's idyllic world.

Even before the United States entered World War II, life for Japanese Americans had become increasingly difficult. Yuri found herself being asked to leave one organization after another as problems between the United States and Japan escalated. About a year before Pearl Harbor, Yuri's friends, White girls a little younger than herself, invited her to join the Women's Ambulance and Defense Corps of America (WADCA), which later became the Women's Auxiliary Corps. Thinking about the excitement of learning to drive an ambulance, Yuri began attending WADCA classes on motor mechanics, first aid, and Morse code. She recalled: "I have to admit, at times, the training was hilarious. We'd meet on the high school athletic field and march into the neighborhood, right where we lived. When officers would yell the command to turn left or right, and we'd make a mistake, everyone watching would roar out in laughter; even dogs were barking. We were so embarrassed, but still we were serious about the WADCA training." Yuri noted that everyone in WADCA treated her nicely, except for one teacher, himself German, who objected to having any Japanese in his class. Even before the bombing of Pearl Harbor, a captain in WADCA told them, "I'm sorry, but some feel a little uneasy because you're Japanese." In a move that typified Yuri's acquiescence in a period of growing anti-Japanese hostility, she explained: "We [four Nisei women] got together to figure out what we should do. As much as we wanted to stay in WADCA, we decided, 'Let's not make a lot of noise. Let's exit gracefully.' So we wrote a nice letter saying we understand that our Japanese background makes us suspect. We wished all the women good luck and thanked them for our short-lived experience in WADCA."[66]

Although Yuri did not know it at the time, war was imminent. Her life was about to change.

2

Concentration Camps
and a Growing Awareness of Race

The fears of the Japanese American community were realized when the U.S. government ordered their forced removal from the West Coast in the spring of 1942. Two months after Yuri's father's death, her family found themselves moving from their well-appointed house to a horse stable at the Santa Anita racetrack. Yuri recalled: "We got our evacuation notices at the end of March. After seeing the Terminal Island people leave, we figured we'd have to leave at some point. But it was hard when it actually happened."[1]

Across the bay from San Pedro, Terminal Island was a fishing colony of some five hundred Japanese American families who had built a fishing industry from almost nothing. They owned their own radio-equipped tuna fishing boats, which cruised as far as Panama. Because of their knowledge of the waters, fantastic and erroneous tales of subversive acts by Japanese American fisherfolk circulated after the bombing of Pearl Harbor. As unfounded rumors spread that these fisherfolk might guide Japanese naval vessels through Pacific waters, the U.S. government and private industry targeted this community. Banks froze their accounts and law enforcement officers restricted their movements. Cash ran out, businesses collapsed, and their fishing fleet was paralyzed. The people were in a dire state. Then, on February 9, 1942, a swarm of FBI and local police descended on Terminal Island and arrested all Issei who had commercial fishing licenses. Without warrants, the agents ransacked drawers and closets and recklessly disheveled family homes. Because many community leaders had already been apprehended following the bombing of Pearl Harbor, this latest round of mass arrests meant that virtually all the Issei men were now gone. On February 14, the government sent a letter to all Japanese American families living on Terminal Island, notifying them that they had one month to pack and leave. Suddenly, with only forty-eight hours' notice, new signs were posted telling them to leave by February 27. Panic ensued as predatory neighbors flooded the island community looking for easy buys on large appliances, cars, and fishing equipment. The quick removal of the Terminal Island Nikkei was an ominous sign for the greater Japanese American community.[2]

In the two months since the bombing of Pearl Harbor, the highest political and military officials had strategized about how to remove the Japanese Americans, including the U.S.-born Nisei, from the West Coast. Their quandary was a legal one: In the absence of martial law, how does one bypass due process to incarcerate U.S. citizens? Their answer came in the form of Executive Order 9066, signed into law by President Franklin D. Roosevelt on February 19, 1942. The order set in motion the procedures for the forced elimination of Japanese Americans through the establishment of "military areas" from which "any or all persons may be excluded." The order was insidious in that it never mentioned any ethnic or racial group, though it was designed with the Japanese in mind. In fact, when Public Law 503, imposing criminal penalties for anyone violating Executive Order 9066, was introduced before Congress in late March, the only member who questioned it, Republican Senator Robert A. Taft of Ohio, declared it "the 'sloppiest' criminal law I have ever read or seen anywhere. . . . It does not apply only to the Pacific coast. It applies anywhere in the United States where there is any possible reason for declaring a military zone. . . . I have no doubt that in peacetime no man could ever be convicted under it, because the court would find that it was so indefinite and so uncertain that it could not be enforced under the Constitution." But since Taft understood that the law was to apply only to Japanese Americans, it passed in both houses without a single dissenting vote.[3]

By then, Lieutenant General John L. DeWitt, head of the newly created Western Defense Command, had already designated military areas in Washington, Oregon, California, and Arizona, suggesting the locations from which the Japanese would be excluded. He also identified the targeted groups: "Japanese, German, and Italian aliens" and "any person of Japanese ancestry." In the end, although the war was also being fought against Germany and Italy, only persons of Japanese descent suffered mass dislocation. Three days after Congress passed Public Law 503, DeWitt issued the first of 108 Civilian Exclusion Orders, each for a particular geographic location, which gave the Japanese one week to pack and vacate their homes. Japanese Americans were first moved to fifteen temporary, euphemistically named "assembly centers" and later to ten more permanent concentration camps.[4] By fall 1942, the U.S. government had succeeded in removing 120,000 Japanese Americans from the West Coast.[5]

Like other Japanese American families, the Nakaharas would have found out about the government's plan by seeing evacuation notices posted on telephone poles and store windows. Yuri's brother Art and a friend also took the initiative to inform the local community. Because the authorities instructed the Japanese to "take only what you can carry," they had the difficult task of deciding what to pack. The selection was made more difficult by the lack of information about their destination and length of stay. Yuri recounted: "All we knew was to be prepared for rough living. They told us to bring hardy clothes like jeans and comfortable shoes like sneakers. We weren't allowed to bring radios and anything that could be interpreted as a weapon, not even baseball bats or knives. People brought their own plates and bedding. So Mom, Art, and I began packing and trying to decide what was most important for us to take." Yuri's choices are revealing of her priorities: "I took pictures of all my friends to remember them by. I also took stationery, envelopes, and stamps so I could stay in touch with my friends. This may seem corny, but my WADCA uniform was really important to me, so I packed it though we really had so little space. The hardest part for me was leaving my friends. San Pedro meant so much to me."[6]

Yuri's priorities, at the age of twenty, reflect the value she placed on friendships. Before leaving, she compiled a scrapbook filled with photos, inspirational poetry, and little sketches she drew to decorate the album. In the introduction, written after her departure from San Pedro, she wrote: "This album is a conglomeration of snapshots and pictures, haphazardly and hurriedly scrambled together in the last week before evacuation. . . . Lack of time and space prevented me from carrying more. . . . However, the fellows and girls in these shots represent the town that meant so much to me when I lived there, and even more so when I left. . . . These pictures have been a source of comfort and pleasure. They gave me something to look back on, something to look forward to, and something to cherish." In addition, Yuri responded to suspicions about her American loyalty in a way that paralleled the reaction of many Nisei: she held on to a symbol of U.S. patriotism—her WADCA uniform. Responding through ultra-Americanism enabled the Nisei not only to ward off accusations of disloyalty but also to maintain the hope for their future acceptance into the dominant society.[7]

On Friday, April 3, 1942, Yuri, Art, and Mrs. Nakahara left San Pedro for the Santa Anita Assembly Center. "Before we left, friends stopped by to say good-bye; it was so good seeing them, but this also left me feeling a little sorrowful," wrote Yuri in a diary she began on this day. Recorded in two volumes (notebooks), "The Bordered World," as she titled her diary, covers her seven-month stay at Santa Anita, with her last lengthy entry in mid-October 1942, as she arrived in the Jerome, Arkansas, concentration camp. Although rich in narrative and subtextual information, there were views, especially negative ones, that Yuri intentionally omitted from her diary. On the cover page she wrote: "Daily Diary of how I think and feel, but may I never put in writing that which would hurt, humiliate, look down, blame, or show dislike for any person, nation, race, religion, or station in life." Not only was she concerned about the feelings of others, she may well have feared, given the circumstances, that her diary would be read by others.[8]

Yuri also documented in her diary the names of each person who visited before she left or whom she saw en route to the Santa Anita Assembly Center. She may have wanted to remember the names of her friends whom she might not see for a long time, or if she allowed herself to consider it, that she might never see again. Still, this record-keeping behavior began before this period—she recorded the names of her classmates in a notebook each year—and has continued throughout her life. The Nakaharas traveled by car caravan to Santa Anita. Along the way, Yuri stayed psychologically connected to her hometown by writing postcards to four friends, which she mailed as soon as they made a stop.[9]

Santa Anita was a shock. Yuri had been excited about seeing the famous racetrack, but her enthusiasm was negated by the presence of armed guards: "Flanked on both sides of us were the soldiers, with gun in hand. . . . We thought they were going to help us unload, but we soon saw they were there to guard us." The soldiers proceeded to inspect their bags. As she watched them confiscate knives, sharp equipment, alcoholic drinks, and even some uniforms, Yuri became alarmed that they might take her WADCA uniform and was greatly relieved when they allowed her to keep it. The Nakaharas turned their attention to their accommodations and learned they were to live in the stables. In avenue 8, barrack 48, room 11, their new home was one large room divided by a partition, with two collapsible cots on each side. Mrs. Nakahara and Yuri slept on one side and Art on the other.[10]

Yuri's diary entries reveal an optimistic naïveté that helped her cope with the uncertainty of their predicament. She saw the world through rose-tinted glasses, constructing a more positive view than existed in reality. While others saw difficulty and aversion in their situation, Yuri saw only the good. She recorded in her diary that first day: "I thought it was pretty good, but it seemed as though most of the people were quite disappointed. My mother complained it smelled like horses were still living in it." Feeling hunger pangs, they rushed to the mess hall where they were served a meal of beans, fish, bread, and water. "I thought the meal was swell, but again there were those who made unfavorable comments," wrote Yuri. They soon discovered that their lifestyle would be communal, eating in army-style mess halls and using community latrines and washrooms. After filling their mattresses with hay, which exacerbated Art's asthma, Yuri finally had time to write letters to friends. The only thing she acknowledged that bothered her was the lack of privacy, but even here she put a positive spin on the situation: "We could hear everything going on in the rooms or apartments next to us. Every word, every move can be heard, even whispers. Around 8:30, the little girl to the right of us yelled out, 'Good-Night everybody over there!' It was cute. We yelled back, 'Good-Night to you too.'"[11]

The day after arriving, Yuri met up with several young women, some she knew from before, others she just met. They decided to welcome new arrivals at the camp's entrance through song, such as this one to the tune of "Yankee Doodle":

We are here to welcome you, as you come here to join us.
We know that you'll cooperate, instead of making fu–uss;
   With your friendly attitudes,
   With your happy moods,
   With your hopes to do your bit,
   Let's show our hearty spi—rit![12]

These words, written by Yuri and her friends, show a youthful simplicity as well as the cooperative spirit of many Nisei. In an environment of intense hostility and in an era before the social movements of the 1960s aroused a consciousness of resistance, many Nisei coped with racism by demonstrating strong American loyalties. These behaviors coincided with the Japanese cultural value of *shikataganai* (it can't be helped), which promoted adjusting to circumstances rather than working for change. Moreover, by focusing on others, Yuri did not have to deal with her own feelings of loss, abandonment, and betrayal. She needed to maintain her faith in America because she had no other belief system with which to replace her notions of a just society. For Yuri, the uncertainty accompanying these changes, on the heels of her father's unexpected death, were magnified by suddenly finding herself in an all-Japanese community. Even today, though certainly more mature and politically astute, Yuri relies on this optimistic, other-focused style. When asked to reflect on the personal impact of incarceration, she stated: "Being the right age for change—young, healthy, excited, and searching—adjustment was not difficult. But I certainly admired my mother, who had just lost her husband and the security of a nice home. She took everything in stride."[13]

Former internees, all Yuri's peers, remember Mrs. Nakahara as being exceptionally supportive of her daughter. Mrs. Nakahara participated in Yuri's letter-writing campaign to Nisei soldiers and volunteered as a chaperon when Yuri was active at the Jerome USO. In fact, Yuri credits her mother with easing the tensions of camp life and crowded living conditions for her family: "Mom instilled in us the need to be mindful of those around us. She impressed on us the need to work together, to sink or swim together as a team. My mother never preached this, but this was how she lived her life. She did a lot for us and always treated everyone who came to our place so nicely." In conversations with Yuri today, it seems that she demonstrated her concern for her mother according to the Golden Rule: Do unto others as you would have them do unto you. Rather than considering the particular needs of Mrs. Nakahara, Yuri supported her mother through her own coping mechanism: by keeping her busy.[14]

It is difficult to uncover Yuri's relationship with her mother, beyond Mrs. Nakahara's support for her activities, and with her brother Art during their confinement. Yuri discloses little about her family, other than standard stories rehearsed for public consumption, and rarely mentioned them in her camp diary. Peter, who was away in the military during the war, was not aware of the details of his family's camp life. And Mrs. Nakahara, Art, and other relatives are no longer living. Yuri's camp friends remember little about Art or Mrs. Nakahara. It appears that Yuri's life in camp, as in San Pedro, centered on her friends and activities. Hanging out and eating meals with friends, rather than family, was common among teenagers and young adults in the concentration camps. Beyond the teenage developmental task of fostering friendships, these conditions were facilitated by the erosion of the Issei family structure, including the loss of the paternal breadwinner role, the communal lifestyle, the removal of some fathers who were incarcerated in separate camps, and the War Relocation Authority's practice of seeking advice from English-speaking youth over their immigrant parents. Yuri recalled that Art too focused on friends and work, though he may well have spent more time than Yuri with their recently widowed mother. But Art was with his family in the Santa Anita and Jerome camps for only fourteen months before he left to work in Chicago in June 1943.[15]

Yuri's community service activities did not go unnoticed. Sumi (Seo) Seki of San Pedro had known Yuri only by reputation—by her service work, friendliness, and popularity. Inside Santa Anita, the seventeen-year-old Seki found Yuri (Mary) to be a source of encouragement: "We were so lonely and so disgusted. We just didn't know what to do with ourselves. But here comes Mary trying to cheer you up. She already knew, 'Don't look back, look forward. Try to do the best you can.' She would start a club and get you going. Then you'd forget about that loneliness."[16]

The group that helped to ease Seki's loneliness was Yuri's Sunday school class of teenage girls, self-named the Crusaders. Like other organizations, the Crusaders met under the grandstands previously filled with horse-racing spectators. Yuri's class was unique in organizing a letter-writing campaign to Nisei soldiers. One of the Crusaders, Rinko Shimasaki, wrote a brief history of the group in August 1942: "The Crusader Club originally began with just five eager girls and a very capable advisor. The group was originally a Sunday School class at the Santa Anita Assembly Center. These girls wanted to do something in the way of service so they organized a club called 'The Crusaders.' This was a voluntary club open to all girls." Yuri's memories of the Crusaders, relayed more than fifty years later, coincided with Shimasaki's history: "Our class started off small, only about five or six girls, but after we started our letter writing, we grew to about ninety. They were just a terrific bunch of enthusiastic, outgoing, inquiring minds; they asked questions like: 'What do we do now?' 'What will our lives be like?' and 'What shall we focus on?' The kids wanted to do something of service. I asked, 'What do you want to do?' They felt there wasn't much they could do. Then one girl said, 'Maybe we should write to our Nisei soldiers. My brother's in the service.'" Many of the girls had a brother or relative in the service, as was Yuri's brother Peter. The Crusaders began by writing to half a dozen soldiers, but their campaign quickly expanded. Yuri recounted: "When the word got around that we were writing to our Nisei soldiers, many girls started pouring into our Sunday school class saying, 'Oh, I want to do that too because I have a brother, cousin, friend in the service.' A lot of Nisei soldiers were only eighteen or nineteen and a lot of the girls were fifteen or sixteen, and they wanted to write to a guy a few years older. Each Sunday, the girls would come with new names and addresses obtained from people in our camp." The Crusaders were soon writing to hundreds of soldiers as well as to Japanese American orphans and tuberculosis patients.[17]

As they left Santa Anita, the Crusaders tried to organize letter-writing campaigns at the various concentration camps to which they were dispersed. Some succeeded in establishing Crusader groups, including the camps at Poston, Arizona; Heart Mountain, Wyoming; Topaz, Utah; and Rohwer, Arkansas. That Shimasaki attributed the inability to establish Crusader groups at every concentration camp to the "lack of advisors" hints at the important role Yuri played in organizing the letter-writing campaign. Yuri got people excited about writing letters, gathered names and addresses of soldiers, wrote form letters and poetry that the teenage Crusaders could copy, wrote countless personal letters, and contributed money to cover postage and other expenses; in short, she provided leadership to this campaign. Predictably enough, the camp to which Yuri was sent—Jerome, Arkansas—had the largest Crusader group. As is typical of Yuri today, she did not exert a controlling leadership style with the Crusaders, but rather led by example through her hard work, dedication, and enthusiasm. "The Crusader group from each camp became autonomous," recalled Yuri. "Because we had so many GIs' names, it was too hard to coordinate our efforts." Still the various Crusader groups did send greetings to one another and shared information about their activities.[18]

As more and more internees of varying ages expressed interest in the letter-writing campaign, Yuri organized the junior high schoolers into the Junior Crusaders and the grammar school kids into the Junior Junior Crusaders. Yuri recounted: "The young ones loved to use their crayons to spice up the cards with their artwork. We gave the older teenage girls a list of addresses to write on the postcards because their handwriting was neater." In time, adults also got involved. Yuri said, "Everyone on my block was so supportive, even my mother got into it." Mrs. Nakahara wrote letters to the soldiers and also assisted Yuri in meticulously recording the names and addresses of each soldier. They were soon sending cards five times a year, at Valentine's, Easter, Halloween, Thanksgiving, and Christmas/New Year's. The following "Thanksgiving Greeting," reprinted in part, is representative of the poetry that was handwritten or typed and copied and sent to hundreds of soldiers. Although the author is not identified, the poetry style and use of shortened words (e.g., "thru") closely match Yuri's writings:

> *And as the days grow nearer to*
> *that great Thanksgiving Day,*
> *We cannot help but think of you,*
> *And try but to convey*
> *That we are grateful for the "stuff"*
> *That Nisei boys like you*
> *Have shown thru your endeavors*
> *To see your duties thru.*[19]

In time, the Crusaders and soldiers began writing personal letters to one another. The Crusaders relayed news about camp life, provided words of encouragement, and at times, sent chocolate candies, dried shrimp, and other goodies, particularly at Christmastime. The letters from the soldiers contained information about military life and news about the war. In one letter, Pvt. Bill Kochiyama explained everyday life, including what they ate and how they got free cigarettes. Yuri printed excerpts from the soldiers' letters in her column, "Nisei in Khaki," published in the Jerome camp newspaper, the *Denson Tribune*. One soldier expressed his appreciation for letters from the Crusaders: "That note came at an opportune moment, in the midst of our fighting somewhere in Italy and to think that you are all back of us and boosting, means a terrible lot to us." Other soldiers' letters conveyed how the connectedness to family and community enhanced their sense of patriotic duty: "Sure, we may grumble and gripe to ourselves at times, but we know that the status of our families back home in Hawaii, as well as you people on the mainland, depends a great deal on our showing here, so we take it and we like it," and "You can rest assured that with all your backing we won't fail you and the public in any way."[20]

The theme of American patriotism runs through the words of the soldiers and Crusaders. Some may question how the Nisei could exhibit such loyalty to a country that unconstitutionally imprisoned their families and for years before that had discriminated against their community. But it was not unusual for a minority group to respond to racism by trying to assimilate into U.S. society, and most Americans of diverse backgrounds saw the war as a popular and just campaign. It is also important to recognize that some Japanese Americans protested their incarceration, just as some had resisted labor exploitation and race discrimination for decades preceding World War II. Still, the majority of Japanese Americans complied with the government's evacuation orders.[21]

There are a number of reasons for this accommodationist stance. Virtually every sector of American society, including the president, Congress, Supreme Court, military, mainstream media, and agribusiness, sanctioned the forced removal of Japanese Americans. The Issei, as immigrants ineligible for U.S. citizenship, were in a vulnerable position and lacked political power. Also, the arrests of Issei leaders immediately following the bombing of Pearl Harbor, left the Nisei, most of whom were young and relatively inexperienced, to provide direction in a period of crisis. Into this leadership vacuum stepped the Japanese American Citizens League (JACL), a middle-class Nisei group that advocated cooperation with the U.S. government as a means of demonstrating patriotism. This view is exemplified in the words of JACL leader James Sakamoto: "Loyalty is shown by obedience to the laws, and we can best prove our loyalty by obeying the orders of those in authority." It was not just the JACL who accepted the notion of law and order. As Jere Takahashi observed, "Many Nisei who were interned said that their fellow Nisei generally accepted what Max Weber called legal-rational authority—respecting the validity of legal statutes and rational rules of behavior." In a period before the social movements of the 1960s promoted the questioning of authority, most Americans, including the Nisei, believed that the law was right. "Before [the war], everybody was a law abiding citizen. . . . Nobody including Whites questioned the 'status quo' and the authority of the FBI and military," explained one Nisei to Takahashi.[22]

Many of the Crusaders matured inside the camps through the process of corresponding with Nisei soldiers. Crusader Dollie (Nagai) Fukawa recalled that a letter she had written was returned with the word "deceased" across the envelope. The realities of life and death became much clearer to the Nisei, to those fighting in the war and those supporting the soldiers. With each GI death, Yuri would have had apprehensions about the safety of her brother Peter and later of her fiancé, Bill Kochiyama. This was another aspect of her growing up, of not living within the sterile cocoon of her hometown.[23]

Yuri not only spent her time and energy on the letter-writing campaign, she also contributed her monthly salary:

What we did was send postcards to the Nisei GIs. Postcards cost only a penny each, so my monthly wage of eight dollars could buy eight hundred postcards. We didn't have to pay rent or buy food, so I really didn't need any of the eight dollars. And it certainly went to good use. We didn't start writing letters and needing money for envelopes for a couple of years. Some internees gave half their paychecks—that's four hundred more postcards. The soldiers themselves started donating money for stamps and crayons for the kids. My brother in the service sent me money for stamps.[24]

In accordance with filial piety, Peter Nakahara sent the majority of his eighteen-dollar monthly wages to his family, withholding only four dollars to buy his favorite beverage, Coca-Cola. Peter and Yuri both acknowledge that this money, at least a good part of it, was being used to support the Crusaders' activities. Although Peter had not intended for his GI wages to be routed for this purpose, he was indifferent as to how the money was used. What was important to him was that he supported his family. Peter said: "At first I was giving the money to my mother. I don't know what she used it for. She might have turned it over to Yuri. I didn't care. It was up to her how she wanted to use that money. [At some point] I must have started sending money to Yuri for the Crusaders when I was overseas." Peter was among the first GIs to receive a Crusader card in those early days when the Crusaders knew few Nisei soldiers. He recalled that their letters wishing him well, inquiring about his health, and informing him about camp life helped to lift his spirits during his overseas tour.[25]

The campaign grew as internees gave the Crusaders the names of more and more Nisei soldiers. Yuri explained: "At first we got them one by one through word of mouth. After we started the Nisei USO [United Service Organizations] in Jerome, the 442nd guys were coming to our USO, one, two, or three busloads every week. We hurriedly jotted down the names of every soldier that came through and even tried to obtain the names of their friends in other platoons. We even started to canvas various blocks, asking the head of the block for names of families who had members in the American service." What is amazing is that in eighteen months, in Jerome alone, the Crusaders and their supporters were writing to, according to Yuri, an astonishing thirteen thousand Nisei soldiers. The figure comes from the compilation of names and addresses she and her mother recorded for each incoming and outgoing letter. This letter-writing campaign served as a training ground for organizing. Yuri learned how to involve volunteers in a project, motivate others, and attend to details; she also experienced the power of collective effort. Years later, she would apply these same skills in her political work.[26]

It is not surprising that Yuri's major service activity would take the form of letter writing. Inside the camps, correspondence became a critical means for internees to maintain contact with the outside world, but even more so for Yuri. She regularly skipped seeing mov-

ies and hanging out with friends so that she could write to her hometown friends or Nisei soldiers. Although Yuri had a history of boosting morale through letters and poems, it was in Santa Anita that she
experienced firsthand the potent and uplifting impact of receiving
letters: "There was mail for me. . . . Gosh! I was so happy. . . . I was
just overcome. . . . I opened up Dorothy Hurley's letter first. She
had sent Friday's sport pages and a note with it. Tears just came to
my eyes. Letters can really bring happiness." "People said the two
things you looked forward to were meals and mail. And maybe the
other kind of 'male' too," remarked Yuri. Other young internees
placed a similar importance on correspondence with hometown
friends but many of their friends never wrote back. Sumi (Seo) Seki
recounted: "You don't know the loneliness when you were in camp.
You think you had friends back home, so you'd write them a post-
card, but they never answered. But Mary, everyone was writing to
her. I'd get so jealous. It was only years later that I found out that
the postman had told them, 'If you write to [Seki], you're helping the
enemy.'" Particularly for those in confined situations, Yuri observed,
"It makes you think how happy, then, a soldier must become when
he receives letters at some camp hundreds of miles from his home."
A couple of decades later, these experiences motivated her writing to
political prisoners.[27]

Yuri's letter writing also reflected her strong Christian beliefs.
Many of the Crusaders' notes contained Christian themes, as did this
Easter message, copied and sent to many Nisei soldiers:

> *May Easter seep within you*
> *And give you strength to dare.*
> *For when our Lord and Savior*
> *Descended to the sky,*
> *He left in body only,*
> *His spirit is still high.*[28]

Yuri's Christian beliefs motivated her community service: "At the
time, being Christian really meant a lot to me. It meant that we were
to fulfill the Gospel mission to be of service to our fellow human beings. The Christian messages also gave me inspiration and hope." The
following excerpt from a creed written by Yuri in 1939 explains her
life philosophy:

I will keep in mind first, that "what I am will speak louder than what I say." Therefore I will strive to live in such a way that what I do, how I think and what I say, will inspire them in a Christian faith [rather] than to destroy it. . . . I will try to make the girls realize, that no matter how much Bible Text-book learning and memorizing they may do, they must LIVE the life of a Christian, not merely STUDY it. They must be thoughtful and considerate of the feelings of others, be understanding of others' way of life; kindly to everyone, not just to a selected few; honest with themselves as well as with others; generous in what they possess; courageous when no one is about; and in short, "do unto others as they would have others do unto them."[29]

"Mary's classes were wonderful," recalled Dollie (Nagai) Fukawa. "Everyone loved it. She didn't talk about the Bible. I don't know if we even opened the Bible. What she did was relate biblical concepts to how to live our lives as good Christians. She really made us believe in God. This was very important to me given all we went through. Mary also made us feel like life was not a waste of time, that every day counted. She kept us going, that we can each live up to our potential even in difficult times." While Yuri may not have taught in a traditional manner, her teachings were not merely generically humanitarian; they had a Christian base. She had attended weekly Bible studies back in San Pedro. And Fukawa herself noted that to this day when she gets frightened, she comforts herself by reciting the twenty-third psalm—a passage she attributes to having learned in Yuri's Sunday school class. Nonetheless, the primary lesson Yuri instilled in her students was to treat others humanely and to make the best of any situation. She continues to draw inspiration in times of hardship from a saying she learned during World War II: "When the great American evangelist E. Stanley Jones came to Santa Anita [during his tour of all the assembly centers], he said, 'It's not so important what happens *to* you as what happens *inside* you and what you do about it.'"[30]

Living inside the Santa Anita Assembly Center, with its daily reminders of racial discrimination, posed a challenge to Yuri's color-blind worldview. For the first time, she was being forced to recognize her own racial identity, to see herself not just as an individual but as a member of a targeted group. As it became increasingly difficult to deny discriminatory treatment, her philosophy gradually transformed into a racialized worldview. Yet it would take another two decades before Yuri developed a political understanding of the significance of race and racism in U.S. society.[31]

On her second day at Santa Anita, Yuri obtained a job as a nurse's aide after hearing an announcement over the loudspeaker. This experience contradicted some of her youthful naïveté and helped her mature as a person. Yuri observed: "Finally, I'm learning a few things I should have learned earlier—to be able to care for people in ill health. I didn't know what nursing really was. I had such a childish conception. I saw only the glamorized and clean side . . . women in neat white uniforms taking temperatures, reading to little boys and girls, feeding children. . . . I forgot to realize, a sick patient can't move . . . or even speak . . . that patients must always be kept clean everywhere or bed sores will result." She filled numerous pages in her diary with these new experiences: "For the first time in my life I got to ride on an ambulance, something I had been wanting to do since joining WADCA in San Pedro." Also, "I had the opportunity to observe the birth of a baby."[32]

Although Yuri does not say so, it is possible that the chronic health problems of her father and older brother motivated her to seek a job in the health field. She had been unable to help her father, but perhaps she could help others. Watching that birth may have been a helpful reminder that death, like life, is part of a natural cycle. As Yuri gained an understanding about the suffering of the sick, she developed a more sympathetic understanding toward the sick in her own family, and her conflictual relationship with Art began to change.[33]

Yuri admired the health professionals working at the camp hospital. "Dr. Norman Kobayashi headed a dedicated staff that went for months without anyone having a day off from a grueling schedule where each physician served an average of twelve hours per day, seven days a week, with twenty-four hour duty every fifth day," explained Anthony Lehman in his study of the Santa Anita Assembly Center. Yuri proudly relayed that two doctors came from her hometown, Drs. Abe and Fujikawa, whose sister is the artist, Gyo Fujikawa. The doctor Yuri most admired was a woman, Dr. Shigekawa: "Her conscientiousness as a health-care professional was extraordinary. Besides her regular hours at the camp hospital, she went on house calls with the aid of an ambulance driver and a medical aide. I understand that years later, after the war, she opened a Japanese American Hospital in East Los Angeles." While internee wages were extremely low—sixteen to nineteen dollars per month for professionals, twelve dollars for skilled labor, and eight dollars for unskilled, according to Yuri—this did not bother Yuri, for whom money held little interest. But after listening to her coworkers talk, she noted: "I see now how important money can be and is. I used to think making money was for luxury, but I see now for many people, it is for *existence*. I also realize what an easy life I led."[34]

It was through participating in many lengthy conversations, or more accurately, listening to the opinions of older internees, that Yuri began to change her outlook. As much as she struggled to hold on to her old color-blind philosophy, she also exhibited an openness to new perspectives. Six weeks after entering Santa Anita, in mid-May 1942, she wrote in her diary: "For the past hour and a half, I've been listening to . . . a conversation of opinions which is undoubtedly the voice of the majority of the people here. I'm slowly coming to understand the problems of the Japanese people; problems I never gave much thought to. . . . The evacuation itself . . . the property and homes that had to be sold at such disadvantageous costs; the unfair dealings by those who were prejudiced; the plans and hopes that are now shattered; . . . the darkness of the future to look forward to . . . and the freedom that is now limited." The ambivalent feelings Yuri experienced as she vacillated between her color-blind and her emerging racial worldviews is evident in her diary entry, recorded the next day: "It's strange. I never felt like this before. In fact, I never gave much thought to the Japanese people. I never thought of myself as being a part of a nation so prejudiced [against]. . . . [I never] thought of people according to their race, but just that they were individuals. I want to keep thinking that way; that we're all Americans here, if we feel it in our hearts; that we're all individuals." This revelation, that one could be discriminated against because of one's race—experienced before, but now in a more meaningful way—was deeply disturbing to Yuri: "Didn't write for three days because of the things that were on my mind. I didn't want my moodiness to write anything I would later regret. . . . I still want to abide by my own creed . . . never to write when my own feelings are rushed, because it is then that it is too easy to hurt someone else."[35]

Yuri's growing awareness of discrimination was reinforced by experiences taking place inside the "assembly center." One impactful event involved a police raid in August 1942, as documented in Yuri's diary:

> Huge excitement!!! Some two hundred policemen from Pomona, unexpectedly came into the center and began a unit-to-unit search, confiscating stoves, knives, scissors, kitchen equipment, hand-tools, and even hair curlers, knitting needles, jewelry and money. Campers were suddenly thrown into hysteria—and then—to anger. Many of the locked units were broken into— and trunks carried out without the occupants knowing of what was taking place. . . . Many reported that even diaries were taken. . . . In one instance, a young girl who was sick in bed had her heating pad taken while in use. Many claimed their money had disappeared after the policemen left the units.
>
> About 2:00 in the afternoon, the excitement reached its height when a hysterical mob of men and boys (numbering over 1,000) ganged up on a Korean [who was half Japanese] accused of being a stool pigeon. Several policemen were also mobbed. . . . Mob hysteria turned into a regular free-for-all riot. The army then took the matter into hand by sending in the soldiers on armored cars. Bayonets, machine guns, and tear-gas bombs ready, the soldiers rode through the camp, poised for action. Never saw anything like this before.[36]

This incident must have heightened Yuri's feelings of vulnerability as an inmate inside Santa Anita and may have triggered some questioning about the role of the police. But, as with the police who detained her for posting alumni flyers in San Pedro, she was able to attribute this to a few bad apples rather than to the function of the police in a class-stratified society. This "few bad apples" explanation enabled her to maintain the belief that American institutions upheld the professed values of democracy and fairness. It also enabled her to support the U.S. military, which Yuri would later contend plays a similar role to that of the police in serving and protecting the interests of the ruling class and in suppressing dissent. While this incident was imprinted in Yuri's memory, at the time she was more absorbed in her own activities. As would be expected of an apolitical young person, when Santa Anita returned to normal functioning four days after the police riot, Yuri's concerns were of a more personal nature. "Missed the mail service most of all," she wrote in her diary.[37]

One other incident significantly impacted Yuri's understanding of prejudice and discrimination, perhaps because Yuri, working as a nurse's aide, could empathize with this woman. In September 1942, a friend told her about a young Nisei women who had applied to fourteen nursing schools, but was rejected from all because of her racial background. Yuri responded with shock: "Could hardly believe that public sentiment could be so strong against Japanese Americans." This event was so noteworthy to Yuri that she recorded portions of each of the fourteen letters in her diary. A letter from a hospital in Idaho reflected the sentiment of the other rejection letters: "We are very sorry to tell you that we are not permitted to take Japanese girls in training for the duration of the war. Our staff, sisters, and nurses haven't anything against your people, but public sentiment is such that we dare not take that chance."[38]

For Yuri to have spent so much time recording these letters probably helped her sort through her own feelings about being part of a targeted group. Still, the process of replacing her color-blind worldview with a race-conscious one was precarious and uneven. Not only did she acknowledge "clinging to the faith I once had," she also wrote, almost unbelievably, "But not until I myself actually come up against prejudice and discrimination will I really understand the problems of the Nisei."[39] It appears that Yuri minimized racism against herself, even as she was beginning to recognize the race problem in her community. It was scary to think that America might not be that land of "justice and liberty for all" as promised in the Pledge of Allegiance, especially at a time when that creed gave her hope that she too could be accepted on an equal footing into the only society she knew. Still, her experiences with race discrimination and the cogent perspectives of more mature internees were having an effect. A couple of days after recording the nursing school rejection letters, she wrote in her diary:

> After listening to Maruyama, just had to write of the many things that are now racing through my mind. I'm getting to see her side of the story—and know darn well she knows what she's talking about. I still believe in my own way, clinging to the faith

I once had. Yet her statements were the feeling of perhaps a good three-fourths of the people here and not just statements made from bitterness, but from summarizing actuality.

Yes, it's true that the Japanese people from the time they came here have had raw deals, one after the other. And it's true that they've tried to fight for equality in chances for good positions, but lost out because of racial prejudice. Yet the Isseis saw to it that their children would be educated. Sacrifice meant nothing to them, and this thru the span of twenty and thirty years. . . . [The Nisei] made good grades in school. . . . Yet what happened when they got into the outside world? Racial prejudice and discrimination told them that the school world and the work world were two different hemispheres; that what Caucasian teachers tried to instill in every student was only meant for the Caucasians; that the black and orientals would be looked down upon; that obstacles would be many.[40]

That Yuri, at least at the moment of her writing, would place Japanese in the same category as Blacks in the racial hierarchy, and both in contrast to Whites, was a marked change from her earlier assimilationist views. At some level, she was acknowledging the system of White supremacy. This newfound awareness of racism led her to want to struggle for justice, "even if it's just writing letters."

And how natural then, that bitterness seeped into the hearts of the great percentage of Niseis long before the war broke out. . . . As I listened to [Maruyama], I'm sure something gripped me and touched me in such a way that I feel I want to fight, shoulder to shoulder with every Nisei for the right to the same opportunity as the Caucasian.[41]

As Yuri wrestled to integrate an increasingly racialized view of the world with her need to believe in American equality, she touched on a way to reconcile these seemingly contradictory views. Race discrimination existed, but as an aberrant glitch in a society committed to "liberty and justice for all." Such irregularities could be eradicated through reforms to the system. Through struggle, Japanese Americans, at least the American-born ones, could obtain "the same opportunity as the

Caucasian." These words are the earliest signs of Yuri's later development into a civil rights activist.[42]

After several months in "assembly centers," the internees were again moved to one of ten more permanent concentration camps, located in the desert, swamps, or mountainous wastelands of Arizona, Utah, Idaho, Wyoming, Colorado, Arkansas, and eastern California. "There, way out in no-man's land, invisible to mainstream America, the Japanese survived dust-storms, sand-storms, torrid summers, and freezing winters," said Yuri. Yuri and her mother left by train on October 12, 1942, and arrived in Jerome on October 16; Art, traveling on a different train, arrived three days later. By this time, most Santa Anita internees had been dispersed to different concentration camps such as Gila and Poston in Arizona and Heart Mountain in Wyoming. The first group left in August. As one of the last groups to depart, Yuri had to endure separating from more friends, not knowing whether she would see them again: "It was sad to see so many friends leave, especially after having just gotten reacquainted or having met new friends. We attended so many going-away parties and had so many tearful farewells." This poem, written by Yuri the night before she left, reveals her need to emphasize the positive:

> For each in turn must leave this camp
> And part with those now near
> And yet we'll take a bit of all
> The things we once held dear. . . .
> Though years and distance lies between
> And paths may never cross
> The richness of our memories
> Will never bring a loss.[43]

Jerome and Rohwer, twenty miles away, were the only concentration camps in the South, in the swamplands of southeastern Arkansas. Racism directed against Black people transferred to the Japanese when they arrived in large numbers. The historian Linda Sue Parker has observed: "The social attitudes in Southeastern Arkansas were that of the Deep South. . . . Racism in Arkansas toward the Japanese was greater than that displayed in the other states." At their peak, Jerome and Rohwer each housed approximately 8,500 internees, a huge jump from the previous statewide population of three Japanese Americans. Although every governor, with the exception of Ralph L. Carr of Colorado, objected to relocating Japanese Americans to their state, the governor of Arkansas expressed particularly vehement protest. For example, from 1942 until 1944, Governor Homer Adkins refused to allow the Japanese to work, relocate, or attend college in Arkansas outside of the concentration camps. There was also strong public fervor against Japanese Americans. The Arkansas public, in general, complained that internees were being coddled in the concentration camps. Some complained that the Japanese Americans ate extravagant food, led leisurely lives, and lived off the government. These accusations prompted several investigations by politicians and journalists, all of whom found no evidence of special treatment. These charges were also countered by Dillon Myer, War Relocation Authority director, who noted that the internees' food ration was the equivalent of Army "B" rations, costing forty-five cents or less per day. Partly as a result of Arkansas hostility, after the West Coast reopened to the Japanese, only 140 of the 17,000 internees in Jerome and Rohwer chose to set up residence in Arkansas.[44]

To those inside the camp, Jerome was similar to Santa Anita in many ways. Communal living was the norm; each block had a mess hall, laundry facilities, bathhouse, and latrine. This meant waiting in long lines to eat, do laundry, even go to the bathroom. As an enclosed community, the camp also had a school, a hospital, Christian churches and Buddhist temples, recreation centers, and an athletic field. In Jerome, Yuri continued to teach Sunday school; to work with the Crusaders, the Junior Crusaders, and the Junior Junior Crusaders; and to supervise a girls' youth group called Twixteens. Children under eighteen were required to attend school, and adults eighteen and over were required to work. So, in addition to her volunteer activities, Yuri, now age twenty-one, worked full-time, first as a block mother, then as a block recreation leader, and finally as a waitress in the mess hall. She especially enjoyed her role as a block mother, which provided an opportunity to nurture children: "I loved it because I got to work with children and make formula for the babies. Whenever anyone was sick, they called us. I mean, we weren't doctors or nurses or anything, but if it was fairly minor, then the block mother would take their temperature and report it." Although War Relocation Authority records indicate her monthly wage was twelve or sixteen dollars, depending on the job, Yuri remembers receiving eight dollars per month, the same as in Santa Anita.[45]

Art, who had graduated with honors from UC Berkeley, worked as a schoolteacher in Jerome, as did other Nisei who had at least two years of college. In contrast to mainstream America, the concentration camps provided a space for Japanese Americans to work in jobs that matched their skills, training, and educational attainment. In the absence of race discrimination in hiring, those trained as doctors and nurses worked in the hospitals; others worked as social workers, teachers, cultural workers, and firefighters. Still others worked in the post office, in the mess hall as waitresses or kitchen crew, as custodians, as clerical workers, and in the war effort making camouflage nets.[46]

In addition to paid work, everyone had to contribute to running the camp. During the freezing Arkansas winters, only the potbelly stove in each barracks kept the internees warm. Yuri relayed how every able-bodied man had to chop down trees for firewood, while women sawed or hacked the logs into usable sections and children counted and distributed the pieces. People helped dredge out a drainage system around the barracks. And women sewed curtains for the partitionless public restrooms so that there could be some privacy. What Yuri admired about the Japanese was their ingenuity and their ability to turn a negative situation into a positive one:

> Though we lived in dismal barracks, men would build beautiful pieces of furniture out of the most useless-looking piece of driftwood. Women would order pieces of material from Montgomery Ward mail-order catalogues and create curtains to partition the rooms, and make bedspreads and tablecloths to brighten up our living quarters. These little touches helped to make this wasteland more like a home. Issei women as well as men planted flowers in front of their barracks, and we enjoyed seeing the bleakness of camp bloom with flowers and greenery. A few Issei women also brought their indigenous Japanese musical instruments like the koto and shamisen and provided entertainment at the Issei events and offered music lessons. Some also taught Japanese *odori* or *nanyuabushi* or *shigin* [traditional dancing]. We learned soon enough that our strongest weapons to sustain

ourselves were teamwork, a cooperative spirit, ingenuity, and concern for others.[47]

In the camps, Yuri gained ethnic pride as she came to admire many qualities displayed by Japanese Americans:

One thing I want to say, I feel that going to camp actually is where for the first time I came to know my own people. And in doing so, I started, finally, to see myself as a Japanese American. In San Pedro, I loved the mixing of people, but then living comfortably in a White working-class area, I didn't have a sense of how Japanese Americans lived, those living on farms and in fishing areas. Before I never thought about being proud of being Japanese because no one chooses their background. But in camp, all of a sudden, I'm interacting with and talking to only Japanese every day. I started to learn about my own people. There's much to admire. They work so hard. And do things, even little things such as serving tea and crackers, with such artistry. In camp, under duress, the best and worst come out. I think it was mostly their strengths that came out. I was really proud to be Japanese.[48]

The individuals she respected most exemplified courage, fortitude through adversity, caring for humanity, and community building. Yuri credits Mary Tsukamoto, whom she calls "one of the most outstanding women in Jerome," with organizing a variety of activities for adults and children to keep up their spirits and occupy their time: "She was afflicted with arthritis . . . was undergoing constant pains. Yet, this woman, almost single-handedly, with tremendous drive and ebullience, managed to organize the PTA, Sunday school, teenage clubs, community activities, and the USO." Tsukamoto also coordinated the numerous girls' clubs, including the YWCA, business and professional women and students, and USO hostesses, all while carrying on her responsibilities as wife and young mother. Yuri said with admiration: "To have watched her, as she spoke with different age groups and interests, arousing, encouraging, involving . . . was something beautiful to observe." Tsukamoto later documented these camp experiences in her book, *We the People: A Story of Internment in America*.[49]

To this day, Yuri regularly tells people about Peter Kondo, a patient in the Santa Anita Assembly Center hospital who was paralyzed from a 1934 car accident: "Peter Kondo, was at first, just another patient in the Men's Ward of the hospital. . . . He was a paralytic, who was totally immobilized. But Peter Kondo had a perennial cheerfulness and a dynamic personality that transcended his helplessness. He was the inspiration of the Ward F, and as such, his influence was contagious. Male patients coming into that ward, seeing his condition would never complain about anything, especially after hearing that Peter Kondo was once one of the greatest Nisei baseball players. He never talked about 'what was,' rather he showed us 'what could be.'"[50]

In addition, Yuri appreciated the people outside her community who supported the Japanese Americans despite potential sacrifices to their financial standing and social status:

> After the Japanese were moved out, Mr. and Mrs. Swearinger took it upon themselves to help the Japanese tuberculosis patients left at Olive View Sanitarium in Los Angeles. On their monthly visits, they took fresh fish and other food, equipment for handwork, and newspapers and magazines for the hospital inmates. A young ten-year-old boy from California traveled alone all the way to Arkansas to visit a school friend in the Jerome concentration camp. The little red-headed youngster spent a week with the Japanese family, and was one of the few outsiders to briefly glimpse wartime camp life. Also, a Mexican teenager from Los Angeles went to camp with a Japanese American family and actually lived there for two years, undergoing the same privations and limited life.[51]

The people and activities that Yuri remembers and the stories she relays reflect her values. She most admired the qualities of fortitude through adversity, humility, and a focus on the well-being of others. It is these qualities that formed the basis of her humanitarian ethics, her community service, and her later political activism.

One of the major crises that hit all the concentration camps was caused by the loyalty registration. The War Relocation Authority (WRA), the civilian agency managing the concentration camps, wanted to determine the loyalty of Japanese Americans in order to permit the so-called loyal ones to work outside the camps. The U.S. Army also wanted to assess their loyalty to form a voluntary all-Nisei combat unit. In February 1943, the WRA administered a questionnaire called the "Application for Leave Clearance" to all adult internees. Two questions were particularly troubling. Question 27 asked if they were willing to serve in combat duty wherever ordered, and question 28, considered the key loyalty question, asked them to swear allegiance to the United States and to forswear allegiance to Japan. It was clear the U.S. government had not put much thought into developing the questions and the questionnaire caused problems in every camp. The Issei were caught in a dilemma. If they answered no to question 28, they would be considered disloyal to the country where they had lived most of their lives; but if they answered yes, they would become stateless people, given that the U.S. government denied them the right to naturalized citizenship on racial grounds. Some Nisei thought answering yes to question 28 might be misinterpreted to mean they previously held allegiance to Japan, a country most had never seen. Most internees were worried that if family members answered the questions in dissimilar ways, the family would be separated. Consequently, people's responses to these two questions had little to do with their feelings of loyalty to the United States. Besides, this was an absurd way to test loyalty. What they put on paper meant little compared to their actions. The majority of Japanese Americans professed and enacted strong patriotism. Even those who expressed anti-American sentiment hardly posed a threat to national security; not a single Japanese American was found to have committed sabotage, espionage, or fifth-column activities against the U.S. government.[52]

Along with the majority of internees, Yuri, her mother, and her brother answered both questions affirmatively. This was predictable enough given the Nakahara family's patriotic and accommodationist stance. In time, Art and Yuri became part of the mass exodus of so-called loyals, who were allowed to leave camp to work. The jobs available to Japanese Americans consisted mainly of menial labor, seasonal farmwork, domestic services, or factory work. By late 1944, after thirty-six thousand internees had left, the concentration camps were transformed into settlements for the elderly and the young. But what affected Yuri most immediately was that those who answered no to question 28 were transferred to the Tule Lake concentration camp in northern California: "For some reason, a lot of families in

Block 3 [where Yuri lived] left for Tule Lake, and many of the children had worked with the Crusaders. It was sad to be separated from our friends yet another time."[53]

The next major crisis in the concentration camps came in January 1944. The reinstatement of the draft for the Nisei triggered hostilities between those who advocated military service and those against it. Sometimes families were split when one son joined the army and another resisted the draft. But this conflict did not directly affect the Nakaharas. Peter was in the army, Art had tried to enlist, and Yuri and Mrs. Nakahara were supporting Nisei GIs. For Yuri, the draft reinstatement signaled an opportunity for Japanese Americans to demonstrate their loyalty to U.S. war efforts. Her support for Nisei soldiers, manifested by her zealous letter-writing campaign, expanded to include working in the USOs in Camp Jerome and in Mississippi. By contrast, in the Heart Mountain, Wyoming, concentration camp, a group of men led a campaign against the draft, arguing that holding Japanese American families behind barbed wire while asking their sons to fight for the United States was the ultimate hypocrisy. The Heart Mountain Fair Play Committee, spearheaded by Kiyoshi Okamoto and Frank Emi, encouraged young Nisei men to resist being conscripted into the U.S. Army until their families' civil liberties were restored. In Heart Mountain, the seven most visible leaders of the Fair Play Committee, including Okamoto and Emi, were arrested, tried using a Japanese American informant's perjured testimony, and given four-year prison sentences. Also arrested was James Omura, a Nisei journalist who printed material about the Fair Play Committee's draft resistance movement in the Denver Japanese American newspaper, the *Rocky Shimpo*. Although acquitted on the basis of freedom of the press, Omura was blackballed from newspaper jobs and ostracized by some in the Japanese American community, especially the leaders of the ultrapatriotic Japanese American Citizens League (JACL). In addition, 85 men from Heart Mountain and 230 from other camps were convicted of noncompliance with the draft. Although the number of resisters pales in comparison to those who obeyed the draft orders, numbers alone fail to capture the significance of this act of civil disobedience. Douglas Nelson observed: "Given the repressive tactics of the administration and the very small likelihood of achieving any practical results, the fact that one out of every nine draft-age Nisei [in Heart Mountain] chose to face jail rather than take pre-induction physical examinations is remarkable." Today, like many other Japanese Americans, Yuri admires both stances, asserting that it took tremendous courage to fight in the war as well as to resist the draft.[54]

In other camps, notably Manzanar and Poston, violence broke out, often between JACL leaders and those opposed to JACL's policy of "constructive cooperation" with the U.S. government. Back then, Yuri had not heard about conflicts in other camps, but she remembered an incident of violence that occurred in Jerome:

A group of ten to twenty Kibeis attacked Rev. John Yamazaki and Dr. Thomas Yatabe, who was past president of the National JACL. Rev. Yamazaki and Dr. Yatabe were very pro-America and encouraged Nisei to volunteer for military service. The Kibeis, however, felt that serving in the American army was a betrayal to Japan. One of the Kibei groups took Rev. Yamazaki out into the forest and before he could take his glasses off, started beating him. He was a frail, elderly person who had been hospitalized in Santa Anita before being sent to Jerome. Our family was very upset. . . . This Kibei group also beat up Dr. Yatabe, a patriotic JACL leader. The way they lay in waiting for Dr. Yatabe was well organized. They had their people waiting in every hospital corridor. I think they locked the doors and waited for Dr. Yatabe to come in. There was no one there who could have helped him. He was just beaten.

Yuri condemned these acts of violence, then and today, despite changes in her political views: "I thought it was terrible, and still do today. These were cowardly acts. My feelings of distress and compassion for the victims have nothing to do with which side you're on. People should have the right to make their choices of loyalty."[55]

Remembering the pledge she made in Santa Anita to support Nisei soldiers, Yuri spent most of her free time writing to GIs and working in Jerome's makeshift USO. Some thirty-three thousand Japanese Americans, including approximately one hundred women, served in the U.S. military during World War II. The irony was that they served their country despite its racist policies against the Japanese Americans. Not only were their families imprisoned in concentration camps under armed guard; the Nisei GIs were themselves relegated to racially segregated combat units. In throwing together men based on their racial ancestry, the military failed to recognize the cultural differences between the Nisei from Hawaii and the U.S. mainland. The mainland soldiers called Hawaii men "Buddhaheads" because they were closely connected to their Japanese cultural roots. And the soldiers from Hawaii called the mainlanders "kotonks"—"a term connoting the sound of an empty coconut hitting the ground . . . referring to an empty head." Thelma Chang explained: "The California boys . . . came in with their 'pachuko' haircuts (slicked back ducktail haircuts), those zoot suit jackets, those great big hats and the pants that came down just tight around the ankles. . . . They were fancy, way out dressed, and the Hawaii boys came in with their bare feet, T-shirts and pidgin English. It was like throwing two roosters in a pen together."[56]

In time, as the two groups learned to work together and trust one another, the cultural differences became points of comic relief. The 100th Infantry Battalion, with its Nisei volunteers from Hawaii, and the 442nd Regimental Combat Team, with its Nisei volunteers from the mainland concentration camps and Hawaii, soon merged. They were sent to Europe and given some of the hardest, most dangerous assignments, which they fulfilled with courage and determination. After Nisei soldiers liberated Bruyères, France, from German control in 1944, the villagers and their descendants built a monument to honor their Nisei rescuers. Less than two weeks after freeing Bruyères, the 100th/442nd, including Yuri's future husband's Company K, was sent on what appeared to be a suicide mission, but they succeeded in rescuing the "Lost Battalion" of 275 Texans trapped in the forest near Biffontaine, France. In what historian Roger Daniels calls "supreme irony," the Nisei soldiers also liberated the 30,000 prisoners at the Nazi death camp at Dachau in April 1945, while their own families remained behind barbed wire.[57]

The men of the 100th/442nd paid a heavy price for their valor. In one month of fighting, from Bruyères to the rescue of the Lost Battalion, the 100th/442nd lost two-thirds of its troops, with casualties estimated at 2,200, including 161 deaths. In the Lost Battalion ordeal alone, the Nisei soldiers suffered more than 800 casualties, a rate three times higher than the number of men they rescued. For suffering this high casualty rate, the 100th/442nd became the most highly decorated unit of its size in U.S. military history, earning more than 15,000 medals for a unit of 3,000 men.[58]

In addition, 6,000 Nisei served with the Military Intelligence Service (MIS) in Asia and the South Pacific, interpreting Japanese communications, translating stolen military documents, interrogating Japanese POWs, and deciphering enemy codes. While most Nisei in the MIS, including Yuri's twin brother, Peter Nakahara, had to attend military language school to improve their limited Japanese and to learn military terminology, their linguistic skills were critical because few in the American military understood the Japanese language. After capturing the "Z" Plan from a downed Japanese plane, the MIS men's translations uncovered Japan's naval strategy for defending the Marianas (Guam, Saipan, and Tinian) and the Philippines against the Allied Forces. Knowing Japanese military strategy in advance, the United States was able to successfully counter Japan's military aggression in the Pacific Theater. U.S. military historians have declared the "Z" Plan the most important enemy document captured during the war. In daring feats, the Nisei intelligence men crept within hearing distance of Japanese troops to learn of their plans. One MIS man even swam across a river in Burma to a Japanese-controlled area and by impersonating a Japanese officer, commanded the soldiers to surrender. The men of the MIS have been credited with shortening the war by two years.[59]

The Nisei soldiers of the 100th/442nd in Europe and the MIS in East Asia fought courageously, becoming distinguished for unprecedented military achievements. Yuri believes that the valiant efforts of the Nisei soldiers were instrumental in changing mainstream America's views toward the Japanese and opening opportunities for later generations of Japanese Americans. The superior performance of the Nisei soldiers was not lost on the War Relocation Authority and the Office of War Information, who championed their achievements, as well as their fundamentally middle-class aspirations and behaviors, in a postwar propaganda campaign designed to create a positive image of Japanese Americans and facilitate their resettlement. Roger Daniels contends that "although the term 'model minority' was not coined until 1966, the seeds of the concept were planted in the waning years of World War II."[60]

In Jerome, Yuri, then twenty-two years old, applied her journalism experience to writing a column, "Nisei in Khaki," which appeared in each issue of the camp newspaper, the *Denson Tribune,* published twice per week by the War Relocation Authority. Through her writing, she worked to inform the camp residents about conditions facing the Nisei soldiers, to report excerpts from soldiers' letters, to boost the morale of soldiers and internees, and to address issues of concern to Japanese American soldiers. One of the themes that ran through her articles was that of nondiscriminatory treatment of soldiers, regardless of their military ranking, their perceived degree of patriotism, and any cultural differences. "A month or so ago," wrote Yuri, "a visiting soldier wearing a service unit insignia was stopped by a Center resident and tagged a 'sissy' for being under the service command and not in the combat team. . . . He is one of hundreds of other nisei boys who . . . had high hopes of going across to convey his loyalty, but who . . . was assigned only to tasks such as working in service clubs." Her advice to these soldiers embraced an accommodationist stance: "Let us realize that a good soldier isn't one who can just show himself well in battle, but is one who will do his duty well. . . . Our nisei service unit men may never receive recognition for the part they are playing at the moment, but they are as valuable to the army as that of any other branch of service."[61]

Yuri used her column to encourage readers to reach out to those in need: "Every serviceman must take back with him some little incident that he experienced on his stay here. Who knows when such memories may lower or raise that soldier's morale. And what of 'not knowing the soldier?' We need not know a person to be kind to him." Drawing from her own experiences in understanding the power of letters to the confined, she passionately urged her readers to write to the soldiers: "If some of you girls knew what letters can do for a soldier's morale, you wouldn't let one day slip by without writing some 'dog-face' a few lines." Some found Yuri's forthrightness not only unusual but downright pushy. Yet others agreed with her rationale for promoting letter writing. "I was stunned that a perfect stranger would ask me to write to GIs," recalled Dollie (Nagai) Fukawa, who was soon an enthusiastic member of the Crusaders' letter-writing campaign.[62]

It was not unusual to find quotes from mainstream American figures in Yuri's articles. Not only did she admire the messages contained within these quotes, but given her patriotic values, she also respected the men and women behind the words. Sports was another common theme. She wrote: "In connection with the importance of athletics in high school, General MacArthur made the following statement: 'Participation in athletics is the planting ground for character buds to grow and develop that the individuals may bear fruit on other fields in other years.'"[63]

Shortly after the formation of the 442nd, Camp Shelby in Mississippi became the training site for the Nisei soldiers from the 100th Infantry Battalion and 442nd Regimental Combat Team. In Mississippi, there was strong racial hatred, harassment, and violence against anyone with an Asian face, even in uniform. And though the Nisei soldiers had authorization to use the USO in Hattiesburg, they were often uncomfortable in that USO predominated by White soldiers. So the Jerome YWCA issued a call for young Nisei women to visit Camp Shelby for a weekend in June 1943. At Jerome, posted flyers read: "Girls! Let's do our part! 100 girls invited to Camp Shelby, Miss. . . . All expenses paid. All girls 18 years of age and over, get your application from Mary Sato. . . . 3 buses to be provided. One Caucasian Personnel and one Evacuee Mother will chaperone each bus." Despite the enthusiasm of the organizers, only eight girls responded to the first call. But, after repeated appeals to their patriotic and feminine duty, eighty-three girls eventually signed on. "Showing no fatigue from their long trip, the girls danced the night away with two hundred or so lucky Japanese American soldiers, selected by lot, each of whom had paid ten dollars to cover the cost of the trip," wrote Masayo Umezawa Duus.[64]

After the young women visited Camp Shelby, Nisei soldiers began weekend excursions to Jerome. Unlike other soldiers who could visit their families or roam freely, the Nisei soldiers had nowhere to go when on furlough. Their families were scattered across the United States in different concentration camps or were far away in Hawaii. And those with families in Manzanar or Tule Lake, the two California concentration camps, were forbidden to visit there because the West Coast was off limits to Japanese Americans until early 1945. Thus, the only home for Nisei soldiers was the Japanese American community inside the concentration camps. Jerome and Rohwer, a fifteen-hour bus ride from Camp Shelby, were the closest. As increasing numbers of Nisei soldiers spent their weekend furloughs at the two camps, internees worked to set up services and activities for them. The Jerome YWCA staff, particularly Mary Tsukamoto, who served as its first director, and her husband, Al, played a key role in establishing the Jerome USO.[65]

The USO organized activities, especially dances, for the soldiers during their stay at Jerome. The young Nisei women worked as hostesses and dance partners, while Issei women and men served as chaperons. Yuri recalled: "There were rules like the girls had to be seventeen or over; most were between ages seventeen and twenty-five, though I guess they could be older if they wanted to be. At the end, I think the age was dropped to sixteen because younger girls wanted to go to the USO dances. I think soldiers were getting younger too. An eighteen-year-old guy would rather have a sixteen-year-old dance partner than a twenty-five-year-old one."[66]

The young men in camp also supported the USO, notably by organizing baseball games between the Jerome All Stars and the Nisei soldiers' Aloha Team. Over one memorable Fourth of July weekend, baseball games were played during the day and a USO dance was held Saturday night. On Sunday morning, some four thousand people, almost half the camp population, came out to the playoff game. The Jerome All Stars became the champs, but no one cared who won. It was a friendly competition, unlike the real-life battle taking place on the war front.[67]

Yuri recounted her participation in this USO:

All of Jerome really came together and supported our GIs. We had to find housing for the soldiers when they came to Jerome for their weekend visits and organize activities like the dances for them. As families left camp, the soldiers would stay in their vacated barracks. This meant lots of people were involved because every block had to let the USO group know how many units in their block were vacant. Each week one, two, or three buses came, each holding forty-five men. So we had to find a hundred or so beds scattered throughout the camp. We each had different responsibilities. Mine was to greet the soldiers when they came in and determine how many beds were needed and where they would stay. We'd look at the map of the camp to find the number of beds available at various barracks. The buses usually rolled in at 2 a.m. and the camp Niseis took the soldiers to their barracks.[68]

Hearing the story in her own words, one fails to understand the central role Yuri played in the USO. USO director Mary Tsukamoto described Yuri, then Mary Nakahara, in these terms: "When the soldiers came to Jerome . . . it was Mary who met them at the gate long past midnight, welcomed them and arranged places for them to stay. . . . This one woman USO, Mary Nakahara, inspired many with her deep spiritual message and her compulsion to teach. She invoked a spirit of gladness and appreciation. A sense of values accompanied her cheery smile and her creative attempts to bring joy into the lives of so many." Masayo Umezawa Duus concurred: "Of all the girls who helped out at the USO, few were more dedicated or enthusiastic than Mary Yuri Nakahara. . . . The [Aloha] team spent only two nights there, but their memories of Camp Jerome were mingled with memories of Mary."[69]

In serving others, Yuri discovered personal benefits. Working late at the Jerome USO one night, she met the man who would become her husband.

3

New York, New Life

On November 20, 1943, working her usual 10 p.m. to 6 a.m. shift at the Jerome USO, Yuri was busily logging in the two busloads of Nisei soldiers from Camp Shelby, Mississippi, and assigning each GI to a barracks for the weekend. In response to her standard question inquiring where each soldier was from, Pvt. Bill Kochiyama, a New Yorker with a cigarette dangling from his mouth, answered "Manhattan Island" to flirt with the pretty USO worker. Yuri took the bait; she assumed he was referring to one of the Hawaiian Islands. Bill also told Yuri that he was a student at New York University, which he was not. Years later, filmmaker Renee Tajima-Peña asked him why he made those remarks. "Smart-ass," he replied. At the age of twenty-two, Bill was mischievous, charming, and strikingly handsome. And he succeeded in winning Yuri's affection that weekend. About their meeting, Masayo Umezawa Duus wrote: "At the dance that evening the soldier turned out to be a splendid dancer too. . . . The USO hostesses were all aflutter at the sight of this dashing and refined New Yorker. Mary [Yuri] was one of them. To the disappointment of the Hawaiians the soldier from New York quickly swept her off her feet." Sumi (Seo) Seko recounted: "Though Mary had already exclaimed, 'That's the man,' she kept telling all the girls to ask him for a dance instead of keeping him to herself." Yuri recalled: "I thought he was such a handsome and distinctive-looking city slicker. It was love at first sight for me. I knew immediately, he's the one."[1]

Yuri placed Bill at the top of her GI letter-writing list and began writing to him every day, sometimes as often as three times in a single day. Their relationship quickly developed into a romance. When Bill wrote to the Crusaders, he began signing off on his letters as "Mary's Bill." And Yuri became known as "Bill's Mary." After a short court-ship of four months, during which time they saw each other three more times, they decided to marry before Bill left for an overseas assignment. The swiftness with which their relationship proceeded can be understood by at least three factors. First, in the context of the 1940s, "ours was a typical wartime romance," observed Yuri. "Back then, young men and women were really serious about rela-tionships. Lots of girls were quickly getting married, and because you never knew if the guy would come back or not, you were willing to give him a total commitment and wait for him. I was one of the lucky ones, because too often, my girl friends were devastated when their guys were killed in action." Second, Yuri was, and still is, a romantic at heart. Back then, among the five holidays that were special to the Crusaders was Valentine's Day. Even to this day, Yuri, now considered a hard-core political activist, continues to send Valentine's cards not only to her grandchildren but also to friends and political associates. On envelopes, she draws a heart instead of "and" between the names of the couple. And in her political writings, she covers romantic rela-tionships in addition to political material. Third, it was characteristic of Yuri to throw herself wholeheartedly, almost impulsively, into new situations, as she had done with her community service work. This is not to imply that she was impetuous with men, despite having been "boy crazy" since her teen years. Still, given her tendency to know her mind and to act boldly with service activities, it was also not entirely surprising that when she did fall in love, the relationship progressed rapidly.[2]

Yuri and Bill, both age twenty-two, had planned to marry in April 1944, at Camp Shelby, Mississippi, where Bill was stationed. They had received their parents' approval, completed all the paperwork, obtained permission for Yuri's temporary leave from Jerome to Camp Shelby, and arranged for the army chaplain of Bill's unit to marry them. But on the morning of their ceremony, the chaplain received a telegram from Bill's father, requesting that the wedding be postponed until he could meet his future daughter-in-law. Yuri was hurt and dis-appointed, not only by the delayed wedding, but also by what she inter-preted as Mr. Kochiyama's condescension:

Bill's father . . . came from a samurai family and was full of tradition. My family came from the same background, so I knew what it was about. But what I hated about that tradition was the place it gave to pride. To me it was false pride. When I would go to J-town, I loved to see what the Japanese call *ojigi*, the way they bow to each other. But what I could see, too, even when I was young, was that tradition required you to bow lower to people who had more prestige in life. You didn't show the same courtesy to a fisherman or a farmer as you did to a doctor. I didn't like it. Bill finally convinced me that although his father had a lot of pride, he was humble about it and not arrogant, and that I would see it when I met him.

In abiding by the Japanese cultural value of filial piety, Bill and Yuri agreed to honor Mr. Kochiyama's request. They would wait to marry until Bill returned from his overseas military service.[3]

While in Mississippi for her wedding, Yuri met with an opportunity that enabled her to continue her service work for Nisei soldiers and made the long and anxious wait for Bill's return more bearable. The director of the USO's Japanese American Unit offered her a job at the Aloha USO in Hattiesburg, Mississippi. "This special USO for Nisei GIs was established by Hung Wai Ching, the Chinese American director of the YMCA in Honolulu, Hawaii," explained Yuri. "Concerned that the Japanese American soldiers would face opposition and a cold reception while training in the South, Mr. Ching flew to Washington, D.C., and received approval to establish a Nisei USO in Hattiesburg." Yuri left Jerome on Mother's Day, 1944, which, as she noted, "was kind of a sad day for Mom because all her children were gone."[4]

Yuri would also be leaving the Crusaders in Jerome. To ease that transition, she wrote these girls a lengthy group letter in which she explained her philosophy about teaching Sunday school, encouraged her Sunday school girls to live life to the fullest, and expressed her patriotic views. In addition, she spoke to them "not as a teacher, but just as 'another' love-hit, sentimental, khaki-wacky gal." She exclaimed, "I'm the happiest girl in the world," who "[s]ome day . . . hopes to be Mrs. B.K., ideal housewife." This last statement might strike one as being rather sappy. Even Yuri recognized this as she added parenthetically, "no comments please." Still, this statement accurately conveyed her goals and aspirations. She had dreamed of getting married since high school. She viewed her junior college tenure as a way to get some educational and vocational skills until she married, at which point she would devote her life to family and home. This statement is ironic because while she longed for marriage, she did not spend her teenage years training to become that "ideal housewife." Rather than staying home and learning to cook and clean from her mother, who indeed fit the nuclear family mold of an "ideal housewife," Yuri was out running around, involved in numerous extracurricular activities. It is possible that Yuri's definition of ideal housewife differed sharply from the traditional sense of this word. But this is unlikely. She did mean that she would cook, clean, take care of the children, and meet her husband's needs. And Yuri did manage these tasks, particularly in the first fifteen years of her marriage, before she became political. But even then, her "ideal housewife" image was complicated by her desire to participate extensively in community service activities and to play hostess to hundreds of visitors and overnight guests. Her notion of family extended beyond her nuclear family to anyone in need. Moreover, economic necessity dictated that Yuri work outside the home, even if this remained her secondary role. So while she did attend to her family's needs, she did so on her own terms. In this sense, she managed to fulfill her role as a "good mother" and "good wife," while not submerging her own needs to that of her family, as the term "ideal housewife" implies.[5]

When Yuri left for Mississippi, her mother expressed concerns about Yuri's ability to manage her life, especially her finances: "I know Mom was worried about my being out on my own. She told me to find out how much money I was to make, and offered to give me money if I needed it because she had money in the bank. I had no idea how ignorant I was about many things until I had to live on my own in Mississippi." Yuri, then a week shy of her twenty-third birthday, was more naive than most about economic issues. She acknowledged that her class privilege enabled her to disregard financial concerns. "I had lived so comfortably in San Pedro and my folks bought us clothes and whatever we needed. Like almost everything in life, I came to understand these things late in life." It was not simply the limited use of money inside the concentration camps that explained Yuri's lack of financial know-how. It was as if she did not want to get bogged down with mundane matters. Her objective was to help others; worrying about money was a nuisance. Throughout her life, she has had others—her parents, her husband, and then her children—handle her finances. The following story, told by Yuri, further illustrates this point:

> When I went to see Pete off before he departed overseas [in the mid-1940s], I stayed with Art in Chicago. Art would treat me to dinner and let me stay at his place. Art often said, "If you want to invite a friend, I'll treat you both to dinner." At the time, I didn't appreciate his generosity because in camp we didn't use money. Then one time, I ran into eight Nisei soldiers who we had been writing to. I invited them to eat with us and even told them, "Oh, my brother will treat you." When he walked into the restaurant and Art saw all those people, he pulled me aside and said, "Wait a minute. What are those soldiers doing here?" I said, "Oh, I thought you wouldn't mind treating us all." He said, "I'll treat you to dinner but I'm not going to treat anyone else." I said, "Oh gosh. I don't know." So he asked, "What did you tell them?" I don't remember what happened, but this shows how I didn't understand the value of money.[6]

At the Aloha USO, Yuri was responsible for finding housing for the wives and families of Nisei soldiers, but she quickly bumped up against the barrier of racism. "Hattiesburg probably had more USOs, percentagewise, [than any other place]," she recounted. "Yet we were told Japanese Americans, probably Asians in general, were not welcome. Of course, Black and Latino soldiers were not welcome. That's why for us to find a place to take a shower was not easy. . . . In Hattiesburg, the only two USOs that welcomed Asians were the Catholic USO and Jewish USO."[7]

Residential discrimination in Hattiesburg also affected Yuri personally. She did not have a home, for example, when Mrs. Nakahara obtained a weekend pass to visit, so they stayed at the Aloha USO. Yuri recounted: "After everyone was gone, we slept on the floor. Mom was so game about everything. Here she grew up very well, had lived comfortably in San Pedro, but she took everything in stride. She didn't think anything was beneath her." Yuri moved several times in Hattiesburg until Earl Finch, whom the Nisei considered the "Godfather of the 442," allowed her to stay at his home. Before that a couple from Hawaii, Yuri and Bones Taono, provided Yuri with a place to stay. Later on, Yuri stayed with Tak and Kei Ishikawa and Kei's sister, Betty. While her own migratory experiences likely contributed to her growing awareness of race and racism, it seems that Yuri consciously focused her concerns outward. By working for others, she would not have to reflect upon her own difficulties, on the meaning of these experiences, or on the feelings of inferiority that often accompany being the target of racism. So she busily worked to find housing for the Nisei soldiers. At times this meant bringing soldiers to her residence. When she stayed in the front room of the Ishikawas' house, for example, Yuri invited so many Nisei GIs to spend the night that "they were sleeping in sleeping bags all over the dining room," recalled Kei Ishikawa. While Yuri may have placed a burden on her hosts, it seems that they also supported efforts to house Nisei soldiers. Ishikawa, whose husband was a military officer, stated: "I didn't mind the soldiers being around. They were well behaved. Some boys wanted to cook their own Japanese food, which they couldn't do elsewhere. So I let them." Rather than feeling encumbered by the soldiers, Ishikawa seemed to appreciate Yuri's dedication and hard work.[8]

In her role as a Japanese American USO worker, Yuri was also asked to speak about the Nisei soldiers at local churches a couple of mornings a week. Because she had taught Sunday school, told stories at the Homer Toberman Settlement House, and taken speech classes in school, it was not difficult for her to speak to the small groups of school-age children. Based on what she knew, she explained the immigration history of Asian Americans, the formation of the all-Nisei 442nd, and the incarceration of Japanese Americans. Yuri said: "I didn't know that much; none of us had had the benefit of ethnic studies courses back then. But I discussed what our Japanese American soldiers were fighting for, and that we hoped after the war was over, life for Japanese Americans would be better. We knew a lot of our Nisei soldiers would be killed, but we hoped their courage and service would open doors for the rest of the community." Yuri's pro-American fervor made her a well-selected choice to promote the patriotic goals of the USO.[9]

After working in Hattiesburg for a year, Yuri traveled to Minneapolis, Minnesota, to help set up a service program for Nisei soldiers stationed at Camp Savage. In Minneapolis, she also worked part-time doing domestic work, laundry, and waitressing—jobs that were typical of the low-income, menial positions held by Japanese Americans during the war. When the war ended in 1945, Yuri's family decided to return to their home in San Pedro, California. By then, Jerome had already closed and the remaining internees, including her mother, had been transferred to the camp in Rohwer. So Yuri went there to accompany her family back to California. Her brother Art also went to Rohwer from Chicago, where he and his fiancée were working. While in Rohwer, he married Chiyo Ogata, a friend of Yuri's who had lived in a nearby barracks in Jerome. It is unclear why Art and Chiyo married inside the concentration camp when both of their families would soon be returning to Southern California. Could it be that they were simply anxious to get married? Or could it be that Art and Chiyo had wanted to remain in Chicago? If the latter were the case, it could explain why they married in Rohwer before both of their families returned to California. Perhaps after they married, Mrs. Nakahara convinced them to move to San Pedro so that she would not have to be alone in such a big house. According to Japanese custom, it was the duty of the firstborn son to care for elderly parents. Yet according to American custom, it was the daughter who usually cared for aging parents. But Mrs. Nakahara knew that Yuri was planning to move to New York when Bill returned from overseas. And Art was probably easier to direct, given his tendency toward Japanese cultural values and given Yuri's independent and stubborn streak. While Yuri expressed that Art and Chiyo had wanted to return to San Pedro and encouraged Mrs. Nakahara to live with them, it is possible that this is what she wanted to believe to justify the long-term care her brother and sister-in-law provided to her mother. Mrs. Nakahara ended up living with her elder son and his wife in San Pedro until she died in 1963.[10]

In October 1945, the Nakahara family, including aunt Tama Kondo, traveled from Rohwer to San Pedro by train. Yuri recalled her feelings about returning home: "We were filled with hope, excitement, relief as well as apprehension and fear as we made the long journey home. We had heard stories of Americans treating returning Japanese poorly, both on the West Coast and throughout their travels. We knew that anti-Japanese feelings ran high. Yet we were thrilled to leave the camps and to return to our beloved hometown."[11]

The Nakaharas were more fortunate than most. Their neighbors, the Stevenses, had kept a watchful eye over their home and yard. When they learned the Nakaharas were coming back, the Stevenses notified the tenants who were renting their house that they had to leave. But other Japanese American families faced a hostile homecoming. Dwellings had been vandalized, and some even recognized their neighbors using the stolen goods. Life savings were depleted. They were not allowed to enter certain business establishments. Japanese American farmers and businesses were boycotted. Yuri and her family experienced both the good and the bad upon returning to the West Coast. Remarking on the positives, Yuri said: "Many local people were kind to us. I enjoyed seeing many of my friends and the girls who were in my Sunday school, Girls Scouts, Girl Reserves and other clubs. Everyone had grown up so much during the three and a half years we were gone. And many strangers went out of their way to help us." But, the flip side also occurred, as Yuri recounted:

> One of my Nisei friends called and told me how, when she went to our place thinking we were already home, the woman who was living there just opened the door and slammed it in her face when she saw her. Other Japanese said they had come over to San Pedro to see if we were there and, when they didn't find us, went to shop. They went to get groceries across the street from our house, but the shopkeeper didn't want to wait on them. When I heard this, I was furious. This was the town that I loved and that I kept bragging about, that was a haven with no racism.[12]

The full force of postwar animosity hit her when she began to look for a job. Her goal was to find a waitressing job so that she could earn a little money while waiting for Bill to return from the war front. Yuri thought it would be easy to find such a job, but she soon discovered otherwise:

> I think I tried every single restaurant in San Pedro, on all the main drags, and not one place would hire me. They said, "If you're Japanese, forget it." Or else it was, "If you're not in the union, don't even try here." How the heck could I be in the union when I had just gotten there and they didn't let the Japanese in the union anyway? Finally I went to Skid Row. I remember Walter Winchell saying that San Pedro's Skid Row was the roughest in

the world. At least, I thought, that would be one place that would take anybody. It was rougher than I imagined. I guess because the war was just over and people regarded us as Japanese, not Americans, they treated us like we were the enemy.

The first weeks were the worst. I'd go out looking for a job every single day, and even when I actually got jobs I would last anywhere from an hour to before-the-night-was-out. I would take night jobs starting at six in the evening until three or four in the morning because that's all that was available. Every night, as soon as a few people would start complaining—"Is that a Jap?"—the boss would say, "Sorry, I can't keep you, you're hurting business." First time around, most places didn't want to even take a chance. But gradually, because they were so hard up for waitresses for those hours, I became employable. They said, "Okay, you can stay until we get too many complaints, and then you've got to go." The first job that I got I was so excited! I rushed home to tell my mother and to get a uniform together. And I made it through the first night. I felt so proud. But when I finished, the boss said, "Don't come back, your presence here made me lose two of my regular waitresses." He said they absolutely refused to work with a *Jap*. I was so busy, I hadn't even noticed.

Every day I'd work a few hours, until I'd get the "go" sign. One time, I went into a restaurant for the first time, and every person sitting in the place looked at me, rose up, and yelled, "What's this? Do I see a Jap?" Some places were nice. The owners would say, "If you can take it, just stay here until someone throws a cup of coffee at you." But that would happen, and then the boss would say, "No, you'd better go, for your own sake."[13]

It was difficult for Yuri to reconcile such blatant discrimination with her previously unwavering views of a perfect hometown. But in the three and a half years since she left, Yuri had matured. She could no longer deny that U.S. society treated people differently on the basis of race. Still, she attributed much of the discrimination to postwar hysteria. Like many Nisei, especially the more patriotic ones, Yuri believed that America would soon change and live up to its professed values of democracy and justice for all. The Nisei had to wait patiently and prove their good citizenship, and in time, America would embrace the Nisei as the good Americans that they were. Hers was not yet a philosophy of active resistance. That would take a couple of decades to develop. As Yuri observed, "[Those experiences] made me aware of racism, but [they] didn't make me political because I didn't understand the politics of why these things happened."[14] But becoming aware of racism was the first step in Yuri's political development. And in the context of the emerging Civil Rights Movement in the United States and national liberation struggles in the Third World, Yuri too would develop a political understanding of world events. But before that would happen, her story involves marriage and children and a move to New York.

The day Yuri had been waiting for finally arrived: Bill returned. He arrived in New York on Christmas Day, 1945, and was discharged from the military on December 31, 1945. Bill wrote, asking her to come to New York as soon as possible so that they could get married. Ecstatic, Yuri left San Pedro on January 23, 1946, to move to New York City. Along the way, she experienced several mishaps:

> I had been saving my waitressing money, so I caught a bus to New York. The trip took several days and had some unexpected events. In Idaho, I went out to get something to eat at midnight, when all of a sudden the bus took off. I ran after it, screaming, "I'm supposed to be on the bus." But it left, taking my suitcase and heavy coat with it. It was so cold and I got sick. [By the time I reached] Chicago I had to run out to buy any coat on the street to keep warm. By that time I was really sick. I had sent Bill a telegram indicating the date and time of my arrival, but when I finally arrived in New York, Bill and I were both confused about where he was to pick me up. Bill went to get me at Penn Station at 11 p.m., but I wasn't there. So he took off to the next station, but again I wasn't there. Bill was really boiling. The next morning he got up early and waited at every bus station. But I had arrived the night before and somehow we had missed each other.[15]

After finding one another, Yuri and Bill hurried to plan a small, simple wedding. They were married on February 9, 1946, by Rev. Alfred Akamatsu in the St. James Chapel of Riverside Church. Dressed in a brown suit and hat, Yuri was elated to be marrying Bill, especially after waiting almost two years since their initial attempt. Seventeen people attended their wedding, including Bill's best man, Ken Hayashi; Yuri's matron of honor, Monica Miya (Miwako Oana); Bill's father, Yutaka Kochiyama; Bones and Yuri Taono; and Tad Miya, Monica's husband. Yuri remembered that in their hastiness: "We forgot about a reception; we didn't even have a tea and coffee reception. Bill just grabbed his best man and said, 'Let's go eat somewhere.' We didn't realize there was certain wedding protocol we were supposed to follow."[16]

William Masayoshi Kochiyama, the child of immigrants from Japan, was born on May 10, 1921, in Washington, D.C., and raised in New York City. His father's family descended from the samurai class and his paternal grandfather was a doctor. Yutaka Kochiyama's class background, unusually high among the Japanese immigrants, afforded him the opportunity to study at George Washington University, in Washington, D.C. But in the United States, race discrimination closed many doors, with the exception of low-status, low-paying work. Domestic work was one job that was available to Japanese immigrants, men and women alike. Mr. Kochiyama fell into this category. The resulting downward economic mobility was hard on many. Bill's father tried to conceal his menial and feminized work, so much so, relayed Yuri, that his impeccable attire fooled some people into believing he was an ambassador from China. Mr. Kochiyama was also an art collector and a skilled photographer. And much of his leisure time was consumed studying hummingbirds, a subject on which he became a near expert; even the Audubon Society and the National Geographic Society consulted with him.[17]

The Kochiyamas' lives changed drastically when Bill's brother and sister, one a year older and the other a year younger than Bill, then age two, died in the post–World War I flu epidemic. Bill never understood what happened to his mother, whether she got ill, died, returned to Japan, or otherwise. Yuri explained: "A couple of times, Bill asked his father, 'Where's my mother? What happened to her?' But his dad just looked sad and never answered. Bill never asked again."[18]

When Bill was four, his father moved them to New York, where Mr. Kochiyama found work as a domestic servant. His long hours, however, prevented him from attending to his young son, and he placed Bill in a Protestant orphanage called Sheltering Arms. That the institution was designed for "half-orphans," or children of single parents, reflected in part society's idealization of the nuclear family. Racially, the orphanage catered to poorer, White families. Although the only non-White resident, Yuri stressed that, "Bill was well accepted, very popular, a good athlete, a good student, and a good dancer. He grew up with many 'brothers' and 'sisters,' some 120 of them, and made close lifelong friendships there." Except for a brief stay with one family, Bill lived in the all-White environment at Sheltering Arms from age five until eighteen. Despite his Tuesday evening dinners with his father, usually at a Japanese or Chinese restaurant, "Bill grew up almost thinking he was White," remarked Yuri. She also added, "But then, I also ran around with mostly Whites, though my closest friends were Niseis." Yet years later, Bill candidly reflected on how this racial environment affected his self-concept: "While growing up, I subconsciously knew that I was 'different.' Therefore, I tried to become 300% American—in every way by rejecting anything and everything 'Japanese.'. . . I adamantly refused to re-learn the Japanese language, or read Japanese history, or even practice Judo, which was then the 'in-thing.' To whitewash my Japanese appearance even further, I attempted to dress . . . 'sharper' than my youthful white peers; tried to excel in sports—particularly baseball, basketball, swimming, track, and ice hockey; and, of course, to 'be-with-it'—to dance the Lindy, Big Apple, Shag, and the Peabody."[19]

Bill began hanging out with Japanese Americans, for the first time, when he moved to California in the spring of 1940 with the intentions of enrolling at the University of California at Berkeley. As Bill understood from his father, "someone" had left him money for college. But he never realized his goals. "When Bill first arrived in Oakland," Yuri said, "he started running around with these Nisei guys who went out all the time. He spent all his money on wine, women, and song. And the money ran out fast." When he started looking for a job, he bumped up against the intensity of anti-Japanese hostility, particularly virulent on the West Coast. He eventually found a job at a Japanese-owned laundry and dry cleaning business. Knowing how disappointed Mr. Kochiyama would be, Bill never told his father he did not attend college. Yuri recounted: "When we printed our marriage announcement in the paper, he asked his best man to write that 'prior to service, Bill attended the University of California at Berkeley.' His father felt so good to see that in the paper." Because Bill was residing in California in 1942, he was moved to the "assembly center" at the Tanforan race-track in San Francisco and later to the concentration camp in Topaz, Utah.[20]

Yuri's life in New York City diverged sharply from her experiences in San Pedro. She had grown up in a well-appointed, eight-room house in a serene small town. Yuri's youth had been carefree and easy. By contrast, her first three homes with Bill in fast-paced New York City were tiny one-room sleeping units, with a communal kitchen and bathroom shared with other tenants. For the first time in her life, she had to worry about how to make ends meet. One would predict that a middle-class woman would have difficulty adjusting to this downward mobility, perhaps blaming her husband for their financial deficiencies. But this did not seem to be the case. Friends from San Pedro and New York remember that Yuri appeared rather oblivious to social etiquette and economic status, except to shun the wealth and high-tone lifestyle of her parents. Perhaps her Christian background encouraged her to avoid coveting material possessions. Rather than pining after the things they did not have, Yuri chose to focus on what she did have: a wonderful husband, a new, exciting environment, and the blessing of supportive friends. She recounted: "I loved New York from the moment I arrived. There were so many interesting people, so kind and generous, and from all parts of the world. It was a much bigger world than San Pedro. Within the first week, we got to know everyone on our floor. We learned so much from all the folks there, mostly older people who had rich life stories to share."[21]

In New York, Bill's first priority was to find a job. He quickly experienced what Yuri already knew—that virtually all Japanese Americans faced employment discrimination in the postwar period. Having fought in the military meant little to employers, as many Nisei veterans discovered. They were seen as Japanese first, and that closed many doors. Bill found his first job polishing stones in a lapidary, work that, according to Yuri, many Nisei were doing at the time.[22]

As was common among returning soldiers, Bill attended college with the aid of the GI Bill. While working part-time, he enrolled at Long Island University in Brooklyn in fall 1946, majoring in journalism. By taking a full course load and attending summer school, Bill graduated with a bachelor's degree in three years. During this period, Yuri followed a typical employment pattern among Nisei women: she engaged in full-time waged work, in her case as a waitress, until she had a child, after which her primary role consisted of child care and housework.[23]

The waitressing work afforded more than a source of income. By putting Yuri into contact with the Black community, she gained a political and cultural education. About her first job in New York at a Chock full o'Nuts restaurant, Yuri recounted:

> All the workers called it "the plantation," because the owner and managers were White while almost all the workers were Black; the customers were also Black. This was my first experience working with Blacks and did I get educated. . . . At Chock full o'Nuts, I became acquainted with a couple of Black guys who, like my husband, had been trained at Camp Shelby, Mississippi. I told them that I worked in Hattiesburg, Mississippi, and we wondered why no Black GIs came into our Aloha USO. They asked, "Where was it located?" When I told them, "222 Pine," they explained: "Pine? That's the main drag. Colored soldiers couldn't walk on any main drags in the South, even in uniform." I was stunned. I never knew that, and wondered if our Nisei GIs were aware of that. Then I started to remember that in the year I was at the Aloha USO, I hardly encountered any Blacks, which seemed strange in a state that was heavily Black. I only saw them at the bus terminals and train stations.[24]

As Yuri connected with her coworkers and customers and the low-income tenants in her building, her understanding of race and class discrimination expanded:

> I was learning a great deal by interacting with people in the projects. The vast majority, some 95 percent, of the tenants were Black and Puerto Rican. They told us stories about their everyday lives. From them, I learned about the Jim Crow laws of race segregation: Blacks in the South couldn't use swimming pools or libraries; couldn't go to certain parks; had to sit only in the balcony of theaters; had to ride in the back of the bus; had to drink out of separate drinking fountains; use separate toilet

facilities; wouldn't be admitted to public facilities like hospitals, hotels, restaurants; had to go to separate schools; could not vote; had limited jobs; could not live wherever they wished—all because of racism. I also learned that institutional racism is practiced not only in the South, but also in the North, East, and West. Of course, back in the 1950s, I didn't use the term "institutionalized racism," or even understand what it meant. I just knew that people weren't being treated fairly simply because of the color of their skin. I didn't understand the systemic forces of racism and imperialism behind this discrimination, but I knew that discrimination was wrong.[25]

While Bill was in college, their first two children were born. As it was for many American couples at the time, children came a year or two after the wedding. "Bill and I both loved children and wanted to start a family right away," said Yuri. Their first child, William Earl, was born on May 1, 1947. He was named after his father and Earl Finch, Yuri's USO adviser in Hattiesburg. Their second child was born June 30, 1949. Audee Tsuma's first name is a combination of the Kochiyamas' friends Audrey (Chavez) and Dee (Yuri Taono) and her middle name honors Yuri's mother. With a growing family, the Kochiyamas could barely squeeze into their one-room unit. So in 1948, before Audee was born, they moved to a three-bedroom apartment in the government-subsidized Amsterdam housing project in midtown Manhattan. The Amsterdam Houses were a large complex, spread out from Sixty-first to Sixty-fourth streets and from West End to Amsterdam Avenue, situated across from what became the site of the Lincoln Center. This predominantly Black residence would be their home for the next twelve years.[26]

After Bill graduated from college in 1949, the Kochiyamas had hoped their financial situation would improve. But, unforeseen at the time, financial hardship would plague them in the years to come. Apart from coping with poverty, what most concerned Yuri was how bad Bill felt about being unemployed. Nisei men, like most men in the United States and Japan, were socialized into their prescribed masculine role, which centers on providing for their families. Consequently, America's racial barriers to employment undermined a sense of self-worth in many Japanese American men. From Yuri's perspective, "Bill's dream was to be a reporter. He was such a talented writer, I mean really good. If he had graduated ten years later, he probably would have worked as a journalist. The jobs were opening up for Third World people ten years later. But when he got out of school, the job market was closed to minorities. Everyday for nine long months, he'd go out looking for a job, but nothing was available. After job hunting all day, he would come home so discouraged."[27]

Yuri, ever the optimist, managed to learn important life lessons and to find the beauty in humanity through these trying circumstances:

> Out of this, we learned the goodness in people's hearts. We had to lean on friends and many people helped us. There was this Irish guy, Bill Sweeney, who slipped in some money every time he gave Bill a handshake. At the Amsterdam housing project, everyone was so generous and helpful. A Black guy, Russ Robinson, and a Greek guy who we knew as Mike gave us onions and potatoes from the vegetable stand they owned. This Italian guy who worked at the A and P gave us canned goods where the labels fell off. And almost every Catholic family in the building, and there were plenty of Spanish, Irish, and Italian families, seemed to make spaghetti with meatballs on Thursday night. Because Catholics don't eat meat on Friday, they'd bring all their leftover spaghetti and meatballs to us for our Friday night meal. Bill's dad and his friends, who also worked as domestics, would sneak all kinds of food out of the kitchens where they worked. We got eggs, bread, whatever we needed. There was also an Italian woman whose son went to Sheltering Arms. She worked as a domestic for a wealthy family, and she brought us really fancy things like artichoke hearts and caviar. We learned that even when people don't have much themselves they find ways to help those in need. I think the poor are some of the most generous and compassionate people. We really appreciate all that they did for us.[28]

These experiences were more valuable to Yuri than any measure of financial success. This is what was important in life: people sharing their time and resources to help others in need. Whether the giver or the recipient, Yuri enjoyed this sense of interdependence and the opportunity it afforded to witness other people's generosity. Many Nisei might have been embarrassed to accept handouts, but Yuri never saw herself as any better than the recipients of her service work. Like them, she could accept help when in need, although she felt more comfortable in the giver role.

Yuri also found ways to contribute to the family finances by working at home:

> All of us housewives in the projects were looking for jobs where we wouldn't have to leave our home. One of the women had a typewriter, so we took turns using it. We agreed that each of the four of us could take the typewriter for three hours and do as much work typing envelope labels or whatever job we got. I also worked making ribbons for Orchids of Hawaii. And then, after Bill graduated and couldn't find a job, we both started selling plastics—plastic aprons, plastic curtains, plastic tablecloths. It got to the point that people would avoid us. We carried these plastic goods everywhere with us, and as soon as they'd see us, they'd turn the other way or cross the street to dodge us. Finally, we got so tired; maybe we did it a year. Then I wrote my mother, "Gee, Mom, can you help me? You have so many friends there. Could you help sell these aprons and curtains and stuff?" She told us to send them. I sent just about everything we couldn't sell, and she sold them all. She was terrific.[29]

After nine months of looking for journalism-related work, Bill found a job in public relations at the Japan International Christian University Foundation (JICUF). There, he was responsible for writing brochures and different kinds of publicity about a new university that was being built in Mitaka, Japan. Yuri commented: "Bill liked being able to write and design the publicity materials. He had so much creativity and was a clever writer." But she also noted that during the fifteen years he worked at JICUF, Bill resented the fact that they never once sent him to Japan: "Every time they sent a White person, and it was generally his boss. Though Bill was the PR person, his boss would go to Japan and bring back materials for Bill to write up. After years of this, he got disgusted at how JICUF did things. He felt that JICUF didn't live up to its Christian ideals, at least not to him."[30]

In referring to Bill's work at JICUF as well as other public relations jobs, Audee observed: "My father always had a white-collar job, but for some reason it was a struggle for the family. He did PR work, which would normally pay more of a middle-class salary. For some reason, wherever he worked, he had full responsibility, but was always underpaid." A combination of factors may well explain the Kochiyamas' financial struggles, despite Bill's educational attainment and professional status. Racism in job hiring and promotions could have been at play, as Yuri and others in the family believe. Regardless of their English fluency, Asian Americans, even the U.S.-born like Bill, are regularly viewed as perpetual foreigners whose presumed English language deficiencies render them unqualified for verbally based jobs such as public relations. Asian Americans are also stereotyped as passive nonresisters who will not make waves no matter how unfairly they are treated. There is also some indication that Bill may not have been very ambitious in the workplace. So the combination of structural factors such as racism and personal factors may have kept Bill in lower-echelon white-collar work, as was common for many Asian American professionals at the time.[31]

Moreover, the Kochiyamas had heightened expenses that accompanied raising a large family in New York City. They also incurred costs from extensive community service activities and from housing and feeding the constant houseguests and large crowds that attended their weekend open houses. Dollie (Nagai) Fukawa, for example, recalled that when she visited the Kochiyamas at a time when Bill was a full-time student, Yuri served veal, a rather expensive item that was certainly not a staple at the Kochiyamas' dinner table. In addition, both Bill and Yuri wanted their family to enjoy life. Their children were exposed to diverse activities, and Bill hung out with his veteran buddies at a bar every Friday night. Yuri's niece Elizabeth Nakahara, the daughter of a lawyer, noticed differences in lifestyle between her New York relatives and her own middle-class family in San Jose, California: "New York was just so different. My cousins would take cabs to go downtown to see movies. I remember they saw a lot of movies. . . . My parents didn't do that. My parents lived very frugally. . . . So they didn't really enjoy the present that much. We didn't go to concerts, restaurants, or much entertainment at all. It was a very boring life compared to the Kochiyamas."[32]

After Bill started working at JICUF and the family finances improved, Yuri and Bill had four more children. Their second daughter, Lorrie

Aichi, was born on June 28, 1952. Her first name is the combination of Terry Croskrey, Yuri's childhood friend, and his wife, Gloria, and her middle name is a fusion of the names of Yuri's sisters-in-law, Aiko and Chiyo. Then came three boys. Edmund Yutaka was born on June 16, 1955, weighing a mere three pounds, fourteen ounces. He was named after Bill's Sheltering Arms buddy, Edmund Singleton, and after Bill's father. Born April 28, 1957, was James Wade, named after his obstetrician, Dr. James O'Rourke, and his pediatrician, Dr. William Wade Glass. Their last child was born on April 1, 1959. Thomas Seiichi's first name is the Anglicized and masculinized version of Tama, the first name of Yuri's aunt, Kondo-no-obasan, and his middle name honors Yuri's late father. To this day, all of the Kochiyama children are called by the informal versions of their names: Billy, Audee, Lorrie (who as a teenager began using her Japanese name, Aichi), Eddie, Jimmy, and Tommy.[33]

Although a family of six children was unusually large for Nisei parents, Yuri would have liked to have had even more children:

> I loved having lots of children around. Right from the beginning, I said let's have six children—at least. I actually wanted a few more kids. I think Bill also liked having a big family; after all, he grew up in an orphanage with more than a hundred other kids. But, we let our children decide. Aichi was the only one who wanted more siblings. The others said, "No, we are having a hard enough time, and you can't give us all the things you said you wanted to give us."[34]

What were most of the Kochiyama children not receiving enough of? Were they feeling deprived of material goods, activities, or parental attention? Yuri and Bill would have posed the question about having additional children in the late 1950s or early 1960s, since their last child was born in 1959. So the children's response was in reference to their family life at the Amsterdam housing project in midtown Manhattan, or possibly also to their first year or two at the Manhattanville housing project in Harlem, where they had moved in December 1960. In either case, they were referring to the Kochiyama family life prior to Yuri's involvement in the Civil Rights Movement. In the 1950s, "Mary [Yuri] was just like any other housewife in the Amsterdam housing project, except busier. She always liked to be around people, and people were always around her," remarked neighbor Betty Robinson. Understanding the meaning of Robinson's observation and of the Kochiyama children's remarks requires a discussion of the Kochiyamas' marital roles, family life, and the activities that kept Yuri so busy.[35]

The Kochiyamas had a fairly typical marriage for the times. They were raising children in the 1950s during a time when the nuclear family was socially constructed as the ideal in American society. This ideal, with its gendered division of labor, dictated that "good husbands" provided financially for their families and "good wives" worked in the home taking care of their children and household. Nisei marriages were characterized by this gendered division of labor, and Bill and Yuri fell into their prescribed roles. Bill was the primary breadwinner. Yuri's domain was the children and home.[36]

Class distinctions affected the extent to which Nisei husbands and wives could, in practice, conform to the 1950s ideal of the nuclear family. In contrast to the middle class, working-class Nisei behaviorally enacted more flexible gender roles, often a result of economic necessity rather than the adoption of egalitarian values. When race and class discrimination, in part, rendered Bill's income insufficient to sustain the family, Yuri engaged in paid work from their home and did part-time waitressing when the children got older. But doing this work did not detract from her primary identity as wife and mother. To Yuri, paid work was secondary: "What I made hardly helped our family's budget at all." That Bill did more domestic work than the average Nisei husband partially reflected the dictates of their working-class background. One task that Bill did throughout their marriage was the grocery shopping, largely owing to Yuri's limited financial know-how. Yuri recounted: "I never did go grocery shopping. If I ever went, I was always spontaneously picking out things not on the grocery list, whatever I thought my family would like—cookies, candy, special food—without regard to cost or need. So Bill was the one who put together the grocery list, checked out what was on sale, and he stuck to the items we needed." Because most Nisei believed that domestic tasks fell in the woman's realm, food preparation, including grocery shopping, was almost always part of the wife's duties. While a husband may have occasionally helped out by shopping from a grocery list prepared by his wife, it was highly unusual for a Nisei man to create the list, look for sale items, and complete the grocery shopping. Had the Kochiyamas had money to spare, it is possible that Yuri might well have abided by her prescribed gender role in this area. Bill also managed the family finances, paid the bills, and did the banking—tasks considered neither male nor female by Nisei couples, according to Sylvia Yanagisako.[37]

In addition to class dictates, Bill's and Yuri's upbringings help account for their more egalitarian behaviors. Bill was raised in an orphanage, with a margin of freedom from traditional gender role socialization, and by a father who did the feminized work of a domestic. As a child, Yuri often stepped outside her prescribed gender roles, despite being the only daughter. These economic and socialization factors affected the kinds of roles Yuri and Bill practiced in their relationship. While Yuri believed that the home and children were her responsibility and she certainly did more domestic work than her husband, she also did much less housework than most Nisei wives. Not only did Bill do more domestically than the average Nisei husband, the numerous houseguests who continually stayed at the Kochiyamas'—some eighty overnight guests in 1954 alone and hundreds of visitors each year—provided extensive help. As Yuri noted, "These wonderful 'temporary homesteaders' would do all the domestic chores." Friends also pitched in. Yuri's niece recalled: "Yuri told me that when her kids were small, the laundry was just unending. So neighbors and friends would come by and do the ironing for her." Other friends helped the Kochiyamas by providing child-care services; transporting groceries (in a city based on public transportation); donating, sewing, and mending clothes; cooking; mopping the floors; and helping Yuri and Bill organize their community service activities.[38]

For most people, friends and extended family members are occasionally willing to lend a helping hand. But the extent to which friends helped the Kochiyamas was unusual; some were even willing to scrub floors. What was it about Yuri and Bill that drew people to them in such ways? The primary explanation is that Yuri and Bill did so much for other people that friends and guests wanted to reciprocate their services. Plus, it was easy to figure out how to give assistance to the Kochiyamas, who as a working-class family could not afford to pay for housecleaning services. Moreover, Elizabeth Nakahara observed: "When I stay with Yuri, I have noticed that what she does is make it very enjoyable for people to come by. She puts out a nice little spread of food. She sits and talks with them, and tells her zillions of funny anecdotes. They really have a good time when they come over. And then they get some work done. So I guess that's it, people enjoy it because it's a pleasant experience."[39]

It certainly seems as if Yuri has disliked doing housework throughout her life, and she has managed to escape having it, in practice, be her exclusive domain. Still, unless one can pay for domestic workers, housework cannot be avoided. This is particularly true for women, given that the home has been constructed to be their domain. Moreover, given the politics of housework, it is questionable whether Yuri would have hired a housecleaner even if she could have afforded to do so. Even prior to her politicalization, Yuri disliked unequal relationships, such as that which exists between a middle-class family and its housecleaner, often a poor immigrant woman of color. And after becoming political, she would have had additional reasons not to do so.[40]

The Kochiyama family's social life and the children's extracurricular activities were typical of Nisei families in the 1950s. Yuri recalled: "When our kids were growing up, we did lots of things together as a family. Every weekend, we'd go to the parks, beaches, birthday parties, baseball games, swimming, you name it. We took the kids everywhere." The Kochiyama children were also involved in organized sports, including baseball and judo. Billy was in the Boy Scouts, Audee in Girl Scouts, Aichi in Brownies, and Eddie, Jimmy, and Tommy in the Boy Commandos.[41]

Throughout the 1940s and 1950s and into the mid-1960s, the Kochiyama family also participated in the Christian church. Upon moving to New York, Yuri taught Sunday school at the Japanese American Christian Church and then at a predominantly White Presbyterian church. It is not clear when she stopped teaching. Although uncertain, Yuri presumed she had taught Sunday school until she got heavily involved in political work in the early 1960s. The family newsletter indicated that all six children attended church, Sunday school, and Christian summer camp throughout the 1950s and into the 1960s. But Betty Robinson recalled taking Billy and Audee to church every Sunday throughout the 1950s, but did not remember seeing Yuri or Bill there. After becoming involved in other activities, Yuri's religious participation seemed to have decreased from its peak in the 1930s and

1940s. Still, it was important to her that her children develop a moral foundation and sense of community. And she continued to embrace the humanitarian ethics derived from her Christian training, even as her views became less Christ-centered. In their 1964 family newsletter, Yuri or Bill—most likely Yuri—commented, "We must also recognize that there are those who can and are living by the highest ethics of moral principles without church or religion, by merely following their conscience developed by experience of man's relationship to man, and by their concern for others."[42]

In addition, the Kochiyama children have had the unusual opportunity to dance and model professionally and to work as extras in television shows and advertisements. Since they lived in New York City, a performing arts mecca, it was not entirely surprising that many of Yuri's and Bill's friends, visitors to their weekend open houses, and community service associates were in theater and the arts. The few agencies looking for Asian models or actors regularly called the Kochiyamas, who were known for helping people find jobs. When there were roles for children, the Kochiyama youngsters sometimes participated. Among many other parts, Billy had a minor theater role as a Korean street urchin, Billy and Audee had roles in *Two for the Seesaw,* Aichi and Eddie modeled in a Dacron ad, Jimmy and Tommy were in an Esso Oil ad, and Tommy had his picture taken for a nationally known baby food ad. Back in the 1950s and early 1960s, Yuri noted, "The kids had great fun and it was a boost to their self-confidence." The extra money also helped the family's tight budget, enabling the Kochiyamas to buy school clothes, feed visitors, and pay the phone bill. Yuri said with appreciation, "Our kids have always been generous in contributing to the family budget; they put in the money they made modeling or working as extras or from other jobs, as well as their Christmas and birthday money and weekly allowances." As Yuri's political consciousness increased throughout the 1960s, the contradiction heightened between her anticapitalist views and her children's involvement in corporate advertising campaigns. In time, the children appeared in fewer and fewer commercials.[43]

The Kochiyama girls also had the extraordinary experience of attending a professional ballet school in the early 1960s. Barbara Bartlett and Helen Milholland, professional dancers and mainstays at the Kochiyamas' weekend open houses, coached the girls every Saturday for five months to ready them for an audition with the Metropolitan Opera Ballet School. Their rigorous training paid off when Audee and Aichi, then preteenagers, made the prestigious school. The two women also facilitated the Kochiyama girls' training by giving them ballet shoes, providing babysitting jobs so that they could pay for their dance lessons, and taking them to several ballet performances. Audee remarked: "My parents wanted us to engage in cultural activities. And ballet gave me the basis for all dance—for the jazz, Hawaiian hula, and other dances I did. I really enjoyed it." To this day, Yuri is proud of her daughters' dancing abilities:

> The girls were into dancing. And they were really good. They'd put the dancers in line according to their talent, with the best dancers at the beginning of the line—and that's where Audee and Aichi were placed. Audee was an especially talented dancer; Aichi was the singer. Aichi even got into one of Harry Belafonte's television specials with children dancing and singing. I think it was called *New York Nineteen*. The girls even got to dance in an opera. It was one of the German musician Wagner's operas.

But by the mid-1960s, as the Movement around them intensified—as did their mother's activism—Audee and Aichi decided to forgo their dancing to concentrate on their political activities. Three decades later, Yuri said regretfully, "I wish they hadn't dropped dancing altogether." Yet by her own activities, priorities, and example, she sent the implicit message that political activism was of ultimate importance.[44]

Throughout the 1950s, the Kochiyama children led very full lives, filled with family outings and extracurricular activities. As Yuri observed, "Our kids, especially the older ones, had an ordinary kind of family life." Yuri's parenthetical remark about "especially the older ones" is telling. After becoming politically active in the early 1960s, Yuri's priorities changed. While her primary identity was still as a mother and wife, she spent increasing amounts of time on her political activities. As a result, the younger Kochiyama children, born in the late 1950s, were not involved in extracurricular activities or family outings to the extent that their older siblings were. This had an effect on how these younger children viewed Yuri's political activities and their own activism, as discussed in the next chapter. But around 1960 when the Kochiyama children said to their parents, "you can't give us all the things you said you wanted to give us," they were certainly not feeling deprived of extracurricular activities. They may well have been concerned with the lack of material goods the family had, especially when they were counted on to contribute their work money, birthday gifts, and weekly allowance to the family finances. But probably just as important, the children were ambivalent about having to share their parents' time with more siblings, in addition to the multiple visitors and overnight guests who were constantly in their home.[45]

The Kochiyamas' home, with its relentless flow of visitors, has been dubbed "Grand Central Station." Over the years, thousands of people—friends and strangers alike—have dropped by. Every Friday and Saturday night, the Kochiyamas held social gatherings where 442nd/100th veterans and USO friends, Korean War soldiers, Sheltering Arms old-timers, San Pedro visitors, local college students and friends, and students from Hawaii and the West Coast would show up. Prominent people such as Japanese Supreme Court justice Mansaburo Shoda and Ishwar Gulati, adviser to Indian Prime Minister Nehru, also were among their visitors. In one year, guests from some twenty-five different countries stopped by. In a highly unusual manner, the Kochiyamas' invitation was extended to all—their 1959 *Christmas Cheer* newsletter stated, "Saturday nite is open to any and all who enjoy people"—and about half the visitors each week were newcomers. Yuri commented: "We talked and ate and had fun. We didn't have much money, so this became an affordable way to socialize." Even though their visitors often brought food and drink, Yuri and Bill, with their hospitable streak, would have felt obligated to provide for their guests. So rather than simply being "an affordable way to socialize," a house filled with people from diverse backgrounds, interesting conversations, laughter, entertainment, and good times would have been enjoyable. This was a reflection of Yuri more than Bill. Amsterdam Houses neighbor Genevieve Hall-Duncan recalled: "Yuri was the key person who made things happen. Bill made sure everyone was comfortable and had a drink. He was able to fill in if conversations started to lag. But Yuri was the one who brought people in from all over. People would say, 'Are you going to Yuri's?' more than 'Are you going to Yuri and Bill's?'" Another neighbor, Betty Robinson, remarked: "Yuri and Bill got the open houses started. But I think it was more Yuri because she never forgot a person. She knew thousands of names. She was the more outgoing of the two. She never seemed to tire, but always had so much energy."[46]

Extending weekly invitations to friends, and especially to strangers, was certainly not common. But coming from Yuri, it was not entirely surprising. Throughout her childhood, Yuri's parents regularly entertained Mr. Nakahara's business associates. In the postwar period, marked by intense anti-Japanese hostility and a severe nationwide housing shortage, Mrs. Nakahara opened up her home to Japanese Americans in need of shelter. Following in her parents' footsteps, Yuri invited her teenage Sunday school girls to her family's home for slumber parties. In the Jerome concentration camp, the Crusaders regularly hung out at the Nakaharas' barracks. And in Mississippi, Yuri invited Nisei soldiers who could not find housing elsewhere to stay with her (and the people with whom she was temporarily residing).[47]

When Yuri got her own place in New York, her hospitality multiplied. About the weekly social gatherings, she recounted, "First there were only a few people, but as more and more people heard about our open houses, we soon had 100 people in our small apartment." In time, the Kochiyamas designated Friday nights for their Nisei Sino Service Organization and 442nd friends, and Saturday night for everyone else. Betty Robinson attended many Saturday night open houses: "There was lots of food, singing, dancing going on. Sometimes someone brought a guitar or sang or performed. And there were always a lot of people. The house was so full you couldn't move. It was a fun time." The social gatherings later turned into cultural and educational programs. "We started thinking, if we're going to get all these people together, why not do something worthwhile," said Yuri. They held talent nights with invited artists as well as the regular weekend crew performing on the Hawaiian ukulele, the guitar, hula dancing, singing, and so forth. They also scanned the newspapers to see who was scheduled to speak at local universities or community events, and invited them to speak to what Yuri and Bill called the "Saturday Nite" group. As Yuri listened to these speakers, some of whom discussed the social issues of the growing Civil Rights Movement, her social consciousness slowly began to grow.[48]

In addition, the Kochiyamas had numerous overnight guests. Soldiers who had come to town, mothers and children who had no place to go, vacationing friends, students, and even strangers stayed at their place for days, weeks, or months at a time. Dollie (Nagai) Fukawa recalled Yuri's hospitality when she visited in the 1950s: "Even though Mary was so busy, she came to the train station to meet me. And she had cooked a fancy dinner. I was a young woman at the time, and met so many people through Mary and Bill. Mary was always willing to help. I remember once when I was getting ready for a date, it was Mary who ironed my dress." The entire family pitched in to accommodate their guests. The Kochiyama children would double up so that there was room for guests in their three-bedroom apartment in the Amsterdam housing project and, after they moved to Harlem in 1960, in their four-bedroom unit in the Manhattanville housing project. That some eighty people stayed overnight in 1954, as reported in the family news-letter, is indicative of the huge number of people who passed through the Kochiyamas' home over the years.[49]

"We took in almost anyone who needed a place to stay," said Yuri. It seemed as if she could not turn down a person in need, although she added, "We appreciated if they called ahead because if our kids were sick or we had too many guests already, we'd have to say, 'No, sorry, but we can't accommodate you this time.'" Because of the numerous guests, Yuri relayed:

> We had a lot of funny situations. Once we had to put somebody in the bathtub on a mattress, and because I'm small enough, I had to sleep with the baby in the crib. Then there were times when we took whoever was the youngest child at the time and went to some friends to sleep over. Our friends would always say, "Gee your place is so crowded, why don't you come over to our place and bring the youngest one." At our place, people just had to sleep on the floor. But we were lucky in that the people who stayed over weren't too particular.[50]

More than four hundred children and youth stayed with the Kochi-yamas over a seven-year period in the 1950s. So in a way, Yuri did get her wish for more children. Some houseguests were friends of the Kochiyama children who had fun spending the night. Others were chil-dren and their single mothers who needed a place to stay. Still others were children whose parent(s) could not care for them on a continuous basis—perhaps similar to Bill's father's situation. Describing two of the more remarkable situations gives a sense of the extent of Yuri's hospitality and of her admiration for those coping with adversity.[51]

To Yuri, "The most unusual child who stayed with us was Hiroshi, a young boy from Japan whose face was badly burned. One day when he fell asleep studying and his face fell on a hot hibachi, his mother picked him up and his face tore off." Hiroshi came to the United States for plastic surgery, under the care of the same surgeons at Mount Sinai Hospital in New York who had treated twenty-five atomic bomb survivors known as the "Hiroshima Maidens." It was one of the Hiroshima Maidens, Shigeko Niimoto, who asked the Kochiyamas to house and care for Hiroshi. Arriving in 1961, he lived with the Kochiyamas for about a year while he underwent ten operations. Yuri said: "Of course, at first, he must have been very, very hurt and angry at what happened to him. Plus, he only knew a couple of English words, so the adjustment here must have been hard. It's interesting how our kids didn't know Japanese and he didn't know much English, but they were able to communicate. He loved being with our kids, not with the older kids though he was Billy's age and not with the girls, but he went everywhere with Eddie, Jimmy, and Tommy. Hiroshi was terrific to the kids."[52]

Mike Hernandez, a sixteen-year-old Chicano from Wilmington, California, stayed with the Kochiyamas for sixteen days in November 1962. After learning that Mike's Hodgkin's disease had progressed to the terminal stage, his teacher, Irene McKenna, arranged for his dream trip—a visit to the galleries and museums in New York City. McKenna did not know the Kochiyamas but had heard of their extraordinary hospitality, and she wrote to ask if they could accommodate Mike. Yuri exclaimed: "We were excited and said, 'Of course he could stay with us.' Mike was the same age as Billy, but he looked four years younger because of his illness; he just didn't grow. When we first met him in the airport, the first thing he said was, 'I don't want you to think I look like this. I don't look like this. It's the medication.' He showed me a picture of what he used to look like—a very lean, handsome face; but when we met him, he was bloated from the medicine." Prior to his arrival, Yuri and Bill had sent their friends letters asking if they would serve as volunteer tour guides. Yuri noted their enthusiastic response: "Countless Saturday Niters, students, and community activists volunteered their services, purchased tickets, provided transportation, invited him to luncheons and dinners, and took him all over town. He had a wonderful time, but he was undergoing a lot of pain because of his deteriorating condition. As we were instructed, we told people to stop and rest if Mike says he's tired. If he wants to be alone because he's in so much pain, give him his space. And if he's really bad, take him to the hospital." His trip climaxed with a "Mike Hernandez Nite," where his newfound friends avalanched him with gifts at a surprise potluck dinner. Less than two months later, the Kochiyamas received the news that Mike had died.[53]

Mike Hernandez made an impact on Yuri's life. Not only did she feature stories about him on the front page of the Kochiyamas' annual newsletter for two consecutive years, she also asked some of her California friends to visit him when he was in the hospital. Some may well have interpreted this as a forward, even pushy, request; after all, they were being asked to visit a perfect stranger. But Yuri saw a teenager with a terminal illness. And that need superseded any discomfort her friends may have felt. Perhaps the Christian belief in serving the sick, the poor, the imprisoned, and others whom they do not know may have influenced her views. Yuri certainly admired Mike's courage, first battling being abandoned as an infant and fostered as a child and then fighting against a terminal illness. She also admired his adoptive family, who gave him loving care. Rather than seeing Mike's visit as an obligation or burden, Yuri felt blessed to have met him as well as his family when the Kochiyamas visited Southern California in the summer after he died. She noted, "Mike enriched our lives and taught us so much about living life to its fullest."[54]

How did the Kochiyamas feel about the constant presence of visitors in their home? For the family as a whole, it was a mixed blessing. Certain visitors made notable efforts to attend to the children, especially Al Karvelis and several friends from Hawaii, and took them on special outings. Billy, a sports fanatic, was thrilled when Baltimore Orioles outfielder Earl Robinson stopped by. Robinson as well as other visitors made it possible for Billy to attend several Yankees games, including a cherished World Series. In a family of modest means, the children also enjoyed receiving treats of chips and soda from some of the guests. And the Kochiyama children learned to be hospitable, sociable, and thoughtful toward others—characteristics they embody to this day. But everybody in the family felt the strain that came from having little privacy in a small apartment already overflowing with a family of eight. Jimmy noted how hard it was for him, an admitted introvert, to play host to the numerous guests. Audee concurred: "I was really shy, and felt uncomfortable being out with people, so I retreated to the back [of the apartment]. I guess all of us kind of did that. It's just so funny being in your house, with all these people, and you just stay in your room." Yuri acknowledged: "I'm not sure how our kids felt. I would imagine that sometimes they weren't too happy because they never knew who would be staying with us, who would be sleeping in their room or sharing their bed. But I also think the kids had fun and liked having so many 'brothers' and 'sisters' to play with, and 'aunties' and 'uncles' taking them places. I think Bill was used to having lots of people around from growing up in an orphanage with a hundred 'brothers' and 'sisters.'"[55]

That Yuri expressed an uncertainty about the feelings of her children reflects her way of deflecting a topic more than an actual lack of knowledge about her children's views. Over the years, her children have unambiguously articulated to Yuri how they felt. Her choice, perhaps unconscious, to impart an overoptimistic outlook helps her reconcile the sometimes conflicting needs of her family and of the larger community. Rather than having to think that her family suffered, she can justify housing friends and strangers by remembering the positive benefits for her own family:

Each person was a learning experience for our family. Many of Bill's friends came back from the war with disabilities. Sanji Kimoto, a blind 442nd vet, taught us how to arrange the food on his plate; to put rice at twelve o'clock, meat at six o'clock, and so forth. Wilson Makabe, another vet, also stayed with us from time to time. He was an amputee. One time, we were sleeping when all of a sudden this huge clackity-clack noise came and we jumped up wondering what happened. Billy, who was about three years old, came running in and said, "There's somebody standing in the bathroom." The thing that clattered to the floor was Wilson's artificial leg. His prosthesis had fallen down. He had hung his prosthesis inside his pants on the bathroom door, so when he got up in the morning he could slip it right on. We explained to Billy that it's Wilson's leg. Little Billy was so surprised, "You mean Wilson can take his leg off?" So we had to explain to him that he lost his leg in the war and had an artificial one. It seems strange that some twenty-five years later, Billy was the one who lost his leg and had to have a prosthesis.[56]

Yuri recalls that she "loved having people over." Others also remember her enjoying the open houses, never tiring of playing hostess, and having an abundance of energy. "Mary was so warm and friendly to everyone. She never forgot a person. You couldn't ask for a nicer person," noted Betty Robinson. It seems that Yuri believed that housing people who had nowhere to go was simply a duty that had to be done, and she was happy to oblige.[57]

Yuri and Bill stayed connected with their large circle of friends by producing and distributing an annual Christmas newsletter. "We wanted to be able to keep in touch with the friends we've made over the years," Yuri recounted, "but found it difficult to return the hundreds of letters we'd receive each year. Bill and I were both into journalism, so we thought why not start a news-sheet?" Their first *Christmas Cheer* came out as a two-pager in 1950, the year after Bill graduated. The newsletter jumped to eight pages with the next issue, and then to twelve pages in 1958. The newsletter primarily consisted of social news: stories and photographs detailing the activities and accomplishments of friends, the Kochiyama children, and Nisei veterans and soldiers; marriage and birth announcements; and trips to California to visit Yuri's family. In a way that reflects the borderlessness of Yuri's definition of "family," the newsletter is more about the activities and accomplishments of others than it is about the Kochiyama family.[58]

Each newsletter had a different theme—such as sports, cartoons, Davy Crockett, Disneyland, and corporate logos—and carried that motif throughout the issue in the titles, framing of the stories, and illustrations. While Bill originated the theme and designed most of the layout, he and Yuri worked as a team in producing *Christmas Cheer*. According to Yuri: "One thing that made it easier was that Bill's writing and mine were so much alike. One of us could start an article and the other just continue writing it. You couldn't tell when the second writer began. A lot of times, we would write on a topic separately, but when we brought them together we couldn't believe how similar the articles were. We split the writing and the work pretty evenly. It was fun working together." The children also got involved, folding newsletters and stamping envelopes as youngsters and writing their own columns as they got older. "It was thrilling to watch the kids get so excited when our newsletter came out," exclaimed Yuri.[59]

While Nisei families regularly sent Christmas cards, the size of the Kochiyamas' Christmas greeting and the magnitude of their social network were phenomenal, with annual mailings of some three thousand newsletters. "From September until the printing deadline in late November, we worked nonstop," recalled Yuri. They managed to send out *Christmas Cheer* for nineteen consecutive years, ending in 1968. A passage in one issue gives a sense of the process involved in producing the newsletter: "After another hectic session of gathering materials, re-reading accumulated letters, going through snapshots and news-clippings, writing and re-writing, typing and column typing, and pasting and ripping, and frantically working into the wee hours of the morning in November, *Christmas Cheer* went to press. . . . The apartment cluttered for three months with 'no visitors' sign periodically on the door [so] that progress could be made, this project has erupted and disrupted the K's household and home life on many occasions."[60]

The business of producing and distributing the newsletter and of maintaining a family was made more difficult by Yuri's periodic health problems. Although she claimed to have been healthy over the years, articles in different issues of *Christmas Cheer* indicate that she had several bouts with extended illnesses and hospitalizations, the descriptions of which were vague. Yuri was ill for the first six months of 1951, which required a one-week hospitalization. In 1955, a few months after the birth of their fourth child, Yuri was ill for two months. In 1957, "during drawn-out and recurring illnesses," a Dr. Glass provided medicine and vitamins as well as several months worth of lactum for their newborn. Yuri's tendency to deny health problems may well stem from her desire to see herself as physically fit, having grown up in a family with chronic respiratory ailments. This tendency also reflects the obsessive manner with which she pushes to attend to the needs of others, even to the point of neglecting her own health.[61]

Yuri's health problems, frequent visitors, active community service commitments, and extensive child-care demands, on top of limited finances, forced Yuri and Bill to rely on their friends for help, as illustrated in the 1954 *Christmas Cheer* article "Counting Our Blessings":

> This year, three costly, necessary articles were given to us as surprise gifts; three things we longed to buy ourselves for many years and could not. . . . The coffee-table was presented to us by John Tsukano and his Goodwill Ambassadors (Charlie Taketa, Ato Umeda, Jiro Watanabe, Kazuo Tojio, Emi Aki, and Merna Tilton) just before their take-off for their entertainment tour of Europe. The washing-machine was left to us by Ralph and Wini Toyota for just a fraction of the original cost. The gray wool over-coat was given by Jin Kozuma, who said he knew how much Bill needed it.
>
> This year, the monthly bill that staggered the K's budget the most was the telephone bill. In May, thanks to money-gifts given to Billy for his birthday from Clancy Takano, Chiri Tsuji, Smoky Nagao, and Herby Karimoto, that month's bill was defrayed. (Thanks to Billy too). In July, the little white sheet from the Telephone Co. was enough to force us to disconnect the phone for August. In the midst of this predicament, came a 100th-Infantryman whom we had never met before, Dick Sasabe. With no thought of repayment, Dick came to our rescue.

The acknowledgment of individuals by name is characteristic of Yuri's—and presumably Bill's—style, as is their tendency to refrain from mentioning their own generosity.[62]

Being able to finance the production of *Christmas Cheer* also required a pooling of resources: "Because of Bill's connections through his public relations work, we were able to get good prices for printing. For the mailing, we were indebted to our cousin, Kathy Muto and her friend, Emi Ikemoto, for typing C.C. addresses. As friends and family received *Christmas Cheer,* they wanted to make monetary contributions, some big, some small, but every bit helped." After a few years, hundreds of people were sending contributions. Since the Kochiyamas absorbed half the production and distribution costs, the contributions made it possible for them to donate the surplus funds to various charities. They also received help from friends and family who wrote out addresses, cooked and cleaned, and babysat the children every Sunday for the few months preceding the deadline so that Bill and Yuri had time to devote to *Christmas Cheer*. Still, Yuri recounted, "Even with this tremendous help, I don't know how we managed to get out the news-sheet each year in between taking care of our kids, working, and service activities." Despite the difficulties of publishing *Christmas Cheer*, she and Bill enjoyed the creativity and writing, the togetherness it promoted, and the means it afforded to stay connected with friends.[63]

The wartime experiences of living together under life-threatening circumstances and depending on each other for survival created a lifelong bond among the men of the 442nd Regimental Combat Team. So when Bill returned home, he helped establish the New York 442nd Association and served as its first president. The association grew out of efforts to organize a 1951 New York premiere for the MGM Studios film about the 442nd, *Go for Broke*. The new formation suc- ceeded in convening more than two hundred ex-GIs to attend the opening night as well as the first East Coast 442nd reunion. The New York 442nd Association was different from most other Nisei veterans groups because, with so few Japanese Americans locally, they allowed American Black, Cuban Black, and White veterans to join. These war buddies became social companions to Bill, hanging out together at a bar every Friday night and playing softball regularly.[64]

Bill was a baseball enthusiast. Always the catcher, he first played for the 442nd Association team and later was the oldest player on the United Asian Communities Center team. When that team disbanded, a group got together to form a multiracial ball club, self-named Ronin, meaning "masterless samurai" in Japanese. Yuri thought the name was fitting. "It was perfect for them because they had no masters, no organization, just guys who came together to play ball." When Eddie got older, he played shortstop on the same team as Bill, and the younger Kochiyama children enjoyed going to the park to throw the ball around. For some twenty years, every week from April through June, Yuri and the children rooted for Bill at his ball games.[65]

As New York became flooded with Japanese American GIs, many from Hawaii, who faced discrimination en route to the Korean war front, Yuri, Bill, and other veterans decided to organize USO-type services and activities for those soldiers. Initially formed as the Nisei Service Organization (NSO) in 1951, they became the Nisei Sino

Service Organization (NSSO) in 1956, after recognizing that Chinese American soldiers encountered similar racial conditions. The pan-Asian nature of this organization is significant, formed more than a decade before Asian American panethnicity became popularized through the emergence of the Asian American Movement. The organization also expanded to provide services for nonmilitary constituencies as well, often taking children with disabilities to the baseball games so loved by the Nisei veterans.[66]

In time, the NSSO became better organized, adding officers and directors, most of whom were World War II veterans, although they remained a fairly loosely structured group. As written in the Kochiyamas' 1960 *Christmas Cheer*:

> The NSSO's aims are still the same—fellowship, service, and personal growth. There are also still the old trade-marks: no membership, but open participation to all; no dues, but support of dances, candy-sales, and other fund-raising projects, and voluntary donations. This loosely-knit group's services and program include giving help in housing and job contacts; befriending and orienting newcomers; sponsoring dances, outings, get-togethers; entertaining hospital patients; giving annual Easter parties to underprivileged children; acting as liaison to other clubs; and supporting and cooperating with the 442 Association.

The Kochiyamas' apartment in the Amsterdam housing project was the scene of NSSO socials every Friday night. And Bill and Yuri acted as chaperons for the young people, mostly women between the ages of seventeen and twenty-five, who organized the social outings for Asian American soldiers.[67]

Yuri emphasized that it took many people working collectively for the NSSO to function. To find housing for GIs passing through New York City, she recounted: "The NSSO families who were involved were so generous, opening their homes to complete strangers. One time when our place was already filled up with GIs sleeping on the floor everywhere, we called a family to see if some soldiers could stay at their place. This one family from Hawaii said, 'OK, but don't send over too many. We already have some soldiers staying here.' I asked them, 'How many are already there?' They said, 'Seventeen.'" Yuri found this generosity typical of veterans from Hawaii. Another time, a whole troupe of Hawaiian hula dancers and drummers stayed at the Kochiyamas': "I don't know how we put them all up. There were two or three hula dancers and five musicians." By contrast to their flamboyancy onstage, Yuri noted: "At home, they were all 'kanakas'; they were so down to earth. They took care of our kids, played with them, and took them out. . . . And they even got down on their hands and knees and scrubbed the floors."[68]

In July 1953, the 442nd Veterans Club of Honolulu hosted a Tenth Anniversary Reunion, commemorating the formation of the 442nd. The generosity of friends, and child-care services provided by Mrs. Nakahara, Art, and Chiyo, enabled Bill and Yuri to travel to Hawaii: "The biggest thing that happened to us, wasn't that we made the trip to Hawaii, but the way that this trip was made possible. It was only through the kind remembrance of the 442 veterans in Hawaii; and the newly-made friendships of Korean War GIs, vets, and NSO hostesses on the East Coast, who raised a fund in our behalf." Several articles about the reunion filled the Kochiyamas' 1953 *Christmas Cheer*, as in this article most likely written by Bill: "Hawaiian hospitality and Primo Beer poured out endlessly when 442 Island Buddaheads played host to the mainland Kotonks and Haoles . . . representing 20 states. . . . The luncheons along Waikiki area; . . . banquets at exclusive nite-clubs; . . . all-day outings. . . . 1500 strong, Island and Mainlanders whooped it up in style."[69]

Five years later, the Kochiyamas traveled to Los Angeles for the Nisei veterans' fifteen-year reunion. The five hundred veterans and their families enjoyed, among many other activities, tours to Disneyland and a welcome dinner dance at the Moulin Rouge in Hollywood. The reunion also had its serious moments, particularly the Memorial Service at the all-Japanese Evergreen Cemetery, where more than fifty Nisei veterans were buried.[70]

These reunions were important to Yuri because they afforded her the opportunity to be with her family, all of whom lived in California. In contrast to the weekly visits with their Kochiyama grandfather, the children came to know their Nakahara relatives through these periodic trips to California, which occurred every couple of years in the 1950s but decreased in frequency following Mrs. Nakahara's death in 1963 and the increased pace of Yuri's political activities. Yuri's mother lived in the family home in San Pedro with Yuri's older brother Art, his wife Chiyo (Ogata), and their four children, Eric, Myra, Della, and Nora. After marrying in the Arkansas concentration camp, Art and Chiyo returned to Southern California, where racism limited job opportunities for Japanese Americans. So Art, who had graduated with honors from UC Berkeley, opened up a small business making salads in the Black community of Watts. Later on, he worked as a cashier at Safeway. As for Yuri's twin brother, following his military service in the Far East, Peter traveled to Japan where he married Aiko (Umino), who originated from Seattle. When they returned to the United States, Peter attended Stanford Law School, graduating in 1954. They settled in San Jose in northern California, where they had four children: Elizabeth, Bill, Bob, and David. Although Yuri's mother and two brothers never traveled to New York, and she maintained sporadic correspondence with them, *Christmas Cheer* contained lengthy descriptions of family vacations to California and happy recollections of these visits in the children's columns.[71]

Knowing Yuri would be in Los Angeles for the 442nd reunion, her childhood friends organized a picnic in her honor, including a mock version of the popular Ralph Edwards television program, *This Is Your Life.* As with the television show, Yuri's friends wrote an eleven-page script documenting her life and had her mother, brothers, and friends describe the "greatness of your heart and soul—the way you put all others before self." The program walked the audience through Yuri's early family life, church work, sports coverage, World War II incarceration, letter writing to friends and Nisei GIs, romance with Bill, and current work with the NSSO and Hiroshima Maidens. Various friends and family members came out to tell stories—sometimes humorous, sometimes touching—of Yuri's extensive service work. Her friends also showered Yuri with numerous gifts, including a Polaroid camera and film, a plaque with the Sportsmen's Prayer, San Pedro High School varsity letter, orchids from Bill's 442nd Company K and Earl Finch, and a sizable check. In their *Christmas Cheer* newsletter that year, Yuri wrote an open letter of appreciation, recognizing each of the main organizers by name and thanking "the 200-plus families and individuals who gave of their gifts, time and talent." "To have been remembered in such a way was an unforgettable experience," she exclaimed.[72]

To have one reunion organized by childhood friends is unusual in itself, but Yuri had a total of three. In 1984, eighty people came out for a spur-of-the-moment luncheon for her. During a 1989 visit, which coincided with her fiftieth high school reunion, friends organized a banquet to honor Yuri, "a legend in her own lifetime," pronounced one of her high school teachers. Sam Domancich tried to explain to a *Los Angeles Times* reporter why more than two hundred San Pedro High "Pirates" from the 1930s and 1940s would attend a homecoming bash in Yuri's honor: "She always made you feel as if you were someone great. Whether it was in football, or basketball, or track—maybe you scored two points, but she would say, 'That was great.'" Perhaps one teacher summed it up: "It's hard to express in words the impact Mary had on the community and school. And it goes on, 50 years later."[73]

In the mid-1950s, the NSO and New York 442nd Association began organizing support services to the Hiroshima Maidens, twenty-five atomic bomb survivors or *hibakusha,* who came to the United States for a year of intensive reconstructive surgery. Although Yuri was drawn into this project for humanitarian reasons, there were obvious political implications. The experience of coming face-to-face with the human cost of war would shape her worldview and, after becoming politically conscious, affect the work she chose, including nuclear disarmament.

The Maidens were teenagers when the United States dropped the atomic bomb on Hiroshima on August 6, 1945. Many had turned to look at the familiar sight of B-29s, but this time a blazing flash broke the sky and instinctively they raised their arms to shield their faces. Their faces, arms, and hands were most severely burned by the radiation. Their scorched skin and extreme scarring caused gross deformities in their facial features and, in some cases, significantly impaired the use of their arms and hands. Many had undergone unsuccessful and painful reconstructive surgery in Japan, sometimes without the benefit of anesthesia. A Methodist minister, Rev. Kiyoshi Tanimoto, had been working hard to bring healing and hope to the suffering people of Hiroshima. One person whom he inspired was a teenage girl who had survived the bombing. Shigeko Niimoto, after living an isolated and hidden existence with her family for five years, conceived the idea of gathering together other young *hibakusha* female survivors to support one another. Through this group, facilitated by Rev. Tanimoto, many of the young women gained confidence and a sense of camaraderie. Rev. Tanimoto also tried to meet the young women's material needs by finding them jobs. But he felt that to fully function in a society that emphasized female beauty, these young women also needed reconstructive surgery to reduce their disfigurement. Because Japanese plastic surgeons' techniques lagged behind those of their American counterparts, he looked to the United States for help.

With hard work and determination, Rev. Tanimoto was able to set the plan in motion when Norman Cousins, editor of the *Saturday Review* and an avid antinuclear advocate, commited to the project. Cousins arranged for a plastic surgery team, headed by Dr. Arthur Barsky and including Drs. William Hitzig, Sidney Kahn, and Bernard Simon, to provide their services gratis at New York's Mount Sinai Hospital. Cousins also found Alfred Rose, who agreed to pay for all hospitalization costs but wished to remain anonymous; arranged with General John E. Hull for the U.S. military to provide transportation; coordinated with Ida Day of the New York American Friends Service Committee to provide homes and hospitality for the women's yearlong stay; and recruited Helen Yokoyama to serve as interpreter and counselor to the young women. On May 9, 1955, the Hiroshima Maidens, as the newspapers dubbed them, arrived in New York. The twenty-five women stayed with Quaker families while they collectively underwent 138 operations.[74]

The New York 442nd Association had the opportunity to support the Hiroshima Maidens. At first, Yuri relayed, these women did not want male visitors, given their disfigurement, nor did they want young female visitors who might remind them of their lost beauty. But Yuri, visibly pregnant with her fourth child when the women arrived, said: "Since I was older, I got to visit them early on. But as their surgeries partially improved their appearance, the women gained self-confidence and more visitors were included." Even when a particular surgery did not change their physical appearance much, the process of the program resulted in psychological healing. The Nisei veterans were then allowed to visit. The 442nd men, who knew how to throw a party, organized a celebration and taught simple dance steps to the *hibakusha,* who had never attended a dance. Yuri noted, "Though all us wives also attended the dance, the 442nd men danced only with the Hiroshima Maidens. The Maidens were made to feel really special." When the women left for Japan, Yuri recounted: "The two things they chose were an iron and a pair of scissors for sewing. They chose practical things that could help them earn a living in Japan. So it was good the 442nd asked them rather than getting them something like perfume or makeup that they really didn't want."[75]

Yuri and Bill wrote about these courageous young women in their 1955 and 1956 *Christmas Cheer* newsletters. A 1956 article, "The Hiroshima Sequel: Scars Diminish as Love Mushrooms," reflected:

> There are powers mightier than the forces of atomic energy. The story of the Hiroshima Maidens radiates this power, generated by the reactor in human hearts. . . . As the months passed and after many operations had erased some of their scars, another transformation was taking place—beneath the surface. The girls were no longer withdrawn or shy. Smiles replaced tears, as were fears with laughter. . . . To the K's who experienced one year's bedside acquaintanceship with the Maidens, the unraveling of their ten years—of mental anguish and torment . . . quiet courage and faith, series of surgeries . . . and finally, the healing, convalescing, regaining confidence, and blossoming anew—is a manifestation that there are powers mightier than atomic energy.[76]

The Hiroshima Maidens made a lasting impression on the Kochiyamas. When Tommy was born in 1959, Yuri and Bill asked Lani Miller, beloved nurse for the women at Mount Sinai Hospital, to be his godmother. And Hiroshima Maiden Shigeko Niimoto, who returned to the United States to live with Norman Cousins's family, was selected as the 1959 "Queen of the 442nd" at the annual dance organized by the New York 442nd Association. Finally, though they did not know it at the time, their interactions with these young women would grow into decades of organizing against nuclear weapons; "No more Hiroshimas" would become their slogan.[77]

4

Plunging into Civil Rights

In 1960, the Kochiyamas made a move that dramatically transformed their lives. They relocated to Harlem. Without any inkling of the changes to come, their decision was based on the availability of larger units in the newly opened Manhattanville housing project. Because Bill worked within a ten-block radius, the Kochiyamas were given high priority for a four-bedroom apartment, a gain of one bedroom over the Amsterdam Houses. Their new residence at 545 West 126th Street, apartment 3-B, on the corner of Broadway, was located one block from where Bill had grown up at the Sheltering Arms orphanage. It was there, in the context of the vibrant Black social movement encircling them in Harlem, that Yuri began her political involvement. Her husband's and children's activism soon followed.[1]

The Kochiyamas were excited about their new home, but the actual move was plagued with problems. They thought the place would be ready in early July, so they disconnected their telephone and packed their belongings, piling the boxes in one bedroom and in the living room. However, the apartment did not become available as expected. For five chaotic months, the five older children, as Yuri and Bill put it, "played, fought, screamed, and slept" in the remaining bedroom, while one-year-old Tommy slept in his parents' bedroom. The move itself was no easier, as Yuri revealed in a speech: "Our family moved to Harlem in December of 1960 during one of the worst blizzards to hit New York. Our children were Billy, thirteen; Audee, eleven; Aichi, eight; Eddie, five; Jimmy, three; and Tommy, one. We moved mostly by subway, hand carried fourteen years of family accumulation. Everybody went back and forth about four or five times on the subway from 66th Street to 125th." They also had a group of friends who endured subfreezing temperatures and seventeen inches of snow to provide their muscles and cars to transport the Kochiyamas' larger items. Plus, as written in *Christmas Cheer,* "Without gas the first six days had the K's subsisting on sandwiches, pizzas, and cold drinks. On Dec. 17, Saturday, however, the K's attended the wedding of Gus Anzai and Phyllis Wright, and thanks to the generous, genial best-man, Dave Lee, all the left-overs from the sumptuous Chinese dinner was carted, still hot, to the K-kids waiting in the gas-less apartment." Despite the disarray, Yuri and Bill somehow managed to produce their eleventh annual family newsletter, writing amidst boxes and having friends type out addresses during the move. That the newsletter came out on time is representative of the perseverance and single-minded focus that Yuri brings to a project.[2]

From the outside the building looks like any other housing project in New York City. Six brick high-rises make up the Manhattanville Houses. There is a small grassy area, but unlike middle-class complexes, there is no well-groomed playground equipped with a jungle gym or sandbox. Because of the sluggishness of the two elevators, it is more expedient to climb the narrow staircase to reach the Kochiyamas' third-floor apartment. In sharp contrast to the starkness of the building's interior walls, the apartment door opens into a home alive with knickknacks, books, and papers—everywhere. Although simple and uncarpeted, their new home was spacious, at least for government-subsidized housing. Upon entering, one faces a long narrow hallway, lined with flyers announcing upcoming events. Six rooms lead off the hallway, three on each side, making for a boxy, rectangular space. To the right of the front door is the living room, sparsely furnished with a couch, a low coffee table, and television, and cluttered—as it probably was in the 1960s—with political posters and pictures, all kinds of mementos, and a dozen yellow metal folding chairs that can be added or removed depending on the number of visitors. By the early 1980s, the room also contained the beginnings of what would become a large teddy bear collection; by the early 1990s, a shrine had been added commemorating family members who have passed on, with large pictures of the deceased throughout the room.[3]

Across from the living room, to the left of the front door, is the kitchen. The sink, stove, oven, and limited counter space line one wall. Across the narrow kitchen, along the opposite wall, are a refrigerator and kitchen table. The table, ostensibly used for dining, is cluttered with Yuri's political materials, letters, multiple colored pens, envelopes, stamps, and so forth; under the table are boxes of material, leaving no room for legs. This kitchen table has been a point of contention in the family for years, with the family wanting to use it for dining and Yuri needing a space for her late-night political work and correspondence. In recent years, the Kochiyamas acquired a washer and dryer, which sit in the crowded kitchen, but ease the laundry work.[4]

At the end of the long, narrow hallway covered with political leaf-lets, pictures of and by her grandchildren, and numerous plaques and awards honoring Yuri and Bill for their social justice work, sits the sole bathroom. Off the hallway are four bedrooms. Until the mid-1960s when Billy left for college, Yuri and Bill shared one bedroom, Billy had his own, the two daughters another, and the three youngest sons had the last room. As family members moved out, the children got their own rooms; later Yuri's political work filled the bedrooms. In the late 1990s, with Yuri as the sole occupant, one bedroom is lined with numerous file cabinets that have enabled Yuri to organize, at least to some degree, her many archives. Although the room is still chaotic with files and paper all over the floor and file cabinets, one could only imagine how Yuri, as a recorder of history, managed to maintain her numerous political materials, collected over the years, without the benefit of file cabinets. Bill dubbed this "the horror room"—a name to which Yuri readily agrees. The other two bedrooms each have a single bed, a desk, and rows and rows of books. One of these rooms contains a computer, copy machine, and fax, acquired in the mid-1990s from a $15,000 Bannerman award for activists of color bestowed on Yuri.[5]

A century before the Kochiyamas' move, Harlem was known for its middle-class and almost exclusively White residents. But beginning in the late nineteenth century, even before the Great Migration of World War I, Black southerners journeyed northward to escape vicious ra-cial violence and to search for expanded economic opportunities. In time, many of the city's affluent Black people, including Rev. Dr. Adam Clayton Powell Sr. and Madame C. J. Walker, as well as almost every major Black institution—social, service, artistic, athletic, and religious—relocated to Harlem. The predictable White flight meant that, by 1920, the center of Harlem was predominantly Black—and flourishing. But in one short decade, observed Gilbert Osofsky, Harlem, formerly known for its profitability among real estate speculators, deteriorated into one of the worst slums of New York City. By 1930, the combination of high rent and low wages resulted, not surprisingly, in overcrowding and other social ills.[6]

But even during its decade of economic decline, events of national and international significance were stirring in Harlem. Marcus Garvey, a controversial Black nationalist whose harshest critics could not deny his worldwide influence, had made Harlem the base of operations for the more than eight hundred chapters of his Universal Negro Improvement Association, located in forty countries on four continents. By preaching Black pride, teaching the achievements of African and African American history, and promoting a return to Africa and Black economic self-sufficiency, Garvey instilled unprecedented cultural pride and a spirit of resistance in Black Harlemites, several decades before the "Black Is Beautiful" slogan gained popularity. The 1920s also ushered in a culturally rebellious, intellectual period in U.S. history. In Black society, the Negro Renaissance, also known as the Harlem Renaissance to locate its nucleus, brought a flowering of influential writers—Langston Hughes, James Weldon Johnson, Zora Neale Hurston, Countee Cullen, and Claude McKay to name a few of the most prominent—who used their literary and artistic works to raise race consciousness. According to historian John Henrik Clarke, they affirmed, "in a poetic way, the same thing as Marcus Garvey: 'Up you mighty race! You can accomplish what you will!'" In short, observed Clarke, "Harlem has been called, and may well be, the cultural and intellectual capital of the black race in the Western world."[7]

In 1960, the six-square-mile area in north Manhattan into which the Kochiyamas moved was predominantly poor and Black. The median income of Central Harlem was 60 percent of the city median; Harlem residents were mainly employed in low-paying, unskilled service occupations; and juvenile delinquency was twice the city average, as was infant mortality. But Harlem was also alive with protests stemming from its history of Black consciousness and cultural pride. The 1960s bore rent strikes, citywide school boycotts, labor strikes, and demonstrations against police brutality and the Vietnam War, as well as a budding Black arts movement.[8]

The political activities taking place in Harlem were part of the worldwide protests emerging since the end of World War II. In Africa, Asia, and the Caribbean, nations were winning their independence against colonial powers. And in the United States, the 1950s was the decade that sparked the Civil Rights Movement. In 1954, the U.S. Supreme Court ruled that "separate but equal" facilities were inherently unequal and legally ended racial segregation in the schools. The next year, Rosa Parks challenged Jim Crow laws by refusing to give up her bus seat to a White man; her arrest sparked a yearlong bus boycott in Montgomery, Alabama. Martin Luther King Jr. was becoming a household name. And three years after the 1954 *Brown et al. v. Board of Education of Topeka et al.* decision, a group of Black students, known as the Little Rock Nine, faced violent attacks when they tried to integrate Central High School in Little Rock, Arkansas. Like many Americans, Yuri and Bill followed these events in the newspapers. Yuri's social awareness was growing, but she was not yet politically active. The closest she came to interacting with the Civil Rights Movement during the 1950s was when she fleetingly met Daisy Bates, the president of the Arkansas NAACP and a key player in the Little Rock Nine case. Yuri recalled:

> After the Little Rock Nine won their case, they came to New York in 1958. I knew one of the Little Rock Nine girls when she had lived with her aunt in our housing project. So when I read about their coming to New York, I asked Juanita Andrade if I could say hello to her niece, Carlotta Walls, when they were staying at the Taft Hotel. Instead, Juanita took me to Daisy Bates's suite and left me there. Daisy Bates was taking a shower. She yelled to open the door and come in. Daisy Bates was one of the big names of the period, and I didn't know what to say. So I said, "I read so much about you, I just wanted to say congratulations." She stuck her hand out of the shower to shake my hand. I couldn't believe I was actually meeting Daisy Bates.[9]

This brief meeting seems almost inconsequential in a life filled with extended interactions with prominent Movement leaders. Yet, this event holds meaning to Yuri, who repeatedly tells this story. Yuri is not trying to name-drop. Even if she were, her telling of this momentary encounter shows that she had only the most superficial of interactions with Bates. Instead, at least two factors help explain the significance of this meeting to Yuri. First, while she already admired the struggles for justice of Bates and other civil rights leaders, she would have been equally, if not more, impressed with Bates's humility. Here was a major civil rights leader greeting a stranger—albeit one who was a friend of a friend—from a position of humility and vulnerability. Although Yuri did not discuss the personal meaning of this encounter, it is likely that afterward she became even more interested in the Civil Rights Movement. Not only would her ears have perked up whenever she heard about Bates or the Little Rock Nine, she also would have remembered the quality of character that marked at least some of the Movement leaders, a trait that made their efforts and motivation appear all the more sincere. Second, Yuri's life intersected with the experiences of the Little Rock Nine in several ways and enhanced her empathy for the plight of poor Black people. In addition to having a personal relationship with one of the Little Rock Nine, she had lived in Arkansas—in a concentration camp—during World War II. And at the time she met Bates, she was living among low-income people of color.

After moving to Harlem, Yuri began to learn more about the Civil Rights Movement and its goal of giving oppressed people a slice of the American pie. But there was now a qualitative shift: rather than simply following events in the newspapers, Yuri was starting to meet people directly involved in the struggle. Her contact with civil rights activists grew slowly at first. In the early 1960s, the only explicitly political information in the Kochiyama family newsletter was a few sentences about their friend James Peck, a White CORE leader who campaigned for integration as one of the Freedom Riders. In 1961, Billy's *Christmas Cheer* column relayed: "We were thrilled to have Mr. James Peck over. He was the one who received 57 stitches on his face when he was beaten up on the first Freedom Ride." Although the Kochiyamas' newsletter contained no other overtly political news, a subtle change, a slight increase in social awareness, was discernible in the contents of *Christmas Cheer*. In 1961 and 1962, for example, there was one article in each issue about the international service activities of the Kochiyamas' friends. One friend helped develop literacy and public health programs in Honduras; another helped construct an auditorium in Nigeria; and yet another taught English and learned about life in Tanganyika, East Africa. But in general, *Christmas Cheer* remained primarily social and service oriented, continuing to feature stories about the NSSO and Nisei veteran activities, news about friends, the Kochiyama children's columns, and birth and marriage announcements. It was not until 1963 that *Christmas Cheer* took on an undeniably political tone.[10]

That year, Yuri, at age forty-two, became involved in several political activities, including protesting the lack of construction jobs for people of color at the Downstate Medical Center, supporting the candidacy of community activist Bill Epton for the New York State Senate, and joining the Harlem Parents Committee. Yuri describes her work with the Harlem Parents Committee as the key activity that launched her civil rights activism. But with her action-oriented inclination, it is possible that she did not work with this school advocacy group until fall 1963, when they initiated a school boycott and opened their Freedom School. A couple of months before that, it seems, she had worked with CORE to protest racialized employment discrimination.[11]

Most likely, James Peck, who began dropping by the Kochiyamas' Saturday night open houses as early as 1961, introduced Yuri to CORE's Downstate Medical Center campaign. Yuri, like many other progressives, would have admired the audacity and success of the Freedom Rides, launched by CORE in May 1961 to challenge the segregation laws governing interstate travel. Thirteen individuals—seven Black and six White—embarked on the first Freedom Ride, traveling as an interracial group throughout the South, even into the fiercely segregated Deep South where the Ku Klux Klan reigned. On that first protest trip, Peck received a severe beating when the Freedom Riders arrived at the bus terminal in Birmingham, Alabama. Another member of their group, Walter Bergman, was beaten so badly he suffered permanent brain damage. It was CORE that initiated this bold challenge to Southern racist rule, a protest campaign that gripped the attention of the nation and one that Yuri no doubt followed in the media. August Meier and Elliott Rudwick, in their study of CORE, posit that this group, more than any other civil rights organization in the early 1960s, played the key leadership role in organizing a massive wave of direct action protests against housing, employment, and educational discrimination in the North. CORE's action-oriented activities would have appealed to a pragmatist like Yuri.[12]

An understanding of CORE's history and politics sheds light on the influences shaping Yuri's politics in 1963. CORE was founded in Chicago in 1942, and its first members were products of the Christian student movement of the 1930s. As participants in the pacifist Christian group, the Fellowship of Reconciliation, they were profoundly committed to studying and then applying Gandhian techniques of nonviolent direct action to resolving racial and labor problems in the United States. CORE had pioneered the technique of nonviolent direct action a decade or two before other major civil rights groups—such as the Southern Christian Leadership Conference (SCLC), which emerged from the Montgomery bus boycott, and the Student Nonviolent Coordinating Committee, formed after the Southern college student sit-ins of 1960—were even established. From its inception, CORE was interracial in membership and ideology. The organization particularly attracted middle-class Whites and in fact, had more White than Black members. Ideologically, observed Meier and Rudwick, "the founders of the organization maintained that it was false to speak of a 'Negro problem'—rather it was a human problem which could be eliminated only through the joint efforts of all believers in the brotherhood of man." It then followed that CORE's statement of purpose, written in 1942, indicated that the group's goal was to eliminate racial discrimination; its method was interracial, nonviolent direct action.[13]

By the early 1960s, however, CORE was embroiled in internal deliberations over the role of its White members. In particular, the debate centered on whether its leadership should be majority White, as it was at the time, or majority Black. Given the increasing emphasis on self-determination in the Civil Rights Movement, as influenced by Black nationalism; the desire to attract Black members, many of whom distrusted White people; and complaints about the paternalism of CORE's White leadership, CORE decided that it was time to have a Black person head the organization. James Farmer, a CORE cofounder and charismatic Black leader, was selected as the national director in 1961. Still, most chapters had majority White membership. Even the non-White-dominated chapters were interracial. Brooklyn CORE, for example, was about half Black when established in 1960. By the summer of 1963, when Yuri worked with this chapter, however, it had become predominantly Black as the Downstate Medical Center protests attracted a heavy influx of Black members. But even then, CORE remained, two decades after its founding, an interracial group. In 1963, when Yuri participated in the CORE-led Downstate Medical Center demonstrations, she supported both the purpose (eliminating racial discrimination) and the method (interracial, nonviolent direct action) of CORE.[14]

That Yuri believed in interracial solidarity was not surprising. Based on her experiences growing up in an integrated, though predominantly White, neighborhood, she felt that cooperation and fellowship among various races were certainly possible. And activists like James Peck demonstrated the commitment on the part of some Whites to fight, and even risk their lives, for racial equality. That Yuri believed in nonviolent resistance was also not surprising. The protest actions that she had seen on television and in the newspapers were those involving nonviolent direct action. The most famous civil rights leader, Martin Luther King Jr., had been offering compelling reasons to denounce the use of violence in any form, reasons that paralleled the religious and pragmatic rationale of the founders of CORE. King argued that "violence solves no social problems; it merely creates new and more complicated ones." Instead, he advocated the use of nonviolent resistance, which he believed was the means for achieving equality for at least three reasons. First, King believed it was necessary to fight for justice because "privileged groups rarely give up their privileges without strong resistance." His method was not passive nonintervention, but an active form of resistance. And it took courage and discipline to resist nonviolently. Second, King believed that violent resistance was immoral because it deepened the brutality of the perpetrator of the violence. King articulated this idea in various ways: "Nonviolent resistance does not seek to defeat or humiliate the opponent, but to win his friendship and understanding"; nonviolent resistance "avoids not only external physical violence but also internal violence of spirit"; and "to meet hate with retaliatory hate would do nothing but intensify the existence of evil in the universe." He further argued that "the [nonviolent] attack is directed against forces of evil rather than against persons who are caught in those forces." Instead, King advocated that the "only cure for fear-hate is love." By this, he was referring to agape, or "the love of God working in the lives of men. . . . We love men not because we like them . . . but because God loves them. Here we rise to the position of loving the person who does the evil deed while hating the deed he does." Third, King believed it was impractical to respond violently against a numerically, militarily, and politically more powerful opponent. Yuri, herself raised on Christian doctrine, would no doubt have been attracted to these ideas.[15]

In the summer of 1963, Brooklyn CORE was leading a campaign to protest racial discrimination in hiring practices at the construction site of the Downstate Medical Center in Brooklyn. Yuri began attending these protests, often bringing her four youngest children, ages four to eleven. Her two oldest children, ages fourteen and sixteen, went on their own to the site. As she got caught up in the frenzy of the activities and in the correctness of the action, she and her children were soon among the approximately two hundred protesters at the site on a daily basis. Demonstrators carried picket signs, marched, chanted, signed petitions, and exerted grassroots pressure on the construction company to hire workers of color. Through this action, Yuri became introduced to the tactic of civil disobedience. The activists decided that they needed to intensify the protest. They began a sit-in at the entrance to obstruct construction trucks. The message was clear: it was going to cost the construction company not to employ workers of color. And Yuri gained a powerful education about the efficacy of collection protest: "That was a lesson for me in how masses of people can put pressure on people in power and force them to change their policies. The construction companies were forced to hire black and Puerto Rican workers that summer."[16]

It was in these obstructive nonviolent demonstrations that Yuri and her oldest son, Billy, got arrested on charges of disorderly conduct, along with more than six hundred others. Yuri recounted: "It was one of the best-organized efforts. It took good organization to keep the protests and arrests going from June to August. At the beginning, mistakes were made. Too many people, like twenty at a time, were getting arrested to stop one truck. Then we realized, you only need two people to stop a truck by lying down across the driveway. Of course, they're not going to run you over. And so they began spacing out the people. Altogether about 650 were arrested. And CORE and Black churches were doing all kinds of fund-raising for the bail and legal fees." After spending perhaps a half-day in jail, Yuri and Billy, like the other arrestees, were released and the charges later dismissed, though they were embroiled in court proceedings for several more months.[17]

How did this Nisei woman, new to activism and civil disobedience, feel about getting arrested? As she explained, "Everybody was getting arrested. It was no big thing. Everybody was taking turns." It is hard to believe that she approached her first act of civil disobedience and arrest so nonchalantly. After all, Yuri grew up in a time when Americans were taught to be law-abiding citizens and she was among the most patriotic of the Nisei—those who equated loyalty to the United States with obedience to the law. But in the two decades since World War II, the social movements taking place in this country and around the world were influencing Yuri's views about political accommodation. Moreover, it was in her nature, if you will, to jump wholeheartedly into a project she believed in. She did not cautiously and methodically become involved in numerous activities as a youth or in the letter-writing campaign to Nisei soldiers. Similarly, after becoming politically conscious, she plunged into activism. While it is likely that Yuri had some apprehensions about participating in her first civil disobedience, since those around her were putting their lives at risk, she would too. And there was an element of exhilaration that surrounded these risky actions: "I think a lot of other people like myself who had never been arrested were excited to be a part of the actions, to be doing something concrete to help fight discrimination."[18]

Inspired by the Southern Civil Rights Movement, including the Freedom Rides, the Kochiyamas decided to take a detour on their trip to visit Yuri's family in California. In the summer of 1963, they traveled by train to Birmingham, Alabama. Birmingham had developed a reputation as, in the words of Martin Luther King Jr., "the country's chief symbol of racial intolerance . . . probably the most thoroughly segregated city in the United States." The Birmingham police commissioner Eugene "Bull" Connor was infamous for his willingness to use any means to enforce segregation, including enabling violent attacks against Black residents. In 1961, White mobs, spurred on by the nonintervention of the police, attacked Freedom Riders in the incident in which James Peck was severely beaten. And numerous bombings in Black neighborhoods earned the city its nickname of "Bombingham."[19]

To push the federal government to enforce Court-ordered antisegregation measures, the SCLC, led by Martin Luther King Jr., strategically selected Birmingham as the site for a prolonged mobilization for the desegregation of public facilities and schools. King reasoned, "We believed that while a campaign in Birmingham would surely be the toughest of our civil-rights careers, it could, if successful, break the back of segregation all over the nation." The SCLC leaders designed a well-organized plan, which included three phases of protest—an economic boycott of downtown stores, mass marches on city hall, and student arrests, in the thousands, to overload the city jails. The boycott was scheduled to begin in early April 1963 to coincide with the Easter shopping period. With careful planning and with the participation of thousands of students, churchgoers, and others in the Black community, within a month, the organized and collective action of the people had done the seemingly impossible. They had forced Connor's police to put down their fire hoses and the economic and political establishment of Birmingham, formerly entrenched in segregation practices, to meet the demands of the civil rights activists: namely, to desegregate public facilities, to abide by nondiscriminatory hiring practices, and to release jailed demonstrators without their having to post bail.[20]

Having been detained by court order for her participation in the Downstate Medical Center demonstrations, Yuri was not able to leave with her family. She departed a few days later and still gained an overall exposure to Southern politics. In Birmingham, the Kochiyamas encountered firsthand the Southern Civil Rights Movement by visiting demonstration sites, burned-down houses, a bombed store, Martin Luther King's organizing headquarters at the Gaston Motel, and several churches, including the Sixteenth Street Baptist Church. Although the front-page article about this trip in the Kochiyamas' family newsletter contained only descriptive information, one senses that it was a moving experience to visit the sites of bombings and civil rights protests that they had read about in the newspaper. The experience became even more significant when, a few weeks after their visit, a highly publicized bombing in September 1963 killed four Black girls at the Sixteenth Street Baptist Church, which served as the headquarters of SCLC's desegregation movement.[21]

Also in 1963, Yuri began supporting the electoral campaign of Bill Epton, who openly ran as a socialist for the New York State Senate in 1964. Epton had recently opened an office of the Progressive Labor Movement (later known as the Progressive Labor Party) on Lenox

Avenue in Harlem to serve as the base of his senatorial campaign and other political projects. Back in 1963 Epton's socialist politics would not have drawn Yuri's support. But he lived in the same housing project as the Kochiyamas, and Yuri probably knew of his work as a community activist advocating for the poor and opposing police brutality. So when Epton formed a committee to promote his candidacy among his fellow residents at the Manhattanville Houses, Yuri offered her support.[22]

As an Asian American and a newcomer to the Movement, she was initially regarded with skepticism. Epton recalled: "It was odd to see Yuri at our committee meetings. In the political climate of that time, the people gathered here were primarily Black and secondarily Hispanic. She was the only Asian and that was sort of different. My wife and I and a few others who were politically active didn't know her politically." Although Yuri may have felt hesitant to involve herself in this new arena, she was not one to act with shyness when she saw a need. She would not have tried to pass herself off as a politically experienced activist, nor would she have tried to act Black to fit in. She would not have done this as a youth, and she certainly would not have created such a facade at age forty-two. Instead, she demonstrated her seriousness through her hard work, dependability, and enthusiasm. And because of this, Black activists grew to trust and respect her. Epton added: "When the political campaign began and Yuri became a part of it, we figured she must be all right. We came to know her as someone who was concerned about the community. And we gave her the blessing. From then on, she just seemed to blossom. The work seemed to energize her." She was soon involved with other projects of the Progressive Labor Movement, including collecting clothing and food to send to miners in Kentucky and the people in Monroe, North Carolina, who had supported the struggles of Robert Williams. That same year, Yuri began working as one of the few Asian Americans in the predominantly Black Harlem Parents Committee (HPC). About that experience, Yuri said: "The people were so wonderful. Even though we weren't Black, we never felt we were different. It was just that we were part of this community." HPC activist Constance Mackey said of Yuri: "I don't think insofar as Yuri was concerned that she was ever viewed as an outsider. She had already established a track record and she'd just been part of the pattern in the weave of her community. And I think most people had already accepted her as that." And in time, noted Epton, "Yuri became a presence."[23]

Yuri's approach to the Epton campaign is revealing of the political changes she was undergoing as well as her approach to entering the Civil Rights Movement. That Yuri's politics in 1963 could be described as liberal-progressive was fairly predictable given the dominance of the civil rights, as opposed to revolutionary, discourse. As a proponent of integration into White America, she had not yet embraced the radical politics of establishing an autonomous Black nation or transforming the United States into a socialist economy. But she also did not reject radicalism as most Americans did after years of anticommunist Cold War propaganda. In fact, she showed an openness to revolutionary ideas, certainly more so than most liberals, and she also did not shy away from associating with and supporting an openly socialist candidate. Yuri looked at Epton's practice and gave him her support, regardless of his ideological stance.

The way Yuri tells the story, it was almost serendipitous that she joined HPC: "We found out that the Harlem Parents Committee office and the Freedom School were located at 514 West 126th street, right across the street and down the block from us. When we realized how close they were, we joined the Harlem Parents Committee right away." Beyond propinquity, the educational goals of the HPC would have also attracted Yuri's attention. As a parent whose children attended Harlem public schools, she would have understood the HPC's position that segregated schools resulted in inferior facilities, textbooks, and learning for inner-city children—a view acknowledged by the U.S. Supreme Court in its 1954 *Brown* decision that declared, "Separate educational facilities are inherently unequal."[24]

Despite the overturning of legal segregation, almost a decade later, segregated schools remained the de facto law of the land. In Harlem, parents, community organizations, and civic groups formed the HPC in spring 1963 with the long-term goal of "'quality integrated education,' a belief that the schools of New York City must be physically desegregated along with the development and implementation of an integrated curriculum." The short-term goal was "upgrading the quality of education within the Harlem community." To achieve their objectives, the HPC called for a boycott of every school in Harlem to commence the first day of school in September 1963. This became the first of many boycotts in which Yuri would participate over her long tenure as a community activist.[25]

After the success of that first boycott, HPC, working in conjunction with the NAACP, CORE, and other civil rights groups, staged what would become the largest school boycott in the history of New York City. This time, the goal was to close every public school in the city until the Board of Education promised to implement integration plans, improve schools, and hire Black principals. Yuri recalled, "Once it started, it was getting up at five or six o'clock in the morning and getting to the school and getting all of our picket signs ready." Bill and the children also participated, with Bill picketing before going to work. Despite efforts by the media, police, and school district to foil the boycott, the citywide action succeeded in drawing in the support of hundreds of thousands of students and more than thirty-five hundred teachers. That the vast majority of students in Central Harlem, an impressive 92 percent, participated in the boycott likely reflects the organizing efforts of the HPC as well as the oppressive conditions in the inner city.[26]

After the HPC demonstrated its effectiveness in organizing school boycotts, the Parents Association asked for its help in what turned out to be a two-year campaign to install a traffic light on the corner of 131st Street and Fifth Avenue, the location of Public School 133 M in Harlem, where cars had killed several children. To symbolize the need to increase children's safety and to stop business as usual, the organizers used a gutsy civil disobedience tactic to confront the city—they had their children do a sit-in in the middle of the intersection. Yuri said: "I remember taking Jimmy and Tommy [ages seven and five]. We put all the kids on the street because children kept getting hit by cars. We couldn't believe it. A lot of these cars, even with all the kids on the streets, would just come through. But we kept doing it until the city said they would put the lights there." Many parents would not have risked the safety of their children even for a cause they believed in. But Yuri would have argued that what she did was no more courageous— or foolish depending on one's view—than the actions of thousands of Southern civil rights activists who faced down police batons, fire hoses, White mobs, and lynchings. Without people willing to put their bodies on the line, figuratively and literally, the community could not effect change, she reasoned. The strategy of the HPC paid off. The mayor promised to install a traffic light, and the HPC kept a vigil to ensure that the city followed through on its promise.[27]

When the HPC announced the opening of its Freedom School in October 1963, it was probably Yuri, in recognizing how little her family knew about Black history, who suggested that they attend each Saturday. The purpose of the Freedom School was to "'teach our children to reclaim and proudly identify with their history and culture'; and to teach all people that the heritage and culture of the American Negro is not a barren one." Students learned the basics about Black history, including Africans in antiquity, the slave trade, the colonial experience, segregation, and resistance. Their instructors were respected Black activists and intellectuals, including James Baldwin, Fannie Lou Hamer, Richard Moore, and John Henrik Clarke. Although the school curriculum was new to Yuri, her experiences living among low-income people of color, her germinating experiences as an activist, and her open-mindedness enabled her to consider these new ideas, which for the most part, made sense to her. Yuri eagerly absorbed the material: "I read everything I could. The reading was really helpful, especially W. E. B. Du Bois's *The Souls of Black Folk*. These readings changed my life."[28]

Although Yuri does not remember the specific ideas that affected her thinking, *The Souls of Black Folk*, written by one of the preeminent Black intellectuals, eloquently explains the effects of racism and economic exploitation on Black people's lives. Much of Du Bois's discussion of racism and poverty in 1903 resonated with Yuri's experiences more than a half century later. As Henry Louis Gates Jr. wrote in the introduction to the 1989 edition, Du Bois "names things that the reader has felt very deeply but could not articulate." Perhaps Yuri as a Japanese American understood what Du Bois meant by the "double-consciousness" of the American Negro. Or perhaps Du Bois's personal testimony about the difficulties he faced as a young schoolteacher trying to educate Black youth up against the powerful limitations of poverty paralleled Yuri's children's experiences with New York schools. Or perhaps Du Bois's discussion of the role of racism—residential, economic, and political—in the lives of Black people or of the role Black slaves and farmworkers played in building the Southern cotton industry gave Yuri a political understanding of the subordination of people of color.

Through the writings of Du Bois and others and through the teachings of Black activist-intellectuals, the HPC Freedom School provided Yuri with her first systematic study of Black American history and culture. As she articulated in the documentary about her life: "Living in the South [during World War II] made me aware of racism, but it didn't make me political because I did not understand the politics of why these things happened." Yuri was now beginning to understand the historical roots of racism and how racism operated in twentieth-century America.[29]

Yuri became so enthusiastic about the HPC that she drew others into the work. Betty Robinson remarked: "I remember going to the HPC school where John Henrik Clarke was teaching. Mary started us going. Although she was about the only Asian—and I don't remember any Whites there—she was the one who got me interested in learning about Black history." This ability to attract others to her activities—be it supporting high school athletes, writing to Nisei soldiers, or attending demonstrations—is a hallmark of Yuri's practice.[30]

This was an invigorating period of transformation for Yuri, one that challenged not only her political beliefs but her practice as well. She ended a consciousness-raising six months with an action that extended her politics into her personal life. At the end of 1963, Yuri introduced to her family a dramatically different idea—that of boycotting Christmas. Since childhood, the holidays had been a special time for Yuri. Her parents had had Christmas parties at their home, complete with a Christmas tree and a suited-up Santa Claus. During World War II, she and the Crusaders made sure they sent Christmas cards to the Nisei soldiers. And the Kochiyama family had been celebrating Christmas with all the fixings, including sending out their *Christmas Cheer* newsletter for years. So when Yuri suggested that her family boycott Christmas in solidarity with the four girls who died in the Birmingham church bombing, it denoted a significant shift in her political development. The primary action was to refrain from exchanging Christmas gifts that year. In this way, the Kochiyamas not only would protest the materialism of Christmas, they also would heighten their empathy with the oppression of others by giving up something of value to them. The children discussed this idea and ostensibly gave their unanimous support. Billy wrote in that year's *Christmas Cheer*:

"This year we're not celebrating Christmas. All of us K-kids agreed to this in view of what happened in Birmingham, and also for what we experienced. We want this to be a year to remember. Even Jimmy and Tommy said they don't want any presents. If any of our relatives or close friends should send us anything not knowing of our plans, we are forwarding these on to a hospital in Birmingham or Mississippi."[31]

Despite Billy's enthusiastic endorsement of this boycott, one wonders about any ambivalent feelings the children may have had. After all, it would have been difficult for just about any child to relinquish gifts. And Christmas was one of the few times the Kochiyama children were showered with presents. Audee recounted: "At Christmas we received a lot of gifts—not so much from our parents, but from their many friends who wanted to thank my parents for their help. They'd give back by giving us kids all these gifts. So at Christmas, we had stacks of gifts." In a family of limited financial means, forfeiting Christmas gifts must have involved quite a sacrifice. Plus, it would have been difficult for the younger children—only four, six, and eight at the time—to understand the reasons for the boycott. Even among the older children who supported the idea of sacrificing material goods, at least one child, then fourteen years old, admitted feeling "surprised" and "a little disappointed" that she missed out on the Christmas gifts. Compared to many other young teenagers who would have protested such a boycott, this Kochiyama child instead felt guilty and a little ashamed at having self-interested feelings. It is hard to disentangle the children's genuine desire to be in solidarity with others who were suffering from their desire to please their parents, particularly their strong-willed mother, whose enthusiasm was contagious and overwhelming at times. After Yuri introduced the idea, it seems likely that there was implicit pressure to do the right thing. There may have been little room for a child to express his or her reluctance to endorse the boycott. What reason could he or she give besides one that sounded selfish? In retrospect, Yuri acknowledges that asking the children, especially the youngest ones, to forgo their Christmas gifts was unfair. She had asked her children to take on a political viewpoint and a non-materialistic stance similar to hers. But she was a mature woman and they were children.[32]

Yuri, and the rest of the Kochiyama family, were learning how to be political activists. Had Yuri thought about boycotting Christmas ten years later, she probably would not have suggested the idea to her family. By the early 1970s, Yuri was an experienced activist, one who had learned somewhat more flexible ways to integrate her political ideas and personal lifestyle. But back in 1963, she was just beginning on her political path. When people are new to activism, they sometimes act in rigid, mechanical ways, upholding the political reason for an action without considering how it affects the persons involved. Even if Yuri had introduced the idea of a boycott ten years later, it is likely that the children would have vetoed the suggestion. By then, the family was making collective decisions and several of the children, especially the feistier ones, regularly engaged in arguments with their mother. But in 1963, a year of dramatic political changes for Yuri and her family, she was discovering how to make the political personal. She was not an activist when convenient, but one who struggled to live her life according to her principles of justice. In doing so, like all of us, she made mistakes. But it is only through such a process of struggle, and of trial and error, that one learns how to be an activist fully committed to social change.

In the context of the 1960s social movements, Yuri infused a political consciousness into all her children, especially the oldest four, who made deliberate decisions to be politically active. "The older kids were excited to be learning new, exciting information and going to marches, demonstrations, vigils, and political talks," recalled Yuri. "And the little ones came with me whenever I went to political events." The older children were active in the progressive-to-radical movements, first participating in the Civil Rights Movement and a few years later in the emerging Black Power Movement. When the Asian American Movement surfaced in the late 1960s, Audee, Aichi, and Eddie became involved.[33]

Two years after Yuri's plunge into political activism, two of her children traveled from New York to Mississippi to help register Black voters. It is likely that the Kochiyamas' visit to Birmingham contributed to Billy's and Audee's eagerness to participate in the South. Yuri proudly relayed that Billy was so keen to help with voter registration that he left for Mississippi as soon as school ended, missing his high school graduation. The Kochiyamas could not afford to finance his travels, but Billy's friends in Students Against Social Injustice (SASI) raised the necessary funds. SASI was a high school group, founded by Billy, Audee, and several of Billy's high school friends, to address social issues. Yuri recalled: "Thanks to all these kids in this really political group, SASI, Billy was able to go to Mississippi. They'd go to the park and some of the girls played the guitar and sang freedom songs. People would just give them money—I couldn't believe it. All the students chipped in money and Billy was able to go." During his five weeks in Rosedale, Mississippi, in the summer of 1965, Billy worked with the Mississippi Student Union, a youth group affiliated with the Mississippi Freedom Democratic Party (MFDP). He lived with the family of Frank Davis, chair of MFDP. In the hostile South, registering Black voters also meant fighting for your very life, as Billy wrote in *Christmas Cheer*: "The terrorism and intimidations were inflicted without holding back their punches. Justice there is something strange and unknown. Poverty was unbelievable. On the other hand, the fearlessness and militancy of the black people was inspiring. They . . . believe, as Malcolm did, that men should have the guts to defend themselves."[34]

A couple of months before Billy's trip, fifteen-year-old Audee went with ten high school students during spring vacation to register Black voters in McComb, Mississippi, under the auspices of the Student Nonviolent Coordinating Committee (SNCC). Bill and Yuri may well have had concerns about the safety of their children in the South, especially after the highly publicized murders of three civil rights workers in Mississippi the year before. By the mid-1960s in McComb, White mob beatings of SNCC activists were regular affairs and the city had gained a reputation as the "bombing capital of the world" for its vicious Ku Klux Klan brutality. Billy and Audee understood the atmosphere of violence surrounding the Southern Civil Rights Movement. Yet both were willing to risk their personal safety. While they may have been worried, Yuri and Bill were also proud of their children's choices. Still, they refused the request of their third child, then only twelve years old, when she pleaded with them to allow her to join her older siblings in their travels to register Black Mississippians.[35]

Even within New York City, the political activities of this third child were restricted, this time by her gender and location within the family and by her age, being barely eleven years old in mid-1963, when the Kochiyamas became politicized. In the 1964 *Christmas Cheer*, Aichi lamented, "[I] couldn't make it to as many demonstrations as

Audee and Billy did because I had to stay home some of the time to watch the three little ones." Still, Aichi managed to participate actively that year: "Eddie and I did picket in the first two [school] boycotts, marched with the Freedom School twice in Harlem, and went over the Brooklyn Bridge with the Puerto Rican silent march. Audee and I went several times a week to the General Motors picket-line back in May." Yuri's political influence on all her children is evident in Aichi's selection of heroes, or perhaps Yuri helped them to write their columns: "As a youth, I also admire such leaders as Stokely Carmichael, Nana Oserjeman Adefumi, Mae Mallory and Bill Epton. The greatest is, of course, Malcolm X, who loved and inspired youth."[36]

Eddie, who was exposed to the Movement as a child, showed a budding political consciousness from an early age. After attending numerous marches and demonstrations, including the Downstate Medical Center and Vietnam War protests, this seventh grader helped organize what he believes was the first antiwar rally at a New York City junior high school, attended by some one hundred students. That Eddie invited his mother to be one of the speakers is indicative of the respect he held for her as an activist. The following day, the school principal suspended Eddie and his two co-organizers for a week for distributing leaflets for the rally. Eddie recounted: "I was thinking, 'I can't believe I got suspended.' The principal's a real jerk. He was upset because the leaflets were printed on red paper. Right in front of the entire school, he says, 'You know what that means—Communists.' I was upset and scared about how my parents would take it, especially my father. I just knew I was gonna get my ass whipped again. When I got home, I decided I'd better tell them the truth. So I did and they were quiet. Then my Mom started crying and said, 'Oh Eddie, we're so proud of you!'" Compared to Yuri, Bill was a stricter disciplinarian and also less enthusiastic about the involvement of his children in political activism. But he too had become politicized during this period and was proud of Eddie's work to organize this rally.[37]

In 1971, a year before President Richard Nixon normalized relations with the People's Republic of China, Eddie traveled to China as part of a political delegation. As the youngest of the four Asian American delegates, he was surprised when Asian American Movement leader and delegation organizer Jerry Tung invited him to give the presentation on the Asian American movement before Chou En-lai and others on the

Communist Party's Central Committee; Mao Tse-tung's absence was explained by illness. In Tung's eyes, it seems, Eddie's substantive involvement in the Asian American Movement made him an appropriate choice. Eddie had joined, for example, Chickens Come Home to Roost, the first uptown Asian drop-in service and political organizing center. This center started as part of the squatters' movement, whereby activists seized abandoned buildings and renovated them to provide housing and services to poor and working-class people being displaced by gentrification. In this way, Asian American activists gained a storefront location for Asian American history lectures, Japanese language classes, martial arts training, political education classes, and a meeting space for different groups, including the Asian Coalition Against the Vietnam War. Chickens Come Home to Roost, named after Malcolm X's famous statement, also helped build bridges among Black, Latino, and Asian communities. When Eddie returned from China and presented a note from his parents, his high school homeroom teacher did not find credible the reason for his three-week absence. As a result, Eddie failed his classes, but as he said, "I didn't care. I knew where I was going to gain a real education and I made my choice." One wonders whether Yuri or Bill intervened on their son's behalf. If they had, their efforts appear to have been unsuccessful. But perhaps they did not intervene. Yuri has mentioned that, as she met West Coast Asian American college students and graduates in the 1970s, 1980s, and 1990s, she regretted not prioritizing education for her children. The early 1970s was also a period of intense political activity for Yuri and of marital discord, as discussed in chapter 7. So it is possible, as one may well presume from Eddie's rendition, that his parents, who a few years earlier might have "whipped his ass," did not confront his teacher or contest his failing grades.[38]

The experiences of the two youngest Kochiyama children differed from that of their siblings. The older ones were showered with cultural and recreational activities during the period prior to the family's political involvement. When Yuri's activism emerged in 1963, their interest in political issues grew alongside their mother's. But Jimmy and Tommy were only six and four years old at the time. While Yuri took them to numerous demonstrations, they often did not want to be outside in New York's blustery winters at places where there were few other children. Although Jimmy and Tommy were involved in various activities—including summer church camp, Boy Commandos, karate, off-Broadway shows, commercials, and the Haryou Act, a federally funded antipoverty program for Harlem youth—they also had fewer extracurricular activities and a less traditional home life. Back in the 1950s, the Kochiyamas spent time together as a family at parks, beaches, and ball games. But as they became more politically active, Yuri acknowledged that their family activities began to revolve around the Movement. Tommy recounted: "We didn't do many things as a family. Dad was in the Niko Niko club, so once or twice a year, we'd go on a picnic. Our family rarely ate out. And at home, we didn't eat together. We'd eat wherever. Dad, Eddie, and Billy played on a softball league and we'd all go to the park to watch them, which I enjoyed. And we did celebrate our birthdays, usually at home with dinner and a cake." Even when she was at home, Yuri's attention was often focused on political issues. Jimmy recalled: "When my friends came over, my mom always lectured them about Movement activities. We hated it, but my friends thought it was OK and a lot of them became involved." The constant visitors and overnight guests were also difficult to contend with, especially for Jimmy, an admittedly shy child. So Yuri's activism had a different effect on her younger children, and consequently these two are the least involved in the Movement.[39]

Certainly not all children of activists have chosen to become active themselves, though it is likely that a much higher proportion of this group, compared to the general population, developed a critical political consciousness. Such is the case for Jimmy and Tommy. This is evident in Tommy's use of political ideas to explain his child-rearing choices: "I was never active in the Movement, never worked on the big causes. By comparison, the problems at home may seem little. But like Che [Guevara] says, one's motive should be great feelings of love. I think that needs to start at home. That's what I'm trying to do with my kids." These two Kochiyama children also stressed their support of Yuri's political commitments. Tommy commented: "I love my mom. I think she has a heart of gold." And Jimmy asserted: "I feel proud of my mother's Movement work. I don't always agree with her, but I respect her for her feelings of wanting to do what's right. Her commitment's real and she's an amazing woman."[40]

Beginning in 1963, changes in the content of the family newsletter were further evidence of the politicization of the entire Kochiyama family. For the first time, the newsletter contained a significant portion of articles with political themes, and the extensive spread of photographs was noticeably darker—Black civil rights activists rather than friends of Asian and other backgrounds. The 1963 *Christmas Cheer* editorial addressed, "The challenge of making the American Dream of 'equality and justice for all' not just a boast or wishful thinking, but a reality in performance." The theme of the 1964 issue—political activism—was markedly different from the previous whimsical, all-American selections. In that issue, Yuri and Bill observed: "Saturday Nites . . . has also during these past two years had the semblance of protest gatherings replete with speakers, folk-singers, freedom songs, soul-spirits, freedom-fighters, peace-workers. . . . The walls came tumbling down as Saturday Nites moved from socializing to social concern." Among the activists who spoke at their Saturday night programs were "James Shabazz, Malcolm's dynamic aide . . . Mae Mallory, Freedom Fighter extraordinary, who related her experience [of being arrested on a trumped-up kidnapping charge in conjunction with Robert F. Williams] in Monroe, North Carolina . . . E. P. Menon who trekked 7,500 miles from Delhi, India to Moscow, Paris, London, New York, and Wash. D.C. promoting world peace." Yuri recalled: "We were meeting so many political activists. They were not radicals; they were civil rights activists [whom we met] through the Harlem Parents Committee and the Harlem Freedom School." And many of these activists attended the Kochiyamas' Saturday night open house. The politicalization of the Kochiyama children's columns was also apparent. Billy, for example, explained the details of his arrest at the Downstate Medical Center protest and made an appeal for people to support political prisoner Mae Mallory. And Audee described her excitement at meeting Malcolm X when he visited the delegates of the Hiroshima-Nagasaki World Peace Study Mission at the Kochiyamas'.[41]

When they moved to Harlem in 1960, Yuri and Bill could not have predicted the reasons they would stop publishing *Christmas Cheer* eight years later. As their interests moved toward social justice, it was natural that their family newsletter reflected these concerns. But this upset many longtime friends, who wrote to the Kochiyamas expressing their indignation at the political turn of *Christmas Cheer*. Yuri recounted: "Our old friends told us, 'We liked when it was just about Xmas.' This is when I decided to put a distance between myself and my hometown. I didn't want them to influence me into their way of thinking. They wanted me to stay the way they knew me. But I had changed." One of Yuri's childhood friends, though reluctant to speak negatively about her fellow San Pedrans, admitted that some were quite outspoken against Yuri's newfound political views. It must have been difficult for Yuri to hear such criticism and to lose old friends. But she understood that good feelings among friends were not enough to rid the world of injustice. In her years as a Christian, she had read about how Jesus was persecuted for his beliefs. As an activist, she understood that staying committed to principles would not always make one popular. But she sought social justice, not social popularity.[42]

The editorial in the final edition, "Why C.C. Went Political," contained Bill and Yuri's reasons for ending the publication of *Christmas Cheer.*

> For some 15 years, C.C. was a comfortable family news-sheet, a way and means of keeping in touch with the myriad of friends who came into our life. It was strictly a "friendship" paper— warm, homespun, individualistic. . . . About four years ago, C.C. became political. That is, we projected social problems and took positions; we vociferated our feelings on ills; we gave exposure to societal prerequisites, reiterating historical and traditional trends of this country. Somehow we could feel that a great number of C.C. readers were upset. Through their letters and from the grapevine, we could sense their feelings ranged from disappointment at our un-Americanism to shock and anger at what seemed like insubordination and subversiveness. . . . Most evident was that the majority of C.C. readers and we were oceans apart in interest and thinking.[43]

The move to Harlem eight years earlier had transformed the Kochiyamas' lives. "Harlem has been my university-without-walls," Yuri reflected. "No college in the U.S. could have taught me so poignantly and effectively about realities in American life."[44]

5

Meeting Malcolm X

Yuri's civil rights work led to her introduction to a person who would revolutionize her political vision. She and her sixteen-year-old son, Billy, were among the more than six hundred arrested during a CORE protest demanding jobs for Black and Puerto Rican construction workers. At their hearing at the Brooklyn courthouse on October 16, 1963, who should appear but Malcolm X. Yuri described their initial meeting:

> He came by himself, no bodyguards or anybody. All the young bloods, the brothers and sisters, ran down. He was immediately encircled by enthusiastic young activists who were eager to talk to him and to shake his hands. They were all young, late teens through twenties and maybe even thirties. But here I'm not Black, so I thought maybe I shouldn't go over there. My mind flashed to [the *Life* magazine story of] the White college student who came to Harlem to ask what she could do for Black people. Malcolm told her, "Nothing," and she left in tears. I hoped I wouldn't say something stupid. But I did want to meet him. A CORE leader encouraged me, "Why don't you try? Whatever happens, happens." I felt funny, but I slowly moved closer and closer to where Malcolm and all his admirers were standing. I remained a little on the outside to give Blacks the privacy they deserve. All of a sudden there was a window of opportunity— Malcolm looked up and seemed to be looking right at me. He was probably wondering "Who's this old lady, and Asian at that."

I stepped forward and called out, "Can I shake your hand?" He looked at me and demanded, "What for?" I stammered back, "I want to congratulate you." And he asked, "For what?" I was trying to think of what to say and said, "For what you're doing for your people." "What's that?" he queried. "For giving them direction." He abruptly burst forth with that fantastic Malcolm smile and extended his hand. I grabbed it. I could hardly believe I was actually meeting the Malcolm X.[1]

In this narrative, well rehearsed through repeated recitations, Yuri's awareness of herself as an outsider to the Black community is apparent. Her experiences in Harlem exposed her to the growing Black separatist sentiments, at a time when Black nationalists regularly condemned the usurpation of Black political organizations by White liberals. But Malcolm, whose race politics were shaped inside the Nation of Islam, would have seen Yuri not simply as a non-Black but, more important, as a non-White. The Nation of Islam considered non-Whites to be Black; in particular, they held that Blacks in the United States are "descendants of the Asian Black Nation." Moreover, in 1942, Nation of Islam leader Elijah Muhammad was arrested and sentenced to four years in prison for refusing to serve in the U.S. military against Japan. Muhammad admitted to sympathy for Japan, whom "Black internationalists" viewed as the leader of colored races against global White supremacy. In addition, Yuri's respect for Black autonomy, perhaps mixed with her fears of being chastised, distinguished her from most White people in the eyes of many Black nationalists. A. Peter Bailey observed: "In the OAAU [Organization of Afro-American Unity], Yuri didn't try to out-Black everyone, like many Whites do. And so many Whites—Right, Left, or center—interacted with the Black movement with such paternalism. They'll do anything for you as long as they run it. That's why most Black people didn't trust alliances with Whites. But people came to trust Yuri, to respect her as a strong supporter of the Black movement."[2]

Still, at the moment of her introduction to Malcolm, it is not surprising that Yuri's politics reflected the civil rights discourse predominant at the time: "I blurted out, 'I admire the kinds of things you're saying, but I don't agree with you about something.' He said sternly, 'What do you disagree with me about?' 'Your harsh stance on integration.'" Within months of that meeting, Yuri began questioning her integrationist beliefs and later adopted Malcolm's nationalist views. Conscious of her transformed ideology, Yuri now prefaces her separatist opposition with a disclaimer: "There was a second part where I said something stupid. I didn't know anything about the Black liberation movement. I had just gotten started in the civil rights movement. . . . It was a stupid thing to say since he was a Black nationalist, but he wasn't even upset. He was so cool, so open. He just said, 'I can't give you a two-minute lecture on the pros and cons of integration right here. If you want, come to my office and we'll discuss it then.'"[3]

Yuri's separatist challenge signaled a boldness in confronting a person of Malcolm's intimidating reputation. Although the written word does not convey the tone of her disagreement, it was, as she tells it today, a mild chastisement. Her modus operandi is to not make direct or harsh confrontations. Rather, she tends to voice her objections in gentle ways. Because of Yuri's tone, Malcolm may well have sensed an open-mindedness in her, and hence his invitation. Malcolm's response impressed Yuri, perhaps because his behaviors contrasted so sharply with the media portrayals of him as a hatemonger: "This just goes to show what kind of person Malcolm was—so open and humble and willing to discuss ideas with people. I was really excited and couldn't wait to tell Billy and the rest of the family. Billy had left the courtroom to take an exam [at school]; I knew how disappointed he'd be to have missed Malcolm X."[4]

The following day, Billy rushed to tell his mother that Malcolm X was speaking on the radio. This was the first time Yuri would hear Malcolm speak. She had assumed he would be debating White people, but the debate turned out to be among Black movement leaders. Malcolm's eloquence and passion as well as his separatist ideas inspired her to compose a letter to him that night:

> My son and I just finished listening to the radio broadcast. . . . I could not constrain myself from writing to you. . . . I shall always admire you and respect you for what you are doing for your people—giving them the "lift," the support, and pride in their heritage. More than that, you are giving much to all of us—penetrating into all the infested areas bloated with pomposity. . . . It may be possible that non-Negroes may wake up

and learn to treat all people as human beings. And when that time comes, I am sure that your pronouncement for separation will be changed to integration. If each of us, white, yellow, and what-have-you, can earn our way into your confidence by actual performance, will you . . . could you . . . believe in "togetherness" of all people?[5]

Even as Yuri promoted an integrationist line, this debate must have challenged, perhaps for the first time, her beliefs. After all, it was Malcolm, more than the civil rights leaders, who captured her imagination—so much so that she "could not constrain [herself] from writing to [him]." Malcolm had moved her. In this Yuri was not alone. Poet Sonia Sanchez, then a member of CORE, was drawn to Malcolm, despite her efforts to ignore this man, demonized by the media as a hater of White people and all things decent. She recalled her first encounter with Malcolm's street-corner orations: "I looked up and looked around, determined not to look at him, determined not to listen. But as he started to talk, I found myself more and more listening to him. And I began to nod my head, 'Yeah that's right, that makes sense.'" After his first experience with a three-hour speech by Malcolm, A. Peter Bailey reflected: "He literally compelled me to question some of the things I had believed. It was like someone pulling up your scalp and just pouring information in that you never, some things you had felt, but you had never heard verbalized before."[6]

As with Sanchez, Bailey, and others, Malcolm's oration and ideas commanded Yuri's attention. "A master teacher" is how Bailey describes Malcolm: "The sheer accurateness and clarity of it made you say 'Ohhh.' And even if you disagreed with every word he said, you had to start doing some things to reinforce whatever you were thinking. He made you think about it." Malcolm had the ability to explain complex ideas in terms that were understandable to the average person on the street. What he said resonated with many in Harlem, including Yuri: "Even though I was new to the Movement, I knew things were wrong with society. Even if I couldn't put it in political terms, I knew there was a lot of racism. So more and more I wanted to hear Malcolm speak." Several months later, in a letter to him, Yuri articulated part of the attraction for her: ". . . you speak for the most downtrodden, shackled, and ostracized. . . . you are not afraid to spell out the grievances as they are, how the injustices are perpetrated and who commits them. People must be made to see the truth." That Yuri admired Malcolm's service to the poor, his search for the truth, and his courage to speak out regardless of potential persecution, is not surprising. These qualities, promoted in the Bible, are traits she had sought to emulate as a young Sunday school teacher.[7]

Although Yuri lived in Harlem, not far from Malcolm's Nation of Islam (NOI) mosque, the opportunity to visit his office eluded her. Six weeks after their courthouse meeting, the NOI issued a ninety-day suspension of Malcolm following his "chickens come home to roost" remark about President John F. Kennedy's assassination. The temporary suspension soon turned into a permanent ouster, accompanied by the equivalent of a death warrant issued in the NOI newspaper, *Muhammad Speaks*. Devastated by the betrayal of his confidants and kicked out of the organization to which he had devoted twelve years of his life, Malcolm agonized, "My head felt like it was bleeding inside."[8]

Until the newspapers broadcast Malcolm's suspension, like the general public, Yuri was unaware of the problems building within the NOI. Much has been written about how Malcolm's previously unwavering faith in his hero and father figure Elijah Muhammad was shattered upon discovering that the NOI leader had committed adultery with several of his secretaries. Also significant to Malcolm's departure, though less discussed, was his growing dissatisfaction with the noninterventionist policy of the NOI leadership. As early as 1962, when Muhammad terminated Malcolm's efforts to protest the police killing of Los Angeles NOI leader Ronald X Stokes, Malcolm privately vented his frustrations to his assistant minister: "We talk about people being bitten by dogs and mowed down by fire hoses, we talk about our people being brutalized in the civil rights movement, and we haven't done anything to help them. . . . And now we've had one of our own brothers killed and still we haven't done anything." After leaving the NOI, it is not surprising that Malcolm founded an organization, the Muslim Mosque, Inc., that integrated his religious and political beliefs. The NOI's continuing influence on Malcolm was evident in the Muslim Mosque's nationalist ideology: "Our political philosophy will be black nationalism. Our economic and social philosophy will be black nationalism. Our cultural emphasis will be black nationalism. . . . The political philosophy of black nationalism means: we must control the politics and the politicians of our community."[9]

During this turbulent period in Malcolm's life, Yuri received a letter from an American peace group explaining that three *hibakusha* (atomic bomb survivor) journalists-writers, Kenmitsu Iwanaga, Akira Mitsui, and Ryuji Hamai, wanted, according to Yuri, "to meet Malcolm X more than anyone else in the United States." When Yuri contacted Malcolm's office, a representative indicated that despite his busy schedule, Malcolm would try to attend their event. The Hiroshima-Nagasaki World Peace Mission Study embarked on a walking tour of the United States, Europe, and the Soviet Union to call for an end to nuclear bombs and weapons proliferation. In the United States, the *hibakusha* writers, translators, and peace activists wanted to see the segregation and slum conditions that motivated the Black revolt. In Harlem, "they saw a community where garbage was stacked high because the sanitation department wasn't picking it up regularly, clogged bath-tubs, toilets that wouldn't flush, broken windows and stairwells because the landlords wouldn't bother to make repairs," explained Yuri.[10]

On Saturday, June 6, 1964, the Kochiyamas' home was overflowing with Black and White civil rights activists, many from the newly formed Harlem Parents Committee and Harlem Freedom School, and concerned Japanese Americans who had come to enjoy a program of singing and poetry, performed by Black and Japanese artists. Despite her hopes for Malcolm X's appearance, Yuri underscored the instability of the times for him: "It's important to understand what a turbulent period this was for Malcolm. He had just been expelled from the Nation of Islam. None of the Blacks who came were Malcolm's people; there were no Muslims, no Yorubas, no nationalists, no radicals. This was really a dangerous time for Malcolm. There were rumors that he would be killed, including death threats by the Muslims, and no one knew who might be out to get him. So we could understand if he didn't show." But all of a sudden, there was a knock on the door and in walked Malcolm X. Yuri relayed the reaction of the *hibakusha* and American activists at meeting the larger-than-life figure: "His appearance electrified the room. But our guests were also apprehensive: Would he be hostile to such an integrated audience? Would he treat the Whites poorly? He was nothing the people expected. There was no arrogance, no egocentricity, no hostility; instead he was gracious, warm, personable. We all noticed that he was as friendly to Whites as to Blacks. He shook hands with everyone within reach."[11]

"When Malcolm began to speak," continued Yuri, "you could hear a pin drop. Everyone was focused intensely on this charismatic speaker. The *hibakushas* asked that the translators not interfere with Malcolm's rhythm once he started speaking." The content of Malcolm's remarks grabbed Yuri's attention, as she remembers the event:

> Malcolm said: "You were bombed and have physical scars. We too have been bombed and you saw some of the scars in our neighborhood. We are constantly hit by the bombs of racism." He candidly described the years he spent in prison and that it was while in prison that he became educated by reading everything he could get hold of. He kept reading even after lights were out by the dim glow of the hall light. He started with the dictionary, reading from A to Z. He loved history and had read a lot of Asian history. He explained that almost all of Asia had been colonized by Europeans except Japan. The only reason Japan wasn't colonized was because Japan didn't have resources that Europeans wanted. All over Southeast Asia, European and American imperialists were taking rubber and oil and other resources. But after World War II, Japan did provide valuable military bases for America, especially on the island of Okinawa. It was because Japan hadn't been colonized that Japan was able to stay intact and become so strong until her defeat in World War II.

"I don't think Malcolm was aware of Japan's similarity to America in its racism and chauvinism—especially Japan's treatment of Koreans," added Yuri, a strong critic of Japanese cultural nationalism.[12]

Based on Yuri's narration, it can be concluded that Malcolm tailored his talk to the Japanese peace activists. Either that, or Yuri's interest in Black-Asian interactions shaped her memories.

> Malcolm spoke highly of Mao Tse-tung of China. He felt Mao had moved in the right direction to simultaneously fight feudalism, corruption, and foreign domination. He liked that Mao showed preferential treatment to the peasants because they were the ones who performed the most awesome task of feeding such

a large population. He also spoke of the war in Vietnam and of his great admiration for Ho Chi Minh. Malcolm had read so much about Asia and the Third World people's struggles; he was really knowledgeable and astute in his analysis. He made the prophetic statement, "The struggle of the Vietnamese is the struggle of all Third World people. It's the struggle against imperialism, colonialism, and neo-colonialism." Though the American antiwar movement hadn't yet started, he said, "All progressive people should protest if the U.S. military makes incursions into Southeast Asia."

"Sadly, he didn't live long enough to see the huge antiwar movement building up throughout the nation and even the world," remarked Yuri. "But it was largely because of Malcolm's vision that Harlem was one of the earliest cities to participate in the antiwar movement. . . . Malcolm was ahead of his time, able to see, to grasp, to understand, and willing to share all that he discerned. The impact that he made on young people, progressives of all nationalities, students, lumpens, street, and intellectuals was unparalleled."[13]

In the eight months since Yuri's courthouse introduction to Malcolm X, they had had no contact, except for letters from Yuri to Malcolm. Malcolm must have received these letters because upon entering her home, he immediately apologized for his lack of response. By contrast, he followed through on his promise to write during his international travels. When he left the next month for his second trip abroad that year, Yuri and Bill were among the people to whom Malcolm wrote in the midst of meeting with national leaders. The Kochiyamas received eleven postcards from eight countries in Africa and the Middle East, as well as England. Each contained a brief message: "Still trying to travel and broaden my scope since I've learned what a mess can be made by narrow-minded people"; "Greetings from Kenya, the home of those great African Patriots, the Mau Mau Freedom Fighters"; and "Greetings once again from the Cradle of Civilization where the recent African Summit Conference was a tremendous success." Yuri shared these postcards with others in her community, not to brag but to convey news from Malcolm. Mae Mallory, a respected Harlem activist, recalled: "Mary [Yuri] was the only person in the area that Malcolm wrote to, except for Mr.

Micheaux [Black nationalist bookstore owner]." Although exaggerated, the perception Mallory voiced exists to this day—that Yuri was special to Malcolm, as expressed in one of his postcards: "I read all of your wonderful cards and letters of encouragement and I think you are the most beautiful family in Harlem."[14]

"I think his coming to our house brought Malcolm much closer to us," reflected Yuri. And Malcolm had an influence on the political growth of the entire Kochiyama family. Billy, for example, had nationalist leanings as a teenager, as indicated in a letter to his parents during his 1965 trip to Mississippi: "I really wish Malcolm could have just made one trip to Miss. First of all, he would have been pleasantly shocked to see how *black nationalist* SNCC was becoming. Secondly, so much of what the black Mississippian want[s] is what Malcolm has said all along. The black people here are always preaching black unity, self defense, and telling the truth just like it is. Malcolm would have found thousands of followers here." Yet only Yuri, Bill, and Audee got to meet Malcolm during his visit to their home: "I'm just sorry that only one of my children was there. Audee was fourteen years old, and we thought she might be helpful as a hostess. Billy was away in Springfield, Massachusetts, with the Upward Bound program. We sent the others to see a movie. It wasn't that we thought they'd be in the way, but a young Black friend, Conway Reddings, son of the famous Saunders Reddings, came and said, 'Look I'll take the kids off your hands.' And he took them to see the movie *Mary Poppins*. I think now the kids are mad that they had to see that ol' movie and missed out on meeting Malcolm X." Malcolm inspired the one Kochiyama child who attended the reception. "The most exciting thing that happened to us this year was that Malcolm X came to our home," said Audee in the family newsletter.[15]

Malcolm's only visit to the Kochiyamas' home was sandwiched between two lengthy international trips in 1964 to advance religious and political objectives. In the spring, he made a pilgrimage to Mecca to recenter his spiritual life and relieve the overwhelming sensation that his head was "bleeding inside." During the first and second trips he met with political leaders, as well as students and journalists, in Ghana, Nigeria, Tanzania, Morocco, Algeria, and Egypt, among other African countries, to gather support for his eight-page memorandum charging the U.S. government with human rights violations against its Black citizenry, as presented to the second annual meeting of the newly formed Organization of African Unity (OAU), held in Cairo in July. Although OAU delegates did not publicly endorse Malcolm's proposal, they did issue a statement expressing concern about racial conditions in the United States. Malcolm left the OAU gathering feeling positive about his impact, as relayed to Milton Henry in Cairo shortly afterward: "Several of [the African delegates] promised officially that, come the next session of the UN, any effort on our part to bring our problem before the UN . . . will get support and help from them. . . . So I am very, very happy over the whole result of my trip here." Others also recognized the potential impact of Malcolm's international activities. M. S. Handler reported in the *New York Times*: "The State Department and the Justice Department have begun to take an interest in Malcolm's campaign to convince African states to raise the question of persecution of American Negroes at the United Nations. . . . After studying [Malcolm's memorandum], officials said that if Malcolm succeeded in convincing just one African government to bring up the charge at the United Nations, the United States Government would be faced with a touchy problem."[16]

Not only did Malcolm influence his African colleagues, they in turn challenged his evolving political ideas about race and class, marking a new radicalization and internationalization that were to characterize his final year and profoundly influence Yuri's political development. She observed: "Malcolm wanted to make things better for his people, and he saw racism and imperialism as the cause of these problems and the solution must be international. It was these revolutionary ideas that I was attracted to, though I didn't know much about them at the time." Although his spring 1964 trip has been interpreted as a transformational moment in Malcolm's political trajectory, Yuri offers a context in which to also see continuity in Malcolm's development: "We never knew Malcolm's private thoughts until he left the Nation, but I believe his ideas were changing throughout his years in the Nation. While his ideas were continuously growing—Malcolm was very open-minded—his fundamental ideas remained the same."[17] Still, Malcolm's thinking shifted in at least two significant ways as a result of this trip.

First, Malcolm's discussions with major Pan-Africanist governmental leaders, including Kwame Nkrumah of Ghana, Ahmed Sékou Touré of Guinea, Julius Nyerere of Tanzania, and Gamal Abdel Nasser of Egypt, served to solidify his conviction that the African American situation was intricately linked to the global African situation. "By internationalizing the American Negro situation, [Malcolm] saw a way of turning the minority into a majority," Theodore Draper noted. Moreover, these same African leaders saw Pan-Africanism not only in terms of racial unity but also in terms of class. As Malcolm learned more about their efforts to create a socialist Africa, he became increasingly anticapitalist and attracted to socialist tenets. Shortly after returning from his first trip to Africa, at an event sponsored by the Socialist Workers Party, Malcolm declared: "While I was traveling I noticed that most of the countries that have recently emerged into independence have turned away from the so-called capitalistic system in the direction of socialism." Characteristic of his rich use of metaphoric imagery, Malcolm continued: "It's impossible for a chicken to produce a duck egg—even though they both belong to the same family of fowl. . . . It can only produce according to what that particular system was constructed to produce. . . . It's impossible for this system, as it stands, to produce freedom right now for the black man in this country. And if ever a chicken did produce a duck egg, I'm quite sure you would say it was certainly a revolutionary chicken!" Malcolm concluded by highlighting the intersection of race and class: "It's impossible for a white person to believe in capitalism and not believe in racism. You can't have capitalism without racism."[18]

Second, after interacting with White Muslims in Mecca, Malcolm modified his view of White people as the devil, a statement he frequently made as a NOI minister. In his autobiography, Malcolm recounted: "In the Muslim world, I had seen that men with white complexions were more genuinely brotherly than anyone else had ever been. That morning was the start of a radical alteration in my whole outlook about 'white' men." In Africa, Malcolm interacted with White and Black people whom he considered true revolutionaries fighting for social justice. He referred to the Algerian ambassador to Ghana, a White man, as "a revolutionary in the true sense of the word (and has his credentials as such for having carried on a successful revolution against oppression in his country)." And upon his return, Malcolm said:

In the past, I have permitted myself to be used to make sweeping indictments of all white people, and these generalizations have caused injuries to some white people who did not deserve them. . . . [A]s a result of my pilgrimage to the Holy City of Mecca, I no longer subscribe to sweeping indictments of one race. My pilgrimage to Mecca . . . served to convince me that perhaps American whites can be cured of the rampant racism which is consuming them and about to destroy this country. In the future, I intend to be careful not to sentence anyone who has not been proven guilty. I am not a racist and do not subscribe to any of the tenets of racism.[19]

Had Malcolm maintained his previous racial views, Yuri probably would not have become such a close supporter. Her initial letter to Malcolm expressed hope for the "togetherness of all people." And today, though she has worked largely in Third World movements, Yuri believes that Whites, especially White radicals, have contributed to the movements for justice. This belief is reflected in her practice, which has included supporting White political prisoners and working with White activists throughout the years.

Whether Malcolm's changing racial views led to a repudiation of Black nationalism remains open to debate and stirs controversy among his closest associates. Trotskyist George Breitman discerned that, after his return from Africa and the Middle East in May 1964, Malcolm stopped calling himself a Black nationalist and never referred to the OAAU, founded in June 1964, as a Black nationalist organization. In his study of the OAAU, William Sales observed that the organization's eclectic radicalism contrasted sharply with the Black nationalism of the Muslim Mosque, Inc., founded just three months earlier. In a January 1965 interview with the Socialist Workers Party, Malcolm revealed: "When I was in Africa in May, in Ghana, I was speaking with the Algerian ambassador who is extremely militant and is a revolutionary in the true sense of the word. . . . When I told him my political, social and economic philosophy was Black nationalism, he asked me very frankly, well, where did that leave him? Because he was white. . . . He showed me where I was alienating people who were true revolutionaries, dedicated to overturning the system of exploitation. . . . So I had to do a lot of thinking and reappraising of my definition of black nationalism. . . . If you notice, I haven't been using the expression for several months." Moreover, Muhammad Ahmad (Max Stanford) disclosed that, in the last week of Malcolm's life, Malcolm told him, "I am no longer a Black nationalist. I consider myself an internationalist." And according to Breitman, Malcolm no longer believed in establishing a Black nation in the United States.[20]

By contrast, A. Peter Bailey, OAAU newsletter editor, claims that Malcolm never deviated from his original position on nationalism: "Because Malcolm only spoke for himself in the last fourteen months of his life, you couldn't really flush out all of his ideas. But you could tell where he was going. Though he never used the phrase 'nation within a nation' when he traveled to Africa, he was treated like a head of state. So he was definitely acting out the concept of nationalism." Part of the controversy stems from the differing definitions of nationalism. Breitman posits that it is still appropriate to refer to Malcolm as a Black nationalist as long as one refers to a commonly used, albeit imprecise, definition of Black nationalism, such as "[Black nationalism] is the tendency for black people in the United States to unite as a group, as a people, into a movement of their own to fight for freedom, justice, and equality." But the debate is fundamentally ideological in nature. The associates of Malcolm who are inclined toward scientific socialism tend to believe that Malcolm had changed. But those who emphasize racism as the principal contradiction in society, as does Yuri, tend to believe that Malcolm maintained his Black nationalist position.[21]

Yuri expressed her views on this debate in a 1993 speech. While claiming that "[Malcolm] was a Black nationalist," even as she mentioned Muhammad Ahmad's view that Malcolm renounced Black nationalism, Yuri's position is that Malcolm was evolving as a person:

Many made Malcolm into whatever they wanted him to be: a leftist, a Communist, an integrationist, a pseudo religionist, a racist, a liberal, a civil rightist, an anarchist. . . . Many nationalists say he remained a Black nationalist; that he never changed on that point. . . . While it is true that he never became an integrationist . . . he did, however, broaden when he met Muslims of all backgrounds in Mecca and Algerians who were light-skinned but were Africans. . . . I feel that Malcolm believed like

Du Bois that "no idea is perfect and forever valid. To be living, it must be modified and adapted to changing facts." Malcolm never stopped growing. He kept developing.[22]

Ultimately, because Malcolm's views were rapidly evolving during his last year and his ideology was somewhat ambiguous at the time of his death, multiple interpretations of his positions have emerged. And such ambiguity is acceptable to an eclectic radical like Yuri, albeit one with strong revolutionary nationalist tendencies.

Perhaps it is most accurate to describe Malcolm's politics in his last year as revolutionary nationalism, in contrast to the cultural nationalism of the Nation of Islam. To Yuri, revolutionary nationalism embraces socialism and internationalism, as discussed in chapter 6. It was this revolutionary Malcolm who shaped Yuri's politics, particularly following his visit to her home. Yuri, at times accompanied by Billy, Audee, or Aichi, made an effort to attend Malcolm's talks. It was at one of these talks, after Malcolm returned from abroad in late November 1964, that he invited Yuri to join the OAAU's Liberation School.[23]

Her first class was on December 5, 1964, in suite 128 at the Theresa Hotel in Harlem. As contained in Yuri's detailed class notes, on this day, James Shabazz, who functioned as Malcolm's chief assistant at the OAAU, discussed twentieth-century slaves. He taught many things: how euphemistic language is used to keep people unaware and downtrodden; how England initiated the termination of the African slave trade for economic—and not humanitarian—reasons; how light-skinned Africans were given preferential treatment over darker Africans in the days of slavery and today; and how the lord-serf relationship has persisted over time, in different forms for different economies (e.g., master-slave, boss-worker, police-Negro). These ideas probably re-inforced material that Yuri had learned in the Harlem Freedom School. In her notes she recorded an experience from her first class that greatly impressed her:

> To my surprise, Brother Shabazz started talking about linkages between Africans and Asians. I was the only non-Black there. I don't know if he spoke about this because I was there, to help me connect my heritage to what we were learning, or if he would have lectured on this anyway. Brother Shabazz, who speaks some

Japanese, Korean, and Chinese, wrote the *kanji* [Japanese and Chinese characters] for Tao and various martial art forms on the board. He explained the spirituality underlying these martial arts—that they were exercises to help one move toward God similar to how Islam did.[24]

James Campbell, the main teacher at the Liberation School, remembered seeing Yuri on this day:[25]

> She came into the class at the Theresa, which was also the OAAU office. Malcolm's office was at the end of the room, a small space, a cubbyhole almost, behind the chalkboard where announcements were made. She just appeared. I don't know how she found out about the classes. But it was significant because there was hardly any diversity in the group. I was gratified to see a person of Asian ancestry there. She also stood out because she took notes throughout the session. Over time, I noticed that she usually stayed to chat with someone after class. Her pattern of attendance, note taking, and chatting with people in class became apparent to me. It was a consistent pattern and I came to see her as a very serious person.

In this unassuming way, she began to interact with Malcolm's associates. In time, she began inviting people she met at the OAAU Liberation School to her weekend open houses. Students at the school as well as OAAU leaders, particularly James Shabazz but also James Campbell, A. Peter Bailey, and others, on occasion spent time socializing with Yuri and Bill.[26]

Yuri attended the Liberation School every Saturday morning until the school closed at the beginning of April 1965. During this four-month period, she learned information that, compared to the Harlem Freedom School curriculum, paid greater attention to international issues, often covering the history of imperialism and resistance in Africa and drawing connections between the struggles of Black people in the United States and in Africa. Yuri was particularly impressed with a series of lectures given by a Mr. Mashashu, a Columbia University student from Zambia, who discussed the history of Africa, including the partitioning of Africa by European leaders at the 1884–85 Berlin Conference into nations without regard to geographic or cultural boundaries or the desires of the people. The OAAU Liberation School also reflected the radicalism of its teachers, ranging from the Marxism of James Campbell and Richard B. Moore to the Black nationalism of historian John Henrik Clarke and Egyptologist Yosef ben-Jochannan. While Yuri saw Malcolm X only once at the school, given his heavy travel itinerary, she was impressed with the intellectuals, highly regarded in the Harlem community, who taught the classes: "Just as Malcolm could speak about almost any topic, all the people closest to Malcolm were the most incredible, well-read, widely knowledgeable people. . . . I couldn't have gotten better teachers within the formal education system."[27]

One of the significant lessons Yuri learned was that racism, rather than being an unfortunate anomaly, was deeply embedded in American society. At her second class, she heard a tape recording of Fannie Lou Hamer, the revered leader of the Mississippi Freedom Democratic Party, describing the life of poverty that she and other Black people experienced in Mississippi. From Yuri's hurried, yet compulsively detailed, class notes: "Mother was paid $1.25 a day (11 cents an hour). Mother chopped up stumps to clear new ground. Mother wore old patch-work clothes, year in and year out. Tried to keep kids in clothes. . . . Mother tried to keep kids in school." What may have been most disturbing for Yuri was hearing Hamer, who like Yuri was a middle-aged mother just four years Yuri's senior, describe how she was beaten in jail by the two Black male prisoners, forced to commit the beating by a police officer, until her "flesh became hard as metal; turned navy blue. Had to have orthopedic care." Yuri's notes for that day contain the remark, "America is a sick country."[28]

In another session, Campbell employed the analogy of a "congenital deformity" to describe the dishonorable conditions existing in U.S. society.[29] Yuri's notes contain the lesson that the United States was born on July 4, 1776, into a society already one hundred years rich in the practice of slavery. But the deformity worsened after the nation's birth, with the institutionalization of slavery through laws like the Fugitive Slave Law, through science, and through the educational system. In the 1960s, slavery continued through the prison systems. These institutions were used to make the oppression in a stratified society seem natural and normal. Campbell noted that radical African resistance to this congenital deformity is symbolized by the Cinques,

Nat Turners, Denmark Veseys, and Frederick Douglasses, as opposed to the assimilationist path of the Booker T. Washingtons. One of the most important tasks for Blacks and other oppressed people, wrote Yuri in her class notes, is "to free our minds, to decolonize our minds"—a theme that runs through many of her speeches today. Campbell raised his students' consciousness about how propaganda, symbolism, and euphemistic language are tools to confuse people at a subconscious level. The public, Campbell reasoned, is taught to admire the Angloesque features of singer Harry Belafonte while belittling the African features of prizefighter Sonny Liston, known as "the big ugly bear." As a solution, Campbell offered that Black people need to control their social institutions and factories and to redistribute wealth equitably. In this way, as Campbell explained about the Liberation School, "the content of the classes tended toward a Marxist analysis of the country in a popular form that was presented in a fashion that was not burdened with the language of classical Marxism." These explicitly anticapitalist and implicitly prosocialist lessons were also contained in the recommended readings, including Frantz Fanon's *The Wretched of the Earth,* Kwame Nkrumah's *Consciencism,* and Herbert Aptheker's *American Negro Slave Revolts.* Over and over again, Yuri learned that this "congenital deformity" could not be reformed; Black people would never achieve equality and liberation in a system built on racism. She began to fathom that an entirely different system needed to be established.[30]

To the revolutionary nationalists of the OAAU, self-determination—not integration—was the solution. James Shabazz, in a 1964 issue of the OAAU newsletter *Blacklash,* wrote: "Economists tell us that the Afro-American earns 20 *billion* dollars annually. . . . Yet the Afro-American controls no factories, no appreciable amount of farmland, builds no schools, has no navy, no army, makes no shoes, no shirts and for all practical purposes has no banks." That Shabazz, one of Malcolm's chief aides, then called for the idealist solution of raising the ethics of Black people ("There can be no betterment of the Afro-American's economic position until there is an elevation of the morality of him") shows the variety of political perspectives in the OAAU. It is likely that James Campbell, who introduced Marxist ideas into the Liberation School, would have called for a materialist solution, such as having Black people control the social institutions—schools, factories, banks, land—within their community. The different perspectives contained within the OAAU reflected Malcolm X's own evolving ideology during this period and helped shape an eclectic radicalism in Yuri. Despite the lack of a singular ideology, the beliefs of Malcolm's organization still differed in significant ways from the integrationist and moderate discourse of the Civil Rights Movement.[31]

Yuri's belief in nonviolent resistance was also challenged by Malcolm X and the OAAU Liberation School teachers. In contrast to many civil rights leaders, particularly Martin Luther King Jr., who raised nonviolence to a principle to be adhered to in all situations, Malcolm X viewed nonviolence as a tactic to be used depending on the circumstances: "We're nonviolent with people who are nonviolent with us. But we're not nonviolent with people who are not nonviolent with us." He elaborated on this concept in his 1963 "Message to the Grass Roots" speech:

> As long as the white man sent you to Korea, you bled. . . . You bleed for white people, but when it comes to seeing your own churches being bombed and little black girls murdered, you haven't got any blood. . . . How are you going to be nonviolent in Mississippi, as violent as you were in Korea? . . . If violence is wrong in America, violence is wrong abroad. If it is wrong to be violent defending black women and black children and black babies and black men, then it is wrong for America to draft us and make us violent abroad in defense of her. And if it is right for America to draft us, and teach us how to be violent in defense of her, then it is right for you and me to do whatever is necessary to defend our own people right here in this country.

Robert F. Williams, the NAACP Monroe, North Carolina, chapter president who gained the respect of Black nationalists for daring to promote self-defense in the late 1950s, concurred with the tactical use of self-defense. "Nonviolence is a very potent weapon when the opponent is civilized, but nonviolence is no repellent for a sadist," he reasoned. "When Hitler's tyranny threatened the world, we did not hear much about how immoral it is to meet violence with violence." Likewise, Williams argued, nonviolence would not prove an effective weapon against White supremacists.[32]

Malcolm remained a staunch advocate of self-defense to the end.

At a speech given at the Audubon Ballroom in Harlem the week before he died, he proclaimed: "You come on in the OAAU and we'll . . . show you how to protect yourself. Not so that you can go out and attack someone. You should never attack anybody. But at the same time whenever you, yourself, are attacked you are not supposed to turn the other cheek. Never turn the other cheek until you see the white man turn his cheek." Malcolm's criticism did not escape Black civil rights leaders who promoted purely philosophical nonviolence, and in doing so, Malcolm argued, functioned to block Black efforts for social change: "If Martin Luther King were teaching white people to turn the other cheek, then I would say he was justified in teaching Black people to turn the other cheek."[33]

Malcolm's message about the use of self-defense contains at least four significant concepts. First, in contrast to the media portrayals of Malcolm X, he did not endorse violence per se. Rather, he supported the tactical use of self-defense by any means necessary, ranging from nonviolent to violent responses depending on the circumstances. Second, Malcolm called out the hypocrisy of those advocating nonviolence for Black people but not for Whites. While U.S. military and police were violently aggressive toward other countries as well as to segments of the citizenry and the Ku Klux Klan attacked Southern Blacks, Black people, but not Whites, were being asked by the government—as well as their own civil rights leaders—to be nonviolent. After hearing how the police forced two prisoners to beat Fannie Lou Hamer, this point alone may have caused Yuri to pause and consider her belief in philosophical nonviolence. Perhaps it did make sense to defend oneself when being attacked. This is the same philosophy promoted in rape prevention classes today.

Third, through his call for self-defense, Malcolm shifted responsibility for the violence from the oppressed to the perpetrators. Should not the aggressor—whether the government or the Klan—be the one to end the violence? Is not the use of violence as a means of self-defense different from aggression used to repress another? Fourth, Malcolm believed that self-defense was an effective strategy, at least under certain circumstances. Frantz Fanon, in his widely read book *The Wretched of the Earth* based in the Algerian struggle against French imperialism, argued that violence is necessary in the decolonization struggle so that, invoking biblical language, "the last shall be first and the first last." In Monroe, North Carolina, in the early 1960s, Robert Williams and fellow Black activists demonstrated the efficacy of self-defense when they returned fire against an armed Ku Klux Klan motorcade and ran the Klan out of town. A few years after Malcolm died, the Vietnamese would demonstrate the effectiveness of the strategic use of armed force in their anti-imperialist struggle. Even the bully on the playground is less likely to be aggressive toward those who stand up to him or her. Moreover, there were psychological benefits to defending oneself, advocated Fanon, a psychiatrist by training: "At the level of individuals, violence is a cleansing force. It frees the native from his inferiority complex and from his despair and inaction; it makes him fearless and restores his self-respect." The experiences of Roy Crowder, a Black teenager trained by Robert Williams in armed self-defense, corroborate Fanon's theory: "Back then, a lot of black people thought things would never get better—they had no hope. But Rob changed that. He gave us confidence to believe that things could get better if we stood up for ourselves."[34]

As Yuri learned about Malcolm X's philosophy on self-determination and self-defense, among other issues, his views gradually began to make sense to her. Still, one wonders: How did a middle-aged Nisei who grew up "red, white, and blue" in a middle-class, suburban neighborhood come to embrace the radical politics of Malcolm X, a man heavily demonized by the mainstream media? One of the most pivotal experiences for Yuri was living in Harlem.[35] Had she not been surrounded by the revolutionary nationalist movement, I argue that her political development would have taken a different path. I believe that, in the context of pervasive social movements, her community service activities could have developed a political edge, but one grounded in the moderate, integrationist civil rights ideology. While her support for the Hiroshima Maidens in the mid-1950s stemmed from humanitarian ethics, it would not have been a far stretch for Yuri to have placed greater emphasis on the political aspects of nuclear proliferation and war. It is possible that the personal experiences of knowing one of the Little Rock Nine high school students and of meeting NAACP leader Daisy Bates could have encouraged Yuri's budding political interest, concomitant with her attention to the newspaper coverage of civil rights struggles. So even without moving to Harlem, Yuri might well have developed into a civil rights activist.

But Yuri did move to Harlem, home of "the most black nationalist movements" in the United States, observed Theodore Draper. There, she worked with CORE in Brooklyn to protest race discrimination in hiring. As a result of the influence of Black nationalists, particularly Malcolm X, Brooklyn CORE was moving toward Black nationalism. So while national CORE promoted interracial, nonviolent direct action, the mixture of Black Marxists, Black ghetto youth, and White militants who composed the Brooklyn chapter was less firmly committed to philosophical nonviolence. The ideas that were brewing in Brooklyn CORE that summer of 1963 planted in Yuri the seeds of self-determination and self-defense, seeds that sprouted when exposed to ideological lessons from Malcolm X and the OAAU Liberation School. The timing of Yuri's entrance onto the political scene, which coincided with the turn toward Black Power within the Civil Rights Movement, is also an essential factor in her development. Yuri was not the innovator but rather was shaped by her surrounding environment. Thus, geography and history combined to set Yuri on her revolutionary nationalist trajectory.[36]

Yuri herself does not explain the forces moving her toward radicalism. Instead, she offers two reasons why she was attracted to Malcolm's teachings. First, as she listened to Malcolm and to his associates at the OAAU, they provided clarity regarding the general notion that, as Yuri put it, "something was wrong with society." Their international contextualization and radical analysis helped Yuri understand the political reasons why racism existed. Second, Malcolm was, in Yuri's words, "the kind of person making his people feel proud to be African," more so than anyone else she had heard. She could sense the swell in self-pride among her Black neighbors and friends as they listened to Malcolm speak. While still a member of the Nation of Islam, Malcolm made statements such as: "[Elijah Muhammad] teaches you and me not only that we're as good as the White man, but better than the White man. . . . That's not saying anything . . . just to be equal with him. Who is he to be equal with? You look at his skin. You can't compare your skin with his skin. Why, your skin looks like gold beside his skin." After living in a country that equated all things black with inferiority, an assessment often internalized by Blacks, such a statement made the applauding audience wild with pride. These were bold ideas in a time before the Black Power Movement popularized them with its "Black Is Beautiful" and "Black Power" slogans. Malcolm's statements were strikingly different from those made by the civil rights leaders working within a racially integrated movement.[37]

The mainstream media labeled Malcolm a racist for, from their perspective, preaching Black superiority. But to Malcolm's followers, his remark had more to do with increasing Black pride than with creating a system of Black supremacy. Even if he wanted to, Malcolm was not in a position to institute systematic oppression against Whites. He did not give jobs to Black people over Whites or allow Black people to use public facilities while keeping Whites out. After Malcolm left the Nation of Islam in early 1964, he was not heard making Black superiority statements like this, though he continued to instill racial pride in Black people. This is why, in eulogizing Malcolm, Ossie Davis proclaimed: "Malcolm was our manhood, our living, black manhood! This was his meaning to his people. And, in honoring him, we honor the best in ourselves." Many Black people wrote to the activist-actor commending him for his words. At the same time, Davis explained: "Most of them took special pains to disagree with much or all of what Malcolm said and what he stood for. That is, with one singing exception, they all, every last, black, glory-hugging one of them, knew that Malcolm—whatever else he was or was not—Malcolm was a man! White folks do not need anybody to remind them that they are men. We do! This was his one incontrovertible benefit to his people."[38]

Malcolm also instilled pride in his people by placing their struggles in a historic and international context. The history of Black people did not begin with their enslavement and end with their current subordination. There were several diverse and flourishing civilizations in Africa before the advent of the Arab and European slave trades. In the United States, there was the Reconstruction period, during which former slaves built communities, complete with schools, banks, and businesses. In the 1950s and 1960s, many African nations waged national liberation struggles, won their independence against imperialist forces, and began the arduous process of building egalitarian nations. In part, because Yuri saw Black people gain pride from listening to Malcolm and from learning their history, she became attracted to nationalism.[39]

Just as many Black people writing to Ossie Davis voiced their disagreement with Malcolm X's ideas, Yuri too would have had points of dissension. Although she did not identify any points on which she and Malcolm diverged other than her initial views on integration, it is reasonable to assume that, while Malcolm was alive, there were at least three such areas. First, Yuri would have cringed at some of the statements Malcolm made, especially his harsh anti-White remarks. Back in the mid-1960s, the boldness with which Malcolm confronted White America was unusual and unsettling to many, Black, White, and Asian alike. Many Black people had learned that "step 'n' fetch it" and other such strategies helped ensure their survival by playing into the racial order. But Malcolm had the audacity to challenge White supremacy and make claims that Black people were just as good as, if not better than, White people. His words created fear—as well as pride—in many Black people who, while they may not have liked being at the bottom of the racial hierarchy, were also not willing to pay the consequences for challenging that system. Second, in 1964 and 1965, Yuri would have disagreed with Malcolm's promotion of armed struggle. In one of his last speeches, an address to an OAAU meeting at the Audubon Ballroom on February 15, 1965, Malcolm remarked during the discussion period: "You need to study guerrilla warfare. Get every book you can find on guerrilla warfare. There's nothing wrong with saying that. . . . Why, the government teaches you that. They draft you to teach you that, don't they?"[40] While Yuri may have, by early 1965, accepted the need for self-defense, she probably would have viewed proactive violence on the part of an oppressed group as equally as wrong as proactive violence on the part of the U.S. government or the Ku Klux Klan. The ends did not justify the means. Third, in the mid-1960s, Yuri would not have agreed with Malcolm's move toward socialism. At a time when she was struggling between ideas of integration and self-determination, it would be surprising if she was ready to embrace a system harshly denounced under Cold War politics. Notice that the first point has to do with style or form, and the last two, with political program or content.

What differentiated Yuri from the many who disagreed with Malcolm, even as they gained pride from his words and deeds, was that she was not afraid to associate with him or to learn more about his ideas. Yuri had a sense that Malcolm was on the right track; she admired that he was "giving direction to his people." Even before she met

Malcolm, she had supported the candidacy of Bill Epton, who ran as a socialist for the New York State Senate. She had also learned about Robert Williams's call for self-defense in Monroe, North Carolina, and supported the case of Mae Mallory, one of the defendants in a kidnapping case related to Williams's situation in Monroe. So why did Yuri support Epton, Williams, Mallory, and Malcolm X at a time when she did not fully agree with their ideology and when *Life* magazine labeled them "violent militants" in juxtaposition to "respectable" civil rights leaders? What is important to understand about Yuri is that she judges people primarily by their practice. She admired those who worked with fierce determination and personal sacrifice, be it a Malcolm, an Epton, or a King. But, given the influences in Harlem, she gravitated toward, in her opinion, the correctness of revolutionary nationalism: "As soon as I started to hear what Malcolm was saying, I could tell that it was more correct than the things the civil rights leaders were saying. Malcolm supported the Vietnamese long before it was popular to be against the war. Just look how many more years it took Martin Luther King before he spoke out against the war. . . . Malcolm read so much. He knew so much about Africa and even about Asia. And he told us who our true liberators were—the Denmark Veseys, Nat Turners. . . . He gave us different heroes."[41]

Yuri gained a significant lesson from Malcolm, one that she recites repeatedly:

> One of the greatest lessons Malcolm taught people was to learn their own history. Know your history. Know the world. Be proud of who you are. He would say, "If you don't know who you are and where you came from, how can you know what direction to go in the future?" Through the process of discovering our own histories, many peoples—Africans, Asians, Puerto Ricans living in the United States—learned to throw off our internalized racism and develop pride in our heritage. But don't stop there. Learn about the histories of other people. And learn about the history of social movements because this is how you learn to create social change.[42]

Yuri took this lesson to heart, studying history at alternative liberation schools and reading whatever she could get her hands on—mainstream newspapers, books, Movement publications. In time, through study and practice, Yuri came to agree with the need for self-determination, self-defense, armed struggle, socialism, and an autonomous Black nation. While she may still cringe when someone makes a harsh remark, a person's approach or style is secondary to his or her overall political practice and ideology.

The ultimate trajectory of Malcolm's ideology will never be known. His life and rapidly evolving politics were cut short by the assassins' bullets. Having been in the audience to hear Malcolm speak at the Audubon Ballroom, Yuri is often asked to recount the events of that day:

> Now, as I recall that date, February twenty-first, 1965, I was sitting in the same booth as Herman Ferguson, which was, I think about the seventh or eighth row. I was with my sixteen-year-old son, Billy. I was taking notes of Brother Benjamin's [Karim's] message. He had just finished saying, just before introducing him, "Malcolm is a kind of man who would die for you." The distraction, a man yelling, "Get your hand out of my pocket," took place across from where we were sitting. All eyes were turned to the distraction. Malcolm tried to calm the people, saying, "Cool it, brothers, cool it." Then shots rang out from the front. Malcolm fell straight backward, and it was right then, all hell broke loose. Chairs crashing to the floor. People hitting the floor. People chasing the killers. A few more gunshots, and something like a smoke bomb was thrown. It was utter chaos.[43]

In the midst of frenzy and hysteria, with bullets flying and people diving for cover, Yuri was one of the few who put Malcolm's safety above her own. She ran onstage to see if she could help: "It was then that a young brother . . . ran past where I was sitting. He was heading for the stage, so I followed him and went right to Malcolm. He was having difficulty breathing, so I put his head on my lap. Others came and opened his shirt. He was shot many times in the chest. And by his jawbone and his finger. I hoped he would say something, but he never said a word." *Life* magazine captured Yuri's action in a photograph showing an Asian woman wearing cat's-eye glasses cradling Malcolm's head.[44]

Most Nisei women would not have considered running onstage to help the dying Black leader. They would have been self-conscious about drawing attention to themselves or presuming their self-importance.

Likewise, they would have felt uncomfortable delivering public speeches, writing articles for newspapers, and writing letters to strangers. As we have seen, however, even as a youth Yuri exhibited a certain boldness, asking to write for the community newspaper, becoming the first female student body officer at her high school, and initiating a letter-writing campaign to Nisei soldiers. Her actions become more remarkable when we consider the racial and gender constraints prevalent in 1930s America. Perhaps Yuri's parents' liberal child-rearing practices or their economic status offset some of the limitations imposed on Nisei women of that time. Perhaps as one of the few Asians in a predominantly White neighborhood, Yuri had the self-confidence that she could accomplish the same things as her White peers. While these might be contributing factors, they fail to fully explain the fearlessness Yuri has displayed throughout her life. Wherever her audacity comes from, it has propelled Yuri to act according to her moral convictions. It was from this motivation that she ran onstage to assist the fallen Malcolm. And it was from this motivation that, after Malcolm's assassination, she wrote a letter to the editor of the Japanese American weekly, the *New York Nichibei*, voicing her support for Malcolm X, a highly controversial figure of that time.[45]

In the short sixteen months between their meeting and his death, Malcolm X provided the greatest influence on Yuri's political life. After his death, she fostered a relationship with Malcolm's family, particularly his oldest daughter, Attallah, who to this day refers to Yuri as an aunt, through regular letters, occasional visits at the Kochiyamas' home, and sporadic phone calls, including when Attallah was in New York in 1997 to attend her mother's funeral. Wherever Yuri goes, in speeches and informal conversations, she eagerly highlights Malcolm's international significance, in contrast to mainstream America's harsh condemnation: "At least three countries have his picture on their postage stamp. . . . Books about his life have been written or translated into Italian, Spanish, German, French, Japanese, and probably a few others. . . . In the late 1960s, Palestinian activists who came to the U.S. told us that names like Malcolm X, Stokely Carmichael (Kwame Ture), and the Black Panthers were used as code names among their guerrilla fighters. In the same period, Vietnamese antiwar spokespersons in the U.S. revealed to us that Malcolm X's name was known in radical circles in their own country." A vigilant observer of Asian-African interactions, Yuri noted that Malcolm's influence also reached Japan: "In the audience at the Audubon Ballroom the day Malcolm was assassinated sat a Japanese socialist journalist who used the pen name Ei Nagata. He was probably the first Japanese writer to bring the story and significance of Malcolm X's life to Japan. It was Ei Nagata who wrote the first book on Malcolm in Japan."[46]

Perhaps because of Yuri's dedication to Malcolm's vision, her steadfast writing, or her attention to human relations, she is regarded as a close associate of his, much closer than their few direct interactions would suggest. This is not simply a case of mythologizing their relationship, as has certainly been done by Yuri's admirers today. But Malcolm's most trusted comrades also consider Yuri to be a close colleague. When Herman Ferguson, an OAAU leader, started the Malcolm X Commemoration Committee in the early 1990s, he listed Yuri Kochiyama on the letterhead as an OAAU founding member. Certainly, he would have known that Yuri was merely a beginning student of radical politics at the time. It appears that the consistency of her political work and her personal connectedness, through thick and thin, have earned her a reputation as a close associate of Malcolm's.[47]

The year Malcolm died, Yuri started a second family newsletter, the *North Star,* its title drawn from W. E. B. Du Bois's newspaper, but so named as a tribute to Yuri's most significant political mentor. In echoing her praise to Malcolm at the Brooklyn courthouse, Yuri extolled him as a guiding light who gives "direction to his people," as indicated in the language, if a bit flowery, of this *North Star* front-page article: "His life is a simile that can only be correlated with the most brilliant of all the stars in the Heavens, the North Star, for the North Star is the one star that does not change position or lose its bright intensity. It is the star that set the course for mariners; that gave direction, from time immemorial, to slaves escaping bondage; and communicated men's hope by allusion. It is, thus, obvious and apropos that we dedicate this first issue of the North Star to him whom we feel, most aptly personifies the significance of this title. Triumphantly illuminating today's stark atmosphere, giving light and direction, invincible and inextinguishable, Malcolm is that North Star shining."[48]

6

Transformation of a Revolutionary Nationalist

By the time of Malcolm's death, Yuri's politics had undergone a significant transformation, moving from integration and nonviolence to self-determination and self-defense. These changes were reflective of and influenced by the nationwide turn toward radical politics, especially in urban areas, where young people, in particular, rejected the moderate goals of the Civil Rights Movement. One of the first contemporary organizations to advocate urban guerrilla warfare was the Revolutionary Action Movement (RAM). At its inception in 1962, however, Don Freeman and Max Stanford had envisioned an above-ground, Black nationalist, working-class group relying on mass direct action and self-defense tactics to push the Civil Rights Movement toward revolutionary goals. As William Sales observed, "RAM was the first of many organizations in the Black liberation movement to attempt to construct a revolutionary nationalism on the basis of a synthesis of the thought of Malcolm X, Marx and Lenin, and Mao Tse Tung . . . [giving] its variant of Black nationalism a particularly leftist character."[1]

Some time after RAM started, Yuri began hearing about the organization from different people, but from no one more ardently than family friend Alkamal (Sheldon) Duncan, a young RAM member whom Stanford described as having "a remarkable sense of leadership among the youth." Yuri relayed: "Alkamal almost had Stanford on a pedestal, and kept telling me, 'Someday you've got to meet Max Stanford and just listen to him. He has so much knowledge about Black history.'" That day came at a time when RAM, frustrated with the Civil Rights Movement and inspired by Malcolm X's emergence as an independent political figure, began using urban guerrilla warfare to create revolutionary change. Yuri recounted her introduction to Stanford with an attention to details and relationships that characterizes her storytelling style:

> I was on a bus going to a big demonstration in Washington, D.C. It must have been before Malcolm was killed, maybe '64. I didn't know hardly anyone on the bus except this one young, very enthusiastic kid who was a senior in high school, Gabre Wolde. Gabre was sort of a son to the Harlem Renaissance writer, Glen Carrington. As I was sleeping on the bus, somebody tapped me on the shoulder and I couldn't believe it. I knew who he was, what he looked like—I knew he was Max Stanford. He said, "Can you come to the back? I want to talk to you." I wondered what he would want to talk to me about. He told me he wanted to talk about the organizing he's doing and how he wants to organize in Harlem. Would I mind listening to his ideas? I was really excited. I had heard only bits about RAM because it was an underground organization. It's the kind of thing that to know even a little about such a group is something. I kept thinking to myself, I can't wait till I get back home to tell Billy and Alkamal.[2]

Just as Yuri expressed surprise, others might question why a Movement leader of Stanford's stature would solicit her help since, in 1964, she was merely a budding activist. Stanford explained that he knew Yuri by reputation. He was under the impression that OAAU meetings were held at her home. But Yuri and several OAAU leaders denied this. Since Stanford, who was working semiclandestinely at the time, did not attend any of these meetings, it is possible that he mistook for OAAU meetings occasions when OAAU leaders like James Shabazz visited the Kochiyamas, probably at their Saturday night open houses. While Stanford may have overestimated Yuri's involvement in the OAAU, he did not overestimate the breadth of her social and political networks. On the bus that day, he made a valuable contact in Yuri, whom he credits with facilitating the formation of the RAM Black Panther Party in Harlem in 1966: "Yuri opened up her apartment as a meeting place, where we met for lunch two or three times a week. She'd fix sandwiches and we would listen to Malcolm's unedited speeches, which would go for maybe two hours or so. And we would have discussions. . . . She could introduce people to us. She would circulate any information that we had to a whole network of people. . . . Yuri was a constant communicator, constant facilitator, constant networker."[3]

That Yuri did not join RAM or any other underground organization is not surprising. In the mid-1960s, at a time when she was developing her own ideological views and raising a family, she would not have been politically prepared for such involvement. More significantly, her strength lies in her networking abilities—work better suited to the above-ground movement. Though Yuri never joined RAM, she supported them by doing peripheral work and over the years developed a close political relationship with Stanford. She pored over the voluminous materials that Stanford sent her and regularly reviewed Stanford's own writings. Yuri credits Stanford (now Muhammad Ahmad) with being one of her most significant political mentors: "One of the most important people that came into my life was Muhammad Ahmad, because I feel the organization he was leading was so outstanding. He's done more study, more reading than just about any other Black leader in the Movement. He's also written extensively, though only one book has been published. He never had the money to get more published and, of course, no mainstream press would print his writings." On a wall in Yuri's living room hangs a picture of Stanford, with Alkamal Duncan in the background, painted by Zayid Muhammed.[4]

Although she could not have predicted it at the time, within a few years of becoming politically active, Yuri would go on to form political relationships not only with Malcolm X but also with RAM's other major ideological mentor. Yuri first heard of Robert F. Williams in the late 1950s, when he garnered international attention for his defense of two Black boys, ages seven and nine, accused of forcing a White girl to kiss them and possibly raping her. As president of the NAACP chapter in Monroe, North Carolina, where the "Kissing Case" occurred, Williams championed a media blitz that got sympathetic, front-page newspaper coverage in the United States and Europe and generated international grassroots protests, resulting in the release of the two boys.[5]

While Williams gained the admiration of civil rights activists for representing the Kissing Case defendants, he also piqued the interest of Black nationalists—and the Ku Klux Klan—for his audacious promotion of self-defense in the South in the mid-1950s. In 1956, when he became president of the nearly defunct Monroe NAACP chapter, he had recruited military veterans, construction workers, female domestic workers, and others previously excluded from the elite, middle-class club and built a chapter sympathetic to self-defense. As a former World War II Marine, Williams also established an all-Black National Rifle Association chapter. The Black community soon began defending itself against the Klan motorcades and succeeded in forcing the Monroe City Council to ban Klan caravans through the Black community.[6]

As Williams trained self-defense teams and struggled to desegregate the library, swimming pool, and other public facilities, an incident occurred that once again propelled him into the media spotlight. In a twenty-four-hour period in Monroe in 1959, two juries separately acquitted a White man charged with the attempted rape of a Black woman and a White man charged with kicking a Black hotel maid down a flight of stairs.[7] After hearing the verdicts, an emotionally outraged Williams stood on the courthouse steps and made this controversial proclamation:

> We cannot take these people who do us injustice to the court and it becomes necessary to punish them ourselves. In the future we are going to have to try and convict these people on the spot. We cannot rely on the law. We get no justice under the present system. . . . Since the federal government will not bring a halt to lynching in the South, and since the so-called courts lynch our people legally, if it's necessary to stop lynching with lynching, then we must be willing to resort to that method. We must meet violence with violence.[8]

Printed in newspapers throughout the United States, this pronouncement had far-reaching ramifications. The *State-Times* of Jackson, Mississippi, for example, announced, "Negro Calls for Lynch of Whites." To disassociate itself from this renegade leader, the national NAACP immediately suspended Williams. But that did not stop the mounting wave of change. Williams's words and armed actions signaled the beginnings of a new era—a more militant period that endorsed self-defense by any means necessary.[9]

In her home in New York City, Yuri read newspaper accounts of Williams's provocative remarks. Not in her wildest imagination could she have foreseen that within a few years she would become an advocate of Williams's philosophy, even going beyond his belief in self-defense to advocate armed struggle. Nor did she understand that a few miles to the north, in Harlem where she would soon live, these same media reports drew the attention of Black activists searching for methods to challenge racial oppression and economic exploitation. Harlem quickly became the strongest support base for Williams outside of Monroe.[10]

Yet, Williams's "meet violence with violence" statement, in fact, did not accurately reflect his views, spoken as it was in a moment of anger, compounded by a sense of failure at having naively misled the Black community into relying on the courts for justice.[11] At a press conference the next day, Williams explained that he did not advocate revengeful actions, but instead promoted immediate physical resistance to White attacks. What he advocated in 1959 was self-defense, not proactive military strikes, though some would call the latter self-defense in the sense of protecting one's community from racist violence or one's homeland from imperialism. Williams clarified his position in his book, *Negroes with Guns*: "I do not advocate violence for its own sake, or for the sake of reprisals against whites. Nor am I against the passive resistance advocated by the Reverend Martin Luther King and others. My only difference with Dr. King is that I believe in flexibility in the freedom struggle. This means I believe in nonviolent tactics where feasible. . . . But where there is a breakdown of the law, the individual citizen has a right to protect his person, his family, his home and his property." He further explained: "When an oppressed people show a willingness to defend themselves, the enemy, who is a moral weakling and coward is more willing to grant concessions and work for a respectable compromise. Psychologically, moreover, racists consider themselves superior beings and they are not willing to exchange their superior lives for our inferior ones. They are most vicious and violent when they can practice violence with impunity."[12]

It was Williams's belief in the flexibility of tactics that led to yet another media flurry and initiated Yuri's connection with this militant leader. In August 1961, the Freedom Riders traveled to Monroe to test the effectiveness of nonviolent tactics in the struggle for racial de- segregation and economic reforms. Williams wrote: "Although I myself would not take the nonviolent oath, I asked people of the community to support them and their nonviolent campaign. . . . I also stated that if they could show me any gains from the racists by nonviolent meth- ods, I too would become a pacifist." But, as Williams predicted and no doubt feared, a White mob, numbering in the thousands, brutally beat the interracial Freedom Riders and local Black protesters during a peaceful demonstration, while the police provided no protection. Experiencing the viciousness of White supremacy and observing the effectiveness of armed self-defense in Monroe not only strengthened Williams's belief in self-defense but also had a profound effect on CORE activists themselves. Within a year, local CORE members at- tended meetings armed with shotguns and many no longer subscribed to nonviolence, even as the official CORE ideology continued to pro- mote nonviolence.[13]

The riot caused by the Klan attack on the Freedom Riders also triggered the need for thirty-six-year-old Williams, his wife, Mabel, and their two sons to take flight from their Boyte Street home. That evening, a White couple, Charles and Mabel Stegall, drove onto Boyte Street. A crowd of Black residents surrounded the car and pulled the wide-eyed and fearful couple out of their car. "The Stegalls, like most white Southerners, felt at ease with their black neighbors only in paternalistic relationships of black deference and white supremacy," observed Timothy Tyson. "Their only other easily imaginable cross- racial encounters evoked frightening images of black savagery." It was the latter imagine that stirred the Stegalls that night. When Williams heard the ruckus, including screams to "kill them," he tried to per- suade the crowd, enraged about the race riot earlier that day, not to use retaliatory violence against the White couple. At the same time, when Mabel Stegall, perhaps seeing in Williams the image of an ac- commodationist Black man, begged him to escort them out of the Black community, Williams retorted, "Look, lady, I didn't bring you in here and I'm not going to take you out. You're free to leave any time you get ready." As Williams turned to enter his home, he found the Stegalls close behind.

Soon thereafter, according to Williams, the Monroe police chief,

A. A. Mauney, called: "Robert, you have caused a lot of race trouble in this town, now state troopers are coming and in 30 minutes you'll be hanging in the Court House Square." Williams took this death threat seriously and made the decision to flee Monroe to save his and his family's lives and to avert a possible massacre. The next day, he discovered that he was charged with kidnapping the Stegalls. But when the Stegalls had left the Williamses' home on their own accord and run into two police officers, they made no such complaint, nor did Mabel Stegall consider herself to have been kidnapped.[14]

The escape of Robert Williams and his family has reached legendary proportions. The Williamses, as if following the path of the underground railroad, went north to freedom in Canada. After traveling westward to the Pacific Ocean, they then, Yuri relayed with excitement and awe, trekked some one thousand miles along the West Coast, from Canada to Mexico, to escape to Cuba. In doing so, they evaded a nationwide hunt by at least five hundred FBI agents. The family's escape was cloaked in fact and fiction for decades, writes Timothy Tyson, until the unpublished autobiographies of Williams and of Julian Mayfield finally revealed the story. The Williams family did travel north, largely through the efforts of Williams's connections in the Socialist Workers Party and the Fair Play for Cuba Committee. While the children were sent off in a different direction for their own safety, Robert and Mabel Williams made it to Canada, where he stayed for about six weeks with a White socialist couple, Vernal and Anne Olsen. Friends were finally able to transport Robert and Mabel, each separately, to Cuba.[15]

That Williams would choose to seek exile in Cuba was not surprising. Even before the Fair Play for Cuba Committee formed in 1960, Williams had been reporting positive portrayals of the 1959 Cuban revolution in his political publication, the *Crusader*. When the Fair Play for Cuba Committee recruited a group of prominent intellectuals and activists to sign a pro-Cuba *New York Times* advertisement, the vast majority of the Black signatories, including writers James Baldwin and John Oliver Killens, came from Williams's support base in Harlem. In June 1960, seventeen months after Fidel Castro took power, Williams flew to Havana, along with CBS's sole Black worker Richard Gibson, at the host government's expense to witness Cuba's transformation. Admired by many in that majority Black country for his armed stance against White supremacy, Williams was instantly "a national hero" in Cuba, observed LeRoi Jones (later Amiri Baraka), who joined Williams on his second trip to Cuba. Williams's popularity was not lost on Castro, who saw in him a golden opportunity to build support for Cuba in American Black communities.[16]

One of Williams's closest supporters in Harlem, Mae Mallory, faced kidnapping charges in the same incident that drove Williams into exile, and Yuri found herself working on her first political prisoner case. A couple of years earlier, Mallory had turned on her radio to hear Williams speak at the 1959 NAACP convention. At the time, she was increasingly dissatisfied with the nonviolent philosophy promoted by the leading civil rights organizations. Perhaps it was her mother's admonition to defend oneself. Perhaps it was her experiences of fighting back against the racist taunts of White children in Macon, Georgia. Perhaps it was the revolutionary ideology she had learned during her short tenure in the Communist Party. Or perhaps it was her feisty personality and quick temper. Mallory liked Williams's message to the NAACP convention of defending home and family and treating Black women with respect. Eager to back up this man targeted by the moderate NAACP leadership, Mallory recounted, "So instead of going to work that day, I got up and went in the streets and organized some support for Robert Williams, a man that I had never met." Mallory and others decided to distribute copies of Williams's political publication, the *Crusader,* and to gather relief donations of canned goods and other food, clothing, and shoes to send to the poor in Monroe.[17]

In the summer of 1961, when Mallory heard that Williams had invited the Freedom Riders to town, she, driven by Julian Mayfield, hurried to Monroe to provide assistance in the anticipated violent encounters with local White mobs. Mallory, who was among the crowd that surrounded the Stegalls' car as they entered Boyte Street and was in the Williamses' home with the Stegalls, was charged with and convicted of kidnapping the couple. So were three other supporters of Williams: John Lowery, who noticed the Stegalls' car was still in the middle of the street and moved it to the curb, and two local teenagers, Richard Crowder and Harold Reape.[18]

By the mid-1960s, Yuri was working with the Friends of Mae Mallory Defense Committee in Harlem. Through the influence of Mallory,

Bill Epton, and Max Stanford (later Muhammad Ahmad), she also began supporting Williams:

> After Rob Williams fled the U.S., RAM helped distribute the *Crusader* in the U.S. I wasn't in RAM, but I worked with people like Akbar Muhammad Ahmad, who was the head of RAM. Akbar told me so much about RAM that I did whatever I could to help, just periphery work. Back then, no one was supposed to know I did those things. One of the things, maybe the only real thing I did with RAM, was to help distribute the *Crusader*. To limit Rob Williams's influence, the government had put a ban on disseminating the *Crusader* through the postal service. So Rob sent it to [his supporters in] Canada. We got the paper out by doing a personal mailing to friends or leaving a bunch at places where political people go.

Defending Mallory appears to be Yuri's first instance of working on behalf of a political prisoner and strengthened her connection with the Black nationalist movement in Harlem. In Yuri's early years of activism, Mallory served as an important political mentor. Not only did Mallory have a visible leadership role, usually reserved for men, she also, remarked Yuri, "taught me how to be a good Movement person. She was always on time, responsible and reliable, accurate in giving out information, and she wanted other people to be the same. She was just a good person to learn how to be a Movement activist from."[19]

In addition to Mallory's organizing mentorship, two Harlem supporters of Williams exerted significant ideological influence on Yuri. In establishing the Black Arts Repertory Theatre/School (BART/S) in 1965, LeRoi Jones helped fill the institutional void in Harlem created by the assassination of Malcolm X. Jones, a prominent poet, dramatist, and writer with origins as a Beat poet, had undergone an ideological transformation from integrationism, when he traveled to Cuba with Williams in 1960, to Black revolutionary nationalism. Jones's first organization in Harlem, On Guard for Freedom Committee, was interracial, a policy he defended when some of the young nationalists in Harlem objected to the presence of Whites at their meetings. But in 1965, Jones argued that BART/S should be, in the words of Harold Cruse, "a black theater about black people, with black people, for black people, and only black people." Yuri witnessed the transformation from integrationism to nationalism, evident not only in Jones's personal development but also in the local Black movement:

> In a short while, BART/S became so well known that black literary people and artists from all over the country came to Harlem to check it out. It was the first kind of institution that upset a lot of people, and certainly it upset whites, because the idea was that it was open only to blacks, or nonwhites. Harlem Freedom School was integrated and most everything else that was political in Harlem was integrated, until this new kind of nationalism emerged. Even a lot of whites who had been in the civil rights movement were upset by it.[20]

The racially exclusionary policy of BART/S and other instances of separatist organizing must have challenged Yuri's own evolving views on integrationism and self-determination. Just two years earlier, she had rebuked Malcolm X for his separatist ideas. But by listening to his speeches and studying at his Liberation School, she was beginning to understand the need for autonomous spaces to solidify unity and realize self-determination. The effects of White supremacy were felt in a variety of ways in the Movement, including White people dominating discussions and leadership positions and Black people, in subscribing to internalized racism, accepting subordinate roles. As a result, autonomous spaces, racially exclusionary ones if you will, served to counter the powerful effects of White supremacy on Black activists as well as on well-meaning White activists, reasoned Yuri. So while she probably disliked that White activists felt hurt, often for the first time in their lives, by being excluded on the basis of race, she also believed that the separation of races was necessary for self-determination, but only as an interim step to achieving the eventual "togetherness of all people" in a transformed society. Yuri's own racial identity placed her in an ambiguous position vis-à-vis Black nationalism. But in a period promoting Third World solidarity, and given Yuri's humble and respectful manner, she was one of the few non-Blacks to be included in BART/S and other Black nationalist formations in Harlem.[21]

At BART/S, Yuri studied political education under Harold Cruse, who also traveled to Cuba with Williams in 1960. Two years after Yuri studied with Cruse, his six-hundred-page, politically penetrating thesis on the limitations of Black intellectuals, *The Crisis of the Negro*

Intellectual, was published. It was Yuri who typed the manuscript for Cruse's second book, *Rebellion or Revolution?* published the following year. Although she would have shuddered at the harshness of Cruse's critique, she also admired his intellectual prowess and was influenced by his revolutionary nationalism: "For me, the big difference between Baraka's school and the ones that had preceded it was a class taught by Harold Cruse. . . . His course encompassed four aspects of . . . struggle, I guess you call it: the history of revolution, the roots of black nationalism, Western political philosophy, and Marxism through black eyes." Perhaps form, more than content, distinguished Cruse's class from those at the OAAU Liberation School. Whereas the latter prioritized accessibility through the use of everyday language and light readings, Cruse required his students to engage in complex and theoretical material. Yuri recounted: "I still couldn't keep up with the heavy reading, and I didn't know enough about leftist thinking. Cruse was just so far ahead. In fact, most of the people in the class were somewhat like me. I don't think that anyone had done that much reading on the subject; it was sort of new to most of us. It was probably unfair to Cruse to have students who weren't quite prepared for all that he wanted us to absorb."[22]

At BART/S, Yuri experienced the first of what was to become many encounters with police and FBI infiltration into revolutionary movements. Activists discovered, for example, that a Black FBI agent posing as an activist not only had attended Cruse's political education classes but also had infiltrated the RAM Black Panther Party and other nationalist organizations. The information about this was so common among revolutionary nationalists in Harlem that Yuri, who is normally conscious about the possibility of public embarrassment or slander, readily disclosed the agent's name. "Don Duncan used to come to everybody's house, like a real good friend," she relayed. "He was here [at the Kochiyamas'] all the time. A lot of the sisters were saying, 'I see him more than my own husband.' [My husband] Bill really liked him, especially because he even joined Bill's 442 baseball team. But at some point, people started getting suspicious of him. He was a good-looking man and we did wonder why he never was with a sister." Yuri's heterosexist assumptions, shaped in the context of nationalism, Christianity, Islam, and U.S. culture, are evident in this passage, even as she opposes homophobia. She continued:

When we first mentioned his name, people weren't quite sure who he was, and no one had seen a picture of him. He never wanted to be photographed. But then one time he came to a birthday party for our Tommy and performed magic tricks for the children. I was taking pictures at the party and was surprised he didn't say anything, so I snapped pictures of him, too. Maybe he thought this will be a good cover for him, playing with the children and all. When we found out [he was an informant], everybody was totaled. We told one another, "If you ever see him again, let me know." And one day, my son-in-law, Terry Williams, called from Manhattan Community College to let me know the guy was in the classroom with him. I told him, "I'm glad you notified me. I'll call so-and-so about this." Terry figured he'd be gone by the time he returned to the classroom, and sure enough he was. I guess he got wind of what was happening and split.[23]

In discussing police infiltration into the Republic of New Africa (RNA),[24] Yuri refused to identify the agent whose testimony about his role as a New York undercover police officer was to be part of a legal strategy to obtain the release of political prisoner Mutulu Shakur. She recounted:

There was even one person who was active in the RNA, who had taught me gun control, who reneged at the last minute and didn't get in the van with us to go to [the 1971 RNA Land Celebration in] Mississippi. We didn't think anything of it. We figured maybe he couldn't get off work. But years later, he turned out to be a police agent. For years, Mutulu Shakur kept telling us about his suspicions of this guy. This guy seemed so dedicated, never missed a meeting, and he sure knew how to teach gun control. One time when he left, a gun fell out of his pocket, a P-38 which only police use. When Mutulu mentioned this, people said, "Nah, he's so dedicated." In every Black movement, the seemingly most dedicated turned out to be police or FBI infiltrators.[25]

Yuri too found herself under the intrusive gaze of the FBI. Judging from the information not blacked out in her FBI files, bureau surveillance began in October 1966, just three years after Yuri's plunge into

activism. The agency became alarmed because "Mary [Yuri] Kochiyama, a Japanese female, frequents the Truth Coffee Shop and . . .
is the only Japanese [the informant] has ever seen there. He added
that rumor among the habitués of the coffee shop has it that Mary
Kochiyama is a Red Chinese agent, but that as many people feel that
she is not." Also, "One member is a Japanese girl who always hangs
around the 'Truth Shop' and who seems to be one of the ring leaders."
Another FBI report that same year suggests that the FBI had been
watching the shop for some time: ". . . an establishment known as the
'Truth Shop' in Harlem, NY, which is the home of the black nationalists. This establishment also represents a haven for a number of 'new
groups.' The 'new groups,' not further identified, are acting in a very
subtle manner and are receiving money from the 'Chinese Reds.'"
Racist and sexist assumptions are evident in these reports. In conjec-
turing that an Asian runs the Black movement, this agent succumbed
to stereotypes about Black intellectual inferiority and Cold War fears
about communist infiltration. In doing so, the agent also conflated
ethnicities, assuming that, as the saying goes, "all Asians look alike,"
and failed to recognize each nation's particular histories, including
the fact that China and Japan were fierce enemies in the 1930s and
1940s. Moreover, despite Yuri's petite stature and youthful appearance, referring to a forty-five-year-old woman as a "girl" reproduces
the patronizing and infantilizing treatment of women in society. Still,
it is not surprising that, given the nature of American race relations,
the agent would find it necessary to explain the presence of an Asian
in, as the FBI report read, a Black nationalist establishment in heavily
Black Harlem. Yuri herself understood this interpretation as part of
the reason for her surveillance: "I think this was because of my association with Rob Williams and because I was about the only Asian
in the radical Black movement in Harlem." The FBI would have concurred, having classified her case under "SM-RAM" and later "Racial
Matters—Revolutionary Action Movement."[26]

Today, we can brush off the bureau's outlandish misinterpretation
of Yuri as a "Red Chinese agent," but back then it was no laughing
matter. The FBI observed her activities outside her home, gathered
information about her from informants and documents, sought new
contacts to evaluate her political activities, noted her attendance at
rallies and other political events, documented the content of her rally

speeches, and so forth. That the Kochiyamas were aware, at least in part, of the surveillance put a strain on the family. Yuri's son Eddie conveyed his fears for his mother's safety: "I was always worried about her, about what might happen if she got arrested. She was on a number of grand jury investigations and there was a lot of police and FBI harassment. Also, when some of her friends escaped from prison, we knew the cops or FBI would be watching our house. That was something that concerned my father—what if she ever got arrested just from knowing certain people?" This was no paranoid concern. Not only had Yuri's father been arrested merely for associating with Japanese ship captains, several of her comrades were arrested, not because of any criminal activity, but because of their political affiliations. Moreover, the New York FBI office had placed Yuri on the Security Index, Category II, as an individual the bureau considered politically objectionable. In the event of an emergency, the government would immediately arrest and detain her, much as it had treated her father in 1941.[27]

These examples of FBI and police infiltration and surveillance were not isolated cases. Through extensive research, Ward Churchill and Jim Vander Wall uncovered hundreds of documents that expose systematic intelligence surveillance and covert actions on the part of the state against the Black nationalist and other social movements. Suffice it to say that not only did the FBI succeed in some of its plots to murder or imprison key Movement leaders, its activities also created an atmosphere of suspicion and intimidation among activists, as explored in the next chapter. To protect themselves, some activists responded through distrust and paranoia. Others went underground. Still others left the Movement. By contrast, Yuri dealt with the situation by trusting everyone until they proved otherwise. Mae Mallory recalled: "I don't know how Bill allowed this, but anyone who came up from the South and said they were in the civil rights movement, Mary [Yuri] let them stay over. Or if they said they knew so-and-so, she'd let them stay."[28]

Given her experiences with police and FBI infiltration and the repeated admonitions by family and comrades to be more security conscious, it is puzzling to find an activist of Yuri's standing so trusting and open, almost naively so. It seems that a combination of personality, psychology, and logic explains her behaviors. Yuri has long displayed a belief in the honorable intentions of others, having opened her home to Nisei soldiers training in Mississippi during World War II and to friends and strangers alike every weekend throughout the post-war years. She also has coped with the constant threat of state repression through denial—or more accurately, by minimizing any potential danger. In part, she saw her own actions as mild compared to those leading the above-ground radical movements or working directly in clandestine struggles or merely living as dark-skinned people in the United States. Why not open one's home to strangers, reasoned Yuri, especially to those in need? After all, her experiences with infiltration had taught her that supposed friends as well as strangers could be dubious, as when she caught a close comrade, who turned out to be an agent, going through her closet one day.[29]

Even if Yuri had fully acknowledged the risks involved, this would not have stopped her radical activism. She was motivated by the fact that she had not broken any moral law and in fact, to the contrary, was striving for justice. Besides, if others were willing to risk their safety, why shouldn't she? Yuri's strong beliefs as well as her stubbornness made it difficult for her family to reason with her. The more Yuri minimized any dangers to herself or her family, the more her family worried about her. And the more her family questioned her, the more she felt compelled, probably unconsciously, to deny the riskiness of her political involvement. In addition, Yuri believes that openness is the best defense: "I remember what [attorney] Conrad Lynn said way back, 'The more open you are, the more people know how you conduct yourself, the more safeguards you have. Those who act most secret, as if they're doing something they shouldn't be, are the ones the FBI watches the most.' I hate when people act so clandestine when there's no reason to do so."[30]

The arrest of seventeen Black nationalists, allegedly all RAM members, in Queens, New York, in 1967, spelled the demise of the RAM Black Panther Party. Afterward, many RAM members went on to join the Republic of New Africa (RNA) and the All-African People's Party (APP), two newly established revolutionary nationalist formations with the goal of building a Black nation in five Southern states. As a testament to his continuing influence on U.S. Black nationalists, Robert Williams, from his location in exile, became the titular president of the RNA and chair of the APP, until he resigned both posts upon his return to the United States the following year. Yuri's decision to place her primary allegiance with the RNA rather than the APP was not ideologically driven. In fact, she believed in the goals and ideology of the APP and actively supported its work, especially since Max Stanford and Alkamal Duncan were APP cadre. The reason Yuri, then age forty-seven, joined the RNA illustrates the personal side of decision making: "The RNA people were more mature, not just in their political experience, but as human beings. I suppose that came with their being older. So, with my also being much older, I just felt more comfortable with the RNA people. I also liked that the RNA was formed by loyal Malcolm followers in the Malcolm X Society."[31]

The Republic of New Africa was founded on March 31, 1968, at the National Black Government Conference in Detroit, attended by five hundred Black activists from all over the country. The conference was organized by the Malcolm X Society, a Detroit-based group formed in 1967 by Gaidi Obadele (Milton Henry), an attorney, former city councilperson, and friend of Malcolm X, and his brother Imari Obadele (Richard Henry). The Malcolm X Society believed the best way to sustain Malcolm's ideas was to put into practice the concept of Black nationhood. Following a discussion about the Black nation position, as outlined by Imari Obadele in a Malcolm X Society document, *War in America,* the conference attendees signed the Declaration of Independence and declared the incipient nation the Republic of New Africa. Gaidi Obadele, first vice president, and Imari Obadele, minister of interior, were the chief architects and foremost theoreticians of the RNA. Prominent men and some women filled other positions, including Robert Williams as titular president in exile, Betty Shabazz as second vice president, Herman Ferguson as minister of education and vice president of the Eastern Region, Amiri Baraka (LeRoi Jones) and Ron Karenga as ministers of culture, "Queen Mother" Audley Moore as minister of health and welfare, Joan Franklin as minister of justice, and Muhammad Ahmad (Max Stanford) of the APP as special ambassador.[32]

When the New York conferees returned, they announced the formation of an RNA support group. Yuri, having worked with many in the RNA and believing in liberation through Black nationhood, was eager to participate: "I went into Friends of the RNA—not the RNA or the Black Panther Party—because I believe in the privacy of individual groups, especially liberation groups. I believe Blacks need their separate space to work for liberation." Echoing the sentiments of many Black radicals, RNA comrade Ahmed Obafemi observed: "Based on [Yuri's] commitment and her work around the question of self-determination and her relationship with Malcolm, based on her practice, she was one of us. She had shown her commitment for the freedom of African people in the United States." It is not surprising, then, that when RNA citizenship was extended to non-Black people the following year, Yuri was among the very few to be invited to join. She explained:

> Mtayari Shabaka Sundiata [head of the Brooklyn RNA] invited me to become a citizen because of my track record with Black nationalist groups for years. They call it "citizens" and "consulates" because they're a nation, not an organization. I asked, "But isn't RNA supposed to be only Blacks?" They explained, "We think you understand what RNA is about." I read their Declaration of Independence and the New African Creed. I really liked what RNA stood for. Of course, they were for freeing Black people from oppression and wanted to do so by building a Black nation within the U.S. I agreed with this then, and still do today. But they didn't only look at political or economic systems, which of course we need to change. RNA also promoted a transformation in the entire person.[33]

The following may well be points from the New African Creed that impressed Yuri: "I will steal nothing from a brother or sister, cheat no brother or sister, misuse no brother or sister, inform on no brother or sister, and spread no gossip"; and "I will keep myself clean in body, dress, and speech, knowing that I am a light set on a hill, a true representative of what we are building." The idea of developing into a new person—one who is freer from the tendencies of individualism, selfishness, and consumerism, all fostered under capitalism—while simultaneously transforming economic and political structures is not new. Che Guevara emphasized the need to build the "new man," or in today's antisexist language, the new revolutionary person. To Yuri, as each of us strives to become that new person, we create the social basis that helps build an egalitarian society.[34]

Yuri recalled with excitement, "I'll never forget the date I became a citizen, September 13, 1969." She took her oath with about five others at the closest RNA consulate. It was at this time that she began using her Japanese name. In the 1960s, many Black activists had given themselves African or Muslim names as an expression of their efforts to decolonize their minds. Yuri's daughter Lorrie began using her Japanese middle name, Aichi, in high school. And as one of two Kochiyama children who did not have a Japanese middle name, Jimmy renamed himself "Chikara," meaning strength. Aichi had been badgering her mother to adopt her Japanese name, so when Mary Kochiyama joined RNA, at age forty-eight, she began using her middle name, Yuri.[35]

After becoming a citizen, Yuri attended the Brooklyn Consulate, which was one of several RNA consulates established in Philadelphia, Pittsburgh, Washington, D.C., Baltimore, Cleveland, Chicago, Los Angeles, and San Francisco/Oakland. Like other RNA citizens, she attended the three weekly classes on nation building, revolutionary first aid, and gun control at the RNA office in Brooklyn. These classes were held on the same night, as Yuri recalls, making it easier for her as a mother of six and part-time waitress to attend. As contained in Yuri's class notes, the nation-building classes introduced RNA activists to political ideology, the history of the struggle for a separate Black state or nation, and the history of New Africans, the term some revolutionary nationalists used to refer to Africans in the U.S. context. The classes also explained the blueprint for financing the nation through reparations from the U.S. government. Although their position is highly contested, RNA "citizens" viewed themselves, as the incipient Black nation, as the representatives of Black people in the United States. As such, they called for Congress to pass an act granting "the peaceful cession of land and sovereignty to the Republic of New Africa . . . and three hundred billion dollars in reparations for slavery and the unjust war against the black nation to the Republic of New Africa." This amount was based on a calculation of ten thousand dollars per descendant of enslaved Africans. Rather than making this demand as U.S. citizens, as Japanese Americans did in the 1970s and 1980s, the RNA claims that previous payments for war damage by one nation to another set the precedent for their demand. Yuri agrees that reparations are due to the descendants of enslaved Africans, an issue she has pushed alongside the later demand for Japanese American reparations.[36]

Yuri found the gun control classes arduous because they were taught in a scientific manner: "We had to learn the velocity of the bullets and how it makes an arc depending on the distance. To me, it was more like learning math and physics. It was really difficult for me. I wasn't interested in all that." She admitted, "I just wanted to learn how to use a gun." Recognizing the negative views of many toward gun training, Yuri was hesitant to discuss this topic. People like to create their own image of Yuri, one that matches their own politics and comfort zone. And she caters to that tendency. When she speaks to people today, she gears her discussion to match her perception of their politics. So she would not talk about armed struggle or her gun-training experiences to most people. As it turns out, back in the late 1960s and early 1970s, she had not even told her husband or children that she was attending gun control classes and target practice: "I never ever told Bill I was learning how to use a gun because I didn't think he would have liked it. It would have worried him. I just said I was going to political education and first aid classes. Even though it's legal to learn how to use a gun, we never talked about these things at home." During a period of increasing marital discord over Yuri's involvement in high-risk political activity, it was easier for this fairly nonconfrontational person simply to avoid conflict. But within the revolutionary nationalist movement, most activists advocated self-defense, not just in theory but in practice: "As for how I felt about learning to use a gun, if you were in RNA, you have it imbued in you how important it is to know how to use a gun. It was to defend your comrades and yourself. We were serious in thinking that if we needed to go to war, we would. Everyone was hyped up about that. The need for self-defense was very real, but in retrospect, I think a lot of Movement people thought the revolution was around the corner."[37]

Although being in the RNA compelled Yuri to take a position on the use of self-defense and armed struggle, this was not her primary motive for joining. Given her pragmatic orientation, it is not surprising that she admired the RNA's practical emphasis, which taught discipline, physical health, and survival skills. She participated in all of the rigorous training:

We'd have to get up early in the morning, 5 a.m., and go to some park in Queens and learn things. They'd teach us how to rescue a person. Could you carry a person on your back? I was small and so it was hard for me. They also taught you about stamina. Some learned how to swim because we wanted to go to Mississippi for the Land Celebration. And you have to be able to swim a certain distance with someone on your back. I don't think too many of us could do all the tasks. . . . And that's what I liked about RNA. They did so much practical skills training.[38]

Despite Yuri's size (she is a slim five-footer) and her age (approaching fifty), she strove to participate in all the training. Not only did she find the physical challenge invigorating, she also never wanted to be seen as too old or too frail to carry out her duties.

It is difficult to ascertain from Yuri the specific role she played in the RNA because of her collective philosophy: "It took everybody working together to get things done. Whether it's making placards or discussing an issue, it's not she did this or he did that. I wouldn't even remember individually what I had done." Yuri readily claimed the ordinariness of her participation: "I was never an officer or leader. I just did what any RNA person would do. I attended meetings, classes, organized certain aspects of the rallies, wrote some leaflets and articles, took pictures—stuff any citizen would do." Emphasizing her belief in self-determination, Yuri added: "But I never spoke. That would be sort of ridiculous for a non-Black to speak for the Black nation." Nonetheless, she did play a unique role in the RNA, which was the same role she generally played in the Movement. "Yuri was our Internet in those days," proclaimed RNA citizen Bolanile Akinwole. Ahmed Obafemi, also in the RNA, concurred: "She was our main communication person."[39] This role took several forms.

First, as Max Stanford recognized as early as 1964, Yuri had extensive social and political networks. Her friendliness, interest in people, and hospitality have enabled her to meet thousands of people over the years, whether at her family's weekend open houses, at political events, or waitressing in community restaurants. This quality predated her political involvement, as seen in the fact that her family's Christmas newsletter was mailed to three thousand people annually. Wherever she went, she carried her notepad, ready to record a person's name and contact information. What made people feel so comfortable with Yuri was her remarkable, almost unbelievable, ability to remember their names, backgrounds, and interests. Since Yuri was constantly meeting new people, she became an important source for recruiting members. Ahmed Obafemi explained: "Yuri would give them the general information about the RNA and then say, 'I can get someone to come talk with you.' She'd always call: 'Ahmed, I just met a couple of people who are interested in the RNA. Can you come by the house and do a workshop with them?'" As reflected in this statement, Yuri's behind-the-scenes work and respect for Black self-determination rendered her less threatening to Black (male) leadership and endeared her to her comrades. Her wide networks also proved useful when planning an event or working on a campaign. She was able to enlist the services of friends to help with the planning; to call on her friends, including distinguished people like Malcolm X's sister Ella Collins, to be a featured speaker; and to bring people to the event. In short, Yuri was a motivator, one who got people inspired to become active or to intensify their commitment to social justice.[40]

Second, Yuri functioned as a communications center. Activists would stop by the various restaurants in Harlem where she worked as a part-time waitress. In a period before answering machines and electronic mail, and in a community where not everyone had stable access to a telephone, Yuri functioned as a message relay center while she worked. Ahmed Obafemi recounted: "Yuri used to waitress at Thomford's. That became like our meeting place. Everybody would come in and talk to Yuri. So when you'd come in, Yuri would have the most recent information for you. If we wanted to set up a meeting, she would set it up. If you had a message for someone, you'd just leave it with Yuri. She must have received fifteen, twenty messages a day." And even when she was not waitressing, Yuri was a magnet for messages. She was known for traveling around town, dropping off flyers or running errands at various Harlem establishments. Although it was unusual for people to leave messages for friends at different businesses and community centers, Yuri became a regular beneficiary of such practices.[41]

Third, when the incarceration of activists escalated in the early 1970s, Yuri became a primary contact for many political prisoners. She was the first person many turned to when arrested or when released from prison, either calling her home or dropping by her work. "When we were captured by the enemy, our first call went to WA6-7412," recounted Mutulu Shakur, rattling off her telephone number from memory thirty years after his first postprison phone call to Yuri. "Everybody just remembered that number," continued Shakur. "Anybody getting arrested, no matter Black, Puerto Rican, or whatever, our first call was to her number. Her network was like no other. She would get a lawyer or get information out to our family and the Movement. You knew she wasn't going to stop until somebody heard from you." Ahmed Obafemi concurred: "Anybody that got out of prison, they'd go right to Yuri. She would know where they were staying and would let everybody know. She had everybody's address and had memorized most people's phone numbers. I don't know how many numbers she had up in her head. She was very efficient, very dedicated, very committed, particularly around the issue of the prisoners."[42]

Fourth, Yuri was a storehouse of political information and updates on political prisoner cases. Not only did she save and file countless Movement documents, her razor-sharp memory enabled her to remember facts about events and cases that eluded most people. That was part of her computerlike function to which Bolanile Akinwole alluded. Akinwole also remembered the clutter of papers that Yuri's packrat behavior created in her home: "She had little cardboard boxes [of files] stacked up everywhere. One of her back rooms was just filled with these boxes. And there used to be boxes in the hallway and in the kitchen. The kitchen table always had bunches of stuff on it and underneath it. But everything was very organized, and it was amazing how quickly she could put her hands on information." As filmmaker Renee Tajima observed, "Yuri remembers virtually everything, and records the rest," referring to Yuri's compulsive note-taking behavior. When activists needed information about a political prisoner case or about an issue, they invariably turned to Yuri who retrieved the material either from her memory, which was quite accurate, or from her files. "You should have seen the files she had on political prisoners. She had everybody's case, when they went to the parole board, their whole file. So if you wanted information on a political prisoner, say to organize a conference or a tribunal, all we had to do was go to Yuri," recalled Ahmed Obafemi.[43]

Yuri also owns numerous personal address books for New Yorkers, out-of-staters, and political prisoners, as well as dozens of outdated ones "just in case." In her books, she carefully enters the names and contact information, not only alphabetically, but also color-coded by race. Brown ink signifies Asians, green for Black people, blue for Puerto Ricans, and so forth. Young people today who are raised in an increasingly multiracial environment, or theoretically minded people who advocate the socially constructed nature of race, or those promoting color blindness might object to Yuri's essentialist coding system. But Yuri is most concerned with getting the work done. To her, much in society as well as in the Movement is racially stratified. So she finds that this race-conscious system facilitates creating mailing lists for events or locating a particular person among the several thousand entries in her personal books. Yuri also meticulously logs every incoming phone call and every letter she receives or sends, including addresses, even though this information is already in her records. While this enables her to keep her contact list up-to-date and to remember who sent a particular correspondence, Yuri's record keeping also has an obsessive quality to it.[44]

Finally, through her writings, Yuri helped to disseminate information and document the Movement. She was a regular correspondent for newsletters of the RNA, the National Committee for the Defense of Political Prisoners, and Asian Americans for Action. She has also submitted numerous articles, letters to the editor, and press releases to mainstream and Movement publications. Moreover, in 1965, Yuri started a second annual family newsletter, the explicitly political *North Star*. As time-consuming as it was to produce one newsletter, Yuri and Bill somehow managed to simultaneously publish both eight-page newsletters, distributed each December, for four years until they ended *Christmas Cheer* in 1968. They then terminated the *North Star* the following year as Yuri's political activities intensified. More than a family news sheet, as Yuri modestly calls it, the *North Star* serves as a chronicle of the revolutionary nationalist struggles in Harlem. There are articles on LeRoi Jones's (Amiri Baraka) Black Arts Repertory Theatre/School, Bill Epton, H. Rap Brown (Jamil Abdullah Al-Amin), and Stokely Carmichael (Kwame Ture). By the third issue, in 1967, the *North Star* focused heavily on political prisoners. Several of the 1968 articles featured the newly established Republic of New Africa. The newsletter also contained information on the revolutionary Puerto Rican and emerging Asian American movements as well as quotes by revolutionary thinkers, including W. E. B. Du Bois, Frantz Fanon, Ho Chi Minh, and Patrice Lumumba, the Pan-Africanist Congolese prime minister who was assassinated by rival Joseph Mobutu's forces in 1961 and whose life and writings influenced Yuri's politics. Yuri, with her ever-present camera, captured the Black movement in pictures. The *North Star*, like *Christmas Cheer*, contained a photo collage, but this time it was predominantly Black radicals who graced the center spread.[45]

Many have wondered how Yuri, as an older Asian American, was regarded by the predominantly Black activist community in Harlem. Her husband, Bill, noted: "[Yuri] was one of the very, very few Asians to mix in with the Blacks. Some may have questioned her, but I'm sure they began to see how sincere she was, how concerned she was in her work." Indeed, activists wondered in astonishment how Yuri could be at so many political meeting and events. Muhammad Ahmad (Max Stanford) recounted: "Yuri worked harder than anyone I have ever seen in life. I mean, we would watch Yuri in amazement. Being such a small woman, we would wonder where all that energy came from. She would be at just about every demonstration." Puerto Rican activist Richie Perez remarked: "Yuri was an activist in the movement to free political prisoners in almost every community. . . . And she approached each of these amazingly with the same enthusiasm as if they were people from her own community." There were also other factors that endeared Yuri to Black nationalists. She became involved in the political struggle at a time when Third World unity was being emphasized. Her self-identification as a supporter of Black self-determination enabled her to display a cultural sensitivity that was appreciated by Black activists. And Yuri's behind-the-scenes work did not threaten to usurp Black leadership. Moreover, as a resident in a housing project, a waitress in neighborhood restaurants, and an activist who leafleted numerous Harlem establishments, Yuri interacted with people locally. The activist community, in particular, grew to embrace her. "[Yuri was] absolutely accepted," exclaimed Nyisha Shakur, echoing the sentiments of numerous Black activists. Undoubtedly, there were some Black activists, usually those new to the movements or with cultural nationalist tendencies, who questioned Yuri's presence at all-Black meetings or functions. But at these times, as invariably happened, a Black comrade would come to her defense.[46]

In the 1960s, Robert F. Williams was considered by many to be one of the most prominent leaders within Black revolutionary nationalist circles, second only to Malcolm X. Shortly after Malcolm's assassination, the journalist Richard Gibson wrote to Williams, "Malcolm's removal from the scene makes you the senior spokesman for Afro-American militants." This is curious to Harold Cruse, who asserted that "Robert Williams himself was never a nationalist, but an avowed integrationist." There is certainly much evidence to support this position. As president of the Monroe, North Carolina, NAACP, Williams advocated integration as the solution to White supremacy, as he worked diligently for the desegregation of swimming pools and other public facilities. Believing that the federal government would defend civil rights activists against the segregationist practices of Southern politicians and the Ku Klux Klan, he consistently informed federal officials and the FBI about local racial problems. He received support from diverse factions, including the interracial Freedom Riders and predominantly White Trotskyists—all pro-integrationist. Moreover, Williams considered the Black nation position unfeasible and was never a nationalist "to the point that I would exclude whites or that I would discriminate against whites or that I would be prejudice[d] against whites." So why, inquires Cruse, were the bulk of Williams's supporters in Harlem in the early 1960s nationalists? And why, I can add, did revolutionary nationalist organizations in the late 1960s invite Williams to be their leader?[47]

Cruse offered a succinct response: "For the young nationalists celebrated Williams as their leader, since his self-defense stand coincided with their rising interests in the adoption of force and violent tactics in the North." Williams's advocacy of self-defense certainly inspired many revolutionary nationalists, including the Black Panther Party's armed stance against police brutality. This position contrasted sharply with the nonviolent philosophy of prominent civil rights leaders and made Williams an adversary of NAACP executive director Roy Wilkins and an ally to revolutionary nationalists. But, Cruse keenly observed, "the social philosophy of Robert Williams is curiously at odds with his tactical ideas." In *The Crisis of the Negro Intellectual,* Cruse argues that nationalism and integrationism are opposing theoretical constructs: "American Negro history is basically a history of the conflict between integrationism and nationalist forces in politics, economics, and culture, no matter what leaders are involved and what slogans are used." Cruse credits W. E. B. Du Bois with identifying "integrationism (civil rights, racial equality, freedom) versus nationalism (separatism, accommodationist self-segregation, economic nationalism, group solidarity, and self-help)" as the two major contradictory forces in the struggle for Black liberation. While many would agree with Cruse's dialectical thesis, there are limitations to his rigid polarization of integrationism and nationalism. To Cruse, the creation of group identity and solidarity is a nationalist desire, in direct opposition to the desire for racial integration. "The very premise of racial integration negates the idea of Negro ethnic identity," he wrote. Perhaps his statement would hold up under an assimilationist model, whereby absorption into the dominant society comes at the loss of minority group identity. But not so, under the more widely accepted cultural pluralist model, where ethnic identity can be retained even as a group is incorporated into dominant society.[48]

In practice, Black freedom fighters have simultaneously advocated integrationist and nationalist solutions as strategies, not intransigent ideological positions. In his testimony before the U.S. Senate in 1880, former slave Henry Adams presented his program for Black liberation: "We first organized and adopted a plan to appeal to the president of the United States and Congress to help us out of our distress, or protect us in our rights and privileges. . . . If that failed, our idea was then to ask to set apart a territory in the United States for us, somewhere where we could go and live with our families. . . . If that failed, our other object was to ask for an appropriation of money to ship us all to Liberia in Africa. . . . When that failed then our idea was to appeal to other governments outside of the United States to help us to get away from the United States and go there and live under their flag." It is clear from this statement that Adams was not pushing for separatism per se. In fact, his first request was for protection from the U.S. government, an integrationist demand. What Adams wanted for his people was freedom and justice, and he was willing to use diverse methods, including establishing an independent Black territory within the United States, to achieve that goal. Almost a century later, Nation of Islam leader Elijah Muhammad, a leading Black nationalist, echoed the sentiments of Henry Adams: "As long as we are not allowed to establish a state or territory of our own, we demand not only equal justice under the laws of the United States but equal employment opportunities—NOW!" Yuri, too, echoes this flexibility in tactics. Simultaneous with her struggle for Black nationhood, she has worked in the integrationist movement for better education, jobs, housing, and so forth to advance racial equality within U.S. society. Although Cruse and others may well see this as a theoretical contradiction, Yuri does not: "Some people divide everyone, but I don't think that's right. On many issues—jobs, housing, education—it doesn't matter if you're a nationalist, a Leftist, or an integrationist, we can all fight together, and we have."[49]

By contrast to Cruse's polarization of nationalism and integrationism, Williams's biographer Timothy Tyson characterized his subject's political philosophy as "eclectic radicalism," influenced by the revolutionary nationalism of his Harlem supporters, the communism of the Socialist Workers Party, and the liberalism of the Civil Rights Movement. In the late 1950s and early 1960s, Williams believed in nationalist ideas about self-reliance, emphasized the militant tactic of self-defense, and strove toward racial equality through integration without fundamentally contesting the economic or political structures of the United States. Yet, neither Tyson nor Cruse adequately articulates the transformation of Williams's ideology as it evolved during his exile in Cuba and China from 1961 to 1969. By the late 1960s, Williams, then RNA president, posited, "I envision a Democratic socialist economy wherein the exploitation of man by man will be abolished." It appears that he had moved beyond the goal of racial integration into the U.S. capitalist economy. Malcolm X too, it can be argued, was moving toward a socialist ideology when he died.[50]

Yuri's political beliefs were profoundly shaped by the eclectic radicalism of Robert Williams and Malcolm X, but a radicalism that can be more precisely described as revolutionary socialist nationalism. She remarked: "We don't understand why others think revolutionary nationalists don't think about socialism. They always have." Still, "many in the Black community wouldn't even want to hear the word," she noted, tainted as the term is under Cold War politics. So outside of select radical circles, she prefers to talk about nation building and self-determination and to use the Afrocentric language promoted by the RNA. RNA leader Gaidi Obadele (Milton Henry) told an interviewer: "We don't have any hang-ups on socialism, which we call 'ujamaa,' which is broader than socialism. It's an African conception of the organization of society. It means we have total responsibility for one another." The RNA Declaration of Independence promotes "plac[ing] the major means of production and trade in the trust of the

State to assure the benefits of this earth and man's genius and labor to Society and all its members." And an RNA political statement holds: "Another aspect of New Afrikan Nationalism is that We are Black Scientific Socialists, that is, We are Black people that adhere to the principles of scientific socialism."[51]

While refraining from using Marxist language, Yuri believes that many in oppressed U.S. communities support the major premises underlying socialist theory, namely, distributing resources equitably among the people, valuing human rights instead of profits, developing a planned economy so that the needs of the populace could be met, providing nonexploitative jobs, and transferring power from the capitalist class to the working class. While Malcolm X and Robert Williams seemed to adopt some generic form of socialism, it is likely that they were also critical of Marxism for privileging class over race. In following Malcolm X, Williams, and the RNA, Yuri subscribes to the school of revolutionary nationalism that emphasizes race as the primary form of oppression. By contrast, other revolutionary nationalists, particularly those promoting scientific socialism or Marxist-Leninist-Maoist thought, view class exploitation as the main source of oppression, even as they recognize the links between race and class. This theoretical contrast underlies differences in ideology and practice, and there have been major struggles within the revolutionary Black movement and among radicals of various backgrounds over the relative importance of class and race.[52]

Still, to many Black revolutionary nationalists, the greater debate within the Black movement involves the struggle to promote an anticapitalist analysis among moderate civil rights activists and cultural nationalists. The distinction between cultural nationalism and revolutionary nationalism is important because, as Yuri stressed: "Nationalism is misinterpreted by so many people. There are all kinds of nationalisms. One type, narrow nationalism or cultural nationalism, is when you think your people are the most important, that you're superior to others." In words that may be surprising to those who misunderstand revolutionary nationalism, Yuri stated, "Narrow Black nationalism can be just as bad as White nationalism." Cultural nationalism is progressive in that it promotes Black or African culture and pride. But, from a radical perspective, cultural nationalism also has regressive elements. Yuri most often denounces the racial chauvinism of narrow nationalism. But she also agrees with the economic critique that cultural nationalism fails to incorporate a class analysis, thereby functioning to promote capitalism for elite Blacks through the exploitation of the vast majority of workers, Black, White, or other. She also agrees with the RNA position, "We are Revolutionary Nationalists as opposed to 'cultural nationalists,' because We understand that while cultural nationalists believe that We constitute a Nation, they are often not clear on what the definition of Nation is, they usually don't talk about a land base, and usually are nationalist in a strictly cultural sense." Although Yuri believes, as does the RNA, that cultural knowledge and racial pride are important components of liberation, she recognizes that those two factors alone will not bring about freedom. Controlling one's land and social institutions are key, hence the RNA's slogan "Free the Land."[53]

Yuri's ideological beliefs challenge another misconception about nationalism. While nationalism has been criticized for constraining liberation struggles within the borders of the nation-state, Yuri argues that revolutionary nationalism embodies internationalism: "If you call yourself a revolutionary nationalist, you must be concerned with all people's struggles. You must think about all nations and people and how you interact. The Black nation would have to be part of the international socialist world." Yuri's ideas reflect the influence of Kwame Nkrumah, a leading Pan-Africanist thinker, who argued that the establishment of an independent, socialist African nation contributes to the establishment of a united, socialist Africa, which in turn contributes to the establishment of worldwide socialism. Most, if not all, revolutionary nationalists argue that the creation of genuinely independent nations—as opposed to the numerous nominally independent, neocolonial governments that emerged following World War II—dictates that revolutions would take place in various countries at different times. This contrasts with the Trotskyist model of creating socialism throughout the world in many countries simultaneously, which revolutionary nationalists argue is imaginary.[54]

While Yuri's radicalism is eclectic, she firmly believes that the road to Black liberation is through the establishment of a sovereign nation in the American South—a highly controversial position even among Black nationalists. Given that the vast majority of American Black people did not migrate to Africa, an incipient Black nation in the United States, or some other area of liberation, Theodore Draper argues that the struggle for Black nationalism, defined narrowly as physical emigration or internal statism, has had stronger support in fantasy than reality. But to Yuri, regardless of its popularity, that Black people have struggled for nationhood lends credibility to this position: "Some people scoff at the concept of a Black nation, but if they knew something of the history of the desire of Black people to have their own nation, they would find that there have been many times in history where Black people have sought a separate government." It can also be argued that Black nationalism—loosely defined as some combination of community control of social institutions, economic self-reliance, cultural pride, psychological identification with Africa, organizational separatism from Whites, and control of a land base—has garnered widespread support. Still, the land question begs for clarification.[55]

The controversy surrounding Black nationhood comprises part of the long-standing Left debate on the dialectical relationship between proletarian internationalism and national self-determination. Proletarian internationalism refers to the need, according to Marx, for the working class (the proletariat) throughout the world to unite against global capitalism. Without international solidarity, the capitalist class pits the workers of one nation against the workers of another. Moving garment factories to Indonesia, for example, enables U.S. corporations to increase profits by cutting labor costs; this results in the exploitation of Indonesian workers as well as in layoffs and reduced wages for American workers. Because of the need for a united working class, some Leftist thinkers believe nationalism is regressive because it separates workers who would otherwise unite against the capitalist class of the dominating nation. In doing so, they fail to recognize the class and race (and gender) differences between the workers of First and Third World nations—as well as within these nations—and the ways in which First World workers benefit from imperialism. Instead, many radicals view proletarian internationalism in a dialectical relationship with national self-determination.[56]

Nations have the right to self-determination, argued Lenin, including the political right to secede from a colonizing nation and establish an autonomous nation. In theory, the struggle for national self-determination in an oppressed nation aids the struggle of the working class in the dominating nation, and vice versa, precisely because both groups face the same source of oppression, the capitalist class of the dominating nation. Yet, even among those who have a dialectical view of national self-determination and proletarian internationalism, there is considerable debate over whether Black people constitute a nation within the United States.[57] This complex discussion contains at least four theoretical positions.

First, the position Yuri advocates is that Black people constitute a legitimate nation within U.S. borders, a nation within a nation. Yuri explained: "As for the New Africans [Black people in the United States], they feel that any land they have lived on, worked on, developed, and fought for, should be their land to establish as a Black nation." As early as 1962, Harold Cruse characterized the situation of American Blacks as "domestic colonialism." Drawing on ideas of Cruse as well as those of Stokely Carmichael and Charles Hamilton in *Black Power,* Robert Blauner further developed the idea of internal colonialism in his classic book *Racial Oppression in America*: "Whether oppression takes place at home in the oppressed's native land or in the heart of the colonizer's mother country, colonization remains colonization. However, the term 'internal colonialism' is useful for emphasizing the differences in setting and in the consequences that arise from it." Because of the historic relationship of Black people to the U.S. government—slavery prior to its abolition and "neoslavery" in the form of racism, economic exploitation, lynchings, and imprisonment since—Black people, it can be argued, constitute an internal colony. Racial dynamics are understood as products of colonialism. The goal of the Black liberation struggle then is to throw off colonial control through a movement for national liberation, self-determination, and political secession.[58]

A second position, advanced by some Pan-Africanists, posits that for Black people throughout the diaspora, their land base is Africa, and their goal is to liberate Africa. This could mean that Black people should emigrate to Africa as advocated by Marcus Garvey or that, regardless of their physical location, Africans should work to decolonize Africa, including ending neocolonialism. A liberated Africa can then be used to help liberate the rest of the world, thus promoting proletariat internationalism. These Pan-Africanists also believe the land in the United States, including the five Southern states claimed by the RNA, belongs to the Indigenous Peoples of that region. Yuri countered this position, albeit not as convincingly as some of the RNA's foremost theoreticians: "If they knew their history, it isn't quite so. So many things have changed. Florida was once heavily Indian. That's why RNA did not include Florida. . . . Back in the mid-1860s is when the Indian Removal Bill forced many Indian tribes out of the South. They forced them out of Alabama, Georgia, and Mississippi into western Arkansas. They wanted to get the Indians out to make room for European settlers who were starting to come in. So people who say what about Indian land? By the mid-1860s, it was no longer Indian land." To this, many would contend that such a forced dislocation did not end the rights of Indigenous Peoples to the land. Even Imari Obadele, former RNA president, acknowledged, "[U.S. Blacks] have a right, based on a claim to land superior to the European's, subordinate to the Indian's, to set up an independent nation." But he too was vague about the how Indigenous People's land rights would affect the RNA's nation-building efforts.[59]

A third position, as advocated by sections of the American Left, posits that Black people are subjugated by racial—not national— oppression; their struggle is intertwined with the class struggle for equality and justice for all Americans. Advancing that nations are formed by objective factors, they use Stalin's definition of a nation, involving common language, territory, economic life, and psychological makeup, to determine that Black people do not constitute a nation in the United States; at a minimum, they lack a land base. Subordinated through both racial oppression and economic exploitation, Blacks are positioned as leaders of the class struggle to build a transformed and integrated socialist America. Note that civil rights activists also support this racial oppression position but, in contrast, advocate racial equality for Blacks within the existing capitalist system.[60]

Finally, some radicals advocate a fourth position on the national question, namely, the right of Black people to choose their own destiny. They believe that in the course of their struggle, Black people will define their own situation, possibly through discussions culminating in a plebiscite. To this day, Yuri agrees with the RNA's call for a plebiscite so that Black people can vote on whether they want to remain U.S. citizens, move to Africa, move to another country, or establish a sovereign nation on land in the American South. The RNA posits that, contrary to the conventional wisdom about the desirability of U.S. citizenship, Black people were never asked if they wanted to become U.S. citizens.

Based on the jus soli rule, citizenship is automatically conferred on anyone born on U.S. soil. But enslaved Black people were brought to this country against their will, and their descendants were born on U.S. soil as a result of this forced migration. Thus, the RNA argues that the Fourteenth Amendment should be considered an offer—and not an imposition—of U.S. citizenship. Notice that this call for a plebiscite is not limited to those advocating a physical Black nation. The Black Panther Party, in Point 10 of its Party Platform and Program, also called for a plebiscite: "And as our major political objective, a United Nations–supervised plebiscite to be held throughout the colony in which only black colonial subjects will be allowed to participate, for the purpose of determining the will of the black people as to their national destiny."[61]

In 1969, after spending eight years in Cuba, China, and Tanzania, Robert Williams decided to return to the United States, though he would have to stand trial on the Monroe kidnapping charges. Revolutionary Black nationalists everywhere were jubilant, but none more so than those in the RNA and African People's Party, who would be welcoming back their leader. Yuri too was anxious to met this man, with whom she had been corresponding during his exile: "Once I started helping to get out the *Crusader,* I wanted to get to know the people at the source. So I started to write to Rob Williams in China. And this is how we started our correspondence. In fact, he's the one who gave me my first *Red Book* [of Mao Tse-tung's thoughts]. That was 1968." Little did Yuri know that a year later, she would have the opportunity to thank Williams in person for the gift of Mao's philosophy:

> When I met Rob Williams, it was such a surprise. RNA citizens brought him and his wife over to our house. I had been writing to him for a few years, since he was in China. It was really exciting to actually get to meet him. About ten of them came walking in—all RNA. Herman Ferguson was one of them. I mean, I never expected Rob Williams. There was this knock on the door, and I thought, "I don't know if I want to see anyone." I couldn't believe it. I saw all these people in the hall, and Rob was the first to walk in. I can't remember all we talked about, but I suppose we said we missed him and I thanked him for writing from China

and for the *Red Book,* told him how much we looked forward to the *Crusader,* asked about his plans, and things like that. He and Mabel were here for quite a while, and Rob was curious to know what was happening locally. In our *North Star* newsletter, you'll see a picture of Rob and Mabel. When I looked at the picture again, I don't know why they looked so grim, tough, military—like the image of Black militants. But they weren't like that at all. They were so warm, really wonderful people.[62]

Although Yuri expressed surprise that Williams visited her, it was in fact not unusual to have renowned political figures at the Kochiyamas'. Activists from all over the world—the known and unknown—would find their way to the Kochiyamas' Friday and Saturday night open houses. "People were everywhere, eating, talking, laughing, spilling out into the hallway [outside their apartment]. People were even in the bathroom. You couldn't close the front door because there were so many people inside," recalled Herman Ferguson. The Kochiyamas' apartment also became a central meeting place for the Movement. Whether Yuri was home or not, members of organizations such as the Black Panther Party, SNCC, CORE, and RAM met at her place.[63]

But soon after the initial excitement of his return, Williams's resignation as the titular head of RNA served to amplify differences that had already begun to emerge between Gaidi and Imari Obadele. Imari Obadele observed: "Much is made of the Constitutional crisis that rocked the RNA Government during November 1969–January 1970, separating those led by my brother, Atty. Milton R. Henry [Gaidi] of Detroit, who wanted to continue RNA work in the North, and those led by myself who wanted to move the center of the struggle to the South. My brother, a Yale Law School graduate and a long-dedicated civil rights fighter, is supposed to have said that myself and those who transferred the struggle to the South had 'too much emphasis on guns.' The *Detroit News* happily broadcast the ideological struggle as a battle between the law-abiding and the gun-happy." The media may well have magnified the dichotomy between the law-abiding and the outlaw, but not the fact that there was conflict between the brothers. Gaidi and Imari Obadele were engaged in a struggle over the form and location of revolutionary change. Gaidi Obadele argued against the five-state position, noting that Blacks have migrated to Northern cities in increasingly large numbers since World War II. Imari, however, asserted that it was problematic to use the North as a land base given its vulnerability to attack. The White power structure could neutralize urban rebellions by shutting off water, electricity, food, and sanitation services and surrounding the contained area with police and the National Guard.[64]

Although Yuri lived in a Northern city and engaged in the urban struggle, she chose to follow Imari Obadele's path, believing that Black liberation would be won through the establishment of an autonomous Black nation in the South. This is the position that prevailed when Imari Obadele became RNA president in 1970, an office he would hold for two decades. Here Yuri's views contrast with those of another Asian American woman who was also deeply involved in the radical Black movement. Revolutionary theorist Grace Lee Boggs, and her collaborator and husband, James Boggs, posited that the cities, where Blacks were fast becoming the majority, represented the core of the Black struggle for self-determination and control of social institutions. The title of an article by James Boggs, conceptualized with Grace Lee Boggs, encapsulates their ideas: "The City Is the Black Man's Land." That Yuri lived in Harlem, a community heavily influenced by a particular form of revolutionary nationalist politics, was a key factor in shaping her views. The RNA nation-building classes stressed the importance of obtaining land in the South, and the OAAU Liberation School also connected liberation to the land question. At the time, many of Yuri's teachers and peers, including Max Stanford (Muhammad Ahmad) and Herman Ferguson, believed in the Black nation thesis. That their position, as they saw it, was based on the ideas of Malcolm X was important to Yuri. In November 1963, from inside the Nation of Islam, Malcolm had declared: "Land is the basis of all independence. Land is the basis of freedom, justice, and equality. . . . A revolutionary wants land so he can set up his own nation, an independent nation." To Malcolm, asserted Imari Obadele's supporters in the RNA, that land base meant establishing a Black nation on U.S. soil.[65]

Moreover, the concreteness of the demand for land was appealing to many, and would have been to a pragmatist like Yuri. RNA citizen Bolanile Akimwole observed: "RNA has a doctrine and philosophy that allows you to be connected to the world, to be international. In contrast, the Black Panther Party's slogan 'Power to the People' didn't give you a foundation. It didn't give you a reference for how to create change. At least RNA had a strategy—reparations, sovereignty, economic independence, and political independence. This is how you get all power to the people. Land is power." Yuri believed in the concreteness and correctness of the demand for land. She avowed: "The Black struggle has involved the fight for land within the U.S. It always will or it will lose its revolutionary potential."[66]

The tranformation of Yuri's politics in the few short years following her introduction to Malcolm X parallels changes in the Black movement. By the mid-1960s, the Black liberation movement superseded the Civil Rights Movements in many places, particularly Northern urban centers. Yuri captured this shift in a 1966 front-page article in her family's newsletter, the *North Star*: "The two words, 'Black Power' pierced the white power structure, cut through the mainstream, sank white security, darkened ivory towers, while it uplifted Black masses, brightened the ghettoes, embarrassed the Toms, and worried integrationists." Just three years since contesting Malcolm X's separatist views, Yuri now promoted nationalist ideas, challenging people to rethink integrationism. She wrote: "'Integration,' [Stokely] Carmichael explained, 'is irrelevant to the freedom of Black people. Negroes have always been made to believe that everything better is always white. If integration means moving to something white is moving to something better, then integration is a subterfuge for white supremacy.'" By contrast, Yuri asserted, "Black Power [is] a way of advocating self-determination. . . . Black Power . . . is an idea to inspire a new image; assert a Black self; create basic changes; govern one's own destiny; achieve, not for personal attainments, but for all Black people." Her belief in revolutionary nationalism, the internal colony position, and the link between national and international liberation are also evident in her 1970 article written for the Asian Americans for Action newsletter:

> Generally speaking, political action during the early part of the "sanctioned sixties" was to expose, challenge, confront, and rectify injustices and discriminatory practices. But in today's context, the issue is not one of civil rights or in terms of individual rights. It is national liberation for the masses of Black

people—that Black people decide their own destiny. Thus, as "colonized" people instead of disenfranchised American citizens, the struggle is one with the struggle of oppressed people everywhere. The oppression has been a combination of economic and socio-political strangulation; physical and psychological brutalitization, all ramifications of racism.

This anti-imperialist, antiracist ideology, in part, drew Yuri into the struggle to support political prisoners.[67]

7

Political Prisoners and the Heartbeat of Struggle

As the Black Power Movement grew, the police and FBI intensified their assaults against Black activists. That Yuri noticed this qualitative shift is discernible in the pages of her family's political newsletter.[1] Beginning with the 1967 edition, the *North Star* contained information on numerous political prisoner cases, including a front-page article titled "1967—A Year of Frame-ups, Jailings." Yuri wrote: "1967 was a rough year; rough in terms of the establishment's unleashing of power. That militants across the country are incarcerated is indicative of the direction the government is moving." While the most famous case that year was of Black Panther Party cofounder Huey Newton, the arrests of seventeen Black nationalists in New York, several of whom Yuri knew, had a more immediate impact on her life.[2]

On June 21, 1967, in Queens, New York, seventeen Black nationalists, allegedly all RAM members, were arrested on the political charge of conspiracy. Max Stanford was also indicted on the conspiracy charges, but went underground to avoid arrest and imprisonment. Among those arrested, Herman Ferguson and Arthur Harris were given the additional charge of conspiracy to assassinate Roy Wilkins, executive director of the NAACP, and Whitney Young, executive director of the Urban League. That there was internal conflict in the Black movement is well documented. For example, after suspending Rob Williams for his "we must meet violence with violence" statement, Wilkins created a tactical alliance with Martin Luther King Jr., based on their mutual advocacy of nonviolence, even as King chastised the national NAACP leadership for not engaging in direct action. But the chasm between political and even personal conflict and death threats is deep and wide. Yuri asserted that the two main FBI targets were Max Stanford (later Muhammad Ahmad) and Herman Ferguson. A 1968 internal memo from Director J. Edgar Hoover reports that the FBI identified RAM and its leader, Max Stanford, as among the four or five "most radical and violence-prone" Black nationalist groups and leaders targeted by the bureau. And Yuri claims Stanford "was the number one person wanted by the FBI." Ferguson's leadership positions in several militant Black organizations made him a strategic target. Moreover, Yuri observed: "Herman took up such a radical position whenever he spoke. He'd say things like, 'There can't be a revolution without armed struggle. We have to learn to fight.' And he would make it specific, 'I don't mean just with words.'"[3]

Yuri wrote a lengthy article on the organizing campaign for the Queens 17 in the *North Star* that year. The group Friends of the 17, which included Yuri, was busy publicizing the event through articles and appeal letters in numerous Movement publications, raising funds to pay for the $200,000 bail bond, packing the courtrooms, and speaking at diverse venues, including Newark Black Power and Students for a Democratic Society national conferences, as well as churches and apartments. As a testament to their organizing skills, at least for this one event, Yuri wrote, "In Queens, where a militant rally was never held before, 2,500 black people jammed an auditorium to hear Rap Brown, LeRoi Jones, Mae Mallory, Conrad Lynn and others." As is characteristic of Yuri, the article highlights the individuals involved in the work, particularly the support committee's chair, Connie Hicks.[4]

It is no coincidence that the Kochiyama family newsletter turned its attention to the issue of political prisoners in 1967. In August of that year, a memo from Hoover to all FBI offices signaled a new era of surveillance for the Black nationalist movement. "The purpose of this new counterintelligence endeavor," wrote Hoover, "is to expose, disrupt, misdirect, discredit or otherwise neutralize the activities of black nationalist, hate-type organizations and groupings, their leadership, spokesmen, membership, and supporters, and to counter their propensity for violence and civil disorder." The goals, according to a 1968 FBI memo, included preventing "the *coalition* of militant black nationalist groups"; preventing "the *rise of a 'messiah*,'" who could unify and electrify the militant black nationalist movement"; and preventing these groups "from gaining *respectability* by discrediting them" to "the responsible Negro community," "the white community," "Negro radicals," and "youth."[5]

As the FBI founder and director from 1918 to 1972, Hoover had already accumulated extensive experience in repressing radical dissent, as seen in the 1919 Palmer Raids, the 1920s campaign against Marcus Garvey, and the 1950s campaigns against the Communist Party, Socialist Workers Party, and the Puerto Rican independence movement. Modeled on these programs, Hoover initiated the FBI's secret domestic intelligence operations, code named COINTELPRO for *counterintel*ligence *pro*gram, against the Black nationalist movement. "While in strict FBI parlance a COINTELPRO refers to a specific secret and typically illegal operation (and there were many thousands of individual COINTELPROs executed between 1941 and 1971)," explained Ward Churchill and Jim Vander Wall, "in popular usage the term came to signify the whole context of clandestine political repression activities. . . . Regardless of its precise technical meaning in 'Bureauese,' COINTELPRO is now used as a descriptor covering the whole series of sustained and systematic campaigns directed by the Bureau against a wide array of selected domestic political organizations and individuals, especially during the 1960s."[6]

By September 1968, the Black Panther Party (BPP) had risen to the top of Hoover's COINTELPRO list, as, in his words, "the greatest threat to the internal security of the country." Hoover explained: "Schooled in the Marxist-Leninist ideology and teaching of Chinese Communist leader Mao Tse-tung, its members have perpetrated numerous assaults on police officers and have engaged in violent confrontations with police throughout the country. Leaders and representatives of the Black Panther Party travel extensively all over the United States preaching their gospel of hate and violence not only to ghetto residents, but to students in colleges, universities and high schools as well." What worried the FBI director was the appeal of the Panthers to so many in the Black communities. A 1970 top secret FBI Special Report for the president identified approximately eight hundred "hard-core members," but "a recent poll indicates that approximately 25 per cent of the black population has a great respect for the BPP, including 43 per cent of blacks under age 21 years of age." To their supporters, the Panthers' efforts to ameliorate

social problems, including their free breakfast programs for school-
children and their armed patrols of the police, demonstrated a more
humane alternative to capitalism and instilled courage to resist in
Black people. It seemed that the FBI was failing to prevent a Black nationalist organization "from gaining respectability" not only among
"youth" and "Negro radicals," but also among segments of "the responsible Negro community" and "the white community."[7]

The FBI, which directed 233 of the 295 authorized Black nationalist COINTELPRO operations against the BPP, was effective in
neutralizing the Panthers. BPP attorney Charles R. Garry announced
that, in 1969 alone, the police killed twenty-eight Panthers, including
Los Angeles Panther leaders Alprentice "Bunchy" Carter and John
Huggins and Chicago-area Panther leaders Fred Hampton and Mark
Clark. The FBI also bombed Panther offices, made multiple arrests,
mailed forged letters, wiretapped phones, leaked false news to the
media, sent in infiltrators and agent provocateurs, recruited informants from within the BPP, created suspicions about legitimate leaders, fabricated evidence used to imprison activist leaders, promoted
or exacerbated internal dissension, created splits between the BBP
and other Black nationalist groups, and harassed Panthers on a daily
basis. Yuri corresponded with numerous imprisoned Panthers, including Geronimo ji Jaga (Pratt), whom the courts admitted to wrongfully
convicting twenty-seven years after his arrest. Yuri was among those
ji Jaga called the day of his release from prison in 1997. Although
they had never met in person, she had supported him during his lonely
prison tenure and helped organize events and wrote articles to educate
the public and mobilize mass support for his case. Ji Jaga expressed
gratitude in a 1991 letter from prison: "You know that you're a hero
to all of us Yuri." At the New York celebration of ji Jaga's release,
Yuri, an invited speaker, returned the accolades: "When we think of
what you have endured, first as an exceptional leader under constant
surveillance and observation; then conspired against by both the
COINTELPRO and sadly some of your own confused comrades; . . .
spending twenty-seven prime years of your life in some of the worst
prisons—and yet, able to withstand all the abject adversities of life,
and emerge from prison, not only strong and spirited, but warm and
loving, and with dignity and humility . . . Your courage, your persis-

tence, your integrity, your faith, your love for people characterize you as someone phenomenal. May we learn from you, and gain some insight on the makings of a freedom fighter."[8]

Yuri felt the effects of COINTELPRO closer to home when, in April 1969, the police arrested the entire leadership of the New York BPP chapter on 156 counts of conspiracy to bomb department stores, the Botanical Gardens, and police stations and to murder police officers. The charges were based largely on the testimony of three police infiltrators, whose statements were called into question under cross-examination. After deliberating for less than one hour, the jury acquitted the defendants on all 156 counts. This was no small victory for the activists who organized protests and aided the legal team. Yuri's support was recognized when, twenty-five years later, she was invited to speak at the silver anniversary celebration exonerating the Panther 21. Despite the acquittals, the police and FBI succeed in their efforts to neutralize the BPP. By imposing excessively high bails of $100,000 per defendant, the court kept the party leadership in prison for two years, and the New York chapter was effectively crushed.[9]

To respond to the arrests of many of their comrades, Yuri and others in New York, including newly released Panther 21 defendants, formed the National Committee to Defend Political Prisoners (NCDPP). Yuri was regarded as one of its most consistent members. "Yuri, out of all of us, was in touch with prisoners and supporters the most," observed NCDPP member Nyisha Shakur. "People would call her relentlessly, just all the time. . . . She was seemingly writing and visiting most of the political prisoners and really staying on top of it." "Yuri diligently wrote, sent information, made sure we were kept up-to-date about different issues," recounted Ahmed Obafemi about his prison time in the mid-1970s. "Yuri communicated with everybody. She was . . . the central figure," he concluded.[10]

Through the NCDPP, and with many of its members before its establishment, Yuri defended numerous political prisoner cases in the late 1960s and early 1970s. She worked on the RNA 11, Harlem 6, Harlem 5, Tombs 7, Rap Brown 4, Carlos Feliciano, Martin Sostre, New Haven 3, Puerto Rican *independentistas,* and numerous Black Panther Party and Black Liberation Army cases. Yuri recounted the intensity of the times:

It would be hard. After all, I'm working, I'm a mother. Number one, I'm a mother and housewife, so there's the house kind of chores. In the evenings, I might attend some meeting, and then late at night, I would be either writing to the brothers and sisters in prison or working on the leaflets of their cases. Then on the weekend, at least every other weekend, we'd visit the political prisoners. Everybody went according to if they had the money because it costs money to go to a prison. So each person went when they could. I mean everybody has their whole life and things they have to do at home. But I'll tell you, we were busy during this time. Every week, more brothers and sisters would be arrested. We were working on scores of cases at the same time—trying to keep up with visiting, writing, attending court hearings. If I could show you all the leaflets we made, you'd get an idea of how expansive the work was.[11]

Beyond a moral outrage and personal concern for her imprisoned comrades, Yuri's personal history holds clues that help illuminate her motivation for political prisoners. "I cannot help but feel strongly about this," she explained, "because I can never forget what we, peoples of Japanese ancestry, experienced during World War II because of hysteria, isolation, and absolutely no support. . . . Yes, we were also political prisoners." Not only was her father falsely arrested, his early death, reasoned Yuri, was caused by inadequate medical care during his imprisonment. An experience inside the Jerome, Arkansas, concentration camp, mirrors the inhumane treatment imposed on some of the political prisoners she has visited: "I remember seeing a Chinese man visiting his [Japanese] wife. . . . There was a table between them. He wanted to hold his baby. The baby was about a year old and sadly the guard came over and said that nothing could go across the table. 'But it's my child,' the Chinese man said. 'Sorry,' the guard said, 'but those are the rules.'"[12]

As with the Japanese Americans during the 1940s, Yuri asserts: "The activities of political prisoners do not embrace crime. No criminal acts have been committed—if crime means violations against humanity." Yuri's position becomes controversial when one realizes that she is not only referring to those, like the Panther 21 or Geronimo ji Jaga, framed for crimes that even the courts acknowledged they did not commit, but also to those who committed illegal actions but, from their perspective, did so in pursuit of justice. Some of the latter group's controversial clandestine activities included bombing military installations, expropriating money from banks, and liberating comrades from prison. While most people would call these criminal activities, former political prisoner Assata Shakur inverted the conventional meaning of criminal, murderer, thief, and bandit in her 1973 message from prison:

> It should be clear to us by now who the real criminals are. Nixon and his crime partners have murdered hundreds of Third World brothers and sisters in Vietnam, Cambodia, Mozambique, Angola, and South Africa. . . . They call us murderers, but we did not murder over two hundred fifty unarmed Black men, women, and children, or wound thousands of others in the riots they provoked during the sixties. . . . They call us thieves and bandits. They say we steal. But it was not we who stole millions of Black people from the continent of Africa. . . . They call us thieves, yet it is not we who rip off billions of dollars every year through tax evasions, illegal price fixing, embezzlement, consumer fraud, bribes, kickbacks, and swindles. . . . They call us thieves, but we did not rob and murder millions of Indians by ripping off their homelands, then call ourselves pioneers. . . . They are the bandits."[13]

The definition of political prisoner is contested, even within the political prisoner movement. There is wide consensus, however, that at a minimum, the term refers to those whom the state incarcerated because their political actions, beliefs, or associations undermined the established racial, gender, economic, political, or religious order. As Yuri wrote in a front-page article in a 1970 *Asian American for Action* newsletter, "[A] political prisoner means that such a person was engaged in some kind of political action." In other conversations, she has added, "and that action was a threat to those in power." Although she did not define *political action,* the meaning can be inferred from her speeches and writings. "It has also become [the Black militant's] role," she wrote in 1970, "to teach the need of defending himself and his community; and to see a greater potential in liberation, whether through separation or confrontation (no longer reform), both of which will disempower the structure that oppressed and suppressed him." At a 1986 forum to support political prisoners Mutulu Shakur and Marilyn Buck, Yuri further explicated what she meant by political action: "It's about replenishing and reinforcing the struggle for self-determination and socialism by example and commitment; making it understandable to the masses thr[ough] an anti-imperialist character, and the highest principles of humanism in conduct and concern for humanity on a daily basis." Yuri agrees with the definition of political prisoners advocated by the Jericho movement, a national formation organized in 1998 to defend political prisoners, in its mission statement: "[Political prisoners] are brothers and sisters, men and women who, as a consequence of their political work and/or organizational affiliations were given criminal charges, arrested or captured, tried in criminal courts and sent to prison." She herself has described political prisoners as "those convicted because of their political activism against policies and practices of the U.S. government, who were committed to struggling for justice and human rights for all people."[14]

Within the national political prisoner movement, some assert that those who become politicized in prison should also be considered political prisoners. Although their initial imprisonment was not related to any political actions, they, like other political prisoners, face retribution by prison authorities for their outspoken advocacy of prisoner rights, among other issues. How could George Jackson not be considered a political prisoner, they would argue, when as a California prisoner, he became the preeminent symbol of the Black and prison liberation movements? While serving a one-year-to-life sentence for a seventy-dollar gas station robbery, Jackson became politicized under the tutelage of fellow prisoner W. L. Nolen and later became a Black Panther Party field marshal. After a guard killed his mentor, Jackson, along with Fleeta Drumgo and John Cluchette, collectively known as the Soledad Brothers, were charged with the retaliatory death of another guard. On August 7, 1970, his brother Jonathan Jackson was killed following an audacious Marin County courtroom entrance, where at gunpoint, he freed three San Quentin prisoners—Ruchell Magee, William Christmas, and James McClain—and took the judge, assistant district attorney, and three jurors as hostages. It was this incident that forced Angela Davis, then head of the Soledad Brothers Defense Committee, to flee underground when the police accused

Yuri Kochiyama's parents, Tsuma and Seiichi Nakahara.

Yuri as a child.

The Nakahara family in their custom-designed home in San Pedro, California, circa 1940. Left to right: Art, Seiichi Nakahara, Peter, Yuri, and Tsuma Nakahara.

This caricature depicts Yuri's numerous travels by bicycle to cover San Pedro High School sporting events for the San Pedro News-Pilot. *Her classmates presented the poster to her at a homecoming celebration in her honor in San Pedro, California, in August 1989. Artist: Peter Bentovoja. Courtesy of Norma L. Brutti.*

Yuri, in her uniform for the Women's Ambulance and Defense Corps of America, and her twin brother, Peter, in his U.S. Army uniform, circa 1942.

Left to right: Bill's father, Yutaka Kochiyama, Billy, Yuri, and Bill in New York, circa 1948.

Yuri with five of her six children, 1957. Left to right: Aichi, Billy, Jimmy (on Yuri's lap), Audee, and Eddie.

Malcolm X visited the Kochiyamas' home on June 6, 1964, to speak at a reception for Japanese hibakusha *(atomic bomb survivor) activists on an international tour to promote peace and nuclear disarmament. He is shown here with Audee (second from left) and three other teenagers. Photograph by Yuri Kochiyama.*

Yuri speaking at a commemoration of Malcolm X's birthday at Malcolm's gravesite in New York, early 1970s. Malcolm's older sister Ella Collins (immediately left of Yuri) headed the Organization of Afro-American Unity (OAAU) following Malcolm's assassination. After Collins's death, James Small (far right) headed the organization.

Yuri was a Sunni Muslim from 1971 to 1975. She traveled biweekly, often with Safiya Bukhari (left), to the Sankore Mosque in Greenhaven prison, Stormville, New York, to study and worship under the head imam, Rasul Suleiman (center). Suleiman was a security guard for Malcolm X and a member of Malcolm's Muslim Mosque, Inc. Bukhari was Jericho cochair, Republic of New Africa (RNA) citizen, and former Black Panther.

Yuri speaking at an event celebrating Robert Williams's return from exile, 1969. Standing behind Yuri are two people who strongly influenced her politics: Robert Williams (left), internationally renowned for his stance on self-defense, and Muhammad Ahmad (Max Stanford), leader of the Revolutionary Action Movement. Photograph courtesy of Greg Morozumi.

RNA *citizen Bolanile Akinwole (left) hands out leaflets at a political prisoner conference in Jackson, Mississippi, 1971. Photograph by Yuri Kochiyama.*

Yuri being arrested in a protest on August 25, 1977, at which twenty-nine activists seized the Statue of Liberty to demand the release of five Puerto Rican nationalists held in U.S. prisons for a quarter century and to call attention to the colonial status of Puerto Rico. Photograph by Mike Lipack, New York Daily News.

On November 23, 1981, Bill testifies about his concentration camp experiences at the New York hearing of the Commission on Wartime Relocation and Internment of Civilians. In defiance of the commission, members of the East Coast Japanese Americans for Redress boldly display the provocative artwork of Byron Goto. Photograph by Corky Lee; copyright Corky Lee.

The Kochiyamas in the kitchen of their Harlem housing project apartment, 1980s. Standing, left to right: Aichi, Akemi, Jimmy, Audee, Tommy, Zulu, Eddie. Sitting: Bill and Yuri.

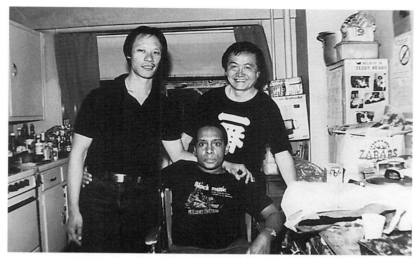

Greg Morozumi (left), close comrade and family friend; Alkamal (Sheldon) Duncan (center, in wheelchair), former head of the Black Guard, one of the youngest members of the Revolutionary Action Movement, and Yuri and Bill's son-in-law; and Bill Kochiyama in the Kochiyamas' kitchen, 1988. Photograph courtesy of Greg Morozumi.

Bill and Yuri being honored for their leadership in the Japanese American redress and reparations movement at a Day of Remembrance program, New York City, 1993. Day of Remembrance events are held in various locations throughout the United States to commemorate the signing of Executive Order 9066, which set in motion the plans to forcibly incarcerate 120,000 Japanese Americans during World War II. Photograph by Corky Lee; copyright Corky Lee.

Yuri surrounded by her teddy bear "family," 1997. Photograph by Diane Fujino.

Yuri visits Dylcia Pagán at the Dublin federal prison in northern California, 1993. Pagán was released on September 10, 1999, along with ten other Puerto Rican political prisoners. Photograph courtesy of Dylcia Pagán.

Yuri sits on a panel discussing the assassination of Malcolm X with Herman Ferguson (center), head of the Malcolm X Commemoration Committee and RNA citizen, and author Zak Kondo (left), New York City, 1990s. Photograph courtesy of Herman Ferguson.

Yuri with veteran activist Iyaluua Ferguson at a Mumia rally, 1990s. Yuri's stylistic printing can be seen at the top and bottom of the sign she is holding. Photograph by Herman Ferguson.

Yuri with Wayne Lum, a leader of the David Wong and Yu Kikumura support committees, in front of the Asian contingent's banner at the Jericho rally for political prisoners on March 27, 1998, in Washington, D.C. Photograph by Diane Fujino.

Gloria Lum (left) and Kazu Iijima, cofounder of Asian Americans for Action, take a break from gathering signatures for a petition to gain release for prisoner David Wong at the Asian/Pacific American Heritage Festival, New York City, 1999. Photograph by Wayne Lum.

After moving to California in 1999 for health reasons, Yuri celebrated Malcolm X's birthday in Oakland at the Malcolm X Jazz Arts Festival, May 20, 2000. Surrounding Yuri, seated in wheelchair, are (clockwise from left): David Johnson, former prisoner with the San Quentin 6 case; former Panther Kiilu Nyasha; poet and revolutionary leader Amiri Baraka; former Panther Yasmin Sutton; and Geronimo ji Jaga, former Panther leader who was released from prison twenty-seven years after being the target of a COINTELPRO frame-up.

Yuri and extended family at her surprise eightieth birthday bash on May 19, 2001, in Oakland, California. Front row, left to right: grandchildren Traci, Maya, Aliya, and Christopher; son Eddie; grandchildren Kahlil and Ryan, and Tia's daughter. Middle row, left to right: niece Elizabeth, brother Peter, Yuri, Peter's wife, Aiko, and son Tommy. Back row, left to right: son Jimmy and his wife, Alison, nephew Bob, Tommy's wife, Julie, daughter Audee and her husband, Herb (behind Audee), Darlene and nephew David, Eddie's wife, Pamela, holding her niece, Pamela's brother, Eric, and his wife, Tia. Photograph by Wayne Lum.

her of masterminding the affair. One year later, on August 21, 1971, George Jackson was killed by a guard in the San Quentin courtyard.[15]

The Jericho movement opposes the inclusion of a George Jackson in the political prisoner category. Their mission statement reads: "While we recognize that there are many people who have become political after their incarceration, George Jackson (murdered in San Quentin) and Ruchell Magee (Angela Davis' co-defendant) for example, we believe that this campaign has to focus on those political prisoners and prisoners of war whose incarceration was political from inception." Those in agreement with Jericho's definition use the term *politicized prisoners* to recognize the political contributions of and potential reprisals toward those who become political in prison, yet differentiate them from those whose political activities led to their imprisonment. In many ways, Yuri agrees with Jericho's definition, influenced in part by her close association with Herman Ferguson and the late Safiya Bukhari, both RNA comrades and leaders of the national Jericho movement. She has upheld the necessity of this narrow definition in order to contest the U.S. government's treatment of political prisoners before international bodies, including the United Nations, which has taken a strong stance against colonialism and racism.[16]

International law has repeatedly affirmed the right of colonized people to fight against colonialism and racism by any means necessary, including armed struggle. The 1970 UN resolution 2621 "reaffirms the inherent right of colonial peoples to struggle by all necessary means at their disposal against colonial Powers which suppress their aspiration for freedom and independence." A 1973 UN resolution declared: "The armed conflicts involving the struggle of peoples against colonial and alien domination and racist regimes are to be regarded as international armed conflicts in the sense of the 1949 Geneva Conventions." Thus, "any attempt to suppress the struggle against colonial and alien domination and racist regimes is incompatible with the Charter of the United Nations." In 1977, the United Nations went even further in "demand[ing] the release of all individuals detained or imprisoned as a result of their struggle against apartheid, racism and racial discrimination, colonialism, aggression and foreign occupation and for self-determination, independence and social progress for their people." To Yuri, these resolutions provide the necessary legal framework to justify the militant resistance of political prisoners and to demand their release and are key to understanding the rationale for Jericho's narrow definition of political prisoners.[17]

But after moving to Oakland, California, in 1999, Yuri began to seriously question Jericho's definition as she heard heated arguments, particularly by "old-timer" ex-prisoners who gained consciousness in prison in the 1960s and 1970s, that politicized prisoners should also be considered political prisoners. Although Yuri will articulate the need for definitional preciseness, her overriding tendency is to avoid alienating people or hurting their feelings. The intense conflict over the definition of political prisoner, as occurred during a Bay Area Jericho meeting to organize an international political prisoners conference in Cuba, is the type of internal movement struggle that deeply distresses her. As one who leaves the struggle over theoretical and strategic methods to others, she has worked to lessen the polarizing effects by, for example, talking to activists on both sides of the political prisoner debate, inquiring about the reasons for their opinions and about their families.[18]

While Yuri is conflicted about whether politicized prisoners should be considered political prisoners, she clearly opposes the idea that all prisoners are political prisoners. The latter position is advocated by some prison activists, who argue that the entire context of imprisonment is political. Economic, political, racial, gender, and religious dynamics beyond the facts of the case affect conviction rates, sentencing patterns, and even the very definition of what constitutes crime. People of color, particularly young Black men, are the most likely to end up in prison, though White people make up the majority of those arrested. Also, prisons overwhelmingly house the poor, though "white-collar crime," often committed by the wealthier class, generates economic losses greater than all burglaries, robberies, larcenies, and auto thefts combined.[19]

Yuri understands the politicized form and function of prisons, but believes a distinction must be made for those who are targeted by the state for their political activism. To her, the term *social prisoners* refers to those whose crimes may well have resulted from their legitimate anger against oppressive conditions, but whose actions did not include efforts to build an egalitarian society. She has heard the charges that such a distinction privileges the role of political prisoners. But Yuri believes that all prisoners, whether social or political, share the loss of control over their bodies; the humiliation of being strip-searched;

the loss of power to make decisions about their lives; physical, psychological, and sexual abuse from prison guards; overcrowded conditions; poor health care; and so forth. To her, political prisoners hardly receive special treatment from prison authorities, except in the form of excessive sentences and unusually harsh treatment, including placement in isolation and experimental control units. These conditions of isolation warrant extra support, asserts Yuri, but many political prisoners languish in prison for years, geographically isolated, and sometimes politically alienated, from family and friends. Moreover, many political prisoners fought for prisoners' rights before they were locked up, and continue to fight for better conditions for their fellow prisoners from behind the walls, including providing HIV and AIDS counseling, facilitating visits for prisoners' children, offering legal assistance, and providing hope and a will of resistance.[20]

Moreover, both political and social prisoners serve the state's efforts to suppress dissent. Former political prisoner Laura Whitehorn expressed: "Political and social prisoners . . . [are] two sides of a program of repression. One is, you terrify communities and tell them the law is all-powerful and people will lose their freedom for many, many years if they transgress. The other is, you give huge sentences to anyone who says, 'There are such egregious social justices that we have to go up against the government.' You lock up those people for long periods of time, and that will prevent the rise of a new generation of leaders or activists. If you leave out one side of that equation, you'll never understand what prisons are." Ward Churchill observed, "The greatest fear of the elite is always that [political prisoners] will be able to galvanize the resentment and inchoate rebelliousness of [social prisoners] into a coherent force for social change." And that is why Yuri advocates the need to support those who put their lives at risk for people's liberation. "Political prisoners . . . are the heartbeat of struggle," she proclaimed. "[They] were the most vocal and visible community activists. They were the most dedicated. They educated and politicized their communities. They are leaders. . . . They are the symbols of resistance and courage. We honor them by remembering them, that their deeds live on."[21]

Malcolm X's influence on Yuri extended beyond the political, and from 1971 to 1975, she practiced Sunni Islam. Not surprisingly, her religious conversion took place at a New York prison, where she visited political prisoner and imam Rasul Suleiman. Suleiman (Robert Smith), Yuri relays, was sent to prison in 1967 after a nationwide search for him in connection with the killing of three police officers. He left the Nation of Islam when Malcolm was expelled and helped Malcolm build the Muslim Mosque, Inc. Skilled at martial arts and at weaponry, he was known as Karate Bob on the street and became one of Malcolm's key bodyguards. Yuri said of Suleiman: "If anyone reached and changed, it was Rasul Suleiman. He, like Malcolm, exemplified what a once negative street blood can do and become when inspired to grow in revolutionary stature."[22]

She explained the beginnings of her Muslim transformation:

A lot of us were visiting Green Haven because it had the highest number of political prisoners incarcerated there. The main person I visited was Mtayari Shabaka Sundiata. In the early 1970s, I was surprised to get a letter from Brother Rasul asking me to visit in Dannemora, all the way up near the Canadian border. He kept asking me to visit him, but I didn't know if I wanted to or not. Finally, I got on a bus at midnight, but had no intention of joining the mosque. When I met him, I was impressed. He wanted to see if I could help get him moved closer to New York City so his family could visit him. I kept writing to him, and worked with the NCDPP to try to get him transferred. Rasul started contributing articles about his case to the NCDPP newsletter. He also wrote to everybody in the prison administration, and they finally moved him to Green Haven. The brothers there were looking for a strong leader to take over the mosque, and they found that leader in Rasul Suleiman.[23]

While Yuri is often portrayed as being unable to refuse help to anyone, we see in her own words, her hesitancy to fulfill Suleiman's request for a visit. Perhaps she was concerned about the cost and time involved in traveling so far. She probably was reluctant to get involved with a prisoner who was already pushing for one thing; who knows what else he would ask? She would have been worried about increasing her political involvement at a time when her family was already upset that her numerous prison visits and other activities took her away from them. While it was indeed difficult for Yuri to turn down a request for help, she did not dole out help foolishly. Still, her fears that a visit to Suleiman would become time-consuming were correct—not because of his political demands, but because of how that visit transformed Yuri's religious life.

When Imam Suleiman invited Yuri into the Muslim faith, she had qualms about joining the mosque. For one, she had observed the unequal treatment of women at the mosques: "Unfortunately, all us sisters put up with a lot of male chauvinism. Men sat up front for prayers, sisters in the back." Her quick insertion, "That didn't bother us because we felt that Black men needed their place since America oppressed them so much," is revealing of a nationalist influence on her thinking. Another issue that concerned Yuri: "What bothered me wasn't something specific about Islam, but rather about all religions. What I didn't like about any organized religion was the chauvinism—as if it is the best religion. I don't think any religion is the best. If religion helps a person to become a better person and if you truly believe in it and that faith makes you not only strong, but makes you feel a part of the whole world, then it's worth joining." Yuri's was a humanitarian religion, centering on concerns for the well-being of others. Her emphasis on good works, more than on theological issues, enabled her to make a fairly easy conversion to Islam, despite her initial hesitation as a non-practicing but still believing Christian.[24]

Yuri's decision to join the mosque was intertwined with her politics, especially her loyalty to Malcolm X: "I also joined the mosque because of the imam. He was so dynamic and represented Malcolm." By contrast to many White Leftists who interpret Marx's widely quoted statement, "Religion is the opiate of the masses," as a condemnation of religion, many groups around the world use religious doctrine as their motivation for social change. Liberation theology, a force in Catholic-dominated countries in Latin America and the Philippines, uses scripture as a guide to the eradication of poverty and oppression. Many activists, including Malcolm X, Martin Luther King Jr., and Cesar Chavez, combined religion and politics in their struggle to improve society. The message of Ahmed Sékou Touré, first president of independent Guinea, sheds light on Yuri's practice: "Revolution and religion influence the nature of thought, the action and behavior of [people] and dictate an attitude of rigorous, honest, absolute fidelity, modesty, and social usefulness." Yuri's religious philosophy, enacted through social institutions or not, laid the foundation for her moral beliefs and community service, which in turn laid the foundation for her political activism. She teaches: "Real revolutionaries should have the highest principles and even standards of morals. This should be expressed not only in their political ideas but also in how they live every day, in their concern for people."[25]

Yuri began making the two-hour trip to Green Haven every other week with her close friend Safiya Bukhari. On alternate Fridays, Yuri attended a Sunni mosque—not a Nation of Islam mosque, she emphasizes in remaining loyal to Malcolm—in Brooklyn:

> Each time I'd go to the mosque, there was no one I could really talk to about my experiences as a Muslim woman, at least not to any Asian. My husband must have wondered, but I never talked about it with the family. I didn't think they'd be interested, and I have to say, I was a little afraid to bring it up because I didn't think they'd understand. Besides, everyone in our house was so busy, we didn't talk about things in detail. They thought I was seeing political activists in prison as I had done for years, but I never told them about my becoming a Muslim. I think Aichi was the only one I told—she was curious. I'd leave home wearing my usual jeans, T-shirt, and sweatshirt. I'd carry all the Muslim attire—skirt, head cover, and so forth—in a bag. If I took the bus, I'd change at the bus station. If someone drove us and we met in Harlem, I'd have to find someplace like a park in Harlem to change. Then I'd have to change again on the way home, making sure I returned in the same clothes I had started out with. It's interesting—I learned that when you change your clothes, you also change your mental attitude. Though I didn't talk about this with my family, my Muslim life was very deep inside me.[26]

The extremes to which Yuri went to hide such a significant experience from her family are striking, but they become more understandable within the context of family conflict over the intensity of her political activities.

Starting in the late 1960s, as Yuri's politics became more radical and more demanding, her family, particularly her husband, Bill, tried to get her to slow down her activism and to spend more time with the family. When the police started arresting increasing numbers of Yuri's comrades and she herself was under FBI surveillance, Bill and the children became alarmed that her political work would jeopardize her safety, the safety of their family, and the security of Bill's job. Having been unemployed for periods, Bill, as the primary breadwinner, was concerned about how the family would fare should he lose his job. Given that when they married Yuri was a more traditional housewife—at least her extensive social activities involved the entire family—there must have been a significant adjustment on Bill's part to the transformation in her political ideology and practice. And there were numerous arguments about the extent of her political involvement.[27]

The first half of the 1970s represented the most difficult years in Yuri and Bill's marriage. This was the period when the advent of the Asian American Movement converged with the radical Black Movement, expanding Yuri's already overflowing political work. Also, by 1968, Yuri and Bill had also stopped producing their family newsletter, *Christmas Cheer,* an activity that brought them together. So not only was Yuri busier, she was engaged in more activities independent of the family. Already frustrated by the amount of time Yuri spent on her political work, Bill now became livid. In a telling commentary, Eddie stated, "My dad was very upset because he felt my mom was not being a mom. She was mostly into her Movement activities." By this time, their two daughters were married with one child each. But their three youngest were teenagers, experiencing their own adolescent problems, exacerbated by their minority status. Their oldest son was on his own, but suffered from depression stemming from a physical disability. To Eddie, the Movement occupied a significant portion of his mother's time; with her "literally going to ten to fifteen meetings a week . . . she just wasn't home." Yuri disagrees with this description, insisting that she was attending "five or more" meetings a week. Whatever the number, it is clear that Yuri's meetings and other political activities consumed her time. "All I remember we did was hear about Mom's political activities," said Eddie, reflecting the sentiments of the other children. Even when home, Yuri was frequently on the phone organizing political activities or sharing Movement information. She also stayed up until three, four, or even five in the morning, writing to political prisoners, addressing leaflets for a mailing, composing articles for newsletters or newspapers, and organizing political activities.[28]

The constant presence of visitors and overnight company added to the family discord. The Kochiyamas' home had already been dubbed

"Grand Central Station" from the time they married. But after Yuri became political, the frequency of visitors and overnight guests increased. There were still many family friends coming over; single mothers and children continued to spend the night, and Bill's father visited every Tuesday evening. Added to this were Yuri's comrades. Despite the enjoyment of having friends over and the excitement of meeting prominent political activists, the cramped living quarters, the nonstop flow, and the militant environment created stress on the family. Yuri's son Jimmy remembered disliking some of the activists, who he thought had "big egos." He also felt unsafe in his own home, worrying that some of the visitors might be infiltrators and that their phone might be bugged. Bill too had strong feelings, as Yuri recounted: "There were a lot of Movement radicals that [Bill] didn't care too much for. He liked ordinary folks. They didn't have to be making a political statement. He thought it was so rhetorical, especially if they were hardlined. He didn't like people who could only talk about politics." Eddie also experienced increased tension: "We had fights about that. . . . Some people said they'd stay two nights and ended up staying a month. . . . I remember one time when I was twelve years old, I came home pretty late and found somebody sleeping in my bed. My mom knew I'd be home later that night but gave my bed to someone anyway. So I slept on the couch. About two in the morning, I hear this woman saying, 'Move over,' because my mother had invited more people to sleep over."[29]

Nyisha Shakur recollected: "When I first met Bill, I was afraid of him. He was always working. He'd come home tired and always have like a million people in his home. He'd just say hello and go to the back of the house. I'd feel bad for him and want him to know that 'I'm not here too, too much. I really love Yuri. I'm not one of the ones taking advantage of her.'"[30] But other activists abused Yuri's generosity. Yet she chose to interpret their actions—dropping by at dinnertime to get a free meal, crashing at her home, selling her already read newspapers, concocting stories to get money—as requests for help. So even if some employed underhanded methods, she considered their needs and their humanity and gave them a meal or money or lodging. As happens in family systems, because Yuri minimized these incidents, it was her family and close friends who became infuriated and felt they had to protect her.[31]

In this context, almost unbelievably, Yuri claimed: "I hardly talked about politics. No one at home would hardly want to hear about politics. Each kid had their own interests, and that's mostly what we talked about." Perhaps Yuri's desire to remember herself, and to be remembered by others, as a "good mother" and "good wife" explains her statement. A woman of her generation would have heard many times that she should be spending less time on political activities and more time with her family. Yuri has not been immune to this chastisement, neither from family nor from others. She acknowledges that she might not have always done as much as she could have for the family—a sentiment that echoes her regrets about her adolescent years. But the dual pressures to be fully committed to one's family and to the Movement are not easily resolved for any activist, especially for women. Because of patriarchal notions that assign women responsibility for children and home, women activists, to a much greater extent than men, face conflict and criticism when they devote large amounts of time to political activities. To be sure, many male activists—Malcolm X, Martin Luther King Jr., and Cesar Chavez come to mind—have spent considerably less time with their families than did Yuri, yet society in general has been more accepting of their commitments to social justice. Over the years many activists, in recognizing this gendered component, have tried to deal with this dilemma. Some believe that having more communal structures, including rotating child care and meal preparation, would lighten the load and facilitate women's fuller participation in the Movement. But there are no easy solutions.[32]

In fairness to Yuri, she did provide for her husband and children. Throughout the 1950s, 1960s, and 1970s, Yuri, with help from her husband, children, and friends, managed to prepare meals, to have clean clothes, and to provide other basic necessities for her family. Audee commented, "Although we sometimes wished we had a more traditional family life, it was a stimulating and actually fairly stable environment." Yuri also helped raise her two oldest grandchildren during the most urgent and frenzied period of the Movement in the late 1960s and early 1970s. Yuri and Bill's first grandchild, Zulu Kahlil Williams, was born in 1968 to Audee and her husband, Terry Williams, a Southern civil rights activist. Three years later, Aichi and her Black Panther husband, Yasin Ladson, had the first Kochiyama granddaughter, Akemi Kochiyama Ladson. Given Audee's and Aichi's involvement in the Movement and location in Harlem, it is not surprising that they married Black activists, choices that are a point of pride for Yuri. That both of the Kochiyama daughters married young, had a child in their late teens, and divorced caused some distress to Yuri and more so to Bill. Yuri heard the whispered criticism, the accusations that she spent too much time on her activism and neglected her family responsibilities, though teenage mothers were not uncommon in Harlem. In a mid-1980s article, "Mothers and Daughters," Yuri defended her daughters' choices and in doing so, perhaps unwittingly, defended her own:

> I am sure there were criticisms of my permissiveness, and queries of "Where was that mother when all this was happening?" Also comments of "What a mistake" when the relationships dissolved. I can understand the criticisms, but saw no mistake because of the eventual break-up. Like my mother before me, I believed in giving freedom and trust when the children were ready. My daughters were ready. Despite the disintegration of both of their relationships with their men (one lasted over ten years), I do not think either of their marriages was a mistake. They were conscious acts that grew out of sincere feelings of love and mutual interests at the time. The dialectics that take place in personal relations, like anything else, bring contradictions that may not be resolved in reconciliation.[33]

Yuri provided not only emotional but also concrete support to her daughters. She supplied full-time babysitting services for Zulu in his first three years while Audee was at work. Audee recounted, however: "Of course, being who she is, it wasn't going to be the kind of babysitting where they stay home and play games all day. My mother took Zulu to demonstrations and meetings. He was going all over. I can't even imagine how she managed or how she and Zulu got around or where they went." And when Akemi was born, Yuri did the same with her. Her daughters appreciate that Yuri, despite heavy Movement obligations, never made them feel bad or encumbered by these child-care responsibilities.[34]

In the 1960s and 1970s, for some twenty years, Yuri and the children attended Bill's softball games every week throughout the spring. She kept score and also covered their games for the *New York Nichibei*.

In a manner that reflected her teenage love for sports, she got excited at Bill's games, rooting and hollering and jumping up and down. Greg Morozumi, who played a couple of seasons with the Ronin during their losing years, remembered Yuri's enthusiastic sports reporting: "Some articles were funny because she played us up even though we were pretty terrible. 'So-and-so made this incredible diving catch!' And then we'd lose the game." So even when Yuri was heavily involved in her activism, she still supported and enjoyed nonpolitical activities.[35]

The family discord, particularly between Yuri and Bill, began to abate by the mid-1970s for a number of reasons. Some of the familial and marital stress was reduced when the Kochiyamas decided in the early 1970s to live more communally. By this time, Billy was out of the house, as was Audee, who had married in 1967. Aichi had also married, and she and her husband lived in the Kochiyama household, now totaling seven. Each person was assigned one night per week to cook and one night to wash dishes. Even the youngest child, then a pre-teenager, participated in the rotation. The family also tried to make collective decisions. Now, rather than Yuri unilaterally inviting activists to spend the night, the family decided who could stay over and when and for how long. This helped ease the influx of overnighters. The communal living also lessened Yuri's domestic responsibilities while enabling the family to function.[36]

Yuri and Bill also struggled to discuss their problems, but there continued to be communication barriers. Bill tried to explain how the family needed her at home more, but his increased drinking during this period made it difficult to communicate. Yuri tried to explain why the Movement work was so important—that unlike their family, who had shelter, food, and love, many people were suffering severely. But to her family, this did not necessarily justify the intensity of her activism. Yuri also made efforts to accommodate her family. To block off time for her family or to get through particularly hectic periods, she regularly placed notes on the door asking people not to disturb them: "We're really very busy. Please don't knock." The people closest to Yuri and those concerned about her well-being left without knocking. But some would rap on the door anyway. A few arrogantly believed the note did not apply to them. In fairness to those who knocked, it was hard to accept the message because Yuri exuded the feeling that she was always available to the Movement. In addition, when they had family gatherings, Yuri often included a close friend or two. So while she tried in ways to oblige her family, it may not have seemed that way to them.[37]

Also important to the resolution of the conflict was that, by the mid-1970s, the Kochiyama children were involved in their own lives. The youngest two, Jimmy and Tommy, had moved to California. Billy, Audee, and Aichi had married, and Eddie was grown. As the need for Yuri to be home for the children decreased, the conflict between Yuri and Bill began to dissipate. Moreover, that both Bill and Yuri placed a high value on family and took their commitments seriously helped them through the rough times. Audee said: "My mother always believed if you make a commitment to someone or a Movement or a goal, you should always stick by that. The last thing to do is to give up." And Bill was the same.[38]

Finally, the advent of the Asian American Movement provided Bill with an avenue for political involvement on issues dear to his heart. He already had a long history of community service, having served as president of the Japanese American veterans association several times. In the early 1970s, he continued these activities, representing Nisei veterans at various functions, organizing the Japanese American softball league, and participating in activities of different Asian American organizations as well as Sheltering Arms, the orphanage where he grew up. Added to this, Bill became active in more political ways. He joined Asian Americans for Action (AAA) and served as the chair of several AAA projects. Notably, he headed the campaign to establish the United Asian Communities Center, demonstrating his leadership skills and commitment to the community. Bill enjoyed working on these projects, hanging out with the people in AAA like Tak and Kazu Iijima, and being actively involved in helping community projects come to fruition. Through his practice in the radically oriented AAA, Bill slowly gained a better understanding of Yuri's political perspectives.[39]

People may wonder if it was through Yuri that Bill started working in the Asian American Movement, and the Civil Rights Movement before that. Bill himself credited Yuri: "I shudder to think that if I hadn't met Yuri, what would have happened to me. When it came to political activities, at first maybe on some of them, I didn't agree with. But in the end, I did because I became educated through her." While Yuri influenced Bill's politics, he also formulated his own opinions and understood racism and economic exploitation based on his experiences. And he developed a political philosophy that was distinctive from Yuri's. Whereas Yuri as a revolutionary nationalist worked on radical and reformist struggles in numerous liberation movements, Bill, whose politics were progressive to radical, chose to concentrate on civil rights and community service mostly in the Asian American community. Bill was more active than Yuri in the Asian American Movement, namely, in AAA and the Japanese American redress struggle.[40]

To understand how Yuri managed family life and political work requires an understanding of her philosophy. Bibi Angola observed: "Yuri was born and never saw herself as an individual. She's always seen herself as part of the collective world. She's always seen herself as a person who wanted to improve the world and felt she owed to give to the world because the world, she felt, had given to her." Audee concurred:

> My mother was always idealistic. As a young woman, she read a lot of inspirational poems. When she met people who she felt faced a lot of adversity and demonstrated inner strength, that was inspiring to her. And around our twelfth birthdays, she made each of us a scrapbook. Some of the things she put in—like poems, photos—represented the values of sharing, of giving to people. She has always believed that whatever you give to people continues to generate itself. I think she has lived her life by that philosophy. My mother definitely has trust in people. She has never lost her faith or her sense of idealism. It's always important to her how you treat people.

Although she would not like to admit this, at times Yuri prioritized the struggle for global freedom and justice above the needs of her own family, and she did so precisely because her vision of humanity extended beyond her immediate family to include the human family.[41]

While it has not been easy, the Kochiyama family has consistently respected and been immensely proud of Yuri's commitment to social justice. "The real difference of growing up in our household was having parents who constantly inculcated us with the idea that whenever and wherever there is injustice, inequality, and oppression—that we all have a responsibility to fight for those who are victimized—whomever they may be," observed Eddie. Tommy noted, "My parents showed us through example the true meaning of humility, sincerity, and genuine

love for people." Yuri's and Bill's promotion of family and community
values also encouraged the development of unusually close relationships among their children. Billy and Tommy, twelve years apart, felt
a close bond. Audee and Aichi were the paragon of sisterhood, according to Greg Morozumi. Today, Jimmy's and Tommy's children
spend so much time together, their relationship resembles that of siblings more than cousins. And Audee's and Eddie's families, living just
minutes apart in Oakland, are regularly at each other's homes. Yuri
has also been successful in passing on the spirit of compassion, kindness, generosity, and a concern for justice, qualities exhibited by all
her children. And this is a testimony to her role as a mother.[42]

In 1975, as some of the marital discord was easing up, a tragedy hit
the Kochiyamas that jolted Yuri into a serious questioning of her political practice and family obligations. Her oldest child, Billy, committed suicide. Billy's problems began with a car accident on the night of
November 4, 1967. Home from college for the weekend, Billy, Audee,
and three friends were going to see an African ballet performance.
Their car stalled on the way, and they got out to push it. All of a sudden, a taxicab smashed into them from behind. Billy suffered the worst
injuries. Yuri recounted how she learned about the accident: "We didn't
even have a phone at that time. So the people upstairs told us there was
a phone call for us. Audee said to come to the hospital; she didn't know
how serious it was. When we got there, Billy was in shock. There was
blood just pouring out of his leg. He kept asking, 'Do I still have my
leg?' We were at a city hospital with many other injured people, so we
were lucky that the doctors picked Billy first. His injuries were so bad he
could have died that night."[43]

After spending the night in the hospital, Yuri departed for her first
day of a new job at Macy's department store. No sooner had she left
the hospital than she received an urgent phone call that another surgery was needed. And so it went for Billy, then age twenty, for the eight
months he remained in the hospital and during the additional two years
of visits to the doctor and hospital, undergoing a total of, according to
Yuri, "eight surgeries, skin grafts, pins in his knee, plastic artery, cast
to his waist, seven-inch plate in his thigh, bed sores, abscessing at the
heel." This was an agonizing process for the entire family, who initially visited Billy at the hospital daily, then several times a week. He also
had many friends visiting. For three years the doctors tried to save his

leg, as Billy's often repeated question, "Do I still have my leg?" echoed in their ears. Yuri questioned whether she and Bill should have pushed for an amputation immediately following the accident. One doctor had recommended this, believing the physical and psychological recovery process would be easier. But Billy wanted to save his leg. In the end, after three years of being in and out of the hospital, of going through so much pain, Billy had a thigh-level amputation.[44]

Following the amputation, life became increasingly difficult for him. This was the son who had been close to all his siblings and acted like a protective older brother. Eddie relayed: "Billy and I were very close. He was like my role model. He taught me how to play baseball. And he was a big brother—if you messed with me, you'd have to deal with him." Billy regularly sent money so that Tommy, Jimmy, and Eddie could visit him at college in Massachusetts. Tommy found these visits comforting when he was experiencing problems in New York: "Billy was always supportive. Though we didn't talk about the fights [I was having with neighborhood kids], I think he knew. And I knew he was proud of me." Billy was also the son who was so politically active that he skipped his high school graduation to help register Black voters in Mississippi. But after he lost his leg, his once gregarious, warm, people-oriented personality changed; he became depressed and despondent. "After the amputation, some people would look at him like he was a freak," Yuri recalled. "I'd get so mad. I remember one time we were at some event here in Harlem, and this guy yelled out, 'Tell the cripple cat to get out of my seat.'" Yuri felt at a loss in not knowing how to protect her son from these hurtful words. "When these things happened, I didn't know how to act, to keep my cool or what. His friends would have taken on the guy, but I thought no, we don't want a fight." Later, Billy became addicted to the painkiller Darvon and had epileptic seizures and anxiety attacks. A short-lived marriage added to his problems.[45]

Despite these struggles, it was hard to imagine that Billy might take his own life. "We didn't understand the effects of the amputation on Billy emotionally. He always seemed so strong and positive. And my parents had met so many people with disabilities that they felt, given Billy's personality and support, he could handle it well," noted Audee. But underlying his positive demeanor, there were signs of the growing difficulties Billy was facing. Audee recalled: "About a year before he died, Billy told me if his life didn't get better before he was thirty, he felt he couldn't keep going on like this. I was really surprised and upset to hear this. But it was still hard to believe that it could be possible. I remember telling my mother, but in her mind, she couldn't imagine that Billy or anyone in our family could consider suicide—we had so much support, a good life."[46]

Billy's troubles deteriorated to the point that he returned to his parents' home from New Mexico, where he and his wife had moved to start a new life. But on October 15, 1975, at age twenty-eight Billy drowned himself in the Hudson River. In a page-long article included in Billy's funeral program, the family disclosed:

> [Billy] was brought back to New York this past June [1975]. We are grateful to Billy for these last four months . . . four precious months that he shared with us . . . of constant changes, upheavals, anguish, and frustrations, but also fleeting moments of joy and sweet hope. Three weeks ago, he even kicked Darvon, cold-turkey. The light at the end of the tunnel, however, suddenly flickered out on Wednesday, October 15. After an agonizing nite of awaiting his return, a pair of crutches was spotted by friends at the ferry-landing's Lost and Found . . . and an eye-witness report to a newspaper confirmed his final act. Many hours later two farewell notes were found at home. Six days later, on October 21, his body was recovered at a pier in Brooklyn.[47]

The loss of Billy, exacerbated by the circumstances of his death, left the entire family shocked and devastated. Bill reacted with more stoicism, but Yuri, at times, just sat and cried, unable to think clearly but needing to let out the pain. She remembered one incident in which she took a friend to the place where Billy died and ended up crying and talking. The person did not say anything, only listened, but Yuri found it comforting to be able to express her suffering to someone who could tolerate the anguish. Perhaps the depth of a family's pain is experienced most severely by the mother, as Yuri has told her friends. Plus, a suicide raises so much self-doubt and guilt—a questioning of whether one was an adequate parent. Yuri must have suffered terribly from this self-questioning, given the criticism about her self-absorption in political activities. But, Billy's final farewell note, found in his pocket wrapped in plastic, let the family know that he loved them dearly and appreciated their support. The Kochiyamas, who gave so much to others, found themselves surrounded by kind, caring, and generous friends who provided emotional and material support. Although it was emotionally hard, Yuri found comfort in hearing friends talk about their memories of Billy. She also began writing a journal to Billy. It was important to her that his memory be kept alive. To this day, she keeps his picture at the family altar. Twice each year, on his birth and death dates, she and Bill went to the ferry from which Billy jumped to leave flowers or pour the Coca-Cola that Billy so enjoyed into the water. There is something about ritualistic behavior that is comforting to Yuri who, for the thirty-four years she lived in New York following Malcolm X's assassination, never missed one pilgrimage to his gravesite.[48]

Today, Yuri wants people to know that Billy was grown and had the right to make his own decisions. In this statement, written in 1996, she defended his choice and inadvertently her own as well: "It's hard to talk about it, and we don't. It's hard for people to understand. Some people think suicide is a cop-out. We don't. It was his choice, tho it hurts us to think about it. He felt he needed to 'liberate' himself. He went through so much. . . . We loved and admired him dearly. He was 28 when he died, but had a very full life; and was very involved in the Movement." Even at the time of Billy's death, Yuri was able to create a liberatory context for her son's life and final act:

> [Billy] raised our humanity by his own suffering. He brought home at the gut-level, humankind's struggle for fulfillment, liberation, and a productive and dignified survival. . . . He felt himself caught in a whirlpool he could not pull out of. He could not see what *we* saw in him: strength, integrity, sensitivity, soulful spirit; a warrior fighting not only a personal battle, but a battle against the evils of society. He did not want to just survive and exist. He wanted this for all others; also never to burden or confine others. He fought hard. He won some battles, and lost some battles. The battle he lost in death was, to him, a triumph that he was in command of his final act. The leap he made was his moment of liberation. He did not *take* his life! He *gave* his life! He *was* and *is* a part of the worldwide struggle raging in many forms throughout this earth.[49]

For Yuri, being able to interpret Billy's life and his death within a political context was important. It was the movement for social justice that helped occupy her time and distract her from her sorrows. Billy's death also served to reinforce Yuri's humanitarian philosophy. "I think all these experiences, especially the tragedies, helped me to grow and my politics to develop," she reflected. "A lot of political people are just on politics and lose a lot of people. Many are so young and have never suffered. You cannot be hard lined; that's why I never take such a hard-line position." Perhaps most significant, the Movement gave Yuri an opportunity to work for something larger than herself that connected her to all of humanity, to work on causes that gave life back to others, and to gain purpose and meaning in her life. Even with a missing person report out on Billy, Yuri maintained her political responsibilities. While distributing leaflets at Harlem establishments, she picked up a phone message at one of the businesses, informing her that Billy's glasses, or possibly it was his crutches, had been located. Bibi Angola, who was with Yuri at the time, recounted: "I'll never forget what Yuri said. She was still so focused on the Movement. Yuri gave me the rest of the flyers and said, 'Bibi, don't forget to leaflet Harlem.'"[50]

It was also helpful to Yuri to see others who, despite suffering tragedies, had not lost their spirit of resistance. Famed Puerto Rican independence leader and political prisoner Lolita Lebron, for example, had lost a son and a daughter under suspicious circumstances while in prison. Knowing this, Yuri gained solace and strength from these words from Lebron in prison: "Receive my profoundest condolescence. Your son liveth in the infinite love and glorious happiness of our Creator. . . . I understand and participate in your pain. I have a son in Heaven. He died on account of the struggle. Imperialism killed him. He was a little boy who said when he becomes a grown man, he would build a house for his mother. He built it: It is a house upon the Rock. I embrace you in these difficult days—courageous as you are and beautiful!" Yuri herself observed: "I don't know what I would've done if I didn't have the Movement. I feel the Movement kept me going and I'm grateful for that."[51]

Following Billy's death, Yuri reduced her activities to devote more time to her family. But even as she ended her Muslim practice in 1975, she found herself caught in the urgency of other issues. Puerto Rican political prisoners represented one such issue. Living in New York City, with its large Puerto Rican population, she had heard about the five

Puerto Rican nationalists incarcerated in U.S. prisons. As she developed a revolutionary analysis of national liberation, she also learned that the United States had colonized Puerto Rico in 1898, as a result of the U.S. victory in the Spanish-American War, and quickly turned Puerto Rico into its economic dependent, with trade between the two countries rising from approximately 15 percent to 85 percent within a short decade. By midcentury, Puerto Rico had become a factory site for U.S. corporations, and Operation Bootstrap attracted labor-intensive, export-oriented U.S. industries through incentives such as tax exemptions, a supply of cheap labor, and a government willing to oblige the demands of the corporations. The United States also sought military interests in Puerto Rico, particularly on the island of Vieques, where the U.S. Navy in 1941 took 26,000 of the island's 33,000 acres and by the 1950s was dropping 3,400 bombs each month. In 1999, in response to the killing of a civilian by a bomb, large-scale, nationwide protest focused international attention on the movement to expel the navy, which continued live bombing practice and nuclear weapons storage on Vieques, despite the presence of more than nine thousand island residents. The resulting toxic wastes and air and water pollution have decimated the local fishing industry and led to health problems, including high rates of cancer. In addition, U.S. policy resulted in the sterilization of 40 percent of Puerto Rican women of childbearing age. As Yuri learned about the history of Puerto Rico, she came to agree with the perspectives of the *independentistas,* as those fighting for Puerto Rican sovereignty were called. She saw U.S. governmental, military, and corporate interests producing impoverishment, political repression, environmental destruction, health hazards, and cultural genocide for the Puerto Rican people.[52]

Yuri would have been moved by stories about the human effects of U.S. policies. Lolita Lebron, a woman she came to revere, described her childhood in the 1920s and 1930s:

> My classmates were very pale, sickly looking children, mostly all barefoot and in rags, with swollen stomachs, skinny bodies, nervous and uneasy. Among the pupils were a few stable, healthy-looking and youthful children. These were the sons and daughters of the landowners. The meals at school were bad, the sanitation horrible, the latrines flooded. . . . Diseases were rampant

among the people. . . . The peons and their families worked long
hours for the landowners. For this they got a few cents. . . . I saw
caskets close to sacks of coffee and of vegetables and fruits—the
produce that the same dead peasants had produced. Yet they died
young because of the lack of proper food, proper human care and
attention. The sight of naked children playing in the mud is heavy
with me.[53]

Lebron responded to those conditions through what most would
consider terrorism. But based on notions of self-determination and various UN resolutions, Yuri contends that the actions of anti-imperialist
revolutionaries in their struggle for national liberation are legally and
morally justified. "I believe in revolutionary nationalism," she declared.
"Those are people who actively believe in armed struggle. And that's
why I support political prisoners and Blacks and Puerto Ricans who
acted out their politics in some way. I agree with their philosophy, but
I myself have never participated in an armed action." She supported
Lebron, who along with Rafael Cancel Miranda, Andres Figueroa
Cordero, and Irving Flores, had entered the House of Representatives
with weapons in 1954 and wounded five members of Congress. She
also defended the actions of Oscar Collazo and Griselio Torresola, who
was killed onsite, when they attacked President Truman's temporary
residence at Blair House in 1950. According to the *independentistas,*
the goal of these armed actions was not to inflict human carnage but
to draw worldwide attention to the devastating effects of U.S. imperialism in Puerto Rico. Yuri reasoned that the *independentistas* would
have preferred nonviolent tactics, but since the U.S. government had
not responded to their peaceful requests, they viewed armed struggle
as a legitimate form of struggle, as sanctioned under international
law. Although highly controversial, *independentistas* and supporters
like Yuri claim that because the U.S. government is responsible for the
conditions of devastation and dependency in Puerto Rico, targeting
the symbols of American imperialism—the president's residence and
Congress—is a legitimate form of resistance, even self-defense, from
a revolutionary perspective. The *independentistas* assert that international law is clear on this point: resisting colonialism is no crime.
Colonialism is the crime.[54]

The *independentistas* gave Yuri strength and courage in her struggles for justice: "Knowing people like Lolita Lebron and Rafael Cancel Miranda—they were our heroes and sheroes. They were fighting for the liberation of their people and warding off U.S. imperialism. They had great leadership. And the spirit of the Puerto Rican people to be free was so strong. We couldn't help but become involved." As Yuri learned more about the Puerto Rican prisoners of war, she began writing to them, particularly Lolita Lebron, the only woman among the five nationalist prisoners and the leader of the 1954 assault on Congress. For years, Lebron had encouraged Yuri to visit her in Alderson women's prison in West Virginia. Though the prison authorized Yuri to be placed on Lebron's visiting list, Yuri never made the visit: "I wanted to see Lolita so badly. But Bill said, 'No, you need to be at home with the kids.' And so I never went." This is one of the ways in the mid-1970s that Yuri relinquished a cherished political goal to appease her family. But it is not clear that, in the midst of Yuri's other activities, her family recognized this sacrifice.[55]

While some Puerto Rican activists in the United States have debated whether their primary struggle should focus on independence for Puerto Rico or on improving local conditions for Puerto Ricans in the United States, Yuri, in accordance with her eclectic radicalism, participated in numerous rallies and events in support of both forms of struggle. One of her earliest actions for Puerto Rican liberation centered on the Young Lords' 1969 takeover of an East Harlem church to provide space for a free breakfast program. Having been transformed from a gang into a revolutionary organization through the influence of Chicago Panther leader Fred Hampton, the Young Lords modeled itself after the Black Panther Party. The group developed a thirteen-point platform delineating their revolutionary nationalist, socialist philosophy and established "serve the people" programs. Based on that philosophy, the struggle for unused church space began.[56]

For her consistent support, Yuri was invited to serve on the board of directors for two Puerto Rican organizations in the mid-1970s. She first worked with the Committee for Puerto Rican Decolonization and then with the Puerto Rican Solidarity Committee, which was associated with the Puerto Rican Socialist Party. But the latter group requested her resignation because of her support for armed struggle, particularly the clandestine armed activities of the FALN (Fuerza Armados de Liberación Nacional, or Armed Forces of National Liberation). Formed in 1974, the FALN assumed responsibility for 120 bombings, inflicting property damage against government facilities, military centers, and U.S. corporations that, in their view, perpetuated colonial conditions. Yuri also supported the actions of the clandestine group Los Macheteros when they expropriated $7 million from a Wells Fargo bank in Hartford, Connecticut, and bombed U.S. military installations in Puerto Rico in the early 1980s. In upholding her belief in self-defense and armed struggle, Yuri left the board of directors of the Puerto Rican Solidarity Committee.[57]

One of Yuri's most memorable experiences was participating in the takeover of the Statue of Liberty to focus attention on the plight of the Puerto Rican prisoners of war. By 1977, the five Puerto Rican nationalists of the 1950s were the longest-held political prisoners in the Western Hemisphere. Had their charges not been of a political nature, they would have been out years earlier, reasoned their supporters. At the time, the average time served for murder was less than nine years, yet the nationalists' principal charge was aggravated assault, which included five wounded but no deaths. In particular, Andres Figueroa Cordero had cancer and the community wanted him released from prison. The Committee to Free the Five Nationalists felt that an audacious, media-catching action was needed to pressure the president to release the nationalists, so they decided to seize the most prominent symbol of liberty and justice. Yuri was one of the few non-Puerto Ricans and the only Asian American invited to participate in this secret mission. Excitement filled her voice as she recalled the events of Tuesday, October 25, 1977:[58]

> We could only tell one person, so I told my daughter Aichi that I may not be coming home that night, that I may be arrested. She was really excited for me. Then early the next morning, we all caught the ferryboat to the Statue of Liberty. We were told not to speak to each other or even look at each other so no one could know we're together. We tried to get to the front of the line, but ahead of us were a bunch of Japanese tourists and all these little kids from a Catholic school. We were told, no matter what, we've got to beat everybody to the statue. We didn't hurt anyone or knock them out of our way, but the young kids had so much energy, so we started running and running to get to the

statue first. When the twenty-nine of us reached the statue, we closed the door.

The young bloods started climbing up the narrow and winding staircase to the top of the statue and hung the Puerto Rican flag on the forehead of the statue, and the other brothers were our internal security. They had to take down the statue's security guards; they didn't hurt them, but took them to another room and maybe handcuffed them. We women moved furniture to block off doors and taped closed windows. The one thing we didn't think about is that we might need food. We could hear the police helicopters overhead and boats coming to the statue and then police landing. I mean, it was exciting! We had planned to give up peacefully when the police came. But we seized the statue for nine hours. We made our point.[59]

Outside the jail where the twenty-nine protesters were taken, some four hundred supporters demonstrated for their release. This arrest was Yuri's second and last to date. All twenty-nine were released on minimal bail the following day. To Yuri, getting arrested and spending the night in jail was, as she exclaimed, "exciting." Taking over the Statue of Liberty symbolized Puerto Rico's control of its own destiny and freedom for the incarcerated nationalists. And those possibilities were exhilarating. Plus, Yuri found her jail stay a learning experience. She recalled that in their group were three White lesbian women who spoke about gay liberation during their detention: "It was good for me to hear about the lesbian movement. Though we knew there were lesbians in the Movement who were strongly committed, we didn't really talk about gay rights back then. These women wanted to be recognized as lesbians." In late 1977, at a time when the women's movement was strong and many were fighting for gay rights, knowledge about gay and lesbian issues was not news to many activists. But, having been influenced by nationalism, Christianity, and Islam, Yuri was a latecomer, though an open-minded one, to these issues.[60]

How did the Kochiyama family react to her arrest? In anticipating Bill's irritation with her for risking her safety and provoking arrest, Yuri recounted: "Aichi told Daddy that I had been arrested, but he wasn't angry or anything. I guess he felt, 'Well, that's Mom. If she thought it was important, she'll do it.' And they had a nice meal ready for me when I came home." This statement is revealing of how Yuri and Bill resolved, in part, their marital discord. It seems that by the late 1970s, he had come to tolerate, at least to a degree, her stubbornness. But more than mere tolerance, it is likely that, himself a seasoned activist by then, Bill vicariously participated through Yuri in the excitement of the seizure of the Statue of Liberty, even if he preferred her noninvolvement. It is also possible that Bill saw this as an effective strategy. Having garnered media coverage from the *New York Times* to the *San Francisco Chronicle,* the image of the Puerto Rican flag draped across Ms. Liberty's forehead imprinted Puerto Rico on the minds of the American public. Yuri believes that their siege contributed to the worldwide grassroots pressure exerted on the White House, which released Andres Figueroa Cordero in 1978 and granted unconditional clemency to the remaining four Puerto Rican prisoners of war the following year.[61]

The release of the *independentistas* was just one of the victories of the political prisoner movement that year. FALN leader William Guillermo Morales and Black revolutionary Assata Shakur separately achieved audacious prison escapes, in New York and New Jersey, respectively. "[W]ho could forget the incredible escape by William Morales from the Bellevue Hospital prison ward in 1979?" exclaimed Yuri. "He baffled the police, the hospital security, and even the movement folks. The daring act was indeed a triumphant feat—in the fact that Morales had one hand blown off and only one finger on the other hand." At Bellevue, where he was being fitted for artificial hands after a bomb he was making exploded, someone slipped Morales wire clippers and "[he] cut a hole in a window screen . . . and—somehow— used elastic bandages to lower himself 40 feet to freedom," explained the *New York Daily News.* Morales, already the FBI's most-wanted terrorist, became a folk hero in segments of the Latino community. But even before then, Yuri had written letters of support to Morales after his arrest. Morales's then wife, Dylcia Pagán, noted that it was a courageous act to write to him during a period when many were frightened by the terrorist label and FBI harassment. But to Yuri, the act did not involve courage; it was simply the right thing to do. "These things could happen," she said referring to her own World War II experiences, "when there is no support; when no one even knows what is happening; and when people are afraid to even know you because they might be found guilty by association. . . . If we don't support one another, and stand by one another, it will be easy for those in power to pick off one group at a time, as they have done so successfully in the past." She continued to write to Morales during his imprisonment in Mexico in the mid-1980s, and to the present, during his exile in Cuba. Morales wrote back: "Every time I receive letters from comrades I feel stimulated to keep on and never give up. Yuri, stay strong. You've done a lot for the struggle and I thank you very much."[62]

Assata Shakur's (JoAnne Chesimard) experiences growing up poor, Black, and female, compellingly described in her autobiography, propelled her into the Black Panther Party in Harlem and later into the clandestine Black Liberation Army (BLA). As early as 1971, explained attorney Lennox Hinds, the FBI sought to neutralize Shakur. Former Deputy Police Commissioner Daley described her as "the mother hen who kept them together, kept them moving, kept them shooting." She was on the FBI's Most Wanted List, a shoot-to-kill target, for alleged bank robberies for which she was later acquitted. In 1973, while living underground as part of the BLA, Shakur and two comrades were stopped on the New Jersey Turnpike. Gunfire ensued. Zayd Malik Shakur (James F. Costan Jr.) and a state trooper were killed; Shakur and another trooper were wounded. Panther 21 defendant Sundiata Acoli (Clark Squire) escaped but was captured a couple of days later. As political prisoners, Shakur and Acoli were treated with unusual harshness. The police beat Shakur, already shot and bleeding, at the scene of the crime and again at the hospital. Acoli was confined in a cell specifically designed to break prisoners, which according to the Society for the Prevention of Cruelty to Animals is smaller than the space required for a ninety-pound German shepherd dog. Both were convicted of murder and given life sentences, despite questionable evidence, including the lack of gun residue on Shakur's fingers. In 1979, members of the Black Liberation Army helped Shakur escape from prison and she now lives in exile in Cuba. After more than thirty years in prison, Acoli is among the longest-held U.S. political prisoners.[63]

Yuri's first extended conversation with Shakur occurred during a visit at Rikers Island—their only prison visit. Yuri came away captivated by Shakur's physical and spiritual presence: "When I finally saw her in prison, she is such an awesome person. I mean, she is charismatic! She was the only woman in the men's prison, the only prisoner kept in that whole building, and when she came out, she was dressed beautifully, almost like a Black queen. She was almost floating in air. At the same time, she was so down-to-earth, so genuine. To me, she's like the female Malcolm, or the female Mumia [Abu-Jamal]." Equating someone with Malcolm X is the highest honor Yuri could bestow. But the admiration is not just one-way. In a 1997 speech before an international feminist brigade to Cuba, for example, Shakur praised Yuri for her tremendous contributions to the political prisoner movement. Yuri has seen Shakur only one more time, when Yuri visited Cuba with the Venceremos Brigade in 1988. But despite the difficulties in communication with Cuba, Yuri writes letters and on rare occasions speaks to Shakur by telephone. She also continues to defend Shakur, for example, in the latest rounds of efforts to extradite her to the United States.[64]

On the heels of these Movement triumphs, the U.S. government arrested eleven FALN activists in 1980 for gun possession and the political charge of seditious conspiracy. Their sentences, ranging from 35 to 105 years, were unusually lengthy when, as attorney Jan Susler reported, "the national average sentence for convicted violent felons was less than eight years." Over the next couple of years, the government arrested more FALN and Los Macheteros activists. Since their arrests, Yuri has supported the fifteen or so Puerto Rican POWs held in U.S. prisons. One of these POWs, Dylcia Pagán, whose life is captured in the documentary video *The Double Life of Ernesto Gomez Gomez*, first met Yuri around 1970 while doing support work for the Panther 21. Since then, Pagán, a fellow New Yorker, remembered seeing Yuri at "just about every major demonstration for Puerto Rican independence." After nineteen years in prison, Pagán and ten other *independentistas* left prison on September 10, 1999. Yuri, along with other supporters, believes that the growing campaign to free the Puerto Rican POWs, in conjunction with the unprecedented massive protests to remove the U.S. military from Vieques, influenced President Bill Clinton's decision to grant clemency. The liberation of the Puerto Rican POWs, along with the release of White anti-imperialist Laura Whitehorn and the transfer of political prisoner Silvia Baraldini to an Italian prison—all in 1999—lifted Yuri's spirits as she battled against physical illness and depression.[65]

Over the decades, Yuri's letters have inspired numerous political prisoners. Geronimo ji Jaga expressed his gratitude by calling Yuri on his first day of "freedom" in 1997. Mtayari Shabaka Sundiata, head of the Brooklyn RNA consulate when Yuri joined and Black Liberation Army member, told Yuri, in a 1975 letter from prison: "After visiting with you Sunday, I felt so good knowing that someone beyond this cement grave knows that I am alive and very much a part of the movement for a better life for all oppressed people. You know Yuri, if it wasn't for you I really don't know what I would do. You are the only person on the outside that I have any contact with. Everyone else seems to have considered me legally dead." These words from a Black movement leader must have saddened Yuri and help explain her motivation for supporting political prisoners, despite her family's objections to this time-consuming activity. Pagán observed: "Yuri has never, never forgotten any member of the Black Liberation Army, any member of the Black Panther Party, that's inside. We're talking twenty, twenty-five, thirty years. That's why in her [semiannual] political prisoner updates she mentions people that others have forgotten about. This shows that she isn't doing opportunistic work. She's been there in the thick and thin supporting all these people for the past thirty years." Today, almost twenty years after the police killed Sundiata, Yuri continues to keep his name and vision alive through her words, such as in an article written for her column in *Nation Time: The Voice of the New Afrikan Liberation Front*. Yuri is not one to forget a person, be it her son Billy, her mentor Malcolm X, or a comrade like Sundiata. Pagán proclaimed: "I have the utmost admiration for Yuri. She is the most incessant activist I've ever met."[66]

8

Asian Americans and the Rise of a New Movement

When the Asian American Movement emerged in the late 1960s, Yuri became a mentor to the youth who predominated this nascent formation. Simultaneously, the Asian American Movement enabled Yuri to rise to the stature of political leader and passionate speaker in ways she could not have in the Black struggle. This movement began to coalesce when Asian American activists united in the late 1960s to protest the Vietnam War, to fight for educational transformation, and to create a political and pan-Asian identity, among other issues.[1]

Few people protested U.S. intervention in Vietnam before the August 1964 Gulf of Tonkin incident. While Yuri was not one of the earliest war protesters, she had agreed with Malcolm X's analysis, expressed at the Kochiyamas' home in June 1964: "The struggle of the Vietnamese is the struggle of all Third World people. It's the struggle against imperialism, colonialism, and neo-colonialism." The antiwar movement accelerated the following year in response to the start of massive, sustained U.S. bombings in Operation Rolling Thunder. A couple of months later, some twenty thousand marchers participated in the first nationwide antiwar demonstration in Washington, D.C. By 1967, hundreds of thousands were attending antiwar rallies in New York, Washington, and elsewhere. And by 1969, a million people attended one antiwar march and millions more participated in the antiwar moratorium. The opposition to the war soon grew into one of the most multifaceted and largest social movements in U.S. history; people of all races, students, workers, youth, elderly, clergy and nuns, intellectuals, and even soldiers and veterans protested American in-

234

volvement in Vietnam. New York City was a hotbed of antiwar protest, and Yuri soon began attending numerous marches and demonstrations there, as well as in Washington, D.C., a five-hour bus ride from Harlem. She also supported the acts of civil disobedience, including burning draft cards and refusing induction into the military, that landed many political activists in prison.[2]

Activists protested the war for a variety of reasons, from saving American soldiers' lives to condemning the violence of war to supporting self-determination for the Vietnamese. Lacking an antiracist program, racism crept into the antiwar movement. After SNCC leader Stokely Carmichael (Kwame Ture) appeared at an antiwar press conference in New York City, for example, an old-line pacifist remarked, "Being linked to the civil rights movement would hurt the infant antiwar movement: the American people might accept peace in Vietnam but they would never accept racial equality." But, activists of color challenged the racism within the movement, as did some radical Whites who pushed for an expansive antiwar movement that included racial minorities as well as communists. Yuri and other New Yorkers in Asian Americans for Action (AAA, pronounced Triple A) situated the war in terms of U.S. imperialist interests. The Los Angeles Asian Coalition echoed AAA's analysis in a 1973 *Gidra* article: "In Vietnam, corporations are financing a war to create new markets and develop a cheap labor force, at the expense of democratic rights of Vietnamese people. The war is a racist, genocidal war that reflects US foreign policy toward Asian countries." Black activists denounced the hypocrisy of the United States for fighting for freedom and democracy abroad while ignoring inequalities at home. Young Black people in McComb, Mississippi, for example, distributed a leaflet in 1965 stating, "No Mississippi Negroes should be fighting in Viet Nam for the White man's freedom, until all the Negro People are free in Mississippi." Black people in Harlem and elsewhere protested the war with placards reading, "No Viet Cong Ever Called Me Nigger." Chicanos held the largest antiwar demonstration in Los Angeles on August 29, 1970, as part of the Chicano Moratorium. Like others around the country, this peaceful demonstration was marked by police brutality, which in this case resulted in three deaths, including that of *Los Angeles Times* reporter Rubén Salazar.[3]

Yuri was also drawing connections between local and international issues. In a 1969 antiwar speech, she proclaimed, "What the United States is doing to the people of the Third World is exactly what the Establishment is doing to Harlem right now." And the Los Angeles Asian Coalition further observed: "In our communities redevelopment is taking place within Little Tokyo. . . . L'il Tokyo will no longer be a place for our community to come back to, but will be turned into a mere tourist trap." This focus on racism at home contrasted with the liberal and predominantly White community's call to "Bring the Boys Home," which essentially meant saving White American lives and helped transform that struggle. The Antiwar Movement was no longer focused solely on saving American lives; it was also about ending imperialism and racism in the United States and abroad.[4]

Yuri's participation in the antiwar movement came largely through the newly formed Asian Americans for Action. Established in 1969, AAA was the first pan-Asian community organization in New York. The panethnic identity embraced by AAA contrasted sharply with the ethnic disassociation characterizing earlier Asian American intergroup relations.[5] AAA was also unique in its multigenerational membership, particularly at a time when youth dominated most pan-Asian grassroots organizations. Two Nisei women with long histories of radical activism conceived AAA over lunch on a park bench. Kazu Iijima and Minn Matsuda were among the Japanese Americans suspended from the Communist Party USA during World War II.[6] They were also active with the progressive Japanese American group, Oakland Young Democratic Club, one of the very few Nisei organizations to protest the incarceration of Japanese Americans.[7] Iijima and Matsuda recruited Asians at antiwar meetings and rallies to attend the first AAA meeting. Iijima recounted, "We'd pounce on any Asian we saw at these events—and some were taken aback, let me tell you, by the sight of two little old ladies babbling about the formation of an Asian organization and requesting their names and addresses." About a dozen people, including a few Nisei, gathered for that first meeting at Iijima's apartment in April 1969. Yuri was not there, but she became active soon after. The majority in attendance were young Chinese American college students from Columbia University and City College of New York, who had been politicized by the radical Black Power and New Left movements. Iijima and Matsuda had initially envisioned a social or cultural group, but were pleased that those at the meeting wanted a political formation. This was actually predictable given that they had enlisted antiwar activists and the period was one of vigorous political activity. AAA became guided by a radical ideology opposed to racism, capitalism, and imperialism and focused heavily on opposing the Vietnam War. To stress the primacy of practice, members named the group Asian Americans for Action.[8]

After deciding its political focus, AAA began forming Asian American contingents to march in New York antiwar demonstrations and to travel to Washington, D.C., rallies, creating the first visible Asian American presence at these East Coast gatherings. Yuri recalled: "The first time we Asian Americans organized for a march against the war, only twenty or thirty people came out. But at every march, we asked every Asian we saw if they wanted to march in an Asian contingent. We kept increasing the numbers, till twice in New York there were two hundred of us, and at one march in D.C., we hit four hundred strong." This was on the East Coast with its relatively small Asian American population. Yuri added: "We didn't just march; we organized so our presence was noticeable. We all wore red headbands, carried bright yellow banners that fluttered conspicuously in the wind, and we marched proud." They also wrote leaflets, written with Asian American concerns in mind, which they distributed as they marched.[9]

In this way, AAA members met other Asian individuals and groups opposed to the war, including Vietnamese, Koreans, and Filipinos. Also, "we met Kampucheans [Cambodians] and found out they had their own group, GKRAM, Group of Kampuchean Residents in America. The only group we never met were Laotians," noted Yuri. By 1971, AAA helped form the Asian Coalition Against the Vietnam War to bring together various Asian groups and individuals, including many students from City College of New York or Columbia University's Asian American Political Alliance (AAPA), to organize major demonstrations and educational forums. Toward this end, AAA members met every Friday night from eight o'clock to past midnight, as well as several times a week, to organize actions and have political education sessions. During this period in the early 1970s, Yuri was active in AAA, but not in the core leadership because of her simultaneous commitments with the National Committee to Defend Political Prisoners, the Republic of New Africa, her Muslim practice, and her family and work. Her main contributions to AAA combined her strengths as communicator and networker: writing articles for the AAA newsletter; giving speeches against U.S. aggression into Vietnam, Cambodia, and Laos; creating artistic leaflets and signs; encouraging new people to attend meetings and demonstrations; and creating alliances among individuals and groups.[10]

Yuri admired the exceptionally democratic way in which AAA operated. The group collectively discussed the points and analysis to be included in a position paper on, for example, an anti-imperialist analysis of the Vietnam War. Although this led to many heated arguments, Yuri believes the process of clarifying ideas was good, as was the experience of engaging in debate, especially for the typically nonconfrontational Nisei. Following the discussion and vote, selected people would write the leaflet based on the majority position and, after review by the group, AAA would print and distribute the material. Many of their position papers were printed in the AAA newsletter. The first issue, published in June 1969, included AAA's positions on various issues: the Vietnam War (immediate withdrawal of troops, support for Vietnamese self-determination); Black liberation struggle; U.S. foreign policy (economically motivated, imperialistic); U.S. domestic policy (no benefit to poor or minorities); the draft (support refusal to comply); and labor (unjust economic system, racism in unions, need for international labor movement). This issue also contained a statement by AAA: "We recognize that this country is racist and that there are contradictions within the society which are responsible for the problems of Asian-Americans. We feel that it is our responsibility to effect changes in this situation. We have united to establish a political voice for the Asian community and a means for group action. We invite other Asians to join us."[11]

Yuri was drawn to AAA for several reasons. Already deeply committed to revolutionary politics, she was attracted to the anti-imperialist and antiracist program of AAA. In a youth-dominated Movement, she also enjoyed working with and learning from older activists, those close to her age like Kazu Iijima but with years more political experience. This was also the first time Yuri was working with substantial numbers of Asian American activists; the same was true for other East Coast Asian Americans. Most significantly, AAA as well as the emerging Asian American Movement gave Yuri an opportunity to work on issues affecting Japanese and Asian Americans and to make linkages between Asian and Black issues.

The advent of the Asian American Movement in the late 1960s enabled Yuri to rise to the stature of political leader and mentor. Young Asian American activists, eager to find their own role models, sought out Yuri, who was already recognized as a writer, speaker, organizer, and dedicated activist in New York and whose reputation stemmed largely from her connections with Malcolm X and the revolutionary Black movement. Through these young activists, Yuri's prominence spread throughout the nation, particularly to San Francisco and Los Angeles, the hot spots of the West Coast movement. When Asian American activists, most of whom were students and youth, traveled to New York, they stayed with the Kochiyamas. And when Yuri was in California to visit her family, Asian American activists would invite her to speak at their events. Japanese American activist Greg Morozumi remembered meeting Yuri when she was visiting her sons Jimmy and Tommy in Los Angeles. When I Wor Kuen, the first national Asian American revolutionary organization, was trying to establish a Third World student coalition at Los Angeles City College, Yuri's sons took her to a house meeting where she talked about the need for Third World unity. Morozumi observed: "Yuri's reputation came from being active in the Black liberation movement. Since the Black liberation movement had such an influence on the Asian Movement, I've always admired her for being such a strong advocate of Third World solidarity. . . . She had a firm identification with people of color in this country and their historically oppressed relationship with the political system, especially in the course of social change. She was not only knowledgeable, but experienced in organizing for change in very practical ways."[12]

Chinese American activist Steve Yip first heard about Yuri in 1969 in his first term at UC Berkeley. He attended a party in San Francisco's Japanese-town for Billy Kochiyama, who was visiting, but he did not know the honoree. A friend admonished: "Whaddaya mean you haven't heard of the Kochiyama family? They're one of the baddest radical Asian American families around!" Yip found out later that "the mother . . . was truly the shining example of what the name Kochiyama really represented." Around the same time, UC Berkeley's Asian American Political Alliance thought Yuri's article on Robert Williams's return from exile, originally published in the AAA newsletter, was important enough to reprint in their newspaper. Yip had the job of retyping the article. In that piece, Yuri not only detailed

Williams's activities and significance but also emphasized his connectedness with Asian peoples. During his exile in China and Vietnam, Williams motivated Mao Tse-tung to publicly support the Black struggle in the United States and he also helped Black people to better understand the Chinese revolution; he refused to denounce Ho Chi Minh in exchange for a chance to return to the United States; and a biography of Williams was published in Japan. Over the next year or two, Yip remembered hearing Chinese American activist Steve Louie tell stories about meeting many Black radicals at Yuri's place. So when Yuri came to speak at UC Berkeley, Yip was excited to meet this woman who was already becoming an Asian American shero.[13]

As a writer and Movement journalist, Yuri made regular contributions to the AAA newsletter, which first appeared in June 1969, followed by twenty-six more issues over the next seven years of AAA's existence. The Kochiyamas' home served as the newsletter contact address from October 1970 until February 1973, when the newly opened United Asian Communities Center became AAA's home base. Yuri's first newsletter article, her Hiroshima-Nagasaki Week speech, was published in October 1969 in the third issue of the AAA newsletter. Her last newsletter article, on Japanese wives of Korean repatriates, was published in the January–February 1975 issue. In between, she wrote thirteen articles ranging from the efforts to save the I-Hotel from gentrification to the political prisoner movement—a testament to her breadth of knowledge and multi-issue focus.[14]

When Yuri communicates about any social issue—whether it be in a published article, in a speech to hundreds of people, or one-on-one with college or high school students—she provides vivid, detailed, well-researched information from a radical perspective. When teaching about social issues, she often imports information that many have never heard. She also humanizes the politics by telling stories and discussing key people in a movement. Her knowledge and humanizing quality, coupled with the passion of her commitment, inspire the audiences about social justice struggles. At a 1993 March on Washington rally, Yuri relayed: "Historically, Asians from many parts of Asia came to this country and contributed to the struggle for a more humane society. . . . There was Sokkom Hing, a Kampuchean [Cambodian], who was a key spokesperson for Asian Americans during the Vietnam War. He went home to Kampuchea because he wanted to rebuild his country after the war ended, but was killed during the awesome, frightening aftermath there. These are Asians who gave totally of themselves, who inspired us with their commitment and dedication because they wanted to bring about a better world for all." Yuri acquired this little-known information, not from reading, but because she was on the ground working with activists from different movements. In 1996, she told an Asian American Studies class at the University of California in Santa Barbara:

> The heroes of Vietnam became our heroes. I hope you've heard about Van Troi. He was a twenty-three-year-old Vietnamese who tried to assassinate a top American official [Secretary of Defense Robert McNamara] because of all the atrocities the American government committed against the Vietnamese people. But he was caught and executed, and the whole world sent their top reporters to take pictures of that execution. To those of us fighting oppression, Van Troi became a hero. Within six months, somebody wrote a story of his life, which was banned in the U.S., so many of us traveled to Canada to get the book. Many Movement people named their children after him. And in Los Angeles, they organized the Van Troi Brigade.[15]

By the late 1960s, Yuri's speeches reflected her now solid commitment to radical politics. At the same time, the antiwar movement motivated her to study the history of Vietnam and thereby deepened her understanding of imperialism in the Southeast Asian context. In a 1969 speech, for example, she asserted that the U.S. government's motives for invading Vietnam were largely economic, in contrast to the official line about promoting democracy:

> Vietnam became a lush prize to Western powers because of its many natural resources: tin, rubber, oil, rice, coal, tungsten, gold, sugar cane, tea, coffee, tobacco, and even citrus fruits. . . . On August 4, 1953, President Eisenhower made the following remarks at a Governors' Conference: If Indo-China goes . . . the tin and tungsten that we so greatly value from that area would cease coming. So when the U.S. votes $400,000,000 to help that war, we are not voting a give-away program. We are voting for the cheapest way that we can, to prevent the occurrence of

something that would be of a most terrible significance to the U.S.A., our security, our power and ability to get certain things we need from the riches of the Indo-Chinese territory and Southeast Asia. And that is the crux of the war in Vietnam.[16]

AAA connected American imperialist incursions into Vietnam with, in its analysis, the U.S. government's plan to politically, militarily, and economically dominate the Pacific Rim. Yuri's November 1969 speech, "Imperialism and the Pacific Rim," reflected these ideas. So in the midst of an intensive campaign against the Vietnam War, Yuri and others in AAA simultaneously protested U.S. imperialist practices in Okinawa, Cambodian, Laos, and other Asian and Pacific Island countries. Yuri, like other antimilitarist Japanese in the United States and Japan, used their condemnation of the nuclear bombings of Hiroshima and Nagasaki to draw parallels with similar atrocities committed against other peoples. This is a common theme in Yuri's Hiroshima Day speeches, delivered annually from 1965 to 1971 and intermittently into the 1990s:

There are many, many Hiroshimas and Nagasakis in modern history—from the kidnapping and enslavement of Africans where untold millions died in the middle passage, the Nanking massacre that took the lives of more people then Hiroshima and Nagasaki combined; the genocide of six million Jews during World War II; the slaughter of two million Kampucheans during the mid-1970s.

Echoing Malcolm X's words when he spoke to Japanese *hibakusha* in her home years earlier, Yuri also saw continuity between the bombs dropped by military aircraft and the bombs of racism and impoverishment:

The violence that befell Hiroshima has fallen time and time again on Asians and other Third World Peoples. Violence means violating humanity, so it comes in all forms; not just in bombs, interrogation by torture, the razing of villages, or incarceration in tiger cages. Sometimes, it is the simple denial of basic rights, the denigration of a heritage, the distortion of history, the super[f]luousness of Madison Avenue commodities; the meagerness of famined lands; the negligence of medical aid to the poor, the old, the mentally maimed; the brutalizing of certain ethnic people; the duality and ambiguity of law and order; the gentlemen's agreement of no jobs and housing; the empty, demeaning lives of those on the periphery of society.[17]

Yuri was particularly drawn to the struggle to remove American military bases from Okinawa, including the repeal of the U.S.–Japan Security Treaty. This treaty, signed in 1952 at the end of the formal U.S. occupation of Japan, authorized the United States to maintain land, air, and sea forces in and about Japan and its territory of Okinawa. Located south of Japan, north of Taiwan, and east of China, Okinawa in particular is strategically positioned to deploy troops to defend U.S. geopolitical interests in East Asia, the Philippines, and the Middle East. As Yuri stated in a 1969 speech: "The bases set up on Okinawa are invasion bases to Asian countries (especially Vietnam, Cambodia, Laos, Thailand, and Korea), to attack, supply military arms and ammunitions, and to transport supplies, and to train and entertain U.S. soldiers. The control of Okinawa is an important role for the U.S. to continue containment tactics on the People's Republic of China and to have Japanese militarism revived with atomic weapons." Okinawa has also functioned as a buffer to protect Japan from foreign invasions. In the notorious three-month Battle of Okinawa, in which one-quarter of its population was killed by American troops, some argue that Japan used Okinawa as a sacrificial lamb to gain time at the end of World War II to defend against a U.S. invasion. So in the interest of both American and Japanese military, the tiny island of Okinawa, making up less than 1 percent of Japan's land base, houses 75 percent of U.S. bases in Japan.[18]

Yuri, in speaking on behalf of AAA at New York's 1969 Hiroshima–Nagasaki Week events, made the following three demands: "The immediate removal of all U.S. forces and all nuclear and chemical weapons from Okinawa, the immediate and unconditional reversion of Okinawa to Japan, and the end of the U.S.–Japan Security Treaty." One might question why Yuri, an outspoken opponent of imperialism—in its U.S., European, and Japanese contexts alike—would support Japanese control of Okinawa. In line with her belief in self-determination—"Just as Africa must be for Africans, Asia must be for Asians," she said in that speech—she would have wanted to promote the demands of Okinawan activists and the leading Japanese trade unions, socialists, and peace activists whom she had encountered in their meetings with AAA. Given the atrocities committed against the Okinawan people by American military troops, the reversion to Japan may well have been a strategic demand, one that was attainable, though not ideal. But these advocates clearly recognized problems with Japanese rule, making the end to anti-Okinawan discrimination one of their objectives.[19]

But the following year, after the U.S.–Japan Security Treaty was renewed under conditions denounced by Okinawan and Japanese antiwar activists, Yuri's Hiroshima–Nagasaki Week speech contained a more critical view of Japan's role in Okinawa: "The U.S.–Japan Security Treaty that was recently resumed is really the combining of American military might and Japanese economic power to rule a vast Pacific empire. The . . . original treaty was simply a base-leasing security, but it has been growing into a blueprint for the U.S. domination of Asia. . . . And now, the United States is encouraging Japan to the kind of rearmament wherein Japan will be used to cooperate in the U.S.'s strategic plans for Asian containment. This will deny the Japanese people's desire to live up to its peace constitution, which renounced wars to settle international disputes." Although they lost this campaign, Yuri and others in AAA challenged American hegemony and in doing so, raised the consciousness of those around them while deepening their own opposition to imperialism. And into the 1990s, Yuri would continue to speak out against Japanese militarism, strongly denouncing war crimes against the so-called comfort women who were kidnapped and held in sexual slavery during World War II and opposing Japan's membership in the UN Security Council based on that country's history of human rights violations throughout Asia, among other issues.[20]

As Asian American antiwar activists made connections between imperialism abroad and racism at home, they focused their attention on self-determination in their own communities. One such struggle, a major focus of the early Asian American Movement, centered on the educational system. In 1960, the California Master Plan for Higher Education created a three-tier college system, placing students on professional or vocational tracks. Predictably enough, people of color and poor students were routed to the lowest tier, the community college system. At San Francisco State College, for example, the enrollment of

African Americans dropped from an estimated 11 percent in 1960 to 3.6 percent in 1968. This raised the alarm of a widening gap between rich and poor and between Black and White. Progressive students, along with faculty and community supporters, waged a struggle over the scope, purpose, and function of public education. Key to this struggle was the fight to establish ethnic studies programs as a means for transforming the curriculum to include the histories of under-represented groups as well as a community service focus, rather than corporate training. At San Francisco State College, an unprecedented five-month student strike, beginning in November 1968, led to the formation of the first ethnic studies program in the nation. The establishment of Asian American and ethnic studies programs at other colleges quickly followed, including an Asian studies program at City College of New York (CCNY) in 1969.[21]

Despite this development, CCNY students were indignant that the Asian studies curriculum lacked community-oriented and Asian *American*–centered courses and asserted that the college administration blocked their efforts for educational transformation. In 1972, Concerned Asian Students at CCNY staged a three-day takeover of Goethals Hall, which housed the Asian studies department, to force the administration to meet their demands for a relevant education and greater student participation in departmental policy-making decisions. Some three hundred students, including Black and Puerto Rican students and Asian Americans from other campuses and community organizations, joined the takeover. When asked by the students, community members from AAA provided food and other supplies, and some members, including Yuri, spoke at their rallies. Yuri expressed to CCNY students: "[AAA has] watched the past several years' development of the Asian studies at City College with keen interest. For the kind of progressive ideas you began with, we felt you would run into trouble. For ironically, and not so strangely, self-determination and self-reliance are something that those in power historically try to keep limited and suppressed." She then encouraged students to maintain the original focus of community service: "Ethnic studies is an important vehicle. It can become a creative, action-oriented, dynamic apparatus for the community, or a stilted, ivory towered institution." The activists succeeded in winning a new department chair, four new faculty positions, a counselor, and a community liaison.[22]

CCNY then needed to find instructors for their Asian American studies courses. That Yuri, who had no formal teaching experience or advanced educational degrees, was among the first people invited to teach a course was a testament to her already prominent stature as a political activist. In her course titled "Social Science Approach to Asia," Yuri taught about the Vietnam War, the movement to remove U.S. bases in Okinawa, the imposition of martial law in the Philippines, and other issues that affected Asians in the United States and throughout the world. She also encouraged her multiracial group of students to build a connection with the community. After the first year, teachers with university-approved academic degrees were hired.[23]

Simultaneous with its support for Asian American studies at CCNY, AAA worked to establish a pan-Asian center to counter the isolation Asians experienced in New York. Yuri's husband, Bill, was elected chair of the Ad Hoc Committee for an Asian Center, comprised primarily of AAA members. After eleven months of planning, the United Asian Communities Center opened its doors in December 1972, with ambitious plans for multipurpose, multiservice programs, including tutoring, counseling, English as a second language programs; cultural and recreational activities; tax and visa information workshops; a daycare center; and a multilingual informational hotline. It was no easy task to raise funds to cover rent, utilities, and services, but managed by Bill and assisted by Kazu Iijima's husband, Tak, the center survived for several years, becoming a nucleus of activity for several Asian American groups, who held regular meetings and events there, as did other ethnic organizations. Kazu Iijima recounted: "It was a humble but incredibly lively and spirited place. . . . There were two floors . . . 250 people would cram in it for parties, and it was used every single night including the weekends."[24]

The center played an important role in the lives of Yuri and Bill's children, who were among the few Asians in Harlem. Even as the Kochiyama children developed close friendships with Black and Puerto Rican children in their neighborhood, at school, and through their extended family via Audee's and Aichi's marriages, they faced regular racial harassment, mainly from other children. The younger Kochiyamas, to a much greater degree than their older siblings, felt the brunt of racial hostility, perhaps because by the mid-1960s, Black nationalism, including its narrow chauvinist variant, was prominent. Tommy, for example, grew up with several close Black and Puerto Rican friends, but also faced hostility as early as second or third grade: "Literally a day wouldn't go by without hearing 'Chink' or some other racist remarks." For Tommy, these racial assaults were made more difficult by his mother's defense of Black people, which on occasion came at the family's expense:

> I remember this one incident when I was about eleven. I was at the train station on 125th [and Broadway, a couple of blocks from the Kochiyamas' home]. I had to call home for something when a couple of [Black] guys started yelling at me, "Ching Chong." Yuri picked up the phone and she could hear them. They were outside the phone booth, talking shit and shaking the booth. As soon as I opened the door, fists were flying. We fought down several flights of stairs and to the corner of the block. I crossed the street and for whatever reason they didn't pursue me. Luckily no one really got hurt. When I got home and told my mom what happened she asked, "Why did you fight back?" She seemed upset that I defended myself. Then she tried to explain why Blacks were angry at Japanese and that I should try to be understanding toward these guys that attacked me. I don't know what she would've wanted me to do, but it pissed me off. We were raised to believe that it was wrong for anybody to be disrespectful of anyone else and to believe as Malcolm taught, that people should defend themselves when attacked and not turn the other cheek. I felt she wasn't being supportive of me and my right to defend myself.[25]

This story was difficult for Yuri to hear, perhaps because it challenged the image of herself as a "good mother." She does not remember this incident or Tommy discussing it with her years later. She also does not recall ever telling her children not to defend themselves. But she thinks she may have asked Tommy and her other children to try to empathize with the plight of Black people. Yet, Tommy, and others as well, recall Yuri defending Black people so forcefully that at times it became difficult to reconcile this with their own identity as Asian Americans. But Tommy is quick to add, "I know if this were to happen today, she would be completely supportive and would never justify racism coming from anyone."[26]

Within the overall environment of American racism, it is hardly surprising that the Kochiyama children internalized, to varying degrees, negative racialized images of their group. But unlike most Asian Americans who are mainly affected by the system of White supremacy, the Kochiyama children grew up in a dual racial paradigm that privileged both White and Black people and rendered Asians invisible. Although the Black community, unlike White society, does not hold structural power nationally to control politics, economics, media, education, and other social institutions, within certain local circles, the Black Power Movement asserted racial pride and power. Tommy recalled: "On the street and at home, what I saw was a positive image of Black people. Strong, beautiful, and cool were synonymous with Black. Never were those adjectives used when it came to things Asian. I thought Asians were weak and unattractive. During those years I wished I was Black."[27]

The Kochiyama children, especially the three youngest, coped with being among the few Asian Americans in New York by finding respite in unusually supportive siblings. They also developed a positive ethnic identity by participating in the budding Asian American Movement. Eddie recalled: "All my best friends were Black and Puerto Rican. I didn't know any Asians outside of softball, but they weren't political. Then in the late 1960s, these two Sansei brothers—Nick Nagatani and Scott Shimabukuro—who were visiting New York asked me to go to LA with them. I spent the whole summer in J-town with all these strong, proud Asian activists. It was great. I felt really proud to be Asian." In New York, Eddie joined an Asian American multiservice center, Chickens Come Home to Roost, which started when activists took over an abandoned storefront. There, Jimmy and Tommy learned about the history of strong Asians and Asian Americans, in part through stories told by Bun Yoshikami, and gained pride in being Asian. The youngest three also went to the United Asian Communities Center, managed by their father, where they played Ping-Pong and hung out with other Asian Americans.[28]

As teenagers, Jimmy and Tommy also visited the Asian American enclave in Los Angeles, but unlike Eddie, they ended up living there permanently. The two youngest Kochiyama children had been fairly unhappy living in New York, where they felt out of place in their own neighborhood. So when they had the chance to hang out in an Asian

American community in California, they jumped. That opportunity came in the summer of 1974 when two Yellow Brotherhood activists visited the Kochiyamas during their cross-country travels. That the Kochiyama children had a chance to meet West Coast Asian American activists was not unusual. Because of Yuri's prominence as a Movement leader, many young, politicized Asian Americans came to New York specifically to meet her or made it a point to visit her while in the city. While visiting, Victor Shibata and Gary Fujimoto invited Jimmy and Tommy to go to Los Angeles to participate in a summer job program sponsored by Yellow Brotherhood, a group formed in 1969 to organize Asian American youth battling drug abuse and school dropout. Yuri recalled: "Victor Shibata asked Jimmy and Tommy if they wanted to go on a Jeep ride. I didn't know he meant to California. But when I found out, I said, 'No, they're too young.' But they were so excited, and the older kids said to let them go." At a time when the Kochiyamas were practicing communal living, Yuri conceded. Jimmy described the impact of this experience on his ethnic identity: "When we got to Los Angeles, we really liked it. We were hanging out in this Asian American community. It was in the Jefferson-Crenshaw area, so there were lots of Blacks and Asians. It was like wow! to see all these proud Asians. I felt proud to be Asian. It was a really good experience and I decided to stay." At the end of the summer, seventeen-year-old Jimmy called his parents to inform them of his decision. In Los Angeles, he lived in a house with several Asian American activists, including Warren Furutani, who served as his guardian. Tommy had also wanted to remain in Los Angeles, but his parents insisted he return to finish high school. Two years later, Tommy moved to California to live with Jimmy. It was a combination of wanting to leave the East Coast to live in an Asian American community, of getting away from problems at home, and, as Eddie Kochiyama and Victor Shibata put it, of wanting to meet "cute Sansei girls" that propelled the two youngest Kochiyamas to California.[29]

Having her children fly the nest earlier than anticipated, with Tommy leaving a year after Billy's death, was not easy on Yuri. She was the one, after all, who wanted to have even more than the six children she bore. That she and Bill refused to let fifteen-year-old Tommy stay in California pointed to their concerns. But several factors eased Jimmy and Tommy's move to California for Yuri. By that time, the Kochiyamas had decided to live more communally, with rotating dinner preparation and other chores. Not only did Yuri have a transition period in which she began to view her children as adults, she also knew that Jimmy and Tommy were capable of taking care of themselves. Because she and Bill had already been listening to and abiding by the input of their children for a couple of years, it became easier to relinquish even more of her parental authority. Yuri also knew the people with whom her children would be living, trusted their judgment as guardians, and liked the activist environment of her children's Los Angeles home. This arrangement also enabled her to pursue her political activities with fewer family responsibilities.

In Los Angeles, with the support of older peers, Jimmy and Tommy supported themselves financially and completed high school. Living in an activist household, they also became involved in the Asian American community. And by being surrounded by proud Asian Americans, they also gained self-confidence and an affirmative ethnic identity. They moved from, as Victor Shibata observed, "hardly leaving the house, always being in the back room" to walking proud on the streets of Harlem. Nick Nagatani recounted: "After living in California, Jimmy and Tommy went back to New York with two of their good friends, both Asian. The four of them walked around Harlem, wearing their leather jackets and their attitude. They weren't going to start anything, but they weren't going to take anything either."[30]

After her children moved out, Yuri felt an emptiness in her home, even though it remained filled with many friends and activists. To help offset that void, in the late 1970s, Bill gave Yuri a special gift that has since turned into a huge collection:

> When the kids grew up and started to leave the house, Bill thought that I might need something to nurture. So when I came home from a pilgrimage to Malcolm's grave [on May 19, the same day as Yuri's birthday], Bill said, "There's someone waiting for you in the bedroom." I thought, "What a crazy place to have someone wait." But I figured it must be a surprise visitor. When I went in, there sitting on the bed was a Care Bear. I loved that cute bear. They say people pick pets that look like them and this bear looked like Bill. The bear had hair coming down, just like Bill's, and his face looked like Bill's. I said, "My God, the

bear looks like you, Bill." I don't know if he liked that. But he was glad I liked the Care Bear. Then about a month later, I came home and there was another bear looking just like the first bear, but smaller. We couldn't call them both Care Bear, so we asked [our granddaughter] Akemi to name them. Akemi was in grammar school, and wasn't too clever with names. She just called the big bear "Bear" and the little one "Care." So together they would be "Care Bear."[31]

Soon people noticed that Yuri liked bears and began giving them as gifts. In a way that is characteristic of Yuri, she named each bear after the gift giver, such as "Barbara Bear," so she could remember each person's kindness. And despite having a collection of more than eighty bears occupying the top of the couch and several other spots in the living room, Yuri remembers each of their names. To her, "The bears aren't really just some fluffy toy bears. They're like extended family." And she gets upset when people push them aside to sit on the couch or treat them like inanimate objects. She sleeps with her two favorite bears given to her by her husband, and until her March 1997 stroke precluded it, she carried them with her whenever she traveled. And when she takes pictures of friends, she insists that a few bears be included in the shot.[32]

Yuri has a long history of picture taking. In the film *My America . . . or Honk If You Love Buddha*, the audience sees Yuri and Bill talking to a redneck-looking White man at the site of the Jerome concentration camp in Arkansas where Yuri was housed during World War II. The man explained that his family owned the land where the War Relocation Authority built the camp. He thought the incarceration was a travesty and makes it a point to greet all Japanese Americans who pass through. Surprised to hear his perspective, Yuri immediately whipped out her camera and asked this stranger, "Can I take your picture?" Yuri is forever taking snapshots of people, Movement activities, whatever catches her eye; many of these pictures were included in her family newsletters. She rarely includes herself in these shots, which explains why pictures of Malcolm X during his visit to the Kochiyamas' home show him with other guests, but not with Yuri. Bibi Angola also observed: "Yuri won't take a picture of just her kids. She believes in putting everyone in the picture. To Yuri, family isn't just her blood.

There's no 'just us.' She was always all-inclusive." The thousands of photographs of political activities that Yuri has taken over the years, if organized, would serve as a chronicle of the East Coast Asian American, Black, and political prisoner movements.[33]

About the bears, Yuri remarked, "We call them our family, our new family since our kids are gone. And our new family has been growing and growing." Not only was Yuri expanding her bear family, she was also expanding her Movement family by nurturing scores of young activists. Yuri's activism includes relating to the entire person. She extends her relationships with people beyond the political, and connects the political with the personal. Nyisha Shakur recalled that Yuri and her family hosted many open house dinners for activists and family members. Despite the age difference, Shakur, a Black activist the age of Yuri's daughters, felt a close bond with Yuri and related to her like a friend. They spent time together talking about personal and political issues, and Yuri consistently remembered Shakur on her birthday by taking her out to dinner. To Shakur, what stands out about Yuri is the caring ways in which she extends her humanity to others.

> Yuri will drop a card for your birthday or a little note to say, "It was great seeing you last week." Or she'll send a thank-you note. I remember one time someone picked up a Movement newspaper for Yuri and she sent them a note, "Thank you for taking the time to pick up a newspaper for me. I did want to see such and such an article." She writes everyone. It's not obligatory. In her heart, she loves people. She'll remember things about people. Her mind is incredible, like a photographic memory. She has an awesome ability to bring out the best in people, to want you to do more. Take politics aside, she's just a very caring person.[34]

Greg Morozumi, a Japanese America activist and close friend of Eddie's, recounted:

> Almost every year, Yuri would throw a birthday party for me and often invite leaders of the Black liberation movement and members of Malcolm's family. Once, she had [political prisoner] Marilyn Buck call [from prison] to wish me a happy birthday. I'd have these conversations with an incredible cross section of people. And for my going-away party, she got all these people

together from all walks of my life—from the post office where I worked and the restaurant where I was bartending, from the Black liberation movement, and the Asian Movement. The party was at her home. And there was over a hundred people in this tight space because she made this amazing effort to find everyone I was involved with.[35]

How was Yuri, already overloaded with family and Movement work, able to find time to organize parties? On one hand, Yuri was simply continuing the tradition she and Bill had started in the late 1940s of having social gatherings at their home. On the other hand, she considers these social activities part of her Movement work. With help from a few friends or family members, Yuri is able to call numerous people and invite them over for a party. And usually people offer to bring food or Yuri indicates that the event is a potluck. By connecting the personal with the political, Yuri helps to build those new social relationships that will form the basis of a transformed society.

To Yuri, one of the major problems in society is polarization; the other is racism. She believes that polarization, or the creation of artificial divisions on the basis of nationality, race, gender, sexual orientation, class, and so forth, substantially impedes the movements for social justice by separating people who might otherwise unify to resist common oppression. Opposing polarization takes on greater significance when one believes, as does Yuri, that social change comes through collective action: "In all the movements, you can't do anything unless there's masses of people." In the words of fellow Harlemite Assata Shakur, "Without the support of the people, no movement for liberation can exist, no matter how correct its analysis of the situation is."[36]

Yuri's belief and practice in opposing polarization contain both strength and weakness. On the positive side, she is a master bridge builder. She has an extraordinary ability to bring people together and to inspire their interest in working for social justice. Yuri is also able to work with people who have fierce disagreements with one another. This is significant, as RNA citizen Mutulu Shakur asserted, "If you consider the tools of COINTELPRO to divide and conquer, Yuri's ability to bring people together was not to be minimized." He elaborated:

Within the Black liberation movement, there were two factions—one, Marxist-Leninist and the other, Black Nationalist. Yuri had no trouble reconciling her work with either faction. Though there were major ideological differences between the two, her predictability, her thoughtfulness, her knowledge of history with every group allowed her to transcend and reconcile those contradictions, if they weren't serious. If they were serious, she could, unlike most, go into either faction and not be criticized or ostracized because of her relationship with the other. So she became a wealth of knowledge, a wealth of example of what a principled, solidarity person should be.[37]

Having worked in various social movements, filled with ideological and personal differences, Yuri certainly is no stranger to intra-Movement conflicts. AAA, for example, had internal clashes shortly after forming when, according to cofounder Kazu Iijima, a handful of Asian members of the Progressive Labor Party pushed their political line inside AAA. Yuri dealt with this by staying on the sidelines. Even in the midst of the 1970s when Asian American Leftists and other activists were trying to determine the "correct line" and at times viciously attacked others who differed from their position, few people verbally accosted Yuri:

I was lucky I was so much older, they didn't really attack me. Usually everyone was attacked by whoever they didn't agree with. A lot of people think, oh my God, Yuri, she just goes for any old thing. I think it's important to know about each group and where their differences are. But I think their [political] differences weren't as great; it became so personal. The personal grievances were heavier than the political ones. People say, how can you socialize with people whose groups you don't work with politically? Why can't we?[38]

In this statement, Yuri expresses the awareness that others may well perceive her as being naive, particularly with respect to understanding ideological and strategic differences. She certainly recognizes the need to maintain political standards, debate ideological differences that guide strategies for social change, condemn unsound tactics, and hold individuals accountable. But it appears that she would rather have other people make the hard decisions and confront comrades on their problematic behavior. She prefers to state her opinions in a soft manner or in personal conversations, so as not to offend. In private, Yuri does raise criticism of groups and individuals, and forthrightly expresses her disdain for people's harsh acts or words or their failure to exemplify a truly revolutionary character, such as when male activist leaders do not take responsibility for their children. Those who are attentive to cultural nuances can tell when Yuri is upset. Nyisha Shakur observed: "I'd see her at meetings and if someone said something negative or racist toward another group, Yuri'd say things like, 'Oh my goodness, how could you say that?' 'You don't really mean that. The brother's not like that,' or 'What?! What do you mean?'" In these ways, Yuri challenges people on their racism or negativism in ways that do not dehumanize them and, in doing so, may well reduce their defensiveness and facilitate self-correction. The downside is that many may miss or ignore Yuri's mild censure. Thus, some say she should speak more directly and that a flexible repertoire of skills involving praise and criticism is needed.[39]

Some interpret Yuri's behavior as a form of liberalism, that is, according to Mao, a tendency to refrain from condemning unprincipled actions for the sake of friendship or unjust peace. But Yuri is a pragmatist and a practitioner of social change. Although she believes that ideology serves as a guide to practice and is willing to engage in ideological discussions, she prefers to find the common goals and concerns among quarreling activists. Moreover, Yuri was often correct in observing that "it became so personal." Distancing herself from personal crusades was a way to remain principled: "I didn't get involved. . . . I saw how many groups judged each other by the organizations they were in, even though in organizations you get all kinds of people. I didn't want to become a part of it." So when meetings involve fierce debates, it is not unusual afterward to find Yuri asking people from opposing sides how they felt about the discussion and listening intently, at times not even inserting her own opinion. Alternatively, she might bring up another political topic of interest or inquire about their family as a way to connect with them on a personal level. Even when Yuri believes a strategy is inappropriate, she is likely to encourage the method so as to nurture the enthusiasm of that individual. In these ways, she validates others and builds positive human relationships.

She also facilitates better relations among activists by encouraging them to keep their eyes on the prize, to remember the larger goal that sometimes gets lost among the details of the struggle. Yuri's behavior consciously stems from her opposition to polarization and her role as a bridge builder.[40]

Yuri's tendency toward nonconfrontation also extended to how she dealt with sexism in the Movement. About the Black movement, she said: "I was never in any leadership position. As the only Asian, I didn't say anything; I didn't think it was my position to do so. That was for Black women to challenge sexism, and they did." But neither did she challenge sexism in the Asian American Movement. It seems that Yuri's unwillingness to confront sexism stemmed, in part, from her misconceptions about feminism.[41]

Like many women of color in the 1960s and 1970s, Yuri equated the women's movement with liberal or bourgeois feminism, which tends to focus on White, middle-class women's issues to the exclusion of race and class dynamics. In addition, many women of color, including Yuri, have equated the women's movement with radical feminism, which views patriarchy as the fundamental oppression. One extreme subset of radical feminism advocates the separation of women from men as a means of contesting sexism. Ironically, even as Yuri advocates nationalist views on race, including the need for autonomous spaces, she opposes the separatist agenda of radical feminism. Yet, the reasoning behind developing autonomous institutions and a distinct women's culture parallels in many ways the Black nationalist rationale for separatist institutions and Afrocentric culture. Drawing an analogy based on Ti-Grace Atkinson's inquiry—"Can you imagine a Frenchman, serving in the French army from 9 a.m. to 5 p.m., then trotting 'home' to Germany for supper overnight?"—radical feminists ask, "Why would you work all day fighting sexism and then go home and sleep with the enemy?" But there is one critical difference between radical feminist and nationalist logic. For many women of color, the institution of the family, often equated with extended family and community, has served as an important source of strength and affirmation, even as there are problems from within. In considering the legacy of slavery, where the separation of husbands and wives was a common method of control and domination; in surmounting legal barriers to family formation, including bans on the immigration of Asian women; and in facing the threat of White supremacist terror, the idea of a self-imposed separation of male and female family members is illogical to many women of color. In short, separatist feminists have failed to recognize, as bell hooks argues, the ways that women of color, subordinated by racism and capitalism in addition to sexism, struggle in solidarity with their male counterparts to fight race and class oppression.[42]

As a result of liberal feminism's neglect of race and class issues and radical feminism's separatist stance, women of color often feel alienated by feminism. This is reflected in Yuri's thinking in the 1990s: "I'm not a feminist because I've always worked with men and women. I see feminism's main priority as fighting for women's rights. But I think we must fight for both women and men. I see my priority as human rights because it's for everyone, on both domestic and international issues." Had Yuri's remarks been made in the late 1960s, at a time when revolutionary Black feminism and socialist feminism were emerging, her misconceptions about feminism would have been more understandable. But an extensive literature on women of color feminism, or womanism, has since emerged, even as liberal and radical feminisms dominate the popular discourse. The Combahee River Collective's statement, written in 1977, contains revolutionary Black feminist ideas that seem consistent with Yuri's politics:

> Black feminist politics have an obvious connection to the movement for Black liberation. . . . Although we are feminists and lesbians, we feel solidarity with progressive Black men and do not advocate the fractionalization that white women who are separatists demand. Our situation as Black people necessitates that we have solidarity around the fact of race. . . . We struggle together with Black men against racism, while we also struggle with Black men about sexism. . . . We are socialists because we believe the work must be organized for the collective benefit of those who do the work and create the products, and not for the profit of the bosses. . . . We are not convinced, however, that a socialist revolution that is not also a feminist and antiracist revolution will guarantee our liberation.[43]

That Yuri did not gravitate toward revolutionary Black feminism was to a large degree because her political priorities lay with the revolutionary nationalist movement, which places greatest emphasis on fighting racism and imperialism to achieve national liberation, sometimes at the expense of gender equality. While Yuri would agree that it is necessary to simultaneously work against sexism, racism, and capitalism, as advocated by the Combahee River Collective, her emphasis on antiracist struggles, as well as time constraints, limited her work for women's liberation. She readily acknowledges that antisexist work is an area of weakness in her political history. Still, despite her ideological shortcomings and her limited collective work against sexism—her work against military rape of Asian women is a notable exception—Yuri has promoted gender equality through her lived experiences. She evaded strict gender roles as a youth and adult and has emerged as a political leader in a generation with few visible women, much less Asian American women, leaders.[44]

Bill's decision to retire in the early 1980s, forced by a period of unemployment, affected the gendered relations in their household as well as Yuri's political activities. After working for the Japan International Christian University Foundation (JICUF) for some fifteen years, Bill got a job at the consulting firm of Tamblyn and Brown in the mid-1960s. There, he also did public relations work, including traveling to various U.S. cities to raise funds for hospitals and schools, and felt respected in ways he had not at JICUF. When Tamblyn and Brown closed in 1974, Bill was forced to search for work again. His next public relations job was at the New Jersey Institute of Technology (NJIT), where after three years, his boss fired him. Bill considered filing a racial discrimination lawsuit, recounted Yuri, but his coworkers, all of whom were White, persuaded him to try to negotiate rather than make waves. Yuri regrets that Bill did not contest the dismissal because after that, "Everything fell apart for him. Every time he almost got a job, there'd be only two job applicants left and Bill would be the one to lose out each time. He'd get excited about interviews, but then feel dejected when he didn't get the job. It was just so hard to see Bill come home each day after job searching. I think he should have started writing because all his life he wanted to be a writer, a reporter. But he was so depressed and beaten down by then. So after three years of not finding a job, he decided to call it quits." Bill faced several obstacles in finding a new job. Yuri believes that Bill's former boss at NJIT blackballed, or as she said, "whiteballed," Bill by writing him a bad evaluation letter. In addition, Bill's age, then approaching sixty, and the fact that people of his generation had not learned the computer skills that were becoming necessary in public relations work hampered his job search.[45]

For the first time since their first child was born, Yuri, then in her late fifties, began full-time paid work outside the home. Before that Yuri had done more than thirty years of part-time waitressing work, but "I never made anywhere near enough to help the family budget." Indeed, out of her minimal wages, Yuri regularly treated unemployed friends to meals at the restaurants where she worked. Yuri recalled the transition into full-time work as being fairly easy for her. Perhaps the most difficult aspect was that the inflexibility of her schedule caused her to miss meetings or demonstrations held during the workweek. But even here, she found that the job gave her a respite from her overloaded activist schedule: "I felt relieved not to have to be running around so much." As someone who has had difficulty turning down requests for help, Yuri has relied on others, particularly Bill, to help structure her time and commitments. The job was another such external aid. Her first full-time job was as a secretary for a Presbyterian church, but she was fired after just seven months. Yuri said, "I was demolished and hurt that they didn't think I had enough initiative and that my office skills weren't up to par." Her friend June Kushino then found Yuri a clerical position with the United Methodist Committee on Relief. She enjoyed sending money and resources to disaster-stricken areas all over the world. She said: "This made me see the church in a different light. The church was there for people all over the world, especially after disasters; also for refugees and those suffering from starvation." Yuri worked at this job for the next nine years.[46]

Despite Bill's desire for full-time work and the ways in which being unemployed undermined his masculine identity, he made a surprisingly smooth transition to become what the family calls "a house-husband." Not only did his orphanage upbringing partially free him from the modeling of traditional gender roles, as did the family's turn toward more communal living in the early 1970s, economic necessity left few options but to adjust. As Yuri worked full-time outside the home, Bill began doing more housework. By then, the household duties were lighter since the children had moved out and the grandchildren were in school. Plus, Bill had long been doing domestic chores in the Kochiyama household. He had been charged with the grocery shopping and family finances and some of the housecleaning since they were first married. After Yuri became increasingly busy with the Movement, Bill took on a greater load in the home. He started cooking some, and "on holidays like Thanksgiving, my parents worked very well together preparing the food," noted Audee. But after he retired in the early 1980s, for the first time Bill began preparing meals on a daily basis. Yuri recalled: "He mostly cooked simple things. But after a while, he got to really like cooking, and he started to open up cookbooks and experiment." And every night, Bill had dinner ready when Yuri returned from work. This shift in gender roles explains why friends remember Bill doing most of the cooking for the many social and political gatherings that continued at the Kochiyamas'. As Bill did more and more housework, it probably came as a relief to him not to have to face the rejection and disappointment of job searching any longer. And he took pride in the work he did to maintain the household.[47]

Bill's retirement coincided with the onset of the New York campaign for redress and reparations for the 120,000 Japanese Americans who, in violation of their constitutional rights, were forced into concentration camps by the U.S. government during World War II. Having flexible time, and filled with a soldier's memories of wartime trauma and of racism, Bill became actively involved in this struggle. Yuri did too, but her work schedule and other political commitments constrained her participation.[48]

The beginning of the redress movement dates to 1970, when Edison Uno introduced a proposal for redress (to rectify a wrong) and reparations (to obtain monetary compensation) at the national Japanese American Citizens League (JACL) convention. Uno's proposal built on a few isolated demands for redress as early as the 1940s by James Omura, Kiyoshi Okamoto, Joe Kurihara, and the Nisei Progressives. In the 1950s, at a time when the Japanese American community, by and large, distanced itself from the stigma of incarceration, only a few people spoke out against their internment. As early as 1951, Yuri and Bill added to these isolated voices through their *Christmas Cheer* family newsletter: "As we look back to Christmas of 10 years ago, we of Japanese ancestry, can recall with almost vivid painfulness, the

uneasy, frustrating, insecure experiences we were forced to undergo."
They provided details of that period, which mirrored their own experiences: "Niseis 'released' from their jobs. Schools reluctant to accept Niseis. A curfew and 5-mile traveling limit. . . . Japanese-run stores were boycotted. . . . Newspapers blared inflammable, untrue stories of espionage and sabotage. Hollywood Class B studios began their production-line of cheap hysteria-filled quickies. . . . Draft boards refused Niseis in service." Given Yuri and Bill's apolitical views at the time and the relative vacuum of outspoken Nisei voices denouncing the concentration camps in political terms, the content and tone of this *Christmas Cheer* article are unexpected. Perhaps their location in New York, away from the watchful eyes of the predominantly West Coast, ultrapatriotic JACL leadership facilitated their coverage. Perhaps Yuri and Bill, both with journalist training, were simply reporting the widespread discontent that existed inside the concentration camps. By the early 1950s, Yuri's experiences living and working with low-income Black people had shaped her consciousness. But even as the article concludes with a demand for "rights still denied," they couch this in terms that Yuri would not later use: "A grateful nation's thanks, her recognition and acceptance of an equally grateful minority completes the wartime saga, and opens the way whereby Niseis may continue their campaign for rights still denied."[49]

As the Asian American Movement emerged, and in the context of the Civil Rights and Black Liberation Movements, efforts to commemorate the concentration camp experience intensified. Starting in 1969, Sue Kunitomi Embrey and Warren Furutani spearheaded annual pilgrimages to the Manzanar, California, concentration camp, with Yuri speaking at the first two. Yuri and other Japanese Americans used their experiences as a rationale for calling for the repeal of Title II of the 1950 Internal Security Act, passed in the McCarthy era of communist witchhunts, to create six concentration camps in which to hold any persons who "might probably" engage in espionage or sabotage. As with the Japanese Americans in the 1940s, the government did not have to provide evidence of any subversive activity or abide by due process of the law. Yuri, whose wartime experiences were published by the Communist Party–led American Committee for the Protection of Foreign Born in their Title II repeal campaign, agreed with AAA's analysis contained in its newsletter: "This is a 'legal' weapon designed to clamp shut and terrorize anyone who dares to question established policy." Their efforts were rewarded when Title II was repealed in 1971. At the same time, fellow New Yorker Michi Weglyn began her research for what developed into a groundbreaking book. In *Years of Infamy*, Weglyn disclosed materials that contradicted the predominant U.S. government and JACL's argument of military necessity and provided substantive material to justify redress and reparations. In this context, Uno presented his proposal to the national JACL, which slowly developed into congressional hearings on the concentration camps. These hearings, scheduled for 1981, provided the impetus that sparked the New York redress movement.[50]

Concerned Japanese Americans (CJA) was one of the main groups organizing for a New York hearing. Yuri and Bill Kochiyama, Sasha Hohri, and others established CJA in early 1980 in response to the American backlash and renewed patriotism generated by the November 1979 Iranian student–led seizure of the U.S. embassy in Tehran and capture of American hostages. CJA provided Yuri with an organizational space to express her cross-racial concerns. CJA's newsletter, for example, "saw an alarming similarity between the hysteria against the Iranians in the U.S. which called for their deportation during the Iranian hostage crisis, and the panic that led to the incarceration of Japanese Americans during World War II." From the highest levels of government, there was discussion about the possibility of incarcerating Iranians in the United States. Ironically, one such call came from a U.S. senator of Japanese ancestry. S. I. Hayakawa, who himself avoided internment in the 1940s by living in Chicago, advocated for incarceration of all Iranians "the way we did with the Japanese in World War II." To counter the abrogation of civil liberties and any potential incarceration or deportation of Iranians, CJA participated in demonstrations with Iranian student groups, invited Iranian speakers to their forums, and were in turn invited to speak on panels organized by Iranian students.[51]

With the January 1981 release of the hostages held in Iran and CJA's Japanese American membership, it was not surprising that CJA turned its focus to the struggle for redress and reparations. In July 1980, Congress established the Commission on Wartime Relocation and Internment of Civilians (CWRIC) to "review the facts and circumstances surrounding Executive Order Numbered 9066 . . . and the impact of such Executive Order on American citizens and permanent resident aliens; review directives of United States military forces requiring the relocation . . . and detention in internment camps . . . ; and recommend appropriate remedies." The commission originally scheduled hearings in eight cities, with Washington, D.C., as the only East Coast site. Some New York Nikkei became alarmed that with such limited testimony on the East Coast, the unique experiences of Japanese Americans who relocated off the West Coast after World War II would be ignored. So CJA brought pressure on the commission to hold a hearing in New York. Their petition drive not only resulted in hundreds of people signing on to demand a New York hearing but also helped educate the public about the formation of the CWRIC. By late summer 1981, the commission announced the addition of New York as a site.[52]

The New York hearing acted as a catalyst to galvanize the Japanese American community in the tristate area. Given the geographic dispersal of New York Nikkei, their sense of community is formed through various institutions, including the Japanese American United Church, the New York Buddhist Church, the Japanese American Association, JACL, service groups, and veterans groups. CJA drew on these institutions as well as telephone book listings to create a broad constituency in support of the commission hearing. "Yuri and Bill played an absolutely pivotal role," observed CJA member Leslee Inaba-Wong. "It was their contacts, their mailing list, their history in the community and their willingness to share it with us that opened all these doors. . . . They gave us an in into the Japanese American community—especially since many of us Sanseis were transplants from other parts of the country." Like the nationwide redress movement, CJA had a predominantly Sansei, or third-generation, membership, reflecting the age and generational cohort that came to political consciousness through the Asian American Movement.[53]

These grassroots efforts resulted in the establishment of East Coast Japanese Americans for Redress (ECJAR) in September 1981, with Sasha Hohri of CJA and Michi Kobi as cochairs. After creating its organizational structure, including logistics, program, outreach, finance, and media committees, as well as a Washington liaison to the CWRIC, ECJAR spent the next two months organizing for the congressional hearing. ECJAR members reached out to former internees as well as to civil rights supporters, to government officials, and to professionals involved in running the concentration camps, encouraging them to submit testimonies and attend the hearing. They held mass meetings to involve the community at the Japanese American United Church. They also helped design the program and logistics for the New York hearing, raise funds, and coordinate activities with the CWRIC commissioners. In short, ECJAR worked to gather broad support by which to influence the commission to recommend redress and reparations for Japanese Americans.[54]

Bill played a leadership role in ECJAR, serving as the chair of the media committee, which was composed of half a dozen people, including Yuri. Bill's committee reports reflect that they mailed press releases to approximately seventy newspapers, radio, and television stations in the metropolitan area; secured radio and television interviews for ECJAR cochairs; cultivated personal contacts with major television networks CBS and NBC; made ten- and thirty-second public service announcements for sixty-four local radio stations; developed press kits to provide the media with background information to promote fair and accurate news coverage; and galvanized international support from Japanese media—actions no doubt guided by Bill's public relations experience. Using Bill's long-standing involvement in the Nisei veterans' community, he and Yuri organized a reception to enlist the presence of veterans and their families at the hearings. For this event, held on Veterans Day, the media committee successfully secured prominent coverage from the *New York Times,* Associated Press, and Kyodo News Service, the AP equivalent in Japan. Yuri and Bill's broad network also included artists who helped organize a theater fund-raiser as well as prominent lawyers and human rights activists, including former U.S. Attorney General Ramsey Clark, who agreed to testify at the hearings.[55]

It may come as a surprise to those who witnessed Yuri's passionate advocacy of Japanese American redress to learn that she viewed monetary compensation for Japanese Americans as a less urgent demand than Black reparations. As she expressed to CJA in the early days of the New York redress movement, Yuri reasoned that if the government were to redress injustices stemming from its racist practices, then the Black community, which has suffered such severe oppression for so long, should be the first to be compensated—a position shaped by her experiences in RNA. An easy interpretation of this is that Yuri prioritized the Black struggle over the Asian American Movement. And some Asian American activists have voiced this concern, though Yuri adamantly denies it. But to interpret Yuri's beliefs solely from a racial perspective is an oversimplification. It is likely that Yuri analyzed the revolutionary potential of various demands. Although far-reaching, some have argued that the goals of the redress movement, even its more militant demand for monetary compensation, were actually fairly moderate. Mo Nishida advocated: "[W]hat they should've also done was raise the demand for return of the land taken from the Japanese [many of whom were successful farmers]. . . . A revolutionary group would have raised the land demand, even if it was a conspicuously minority position, to do revolutionary education work around." Such a demand would have fit the revolutionary nationalist position of the Republic of New Africa as well as some revolutionary Asian American organizations. Still, Yuri expressed her views only to small, selected circles, probably fearing correctly that she would be misunderstood. She was also aware of how potentially divisive her views could be to the blossoming movement.[56]

The diverse politics and purposes of the groups in a coalition like ECJAR at times created internal conflicts. One such conflict in ECJAR involved differences in strategies for creating social change; namely, should the group prioritize working through mainstream structures such as elected officials or grassroots organizing with ordinary people? In New York, the leadership of the local JACL, although not necessarily its membership, tended to represent pro-establishment views and pushed to work within institutional channels. But many in ECJAR were critical of the commission's failure to regularly communicate, consider their recommendations, or fulfill what they felt to be the commission's obligation to the community. When in early October 1981 the commission had not yet set a date for the New York hearing, Bill expressed his exasperation in a media committee report: "The Media Committee . . . is stymied—frustrated because no definite date has yet been set for the hearings here by [CWRIC]. The committee is raring for action. It has drawn up mailing lists [and] prepared a 'canned' press release, which is ready to fly as soon as a definite date is set." In early November, less than three weeks before the scheduled hearing, at a time when the media committee was sending press releases to the smaller media, members were angry and distressed to discover that the professional public relations firm retained by CWRIC to publicize the hearings to the major media had not even written its press release. Ideological differences among ECJAR organizations were another source of internal conflict, and CJA, as the most radical of the groups, experienced red-baiting from a few of the moderate ECJAR members.[57]

As the date of the New York hearing neared, the commission overruled many of ECJAR's recommendations and testimonies. This was disturbing to Yuri, who felt the commission abandoned many of the best statements. These rejected testimonies, according to Yuri, included those of Rev. Arthur Kamitsuka, a Presbyterian minister whose mentally handicapped sister died after being forcibly removed from her internee mother and institutionalized; Thelma McBride, War Relocation Authority nurse and Peter Kondo's partner, who could have relayed her views of camp life from a White woman's perspective; Masato Matt Takashige, a merchant marine from Hawaii; and Ramsey Clark, human rights activist and U.S. attorney general under Lyndon Johnson. In addition, Yuri recounted: "Everybody in the committee was really upset that Bill's testimony was not selected. Here he is a New Yorker [former internee] and that's unusual. All the other New York Niseis were saying there was no racism, but Bill did research and his statement showed there was racism in New York." Through the advocacy of some ECJAR members, Bill's name was added to the hearing.[58]

Controversy also emerged over the political content of an art display at the New York hearing. Artist Byron Goto had submitted several large panels depicting the concentration camp experience to be displayed at the commission hearing. But at the last minute, the commission sent word that they would not allow ECJAR to display the panels. The commission's decision relieved some of the conservative members of ECJAR, who objected to the strong political messages contained within the artwork. But Yuri and other ECJAR members, already angered by the unilateral decisions coming down from the commission, decided to defy the ruling and devised an alternative way to display Goto's work.[59]

ECJAR's efforts bore fruit when on Monday, November 23, 1981, the Roosevelt Hotel on Forty-fifth Street and Madison Avenue was overflowing with people who came to observe the commission hearing. They heard eight and a half hours of historic and educational testimonies, personal stories of hardship and perseverance, emotionally stirring memories from former internees, and a panel of Sansei whose parents had been incarcerated. One of the Sansei testifiers, Greg Morozumi, remarked, "Bill [Kochiyama] gave the most dramatic and moving of all the testimonies." In his statement, Bill detailed how his experiences with racism changed him from a patriotic, all-American kid to an angry and politically conscious individual: "In my quest for a job [in northern California in the early 1940s], I faced an insurmountable wall of prejudice. Unions would not accept Asians as members and the white-collar world was exactly that—for whites only. For the first time in my life, I felt like a second-class citizen." About his incarceration experience, Bill recollected: "[F]our days before my twenty-first birthday, I entered Tanforan Assembly Center. . . . At the entrance of the converted racetrack stood two long lines of troops with rifles and fixed bayonets pointed at the evacuees. . . . Overwhelmed with bitterness and blind with rage, I screamed every obscenity I knew at the armed guards—daring them to shoot at me." He ended by listing his demands, which included fifty thousand dollars in individual reparations and, interesting for its self-determinationist character, "a community trust . . . to help fund programs for the elderly, the sick, the handicapped, et cetera." Yuri recalled that the most exciting incident of the New York hearing occurred during Bill's testimony: "When Bill started speaking, twelve or fifteen of us came marching straight down the middle of the aisle with these huge, militantly political placards made by Byron Goto. We marched right in front of the CWRIC Commissioners and a house packed with seven hundred people. It was really dramatic!" This was how a subset of ECJAR defied the commission's veto, boldly displaying the unsanctioned political artwork, with an introduction from Bill: "As an adjunct to my testimony, I am presenting a visual expression of my feelings. The artist is Byron Goto." Given the successful media coverage of this dramatic event, it was hard for even the conservative ECJAR members to deny the effectiveness of the tactic.[60]

The New York hearing was part of a ten-city tour embarked on by the CWRIC, which heard more than 750 testimonies from July to December 1981. In each location, the hearings were packed with hundreds of people there to hear those unprecedented stories. The hearings were the first time many former internees publicly, or even privately, spoke about the injustice of incarceration. Many told emotionally gripping stories of hardship, fear, illness, and death. The testimony of a dentist in the Poston, Arizona, camp captures the intense emotions never voiced for all those years. Kiyoshi Sonoda described how insufficient supplies created monumental and deadly challenges. A man whose wife had never seen him cry, the doctor shed tears as he bared his feelings of helplessness in having to watch an infant die from dehydration, what should have been an easily treatable ailment. Yuri testified at the first hearing, held in Washington, D.C., in July 1981, describing her father's arrest, imprisonment, and death and ending with an appeal: "We Japanese in America must speak up now. . . . It is a moral duty at this awesome, unpredictable time in history to fight for human rights, human dignity, and human enhancements." By giving voice to their experiences, a healing process began for the Japanese American community. The Sansei generation also began to understand the struggles of their parents and, in doing so, put aside their anger and disappointment at what they, having grown up in the civil rights era, perceived as their parents' timidity and acquiescence to governmental orders. In the end, the shame of incarceration was transferred from the internees to the U.S. government. And many committed themselves to fighting for redress and reparations.[61]

Two years after the hearings, the CWRIC presented its report to Congress. For the first time, a governmental body overturned the government's previous justification and acknowledged the wrong committed against Japanese Americans: "Executive Order 9066 was not justified by military necessity. . . . The broad historical causes which shaped these decisions were race prejudice, war hysteria and a failure of political leadership. . . . A grave injustice was done to American citizens and resident aliens of Japanese ancestry who, without individual review or any probative evidence against them, were excluded, removed, and detained by the United States during World War II." With this report, the issue for redress changed from whether a wrong had occurred to what should be done to right that wrong. In many ways, the commission hearings brought healing to the Japanese American community and provided mainstream corroboration to their fight for redress.[62]

Today the CWRIC hearings are viewed as a pivotal event in the redress struggle, but they were not always so uniformly accepted. The three national formations that fought for redress—JACL, NCJAR, and NCRR—had some conflicting goals and strategies and contrasting views on the hearings. The Japanese American Citizens League (JACL), the largest, most established, and most conservative of the three groups, used its contacts and prestige to work primarily through the political system. After meeting with the four Democratic Nikkei congresspeople in 1979, JACL decided to abide by their recommendation for a congressional commission, whose charge was to "review facts and circumstances surrounding Executive Order 9066 . . . review the directives of United States military forces requiring relocation . . . and recommend appropriate remedies." Although the majority in JACL wanted immediate monetary compensation, they saw the commission as strategically necessary to secure the support of the four Nikkei congresspeople, especially in light of opposition from the national JACL leadership and conservative senator S. I. Hayakawa. Significantly, the hearings could be used to educate the public, especially members of Congress who knew little, if anything, about the wartime incarceration of Japanese Americans.[63]

This move was sharply criticized by the Seattle JACL chapter and by William Hohri, a longtime Chicago JACL member, who split from JACL and formed the National Council for Japanese American Redress (NCJAR). Hohri noted, "The commission bill failed to mention either Japanese Americans or redress." In a February 1981 speech, Yuri voiced her concern that the commission might not recommend reparations, and even if it did, would not have the power of enforcement: "The commission is not a bill to provide redress in any form or manner but to gather facts, hold public hearings, recommend appropriate remedies, and submit a report to Congress." Hohri expressed harsher objections: "It seemed ludicrous to form a commission to determine 'whether any wrong was committed.' Clearly, this was intended to result in having the victims tell their tales of woe while ignoring the actions of the perpetrators." NCJAR went on to file a $25 billion class action lawsuit against the U.S. government that was dismissed and refiled several times.[64]

CJA joined the third major formation fighting for redress. The National Coalition for Redress/Reparations (NCRR), formed in July 1980, disagreed in principle with the commission hearings but saw the strategic need to organize the Japanese American community to influence the commissioners. Yuri, along with others in CJA, not only agreed with NCRR's position on the hearings, they were also attracted to NCRR's grassroots approach. In her book on JACL's redress efforts, Leslie Hatamiya acknowledged: "To a greater extent than JACL . . . , NCRR rallied the Japanese American community behind redress and made people feel they had an important role to play. NCRR drew a large number of people into the movement by sponsoring the lobbying teams, by going out into the community to enlist people to write letters, and by holding rallies in cities up and down the West Coast." Yuri was also drawn to NCRR's efforts to link redress with contesting South African apartheid and the forced removal of the Dineh (Navajo) from ancestral lands in Big Mountain, Arizona, among other issues. While CJA had a strong basis of unity with NCRR's goals, as an independent organization within the coalition, CJA, one of whose founding members was the daughter of William Hohri, also supported NCJAR's lawsuit.[65]

In addition to preparing for the congressional hearing, CJA sought to build a mass redress movement. Toward this end, CJA organized the first official Day of Remembrance celebration in New York in 1981. Not only did Yuri and Bill help organize this event, Yuri was invited to be the keynote speaker. In this talk, nine months before the New York commission hearing, she made an appeal for reparations and introduced the political work of CJA, NCRR, and NCJAR. As was her style, she identified key individuals in the redress movement. She also linked the incarceration of Japanese Americans with the U.S. government's dislocation of Indigenous Peoples, enslavement of Africans, and colonization of Hawaii, Alaska, Mexico, and Puerto Rico. Yuri and Bill also participated in the largest Asian American delegation to ever lobby Congress. Although former internees were not professional lobbyists, they secured congressional votes for redress through their heartfelt appeals, combined with NCRR's strategic game plan, which included having Nisei veterans, whose 442nd Regimental Combat Team rescued the Texas Lost Battalion in France in 1944, speak with Texas congresspeople. Support for redress grew inside and outside the Nikkei community, and inside and outside Congress.[66]

All of these various efforts by diverse organizations culminated in the Civil Liberties Act, which passed by wide margins in the House (243 to 141) and Senate (69 to 27) and was signed into law by President

Reagan on August 10, 1988. Although Reagan endorsed the bill in the end, his administration had posed serious barriers to achieving redress throughout the process, and as late as September 1987, he had threatened to veto the bill. Some suggest that after he recognized that Congress would override his veto, Reagan signed the bill to prevent any loss of votes in California, especially from Asian Americans, for the Republican presidential nominee George Bush in that election year. This legislation granted a tax-free twenty-thousand-dollar payment to each internee alive at the time of the bill's passage (about one-third to one-half of internees had already died by that time), established a public education fund, and offered an official apology from the president. These were essentially the recommendations of the 1983 CWRIC report. It had taken close to fifty years since Japanese Americans were first uprooted and incarcerated and almost two decades since Edison Uno first proposed redress for the government to admit its transgression and offer compensation. This was a major victory for the Japanese American community and gave hope to others struggling for justice, particularly, in Yuri's mind, for Black reparations.[67]

But the struggle for reparations did not end with the signing of the bill. The first battle was to secure funding to pay eligible internees, many of whom were quite elderly. With pressure from the grassroots community and maneuvering by Nikkei congresspeople, the first checks were issued, beginning with the oldest internees, on October 9, 1990. In addition, several groups of people, representing several thousand individuals, have had to struggle to secure their reparations, including "voluntary evacuees" who were pushed out of their homes by the exclusion orders, children whose parents repatriated to Japan, and most notably, Japanese Latin Americans.[68] Because the struggle for redress and other social injustices is ongoing, to this day, Nikkei communities across the nation hold Day of Remembrance events each February to commemorate the signing of Executive Order 9066. For their years of dedicated service, Bill and Yuri were honored at the 1988 New York redress celebration, at the 1993 New York Day of Remembrance, and at the 1996 NCRR Day of Remembrance held in Los Angeles.[69]

As Yuri continued her political organizing, another tragedy hit the Kochiyama family. Yuri and Bill's third child, Aichi, died at age thirty-seven on November 19, 1989, the day after being struck by a taxicab in midtown Manhattan. The night before, Aichi and her brother Eddie had celebrated her daughter Akemi's eighteenth birthday. Eddie recounted:

> We had just enjoyed a great meal. We didn't want the fun to end, so we were standing on the corner trying to decide what to do next—to go to Rockefeller Center, eat dessert and watch the skaters in the ice rink, or go back uptown and have birthday cake with Alkamal and Akemi's homegirls. In an instant, joy turned to grief when a cab jumped the curb and rammed directly into Aichi and Akemi. Aichi was thrown more than a hundred feet down the block as Akemi lay on the sidewalk closest to me, bleeding profusely from the head. At dinner, we had been joined by my best friend Peter [Wong] and [his now wife] Emilie. We said our good-byes after dinner, and Peter and Emilie left to get their car. As they were driving around the block, they noticed an accident scene, so they decided to get out and see if they could provide some assistance since Peter's a medical doctor and Emilie's a nurse. They were stunned to find out that the two victims were Akemi and Aichi. Peter drove me to the hospital and Emilie went in the ambulance with Akemi and Aichi.

At the hospital, Eddie recalled Peter informing him of the severity of Aichi's injuries: "He pulled me outside the emergency room and told me that he doubted Aichi would survive another twenty-four hours. Or if she did, her injuries were so catastrophic that she would have permanent brain damage as well as multiple irreversible physical problems. He told me to call my brothers and sister in California immediately to take the next plane to New York." With Eddie in a state of shock from the trauma of the accident and the horrifying news, Peter made that difficult phone call to Yuri and Bill.[70]

At the memorial service held in New York City, attended by more than one thousand people, Eddie delivered a poignant eulogy to his sister: "Anyone who knows our family knows that we have always been a tight-knit unit. But, I think that throughout the years it was always Aichi who made sure that we took care of one another." Yuri concurred: "Aichi was the one that everybody in the family loved to talk to. She was such a good listener. So when she left, it left such a desolate void for the whole family." Others also noticed Aichi's central role in the family. Victor Shibata recalled: "Aichi was the one who made you feel totally welcomed, who introduced you to new people. So when Aichi died, it was like the life of the family, the centerpiece, was gone."[71]

Eddie continued his eulogy:

> First and foremost was her family. As a mother to Akemi, the two of them shared a most unique relationship. . . . Aichi and [her partner] Alk . . . both talked about how happy they were despite the fact that there has been so much pain and struggle in their lives. If anyone asked me to define the words commitment and dedication, I would answer Aichi and Alk. They have stayed together through one crisis after another. I never once heard Aichi complain about having to take care of Alk. It was Alkamal's strength and courage that gave her inspiration and fortified her spirit.
>
> During the past few years Aichi and I grew especially close. . . . We talked to or saw each other almost every day. We had a lot of fun hanging out, drinking, shopping, and cooking dinner for one another. . . . We could talk about anything. And we did. We talked about politics, music, our jobs, our family and friends and we talked a whole lot about men/women relationships. Man, Aichi gave me advice even when I didn't ask. . . . She didn't *enryo* [hold back] when she thought someone was doing the wrong thing, especially when the subject was concerning how men treat women.

Audee also conveyed the closeness of her relationship with Aichi: "She was my best friend. We could talk about anything. Aichi and I did so many things together. We both worked at the New York Public Library and lived on the same floor of our apartment building. We also joined a taiko group together. There was a strong closeness between us."[72]

In Aichi's death, Yuri lost not only a daughter but perhaps her closest confidante, to whom she disclosed her hidden Muslim practice and secret plans to seize the Statue of Liberty. Greg Morozumi saw Aichi as "a mirror to Yuri in many ways." So did Audee: "Aichi and Billy of all the family were very much a reflection of my mother's politics—very outgoing, very people oriented, outspoken, strong willed. They were also the two that argued the most with my mother. It wasn't that they were very different; they had a similar way of viewing the world and a deep commitment to people. But they could stand up to her."[73]

On the heels of Aichi's death, her common-law husband of fourteen years, Alkamal Duncan, died following a long battle with sickle-
cell anemia. To counter their deep mourning, Yuri and others in the
family gained strength from what would become a complete recovery
for Akemi, the need to provide support to a grandchild who in the
span of five months lost her mother and stepfather, and the ways the
activist community celebrated Aichi's life. Tributes to Aichi were included, for example, in the twentieth anniversary edition of the Asian
American movement publication, *Gidra,* including a moving poem by
Sasha Hohri.[74]

Shortly after Aichi's death, the Methodist Church terminated Yuri's
disaster relief secretarial job. This created a financial hardship for the
Kochiyamas, who relied on Yuri's income and health benefits since
Bill's retirement. Yuri tried to get a waitressing job, but soon recognized
that, given her age and frail physique, no one would hire her for this
physically demanding work. It was at this point that Yuri, then almost
seventy years old, decided to become a full-time activist. By this time,
Bill, having himself gotten more involved in the redress movement of
the 1980s, seeing less need for Yuri to stay at home, and recognizing
the changed political climate, fully supported her activist work. They
also embarked on a second honeymoon, traveling to Mississippi and
Arkansas, where they had met almost fifty years earlier as a young soldier and a USO volunteer. In her film, *My America . . . or Honk If You
Love Buddha,* Renee Tajima-Peña captured, with humor, their person-
alities, quirks, and interactive style. Yuri, a romantic with a razor-sharp
memory, accused Bill of forgetting the date they met. Bill was able to remember the month (November) and to guess at the year (1943 or 1942),
but he could not recall the exact date, even though one senses that the
two have had this conversation many times. Yuri quickly reminded him
that they met on November 20, 1943, adding, "I guess it didn't mean
that much to him. I put it down as something very special." While Bill
may not have shared Yuri's memory for details, he did begin to share
her passion for supporting Asian American prisoners.[75]

9

The Most Incessant Activist

The news that a Chinese national, imprisoned at the Clinton Correctional Facility in Dannemora, New York, had been convicted of murdering a fellow prisoner aroused Yuri's attention. In March 1986, someone fatally stabbed Black prisoner Tyrone Julius. Sixteen months later, an all-White jury convicted David Wong of the killing and sentenced him to twenty-five years to life. But the more Yuri listened to Shelley Wong (no relation) discuss the case, the more alarmed she became that David Wong was wrongfully convicted. Yuri's first step, predictably enough, was to write to Wong, a recent transfer to Dannemora at the time of the killing, who denied ever meeting Julius or killing him. Wong did admit, however, that he had participated in an armed robbery in Long Island in 1983, the crime that landed him in prison. Plans went awry, Yuri relays, when Wong and a coworker threatened their boss for back wages. Although many would not defend a convicted criminal and some accuse Yuri of naively supporting just about any prisoner, she sees the humanity of the prisoner and the injustices in a case, in this instance involving race, immigration, and the criminal justice system.[1]

To solicit legal counsel, Yuri mailed a packet of information on Wong's case to a couple of dozen progressive Asian American and civil rights lawyers in New York and elsewhere, to which she received not a single response. Despite her frustrations, she persisted in telling people about Wong's situation and continued her correspondence with him. Four years later, she met three young people who expressed interest in the case and went to visit Wong. Yuri recounted: "I tell you,

Xuanthao [Nguyen], Steve [DeCastro], and Eric [Hill] were so impressed with David. He was learning English so we were able to converse with him. He was a very quiet person, but honest, and he told us everything very honestly. We liked him, and so on the way back, we said we've got to start a committee for him. We started writing letters and making phone calls, and finally we got about eight people who said they would come to a meeting." With much determination, Yuri and Bill, along with these three, began organizing the David Wong Support Committee (DWSC), formally established in 1992.[2]

After researching the case, the DWSC created a brochure to explain their version of the story. Wong did not receive a fair trial, they assert, and was convicted on questionable evidence, including noncredible witnesses, lack of physical evidence, and an ineffectual translator. The main witness was a prison guard assigned to the watchtower overlooking the recreation yard where the stabbing occurred. From a distance of more than one hundred yards, the guard claimed he could identify Wong, though the seven hundred prisoners were dressed alike in prison greens, with hooded sweatshirts on their heads. Even more suspicious, the guard changed his original testimony from "the attacker appeared to be White" to "the attacker was David Wong." The other major witness was a prisoner who, after testifying against Wong, received recommendation for parole from the district attorney. By contrast, several former prisoners reported that Julius was killed by two Latino men in retaliation for an earlier dispute at Rikers Island prison. *New York Times* journalist David Chen reported: "Mr. Julius' widow said she, too, had heard that her husband was killed because of an altercation at Rikers Island. A friend of her husband's even warned her that his killer had not been caught, and that she should exercise caution in pursuing a wrongful-death lawsuit against the state." A former prison employee also told Chen that "the consensus among employees and inmates was that Mr. Wong 'did not do it.'" The medical examiner also testified that the victim's wound was so deep that blood would have splattered on the killer. But no blood was found on Wong's body, clothing, or the Chinese-language newspaper he was carrying, though he was immediately apprehended and strip-searched. The murder weapon was never located.[3]

Wong was a Chinese national who, Chen relayed, "grew up poor in the rural Fujian province of China and in Hong Kong before being smuggled to New York as a teenager [in 1980]"; his limited English skills, lack of family and friends in the United States, and unfamiliarity with the U.S. legal system made him a vulnerable target. At the trial, for example, Wong could not adequately understand the court proceedings because the state-provided translator had no legal training and did not even speak the same dialect. To Yuri, Wong's situation bore a striking resemblance to that of a Korean American prisoner, Chol Soo Lee, whose case she had worked on a decade earlier. The latter case was significant in that it, perhaps for the first time, galvanized the nationwide pan-Asian community to defend a social prisoner, and in doing so, to challenge the racial, anti-immigrant, and class biases in the judicial and prison systems. While in prison for the 1973 murder of a gang adviser in San Francisco's Chinatown, Lee was convicted of killing a fellow prisoner. Authorities accused Lee, then in his mid-twenties, of being a member of the Asian Family and carrying out a contract for a rival Latino prison gang. Lee and his supporters, however, assert that he was forced to defend himself against an attack by an Aryan Brotherhood prisoner and ended up fatally stabbing his attacker with the neo-Nazi's own knife. Despite problems in the trial, including the alleged coercion of a prisoner who was granted immunity in exchange for his testimony, Lee was convicted of the prison murder. Under California law, a second felony conviction mandated capital punishment and Lee was sentenced to death.[4]

In contrast to Yuri's rebuffed initial requests for legal support for David Wong, Lee's family and friends successfully recruited the Korean American journalist K. W. Lee (no relation) to cover the case. His two-part, intensively researched and poignant account of the prisoner's background and legal case, published in the *Sacramento Union* in January 1978, revealed substantial evidence suggestive of Lee's innocence. In response to the lengthy articles, defense committees sprouted in Sacramento, San Francisco, Los Angeles, and New York; activists also worked on his case in Seattle, Honolulu, Chicago, and Texas, as well as in Korea and Japan. In late 1979, Lee's supporters won a retrial for the Chinatown killing. They reasoned that if Lee had not been imprisoned for a crime he did not commit in the first place, the second killing never would have occurred. The work of the various defense committees resulted in making Lee a cause célèbre by, for example, the New York committee, including Tak and Kazu Iijima and Yuri and Bill Kochiyama, getting his case aired on the nationally televised *20/20* current affairs program. Their combined efforts resulted in Lee's release in 1983 after ten years in prison and inspired a Hollywood movie.[5]

As Yuri had done for Chol Soo Lee, she worked to enlist support for David Wong. Wayne Lum was one of those Yuri drew into the DWSC: "It was 1992 and I had just heard on Pacifica Radio that there was a hearing for two former Black Panthers at the Queens courthouse. . . . I was waiting in the hallway with other supporters, who all seemed to know each other. I didn't know anyone. When the elevator doors opened, Yuri and others came out. I didn't know her or anything about her. But everyone seemed to gravitate to her. She began meandering to me, the only other Asian there. . . . She got my name, address, and phone number, and within a few weeks, I got a mailing from her about the David Wong Support Committee." When Yuri approached this stranger at the courthouse, she could not have known that he was earnestly searching for political direction and had just read Malcolm X's autobiography and listened to several of Malcolm's taped speeches. Although it took several phone calls and mailings to get Lum to attend a DWSC meeting, Yuri persisted. And Lum not only joined the DWSC, but has developed into one of its most dedicated members, presently serving as coordinator.[6]

A friendly ambience and good food characterize the DWSC meetings, held at the Kochiyamas' until Yuri left New York in 1999. "Every meeting is a potluck. And Yuri is always asking how each person is doing. It's like a big party," remarked Lum. This style of organizing has its benefits, particularly in creating a welcoming atmosphere, but the lack of structure also resulted in time-consuming rehashings of the same issues. In time, the DWSC developed a more effective structure, with a steering committee and legal, fund-raising, media, and political subcommittees. The DWSC secured appropriate counsel through the pro bono services of the Center for Constitutional Rights, including the highly respected human rights lawyer William Kunstler. Despite gratis legal services, significant funds, upwards of several thousand dollars, were needed to cover investigation, clerical work, court fees, and so forth. So the DWSC embarked on numerous fund-raising projects. Yuri is particularly proud of one benefit dinner, which grossed eight thousand dollars, even as they kept the price to thirty-five dollars per plate, compared to the typical one-hundred-dollar tickets, as a way to include ordinary people. While the DWSC's various educational forums and brochure distributions have garnered local support, the committee's most far-reaching publicity to date has come in the form of a lengthy and sympathetic article in the *New York Times* in 1999. The campaign is also spreading nationwide, as evidenced by speaking invitations at national conferences and events and by the establishment of a northern California DWSC, but has not gained the widespread support of the Chol Soo Lee case.[7]

The DWSC members, whose ideologies range from liberal to radical, have engaged in debates about the goals of the committee and its strategy for creating social change. One such issue was whether the campaign should focus solely on the legal aspects of the case or also link Wong's case with broader political concerns. Predictably enough, given the desire to overturn Wong's murder conviction, many in the DWSC, especially the numerous law students, emphasized legal strategy. But the more radical members, critical of the criminal justice system, stressed the need to mobilize public pressure on the courts to secure fair legal proceedings. While providing support and legal defense to Wong remains the primary goal, through dialogue and struggle, the committee also decided to connect Wong's case to larger political issues and to implement a two-pronged approach—both in the courtroom and on the streets. These views are reflected in their mission statement:

> The David Wong Support Committee (DWSC) was formed to fight for the freedom of David Wong, a Chinese immigrant who was unjustly convicted of a crime he did not commit. David's case exposes the systemic barriers of the criminal (in)justice system, anti-immigrant sentiment, racism and poverty, that impede justice. DWSC hopes to galvanize the support of diverse communities in collective effort to achieve justice.[8]

It is interesting, though not entirely surprising, that despite Yuri's pivotal role in forming the DWSC and her extensive political experience, she did not provide major leadership in these debates over line and structure. But her influence was felt through the committee's support of Black political prisoners, attendance at demonstrations opposing the U.S. blockade of Cuba, and the selection of anti-imperialist documentaries such as *Panama Deception* and *Act of War* for fundraisers. As supporters discussed the political context of his case and its connections with broader issues of race and class, Wong too became politically conscious. "David has become politicized in his outlook on this legal system and its relationship to capitalism," observed Lum, who considers Wong to be a politicized prisoner. "Through his years in prison, his illusion of being freed by the same legal system that had framed him dissipated with each step of the legal denial of his case."[9]

Unquestionably, Yuri is serious about the issues involved in a cause, in this case, overturning Wong's murder conviction. But one senses that the most rewarding aspect of political work for her is connecting with the individuals involved—the prisoners, the activists, the community. "For all those years before the Support Committee started, David never received a letter, never had anyone to phone, and of course, he never had a visitor. And now he's got so many people supporting him," stated Yuri with slight hyperbole, or more accurately modesty, given that she had already been writing to him. Each year, the committee sends Wong a special Christmas packet filled with Chinese food and other goodies, and visits on his birthday, making the seven- to eight-hour drive from New York City to the isolated prison in northern New York, only ten miles from the Canadian border. Numerous letters have diminished Wong's isolation. "What's amazing," remarked Yuri, "is that David has written to everyone who's ever been on the David Wong committee. I think he's a very unusual kind of guy." It seems that the unexpected support elicited a change in Wong's philosophy. "I look at success or failure not in terms of whether my appeal will succeed," he told the *New York Times* reporter. "I think my success is how much I and those wonderful people accomplish to make the system a little bit better. Before, I didn't care about anybody, and nobody cared about me. But now, they have made me see the good side of human nature." The transformation in Wong was also apparent to his family. "His mother," noted Maggie Ho upon visiting Mrs. Wong in Hong Kong, "had been despondent about her only son, but came alive when she discovered that others cared about him, too. It was extremely emotional for everyone; our eyes were really watery. We basically represented her son, and she didn't want to let go." Yuri has been the main force emphasizing Wong's human side to the committee. "She always mentions the personal," noted Lum.

"If David gets sick, she says we need to send him a card. Or she'll say, 'Oh, don't forget his birthday's coming up.' To me, she helps give a mental image of David. She is always humanizing our work."10

Yuri's work for Wong resulted in the formation of a support committee for another Asian prisoner. Unlike Wong, Yu Kikumura is regarded as a political prisoner by the International Tribunal on Political Prisoners and Prisoners of War in the United States, held in New York City in 1990, and by the Jericho movement a decade later. In fact, Kikumura is currently the only widely recognized U.S. political prisoner of Asian descent, but that will likely change as Yuri and others help to publicize the few other cases, including Tsutomu Shirosaki. Although by the early twenty-first century, Yuri appears to have made Wong the centerpiece case of her Asian prisoner work, including giving the entirety of her speaking honoraria to the DWSC, Kikumura's politics are, in many ways, a closer match to Yuri's. His anti-imperialist politics are apparent, if a bit dogmatic, in a twelve-page handwritten letter composed in 1990, at the time of the Gulf War: "It is crystal clear that, regardless to how this Middle East conflict will be settled, the purpose of domination of the Middle East and oil grabbing by the US imperialists would be to firmly consolidate world economic power in the hands of the major protagonists clamoring incessantly about a 'new world order.'" He strongly denounced U.S., Japanese, and Zionist imperialism and supported liberation struggles in Palestine, South Africa, El Salvador, Peru, Colombia, and elsewhere.11

In 1988, Kikumura was arrested on the New Jersey turnpike for the possession of three pipe bombs. Yuri recounted: "At the beginning, we didn't know anything about him, but it was so big. He was on TV for three days. They showed pictures of him being arrested. He was on the front page of all the newspapers. They were saying they caught a terrorist." Upon the recommendations of political prisoners Mutulu Shakur and the late Nuh Washington, both housed with Kikumura, William Kunstler immediately came forth to represent the Japanese national. It was Kunstler, Yuri explained, who invited her to attend the hearing: "When Yu Kikumura was brought to court for the first hearing, Bill Kunstler called and said, 'Would you like to go with us?' Of course, I was so excited. I had read about it in the paper and all. He said that, 'One of your friends is going to be our translator and

I thought maybe you'd want to go.' I thought it was so nice of Keiko Tsuno to mention me. She's with the downtown TV center."[12]

Months later, as reported in the *New York Times,* Kikumura was found guilty of illegal possession of explosives and fraudulent passports and visas, charges that carried a twenty-seven- to thirty-three-month sentence under federal guidelines. But in the sentencing phase, the prosecution, for the first time, raised the specter of "international terrorism," claiming Kikumura was a member of the Japanese Red Army and was plotting to avenge the 1986 U.S. air raid on Libya. "The bombs were intended and designed for flesh and blood, not brick and mortar," asserted federal district court judge Alfred Lechner, in the absence of evidence to corroborate his statement. He further claimed that Kikumura's objectives were "murdering and maiming countless numbers of people for no other reason than they're American." Reminiscent of Mumia Abu-Jamal's sentencing phase, Kikumura was punished, not for the crimes for which he was convicted, but for his alleged political affiliations and *potential* transgressions—though he was not indicted, tried, or convicted of these charges. The prosecuting attorney, Samuel Alito, admitted as much: "[Kikumura] was sentenced for what he intended to do." Because of the allegations of terrorism, the judge was able to sentence him to thirty years, more than ten times the federal guidelines. Kikumura immediately appealed his sentencing, and continued to do so, for example, in a 1992 letter written from prison : "I was tried and convicted for illegal possession of firearms and passport-visa violations. However, the government criminalized me by charging me with attempted multiple murder, and as an 'international terrorist,' of which I'm innocent."[13]

Kikumura's history of activism, his unambiguous anti-imperialist stance, and the political charges introduced in the sentencing phase were enough to convince Yuri that his unusually long sentence resulted from political persecution, rather than any criminal charges. But as she worked to gather support, she discovered that "it was really hard to get a group going. Many people are afraid to join a support group for someone labeled a terrorist." But after years of persistent prodding, Yuri succeeded in shoring up supporters, mainly radical members of the DWSC and a few Japanese American activists, to establish the Yu Kikumura Support Committee (YKSC) in 1993. "We could only get about seven or eight people, but those same people are still supporting him. So even if it never grew, they have been really loyal," Yuri noted. One of the committee's first efforts was to create a fact sheet to subvert the mainstream definition of terrorism: "[The U.S.] government and its media have no right to complain of terrorism. The US is the most consistent and outrageous purveyor of indiscriminate, reactionary violence seen not only within its own borders—but around the world. From the systematic elimination of the native peoples, to the enslavement of African peoples, to the forcible annexation of Mexican lands, to the fly-by bombings of the Iraqi peoples, and the 'humanitarian' massacre of Somali civilians fighting against foreign military occupation, US imperialism continues to prove that its 'new world order' still dominates and strangles with its iron fist."[14]

That Yuri enlisted a few supporters no doubt provided a morale boost for a prisoner housed in two of the most brutal federal prisons, first in Marion, Illinois, and later in Florence, Colorado, where prisoners are in a perpetual state of lockdown, secluded in cells twenty-three hours per day. Supermax prisons such as Marion and Florence, attorneys Erica Thompson and Jan Susler explained, "employ isolation, control, and behavior modification techniques. Prisoners are not allowed to communicate with other prisoners. . . . [Because they] utilize solid steel doors, rather than bars, complete isolation is virtually assured. Prisoners must eat, sleep, and live their entire lives alone in a cell. There is not congregate exercise or religious service. Censorship of reading materials is strict, and educational programs via correspondence courses are severely restricted, if allowed at all." In his first ten years of imprisonment, the prison authorities allowed only one social visit, which was from Kikumura's now deceased father. Later, a few people, including Rev. Michael Yasutake, were able to visit. Amnesty International, in its investigation of Marion, concluded, "There is hardly a rule in the [United Nations] Standard Minimum Rules [for the Treatment of Prisoners] that is not infringed in some way or other." Though the YKSC has not been particularly active, the work of Yuri and others to maintain human contact through letters and occasional telephone calls and to provide Kikumura with his requested *New York Times* subscription have been instrumental in breaking his sense of isolation and countering what Bill Dunne, then a prisoner at Marion, called "a laboratory for experiments in social manipulation and control."[15]

In addition, the YKSC has organized letter-writing campaigns to support Kikumura's efforts to protest varied civil liberties violations. In one incident in 1994, prison officials raided his cell and confiscated his books, most of which were written in Japanese. The timing of the confiscation, occurring just before the Seventh Circuit Court upheld Kikumura's charge that Marion prison authorities unconstitutionally denied him the right to speak, write, or receive letters and materials in his native language, not even from his family in Japan, raised the idea of retaliation in Yuri's eyes.[16]

Fueled by the success of the lawsuit, support from people in Japan and the United States, and his own rebellious politics, Kikumura filed another civil lawsuit, charging Marion authorities with wrongfully confiscating and later destroying his books. Kikumura assumed that he would lose the case, not only "because of the overwhelming lie by the government witness, the Marion's staff," but also given the unlikelihood of U.S. courts ruling in favor of a prisoner. As one who admires persistence in the face of adversity, Yuri has been moved by Kikumura's determination as well as his ability to remain optimistic. "I comforted myself that losing the case wouldn't matter anymore for me," remarked Kikumura in a twenty-one-page, cogent letter detailing the legal proceedings, "because before the case it had me had a great time for the outing from the USP ADMAX in Florence, Colorado, the highest security prison in US at where I couldn't have seen the outside at all but the concre[te] wall and the blue sky for more than five years." He described the trip to the courthouse with an optimism that defies the isolation of a supermax prison: "Thanks to the US Marshall for their botching handling of my transportation in placing me into two county jails instead of the USP Marion, the driving with a county jail van was also fabulous sightseeing of bucolic picturesque scene along the country road in southern Illinois that everywhere was colored in true green with several tonality." Kikumura's response to an everyday, almost-overlooked experience for many nonprisoners is revealing of the harsh conditions in the Florence and Marion prisons: "At the county jail . . . I touched the green grass first time in five years. I kneeled down to the ground and kissed and chewed the blades."[17]

Contrary to Kikumura's expectations, the U.S. District Court ruled in 2001 that "USP-Marion staff members breached the duty to safely care for Kikumura's property and that they were negligent in allowing the property to be destroyed instead of sending it out of the institution to an address provided by Kikumura. Kikumura's loss of property was proximately caused entirely by USP-Marion staff's negligence." Even though the court set the value of Kikumura's sixty-three books at a mere $144.95, far below the more reasonable $961 claimed by the plaintiff, Kikumura was jubilant about the verdict: "Justice is done. . . . In this sense, I can write to you that I won the case and for which I wish for you to share the joy with me." Yuri was among those about whom Kikumura was thinking when he composed the above letter to his supporters. It is this type of behavior that motivated the YKSC to state: "In supporting Yu Kikumura, a fighter against imperialism, we can do no less out here. Remember that political prisoners are those who put themselves at risk, that we can continue the struggle against imperialism with them." Kikumura is a reminder to Yuri of the kind of strength and dedication embodied by many political prisoners.[18]

At the time Yuri was forming the YKSC, Bill, age seventy-two, unexpectedly passed away. He had entered St. Luke's Hospital with chest pains. The doctors ran routine exams and Bill was to be released in twenty-four hours. But one day turned into two, which eventually turned into an eleven-day hospital stay. Though Bill had developed arrhythmia a couple of years earlier, there were no indications of any serious problem. Even on October 25, 1993, the day he died of multiple cardiac complications, the doctors had told the family that Bill would be able to make the trip to California scheduled in two weeks.[19]

At Bill's funeral, held on Saturday, October 30, at the Church of St. Paul and St. Andrew in New York City, nearly seven hundred people attended from all walks of life, including leaders of the Asian American and Black liberation movements. As difficult as it must have been, Eddie, who followed his parents into journalism, delivered a moving statement on behalf of his siblings and adult nephew and niece that captured his father's personality and character:

> Bill could be as comfortable rapping with his 442 buddies as he would be with Akemi's schoolmates, or Yuri's comrades in the Black liberation movement, or my friends in the Japanese restaurant scene. He had that rare ability to adapt to any scene. He

could do it because Bill was one cool dude. Akemi's friends even called him "Big Daddy Mack," while some of our friends called him "Wild Bill."

It's been said that there are so few positive Asian male role models. We think our father came pretty close. Not only was he handsome, possessed a sharp wit, had good taste in music, kicked our butts in Ping-Pong, and certainly shamed his sons on a dance floor; but he could also put together a pretty mean leaflet for the Day of Remembrance, published a family newsletter that comes out with more consistency than established newsletters, and in his later years, took on a greater role in doing the shopping, cooking, and cleaning, which enabled our mother to do her political work.

. . . We remember the year the Ronins won the championship—when Bill was around 55 years old and then again when the team made the playoffs when he was 60 years old—he had a better batting average than me when I was in my twenties at that time. . . . Thank you for being such a beautiful father in your own gentle and unassuming way. You showed us the true meaning of love for family and humanity. Your spirit will remain in our hearts forever.[20]

Yuri too showed inner strength, as she delivered a eulogy to her late husband. While Bill was a leader in his own right, Yuri also acknowledged the way he enabled her political work: "As a husband, he was phenomenal in sharing the workload at home whether cooking or doing housework. He did not feel that there should be gender borders around work." She further observed: "He was always the 'quiet warrior supporter,' who contributed in his own way to the struggle, especially giving moral support or providing a place for activists to stay." From Guinea, Africa, Kwame Ture (formerly Stokely Carmichael) also recognized the significance of Bill's support in a letter to Yuri: "You and your family are very lucky, especially you. To have had such a comrade in arms by your side. One who never limited your development. . . . For all of us who got a chance to know you, we had to appreciate him without knowing him."[21]

That Bill's life touched many others was substantiated by the numerous feature-length obituaries in newspapers from New York to

California to Hawaii, and several memorials and tributes organized for Bill, including those at the Sozenji Buddhist Temple in Los Angeles, at a David Wong Support Committee program in New York, at the East Coast Asian Student Union conference at Yale University, and at the New York Day of Remembrance program. Bill's generosity and compassion were captured in a newspaper article by Edward Lin:

> Bill never showed any intolerance towards anyone, even in the face of ignorance. When a neighbor fell sick and no hospital would admit her, Bill made endless phone calls and even offered his own medical coverage in attempts to get her treatment. All this, despite the fact that for years, the neighbor had been hurling racist rhetoric at him. . . . We were in his kitchen when I asked Bill why he was trying to help her. . . . "She hasn't a soul left in this world," said Bill, though his expression asked if he even needed a reason to help somebody. He did eventually find a hospital to admit her.[22]

After forty-seven years of marriage, Yuri's life changed drastically following Bill's death. Not only did she experience a huge emotional void, she also had relied so heavily on Bill in certain ways, particularly to handle their financial matters, that she quite literally was at a loss. "Yuri never wrote a check in her life or used a credit card. She barely knew what bank we went to," said Eddie. When Eddie, who succeeded his father in managing Yuri's finances, moved to California in 1996, Yuri was forced to learn to write checks and do her own banking. Still, Audee explained: "We've never taught her to use the ATM. We're afraid she'll stand in line and get flustered and ask the person behind her for help, giving them her access code."[23]

Given Yuri's generous nature—some would call it an inability to prioritize her work—coupled with the constancy and intensity of political demands, she relied on Bill to help set limits on her activism and to help organize her life. Yuri's chaotic state on the eve of her embarkment to the Philippines and Japan, shortly after Bill died, is revealing of her style, as recounted by her niece Elizabeth Nakahara:

> She was very frantic and hyper and high strung. She was going to stay up all night to do the million things she had to complete before getting on that plane. But she got so nervous, "Oh, I've got

to do this." She'd start to work on one thing, and then abruptly say, "Oh no, I've got to do that too." And she moved from one thing to the next without finishing any single task. So I just kind of took over. I put everything out on the couch in separate little piles so we could approach each task in a systematic way. I went down the line and attacked all her tasks. I had to hem her rain-coat. I had to send information out to all her kids. I had to figure out the time difference between the Philippines, Japan, and the US. I had her write a letter to Social Security. So, I did all of those things while she was doing something else. And to her it was just the biggest relief to have someone do that.[24]

Bill also helped keep Yuri focused. At David Wong Support Com-mittee meetings, for example, when Yuri would go off on a tangent, digressing into news on the political front, Bill would redirect her back to the task at hand: "Let's get with it" or "Let's get back to the issue." At the end of the night, when Yuri engaged in long good-byes, inquiring about people's families or reminding them about their tasks, Bill would nudge her, saying, "Will you come on?" Bill also regulated the number of demands placed on his wife. In contrast to Yuri's in-direct and sometimes ambiguous messages, Bill communicated more directly, even curtly at times, telling people that it was time to leave their apartment or not to call. Sometimes Yuri got upset with Bill's intrusiveness, but most of the time she appreciated his efforts to keep her on track and to safeguard her time and well-being.[25]

In other ways, however, Bill's passing allowed for an even greater degree of freedom for Yuri to pursue her political activities. For the first time in her life, she was living alone. She no longer had to worry that staying up to the wee hours of the morning writing letters to political prisoners would bother others. Nor did she have to worry that the constant barrage of visitors and phone calls might disturb her family. And Yuri is fiercely independent—so much so that her chil-dren's efforts to have her visit them in California following Bill's death turned into a major battle. "My mother resented people being protec-tive of her," recounted Audee. "Of course, she also appreciated that so many people were looking out for her. But she thought people thought she was inept, that she couldn't take care of herself. And she argued a lot with us about if we wanted her to stay longer in California." Yuri's defensive position stemmed from her correct reading that her children had misgivings about her ability to manage her finances and to attend to her own health. She also read correctly their preference for her to live permanently in California, but her children were not willing or able to force such a move. It seems that, to varying degrees, they understood their mother's desire to remain in New York, her home of almost fifty years, where she was surrounded by friends and a political community. In the end, Yuri did travel to California for several weeks, providing the respite sought by her children. But the amount of effort it took to get Yuri to take a hiatus from her activism is revealing not only of her political priorities but also of her independent streak, her stubborn side, and the lack of attention she pays to her psychological and physical well-being.[26]

Half a year after Bill died, Yuri planned to travel to the Philippines and Japan to gather support for Abimael Guzmán, a political prisoner in Peru and leader of the Communist Party in Peru (Sendero Luminoso, or Shining Path). Still grieving the loss of their father and worried about their mother's recent bout with ill health, Yuri's children adamantly opposed her involvement in a rigorous international trip, one replete with potential dangers, given that some in the U.S. Congress deemed the Shining Path "the single most dangerous terrorist group and now the greatest threat to U.S. national security in this hemisphere." Eddie, in particular, was so incensed that, rather than engaging in the more typical family discussions or asking a close friend to intervene, he directly involved himself in his mother's affairs. In no uncertain terms, Eddie confronted Phil Farnham, local coordinator of the tour and leader of the New York Revolutionary Communist Party (RCP): "The RCP didn't give a damn about our mom's fragile health, or the fact that we had recently suffered the loss of our dad. No, they did not care one bit about our family situation. All they were concerned about was being able to exploit our mom's name, recognition, and respect she had gained for all the work she had done in the political prisoner and anti-imperialist movements." Predictably enough, the RCP had a different perspective. They remember discussing Yuri's family's concerns with her and stressing the need to preserve her health, which is a memory shared by Yuri.[27]

It was Yuri who was the most adamant about making the trip. She tried to explain the reasons for her decision in a letter to her family:

Eddie felt that healthwise I wasn't ready, but I am fully recovered and well. He thought I was too old to make such a trip, but I am going precisely because of my age. If I don't do it now while I'm 72, I don't think I'll be in shape to travel in a few years. . . . I also feel the reason for the trip is absolutely necessary. The indigenous in Peru, fighting for their life and their future, need to have world support. Their leader, Guzman, must also be seen. . . . His own lawyers have been put in prison for treason because they defended him. So many political prisoners in Peru have been killed. . . . As you know, my special area of work has been with political prisoners. I began with PPs and POWs here, but now have extended the concern worldwide, as some of the worst human rights violations are against those incarcerated and invisible. . . . I hope you'll understand why I think it's so important to go to the Philippines.

The closing sentences of Yuri's letter—"I appreciate all you've done for me in the past two years when I had been hit with illness. . . . Because of you, I can travel again"—shed light on her family's concerns. If Yuri were to fall ill, it would be her family, not the Movement, that shouldered the major responsibility for her care. "I don't think that our family can bear suffering another illness or tragedy," Eddie informed his mother.[28]

In her letter, Yuri also clearly stated her political position. She felt compelled to support a leading international political prisoner as well as the struggles of the Indigenous of Peru. In traveling to Asia, she would be fulfilling an appeal by the shantytown residents she had visited in Peru the previous year. "Go back to your country and tell them what you have seen and what you have heard here," they implored, a message she interpreted without regard to national borders. In April 1993, Yuri had traveled to Peru under the auspices of the International Emergency Committee to Defend the Life of Dr. Abimael Guzmán (IEC). As the leader of the Communist Party in that country, Guzmán was highly sought by the Peruvian government, which succeeded in arresting him in September 1992. For Guzmán, the arrest could not have come at a worse time. Five months earlier, Peruvian president

Alberto Fujimori imposed a military self-coup in which he unilaterally dissolved Congress and the courts and suspended the Constitution to rule by presidential decree. Guzmán was tried before a military tribunal, predictably convicted of treason, and, in the absence of the death penalty, sentenced to life imprisonment. Peter Erlinder, president of the U.S.-based National Lawyers Guild, and Leonard Weinglass, then lawyer to Mumia Abu-Jamal, and other attorneys from France and Germany, all members of the first IEC delegation, asserted: "We have examined international treaties, portions of the Peruvian Constitution, recent decrees issued by the Fujimori government. . . . Based upon our initial investigation, we have concluded that the military tribunal . . . is being conducted in flagrant violation of both Peruvian and international law. . . . Any verdict or sentence in any resulting proceeding should be considered null and void *as a matter of international law*" (emphasis in the original). What Erlinder, Weinglass, and others condemned were, from their view, brazen civil liberties violations. The defendant was not allowed to meet with his lawyers, who were given a mere two days to prepare the defense and were barred from calling any witnesses. The public, including an international delegation of lawyers, was prohibited from observing the trial. A body of anonymous judges, wearing black hoods to cover their faces, presided over the trial.[29]

More to the point, Weinglass stated: "We haven't seen anything like this in decades . . . a prisoner exhibited in a cage, a clandestine summary proceeding, the president of a country announcing the sentence before the trial begins. This is clearly just an index of what life is like in Peru today." Indeed, following Guzmán's arrest, President Fujimori further abrogated the democratic rights of the populace, particularly resisters. Guzmán's lawyer, Dr. Alfredo Crespo, for example, was sentenced to life imprisonment for defending the Sendero leader.[30]

After Guzmán's arrest, Yuri was invited to participate in an international delegation to Peru by Phil Farnham of the Revolutionary Communist Party (RCP), a leading American group supporting the Sendero Luminoso. Given her sparse knowledge of Peru and her awareness of the widespread criticism of Sendero even by other Leftists, particularly its use of indiscriminate violence and authoritarian rule, Yuri was initially reluctant. "What has struck many observers is Sendero's use of violence against a wide range of victims and targets," wrote Michael Smith. "Sendero shows no respect for grass-roots organizations because, from its viewpoint, they are pillars of the old order, tinged by the old power relationships. By patching the system or setting up several networks (soup kitchens or communal development programs), these organizations are merely propping up the government by reducing social tensions." But, recounted Yuri, "[Phil] gave me the kind of reading materials that I could become 'educated' on the real situation in Peru; not the slanted reports of corporate America. The more I read, the more I came to completely support the revolution in Peru." It seems that Yuri came to understand, if not agree with, RCP's contention that Sendero did not engage in indiscriminate violence, but that every liberation movement must deal with counterrevolutionaries masquerading as neutral forces. Moreover, through armed struggle, Sendero supporters asserted, revolutionaries had seized land from the landlords or government and created revolutionary base areas in which collective planting and harvesting resulted in increased food supply and improved human rights for the poor, Indigenous, and women. This in a country where, by the early 1990s runaway inflation (in an extreme case, gasoline prices jumped 3,000 percent in a single day in part owing to a series of International Monetary Fund–imposed austerity programs) and harsh government repression (including among the highest number of detained and disappeared people in the world) had created severe conditions of impoverishment.[31]

In a speech delivered shortly after her return from Peru, Yuri explained her support for Sendero, though she fell short of addressing any specific criticism of the group's tactics and strategy: "What has been taking place in both Peru and the U.S. is a serious campaign to discredit Guzmán and the Shining Path movement, tainting them as terrorists, undermining their struggle with lies, isolating them, and intimidating anyone who might support them." These tactics, no doubt, reminded her of the FBI's COINTELPRO activity against the Black movement. Moreover, Yuri has, at an almost instinctual level, an identification and sense of solidarity with the poor: "The liberation of the most impoverished, the most oppressed, and the most marginalized in Peru must be supported." This is grounded in a class analysis of the Peruvian situation: "An all-out People's War against the rich and powerful was absolutely necessary for the survival of the peasants and indigenous. The main enemies were and are the dictatorial Fujimori government and U.S. imperialism." She also drew on the U.S. Declaration of Independence's petition to "alter or abolish" an unjust government in advocating "the right to rebel when repression becomes intolerable." "Americans must understand," implored Yuri, "that self-determination is a human right; survival is a human right." While Yuri takes a clear political stance on this highly controversial issue, she does so in the absence of any specific ideological position. In explaining why she worked with the RCP to support the revolution in Peru, she said vaguely: "I felt, well, thank God there is a group like the RCP who is working for the revolution. So many radicals talk about revolution, but then don't even support an ongoing revolution like the one in Peru."[32]

By taking time off from work, Yuri joined Phil Farnham and three activists from Mexico, Spain, and England in the fourth IEC delegation in April 1993. The first delegation went to Peru to observe Guzmán's trial but was denied entry. The second, third, and fourth IEC delegations traveled to Peru with the objectives of seeing Guzmán and other political prisoners, investigating human rights violations, and bringing international support to the Peruvian revolution. None of the delegations was ever able to visit Guzmán. In fact, the second delegation was arrested and deported following a press conference denouncing Guzmán's trial. On the day of the fourth delegation's arrival in Peru, Guzmán was transferred to an underground cell at the Callao Naval Base in Lima. The transfer was repeatedly broadcast on television, while newspapers carried front-page headlines blaring, "Bajo Tierra Para Siempre" (underground forever), as if, reasoned Yuri, "to assure the wealthy class in Peru that Guzmán will never be able to escape." Although unable to visit Guzmán or other political prisoners, Yuri said: "Our disappointment increased our understanding of the realities of the invisible, subhuman treatment of political prisoners. No one has been allowed to see Dr. Guzmán since his capture on September 12, 1992. No lawyer, doctor, or family member." To Yuri, the IEC delegation's presence signaled to the Fujimori administration that the world was watching and to the Peruvian people that they were not alone. She emphasized to the people she met that their cause was supported by prominent Black leaders and organizations, including Kwame Ture (Stokely Carmichael), Father Lawrence Lucas, Republic of New Africa president Kwame Afoh, Herman Ferguson, and the Malcolm X Commemoration Committee—all of whose support Yuri had probably enlisted, though she did not credit herself.[33]

Advised against holding a planned press conference, Yuri's delegation was instead invited to visit one of the many shantytowns that have emerged in Peru. The widespread poverty in rural areas, exacerbated by the IMF-imposed austerity programs, has fueled mass migration from the countryside to urban centers in search of jobs. But the cities cannot supply sufficient work, and the poor resort to selling products through the informal economy and to creating their own impoverished communities. The poverty is so great that, as Yuri reported: "In Lima, the largest city in Peru, out of a population of eight million people, four million—that's half the population—live in shantytowns without water, electricity, or a sewage system. Also, of course, [there are] no toys for children, no books, no schools, and often no farming areas. Vegetables and water were brought in by homemade carts." Her respect for Sendero was heightened by what she saw: "We will not forget the visit to one of the shantytowns, one of the best organized because they were under the influence of the Senderos. Their communal kitchen was their apparatus of survival. Everybody helped that everyone could eat. We watched women chopping vegetables as children played underfoot. We also watched men and young boys making mud bricks and putting burlap and cane together to make their huts. Women did sentry duties like the men. . . . The whole atmosphere in the shantytown was so cool. I never heard anyone yelling at each other or fighting." Yuri, who most admires people's efforts to overcome adversity, gained inspiration from the people of the shanytowns, as she has proclaimed in speeches: "The significance of the shantytown is their spiritual strength, their political understanding, their will to undergo difficulties despite lack of material goods, their optimism in the face of extreme poverty, their determination to struggle and win."[34]

In early 1994, at a time when her family was urging her to decline the Asian IEC tour, Yuri was probably thinking about the hardships of the people living in shantytowns in Peru and of their resistance. The primary objective of IEC's campaign—endorsed by prominent people, including Ramsey Clark, scholars Howard Zinn and Manning Marable, William Kunster, musicians Michael Franti and Sinead O'Connor, former South African political prisoner Dennis Brutus, and current U.S.

political prisoner Mumia Abu-Jamal—was to exert worldwide pressure on the Fujimori government to end the isolation of Guzmán, whom no one, not even his family or lawyers, had seen since late 1992. That the IEC would recruit Yuri as one of three delegates for a fifteen-day tour of the Philippines and Japan was not surprising. Not only had she vigorously defended the Peruvian revolution, she was renowned in activist circles for her lifelong work on behalf of political prisoners and her international connections, particularly with Japanese activists.[35]

In March 1994, Yuri and the other IEC delegates visited the Philippines under the auspices of BAYAN, an umbrella formation of some one thousand mass organizations, representing more than one million members, whose objective is to end neocolonialism and semifeudalism in the Philippines. During her ten-day tour, Yuri met with numerous students, workers, urban poor, women, religious workers, news reporters, shantytown people, "comfort women" who were kidnapped and used as sex workers by the Japanese army during World War II, former political prisoners, and revolutionaries. Given the close parallels between Philippine and Peruvian societies (both marked by Spanish colonialism and U.S. neocolonialism) and between the Philippine and Peruvian revolutions (both engaged in armed resistance, grounded in Maoist theory and led by the Communist Party), Yuri noticed: "You didn't even have to tell them that there's no way that Peru is going to change unless it's through revolutionary change. They understood." She also observed: "There [was] great empathy there for people like the Senderos and leaders like Guzmán. The Filipino people (those who fought against a corrupt regime) understand the circumstances of the poor and indigenous in Peru." In Japan, as expected, support for political prisoners like Guzmán and the poor in Peru was greatly diminished; instead, many, particularly the professionals in Tokyo, were proud that a person of Japanese descent had ascended to the presidency. Yuri did find, however, that the working-class and oppressed peoples like the Koreans and *Burakumin* she met in rural parts of Fukuoka and Kyushu showed greater sensitivity to the plight of the poor and Indigenous in Peru. And throughout Japan, she met scatterings of Leftists who were generally supportive of Guzmán and Sendero.[36]

Despite the conflict the trip created within her family, Yuri's letter to U.S. political prisoners reveals why she felt she had made the right decision: "We must defend the life of Abimael Guzmán and all political prisoners in Peru. We must fight for the freedom of all progressive lawyers, doctors, journalists, and Sendero supporters also held in Peru's jails. We must tell the world about the courageous struggle being waged by the most impoverished and marginalized in Peru. . . . It symbolizes the right to live for all indigenous; the right to choose their own ideology; the right to establish their own nation; the right to be recognized and respected in the international community; and the right to sovereignty and independence, but also the right to interdependence—becoming part of the world's family." This statement, made thirty years after her introduction to Malcolm X, reflects her revolutionary nationalist emphasis on self-determination, as well as her continuing hope for the "togetherness of all people," expressed in her first letter to Malcolm.[37]

To Yuri, one of the persons who best exemplifies the "togetherness of all people" is Mumia Abu-Jamal, the U.S. political prisoner and award-winning journalist. In writing about a variety of political issues, from condemning police brutality and the prison buildup at home, to denouncing U.S. political, economic, and military intervention in Afghanistan, Iraq, and Chiapas, to supporting gay rights and national liberation movements worldwide, Abu-Jamal embodies Yuri's vision of global interdependence. She remarked: "Once people learn about Mumia, they can't help but love Mumia because not only was he such a radical and such a courageous kind of guy and his support for the MOVE group has been contagious. He has supported everyone, all the underdogs and the marginalized." On a more personal level, Yuri revealed another aspect of Abu-Jamal's ability to connect cross-culturally:

> People won't believe how Mumia and I got started corresponding. It had nothing to do with the movement. It had nothing to do with political prisoners. I couldn't believe it but one day I got a letter from him and he wrote in Japanese—*Hiragana,* which is one of the forms of writing Japanese. . . . And I said how did you learn? And he said he was studying Japanese just by himself in prison. . . . But how this came about was that I had just read something by Velina Houston, the famous Black/Asian/Indian playwright. She wrote about a Black samurai in the sixth or

eighth century. And so I wrote to Mumia about him and he said, "You won't believe it but I've just been reading about him myself." But just before that he wrote in Japanese, and that's how we got started to know each other.[38]

Yuri may have first heard of Abu-Jamal in connection with his media coverage of MOVE, a militant, antiestablishment group. She supported MOVE in 1978 when hundreds of Philadelphia police officers used fire hoses to flood the MOVE house, directed gunfire at them, and as documented by filmmaker Martin Smith, savagely beat one of its members. A police officer was killed in the incident. Although the judge admitted that he "hadn't the faintest idea" who shot the officer, who forensics indicated was killed by "friendly fire," nine MOVE members were each sentenced to thirty to one hundred years for the murder. The activist community—and this time, neighbors— were further outraged when, in an unprecedented maneuver on May 13, 1985, the Philadelphia police, again sanctioned by city and federal officials, used a helicopter to drop a military-style bomb on the MOVE house and police gunfire prevented its residents from escaping the ensuing flames. Eleven MOVE members were killed and more than sixty homes burned. The only person arrested, tried, and convicted for this atrocity was MOVE member Ramona Africa, the sole adult survivor of the bombing.[39]

Abu-Jamal, having personally experienced police brutality, gave the only sympathetic media coverage to MOVE. Because of his bold radio broadcasts and his cofounding of the Philadelphia chapter of the Black Panther Party at age fifteen, the local police, Abu-Jamal's supporters contend, had been trying for years to neutralize him. And that opportunity appeared in the early morning hours of December 9, 1981. Moonlighting as a cab driver, Abu-Jamal tried to stop the police beating of a Black man, who turned out to be his brother. Gunfire erupted. When other officers arrived, Abu-Jamal was slumped over on the curb, shot in the chest, and Daniel Faulkner, a White police officer, was on the ground, also shot. Faulkner died within the hour, and Abu-Jamal was charged with and convicted of first-degree murder. After prosecutors introduced his political beliefs and former affiliation with the Black Panther Party in the sentencing phase, Abu-Jamal was given the death penalty.[40]

Since 1995, Abu-Jamal has become perhaps the most renowned political prisoner in the world. But in the 1980s, Yuri was among the few defending him and working to appeal his case, based on what she and other supporters saw as flagrant courtroom misconduct, including prosecutorial and police concealment of evidence and coercion of eyewitnesses. For Yuri, Abu-Jamal represents a continuation of the scores of political prisoners she has supported over the decades. What distinguishes his case is the urgency that comes from his location as the only U.S. political prisoner on death row. In addition, "there has been no political prisoner who has been able to galvanize so many people the way Mumia has—and not just here in the country, but all over the world . . . [including] 26 members of the Diet [top government body] in Japan," observed Yuri. In 1995, Yuri gained a compelling reinforcement of her belief that the extent of justice in the courtroom depends on the strength of social movements. In June of that year, newly elected Pennsylvania governor Tom Ridge signed Abu-Jamal's death warrant and unwittingly provoked national and international protest. The sole legal channel for preventing the state execution, scheduled for August 17, 1995, was to gain a stay of execution from Judge Albert Sabo. Not only was Sabo a former undersheriff in Philadelphia County and a member of the conservative Fraternal Order of Police, one of the staunchest advocates of Abu-Jamal's execution, he also had a reputation as the "hanging judge" for his frequent sentencing of Black prisoners to death. Significantly, if Sabo were to grant the stay of execution, he would be reversing the decision rendered in the original trial over which he presided. Needless to say, the possibilities looked grim. But ten days before the scheduled execution, Sabo granted the stay of execution, allowing Abu-Jamal time to file further appeals for a new trial. Some would interpret this reversal as evidence of the judge's change of heart or the sound functioning of the judicial system. But Yuri, who has repeatedly witnessed racial, class, and political biases of the courts, saw a major Movement victory—the power of ordinary people to effect social change.[41]

Wherever Yuri speaks—whether to community residents in Harlem or high school students in New York City or college students in California—she, often donning the same well-worn orange Mumia T-shirt, provides detailed information about his arrest, trial, and the denial of many appeals, and urges people to join the campaign. Her politics spill over into her personal communications and on the bottom of Christmas cards, she has added, "Save Mumia, Save Mumia, Save Mumia." In 1997, she was invited to serve on a distinguished panel of judges for an International People's Tribunal for Justice for Mumia Abu-Jamal, held in Philadelphia. Throughout the lively daylong event, some fourteen hundred people heard respected attorneys and activist-researchers present background information and evidence about specific legal questions concerning Abu-Jamal's case. The panel of judges examined the evidence and, as expected, found the eleven defendants, including Pennsylvania's governor, Philadelphia's mayor, Judge Albert Sabo, and U.S. Attorney General Janet Reno, guilty of violating Abu-Jamal's constitutional rights. Yuri has also marched in numerous demonstrations in support of Abu-Jamal. She was among the twenty-five thousand activists, for example, who gathered in Philadelphia for the Millions for Mumia rally on April 24, 1999, to demand a new trial for Abu-Jamal on his forty-fifth birthday; solidarity rallies also took place in France, Spain, Brazil, Sweden, and most notably in San Francisco, where twenty thousand protesters assembled.[42]

It is not surprising that Yuri has made Abu-Jamal's case a top priority, given the urgency of his situation, his political prisoner status, and the fact that his case embodies issues affecting broad sectors of society, including the persecution of radical dissenters, the racist nature of the court system, police brutality, abrogation of civil liberties, expansion of the prison-industrial complex, problems with the death penalty, and the criminalization of youth, the poor, and people of color. Yuri also sees his case connected to the history of Asian America, as conveyed by Asians for Mumia, a New York–based group that she cofounded with Gloria Lum in 1995:

> As Asians, we are an oppressed community that has endured and resisted the attempts to dehumanize us throughout US history, from racial lynching and Exclusion Acts of the 1800's, to the concentration camps in the 1940's, to the systematic scapegoating of Asians that have resulted in beatings and killings by civilians and police. . . . Mumia not only speaks for the Black community, but marginalized and oppressed people around the globe. The "voiceless" of the Asian and Pacific Islander community are found in abundance in sweatshops, restaurants, farms,

and factories. . . . To silence Mumia is to silence our own voices of resistance.

By the late 1990s, Yuri began to see growth in the number of Asian Americans supporting political prisoners. One of those Yuri drew in, Wayne Lum, concurred: "The Jericho '98 [march and rally for political prisoners] and the Millions for Mumia showed sizable Asian support, but at the Asian roundtable in Critical Resistance [prison conference at UC Berkeley in 1998], the classroom of supporters was standing room only and overflowed into the hallway." Many would argue that Yuri has been the primary force in inspiring Asian American involvement in the political prisoner movement.[43]

Since the 1990s, Yuri has emerged as one of the most prominent Asian American activists. In 1993, Rea Tajiri and Pat Saunders produced an hour-long documentary, *Yuri Kochiyama: Passion for Justice,* about her life and political work. She is featured prominently in other films, including Renee Tajima-Peña's *My America . . . or Honk If You Love Buddha* and Lee Lew Lee's documentary about the Black Panther Party, *All Power to the People.* Yuri's memoir, *Passing It On,* was recently published by UCLA's Asian American Studies Center. She justifies the writing of her memoir, the self-absorption of which embarrasses her, by reasoning that this book is the fulfillment of her family's long-standing request to document the family history. In addition, Yuri has garnered international attention. Journalist Mayumi Nakazawa wrote the biography *Yuri: The Life and Times of Yuri Kochiyama,* published in Japan. She is also the subject of hundreds of articles and interviews. In addition, more than two dozen plaques honoring Yuri alone, or Yuri and Bill jointly, for years of dedicated human rights activism, community service, and leadership, mostly awarded during the 1990s, adorned the walls of the back hallway of her home. And these account for only a portion of the honors bestowed on Yuri.[44]

Since the early 1990s, numerous invitations, often from Asian American college students, have introduced Yuri, previously known primarily in activist circles, to thousands of young people. These youth, even those whose politics are substantially more moderate than Yuri's, overwhelmingly have come to admire her and regard her as a shero. She became so widely sought after throughout the nation, often featured as the keynote speaker, that it was not unusual for her to give multiple talks in a single week. During an intense three-year period, from early 1994, following Bill's death, to March 1997, when she suffered a debilitating stroke, an active but not atypical week might include speaking in New England one day, returning by train to speak in New York the next day, and a couple of days later, flying to the West Coast to deliver yet another talk. Before that, in the 1960s and 1970s, New York City was the main locale of Yuri's talks, often against U.S. incursions into Southeast Asia and Okinawa. By the late 1970s, she began expanding to other East Coast states as invitations rolled in from college students.[45]

Yuri's knowledge, gained through her activist practice and study, has enabled her to speak on a broad range of topics, including Malcolm X, political prisoners, Japanese militarism and sexual slavery, Japanese American redress, and anti-imperialist struggles in Okinawa, Hawaii, Puerto Rico, and Peru. However, the most requested topic, by far, has been various aspects of the Asian American Movement. Another popular topic, African-Asian interactions, may well be Yuri's favorite as it expounds on the theme of, in her words, "break[ing] down barriers, obstacles and phobias" in order that "we must become one, for the future of humanity." As is typical of her speeches, Yuri provides precise details, historical facts, and vivid, well-researched information to reveal, in this case, the solidarity among Asians and Africans: "Much of the history of African and Asian interactions is not as well known as it should be. All peoples of whatever race or color have crisscrossed into each other's lives more than we think. But such history, like all true history, has often been hidden, lied about, or distorted. Malcolm X used to admonish: 'Study history. Learn about yourselves and others. There's more commonality in all our lives than we think.' . . . There is so much that unites us, which we do not learn." Drawing from Gary Okihiro's writings, Yuri explains that the first Asians who came to the United States were Filipino slaves, and that the East African slave trade involved both African and Asian slaves. She describes how Black soldiers sent to the Philippines during the Philippine-American war of 1898–1901 were so appalled at the viciousness of American troops that many joined the side of the Filipinos, who were engaged in a struggle for national liberation. She relays that Japanese immigrant Sen Katayama and Harlem Renaissance writer Claude McKay organized together in the Communist Party in New York. Also by 1920, the future Vietnamese leader Ho Chi Minh interacted with Black people in the ghettos of Chicago and Harlem, and became an admirer of Marcus Garvey. Consistent with her admiration for Malcolm X, she dubs him "the most charismatic Black leader who made the greatest impression on Asian Americans." Moreover, during the 1960s, Black Panther leaders traveled to China and North Korea to learn from their revolutionary movements, and Asian and Africans students struggled together on U.S. campuses in the antiwar and ethnic studies movements.[46]

Through her public speaking, Yuri fulfills her role as elder, sharing experience and knowledge with the younger generations and inspiring them to continue the struggle. Her references to authors and books encourage people to read and learn more about political issues. As before, she continues to personalize political activity by identifying activists and groups and by thanking the individuals, each by name, who arranged her talk. Yuri motivates young people to pick up the baton, to carry on the struggle. She ends many speeches by quoting Frantz Fanon's famous statement, "Each generation must, out of its relative obscurity, discover its mission and fulfill it or betray it."[47]

After more than four decades of activism, Yuri's commitment to social justice is as strong as ever, slowed down only by declining health. The Movement remains her extended family. At the Jericho '98 march and rally in Washington, D.C., for example, Yuri was greeted by a nonstop flow of people of all backgrounds. Old friends came by to give a hug and kiss to their longtime comrade; young people introduced themselves to their shero; still others invited Yuri to speak on their campus or in their community. Yuri's connectedness to people and dedication to enhancing humanity are the hallmarks of her community service in her youth and of her activism in adulthood. In the late 1970s, for example, she had taken her granddaughter, then age six, to a Hiroshima Day rally protesting the building of nuclear weapons. Akemi Kochiyama-Ladson recounted: "I remember that the moment we got to the demonstration site, it seemed like she knew everyone: these people were her extended family. She was in her element, greeting, embracing, and introducing her colleagues to one another, all the while handing out leaflets to every person she encountered."[48]

Today, the life-giving Movement is a major vehicle that sustains Yuri, continuously giving her nourishment, support, and purpose in life. In turn, she is constantly motivating others to join the grassroots struggle for social change and to be conscious of other people's needs and humanity. For Yuri, "The Movement is contagious and awesome because the people in it are the spirit of the Movement. And the Movement will continue because new concerned people will rejuvenate and revitalize this never-ending struggle. It just always makes you want to be part of it." Yuri's passion for social justice is profoundly inspiring. Her life will forever be synonymous with creating a better world for the "togetherness of all people."[49]

Epilogue

The Never-Ending Struggle

Geographic relocation has been a significant politicizing factor in Yuri's life.[1] The forced displacement to a concentration camp in the 1940s facilitated the beginnings of a racialized worldview. Her family's move to Harlem in 1960 sparked the onset of more than four decades of political activism. And her move to Oakland, California, in 1999, fostered Yuri's direct involvement in the progressive politics of the Bay Area, with its large Asian American community, and enabled West Coast activists to have extended interactions with this esteemed Movement leader. This latest relocation was prompted by declining health and a desire to live closer to her four children and their families.

In March 1997, Yuri, then age seventy-five, suffered a stroke that required a one-month hospital stay. Through physical therapy and the support of her two adult grandchildren—her only family in New York—her children, and her many friends, Yuri's health slowly improved. Still, she was plagued with chronic problems. She had frequent shakiness, dizziness, and increased fatigue. She had to rely on a walker for mobility. She was frustrated by the limitations that her physical ailments placed on her work and independence. Although she was forced to slow down, take afternoon naps, and limit her activities, she was still able to participate in Movement activities. She continued, in a more limited way, to organize events, attend meetings, and correspond with political prisoners. She even traveled to Washington, D.C., a five-hour bus ride, for the Jericho '98 march and rally for political prisoners. Visitors and overnight guests also continued to have a presence at Yuri's apartment.[2]

But in the spring of 1999, Yuri's physical and mental health took a turn for the worse and she began to ruminate on her situation. With a strikingly atypical focus on self, she spent two paragraphs in an April 1999 page-long letter discussing her health: "I think I had a mini stroke a few days ago. I could hardly stand up, walk, and had difficulty talking. . . . I'm still very weak. I've never felt like this before. I've never been this wobbly. . . . It's frustrating and a little frightening." Her acknowledgment of being "a little frighten[ed]" spoke volumes to the degree of fear she was experiencing. As she became more anxious and depressed and expressed a desire to spend time with her family, her children helped her arrange an extended visit to California. Yuri left New York a couple of days after making the pilgrimage to Malcolm X's gravesite on their joint birth date, May 19. In California, Yuri stayed with Audee and her husband in Oakland, and saw her other children and their families regularly. Yet her physical and psychological health continued to deteriorate. The most difficult symptom was, as she called them, "head spells," a vague yet intense feeling that something was wrong with her head. She began to dwell on her physical condition, even on small things like having a dry, salty mouth. Before, while she mentioned such discomforts, these ailments seemed inconsequential compared to the larger political concerns that occupied her thoughts. But it became difficult for Yuri to concentrate on anything other than her health problems. In a way that was markedly different from her usual self—many commented that they had never seen her like this—she began to lose interest in talking to people, maintaining her correspondence, reading, or focusing on political issues. She no longer wanted to see anyone except her family and closest friends. She was feeling so miserable, unable to understand what was wrong with her head, that she even began to lose interest in life itself. Compounding her severe depression, in July 1999, she fell and fractured her pelvis, which put her in the hospital for weeks.[3]

A number of factors help explain the onset of Yuri's depression. To be sure, coping with chronic health problems is difficult, involving a sense of loss of one's formerly active life. This would be particularly hard on one like Yuri who was used to having boundless energy. Even though many of her activist friends recognized her frail condition and tried to safeguard her health, there continued to be multiple demands made of her—requests for resources, speeches, interviews, organizing, and so forth—from friends and strangers alike. While this Movement work gave purpose to her life, her declining health rendered her less able to meet these demands. Her inability to regulate her schedule and to turn down many seemingly urgent and important requests added to her strain. Since the neurologists found no physical condition that could explain her problems, family and friends concluded that she was "overly exhausted." She seemed to have physically and emotionally collapsed. In this slowed-down state, one of Yuri's major coping mechanisms, that of staying busy, no longer functioned. During this inactive period, she may have started to contemplate her own mortality, especially since many of her peers were dying; particularly hard hitting was the death of Yuri's friend Michi Weglyn in April 1999. She also may have reflected on the tragedies in her life—the deaths of her two children, her husband, her father, and numerous comrades—as well as past conflicts within her family, areas that have not been fully resolved. Finally, there is also an indication that the medication prescribed to Yuri for two years resulted in a psychological and physical deterioration. Shortly after her California doctor, a 1960s activist and friend, discontinued the use of this medication and placed her on an antidepressant, her depression abated somewhat.[4]

The combination of high-quality medical and mental health care, along with a strong support network of family and friends, enabled Yuri gradually to regain her physical and psychological health. Also, in August and September 1999, three significant advances in the political prisoner movement helped facilitate her recovery. First, Laura Whitehorn gained release from prison on parole. That Whitehorn visited Yuri, bringing handcrafted gifts from the six women political prisoners incarcerated with Whitehorn in the Federal Correctional Institute (FCI) at Dublin in northern California, speaks to Yuri's revered position in the political prisoner movement. Although Yuri only had the strength to visit for a few minutes, seeing Whitehorn freed from prison was a boost to her spirits. Second, Silvia Baraldini, a U.S. political prisoner and Italian national, attained the long-sought-after transfer to Italy to finish her prison sentence in close proximity to her ailing mother. Third, after being incarcerated for close to twenty years, eleven Puerto Rican prisoners of war received presidential clemency and exited prison. That Yuri took a keen interest in these developments also signaled her improving health.[5]

Because Yuri required the availability of round-the-clock care, after being discharged from the hospital, she moved into an assisted-living facility in Berkeley. By September 1999, she realized that she could no longer live on her own and, with no apparent resistance, had her family move her belongings out of her New York home. After she had occupied the same apartment in Harlem for almost forty years, it was hard for many of Yuri's friends to believe that she had actually left New York. By February 2000, as her health improved and as space opened up, she moved to her preferred choice of residence, an independent-living senior facility in Oakland, with an on-site medical clinic and twenty-four-hour care as needed.[6]

To those who have witnessed Yuri's fiercely independent spirit, the ease with which she made the transition into retirement home living in California was surprising. While she would have wanted to remain in Harlem had her health permitted, she was able to accept the limitations of her condition, perhaps because she had hit rock bottom. But as her health improved, having less freedom was frustrating at times. When Yuri first entered the Oakland facility, for example, she was prohibited from leaving the building without an escort. On many days, she looked out her window at the copy center across the street, annoyed that she could not simply go by herself to duplicate political materials for a mass mailing.[7]

But living at the senior home also has its advantages. In the same way that Bill and others helped Yuri manage her schedule, decline requests, and tell visitors it was time to leave, the residential facility provided a framework for regulating her life. She had to eat, take medication, and attend physical therapy and counseling sessions at specified times. The facility's regimented program also enabled this former night owl to turn in early and get much-needed rest. She could justify refusing requests or cutting short phone calls based on her illness and living situation. Being close to family also was useful in this regard, as Audee in particular screened some of the demands placed on her mother. Moreover, when she was living with her family, despite their strenuous reassurances to the contrary, Yuri felt that she was a burden to them. The senior home granted her a greater degree of independence. As her health improved and the home lifted its strict rules, Yuri has been able to come and go as she pleases. And that she does—as numerous friends, activists, family members, and acquaintances visit or take her out to eat or to attend political or cultural events and meetings. Over time, Yuri has also made her small room fit her lifestyle. In addition to the standard single bed, chest of drawers, and kitchenette, there are a computer, file cabinet, small writing table, and a couple of folding chairs crammed into the tiny space to facilitate her political work. Photos of family, friends, political prisoners, and other activists take up much of the wall space. A poster of Mumia Abu-Jamal and flyers of Movement events are taped everywhere on the walls, even in the small bathroom. A few teddy bears also made the trip. Yuri's room has the same warm and cluttered environment that she created in her home in Harlem.[8]

Living in California has enabled Yuri to strengthen her relationship with her family. The proximity and the slower pace of Yuri's political activities has allowed her children and grandchildren to spend time with her in a more relaxed atmosphere. Living close by are Audee and her husband, Herb Holman (and Herb's college-age son Herbie when he visits his parents), Eddie and his wife, Pamela Wu, and Yuri's niece Elizabeth Nakahara, all of whom visit on a weekly basis. Jimmy and his wife, Alison (Murakawa), and their children, Maya, Aliya, and Kahlil, and Tommy and his wife, Julie (Miyashiro), and their children, Ryan, Traci, and Christopher, occasionally make the six-hour car trip from Los Angeles.[9] In May 2000, for the first time in their adult years, Yuri and her twin brother, Peter Nakahara, who lived an hour away in San Jose, were able to celebrate their birthday together.[10] At the celebration, Yuri received a heartwarming gift, a three-volume scrapbook. Audee, Elizabeth, and activist-friend Stephanie Tang collected photographs, letters, and other memorabilia from friends spanning the eight decades of Yuri's life. The following year, her children threw a surprise eightieth birthday bash for Yuri at Pro-Arts, a community art gallery in Oakland. Knowing that Yuri would be self-conscious and upset by having so much attention paid to her, her children used the birthday party to raise funds for prisoner David Wong. In part because of the injustices in the case, and probably even more so, because of their admiration for Yuri, friends contributed five thousand dollars to hire an investigator. It is fitting that her celebration was used in the service of justice as well as to bring numerous people together to share old memories, meet new friends, and strengthen political bonds.[11]

Yuri's passion for justice also returned with her improved health.

Living in the Bay Area, a mecca of political opportunities, has turned out to be an exciting experience. There is one political or cultural event after another, as well as a thriving activist community. Many West Coast activists have eagerly invited this revered Movement leader, now in their proximity, to speak at their programs. Yuri is often featured as the keynote speaker, even if she is able to give only a short speech, or is the first person listed on flyers, not only in the Asian American community but also in the political prisoner and Black movements. In northern California, she has spoken at scores of programs, including a tribute to Albert Nuh Washington, a former Black Liberation Army member and political prisoner who was dying of cancer at the time; a book party in 2000 for the release of *Legacy to Liberation: Politics and Culture of Revolutionary Asian Pacific America*; and a program on political prisoners with former political prisoner Linda Evans, whose sentence was commuted by President Clinton in January 2000. At the second national meeting of the Asian Left Forum in 2000, Yuri received a standing ovation from the predominantly twenty-something-year-old Asian American activist audience. In time, Yuri began traveling to speak throughout California and even to the East Coast. In addition, living on the West Coast has enabled her to meet many West Coast activists, including former Black prisoners with whom she corresponded twenty to thirty years ago. Some of these local activists visit Yuri on a regular basis. And different friends from New York, as well as Los Angeles, have visited almost every week, making the distance between her New York comrades and herself seem smaller.[12]

Significantly, Yuri was instrumental in forming a northern California David Wong Support Committee and initiated broadening the committee's mission statement to address other interconnected political issues. She also organized support for the widely publicized case of Dr. Wen Ho Lee, a Taiwanese immigrant physicist indicted on fifty-nine counts of mishandling restricted nuclear data at the Los Alamos National Laboratory in New Mexico, where he was employed for more than two decades. His case sparked controversy over allegations that China stole U.S. nuclear weapons designs, but Lee was never charged with spying or with passing information to China or any other country. He was fired from his job and sat in solitary confinement in a New Mexico penitentiary awaiting trial for nine months. By contrast, in a comparable case, former CIA director John Deutsch, who transferred top-secret files to his unsecured home computer, received only a reprimand and had his security clearance revoked. The differential treatment of these two men led many, particularly in the Chinese and Asian American communities, to raise the charge of racial discrimination. As is her style, Yuri sent out several mass mailings to generate support for Lee's case. The nationwide grassroots campaign for fair treatment for Lee contributed to his release from prison and the dismissal of all but one of the charges against him.[13]

As the events of September 11, 2001, unfolded, Yuri watched in shock and horror at the mounting death toll at the World Trade Center and Pentagon. But even in the atmosphere of flag-waving patriotism, she began speaking out, as she had done so many times before, against the predictable escalation of U.S. military incursions, this time into the Middle East: "The goal of the war [on terrorism] is more than just getting oil and fuel. The United States is set on taking over the world." Drawing on her own experiences, she made connections between the treatment of Japanese Americans in the 1940s and Arabs and Muslims sixty years later, as relayed in a *War Times* interview: "The United States has gained support for its wars by using media to whip up war hysteria. During World War II they demonized the Japanese; today they are demonizing Muslims and Arabs. And just as the war against Japan . . . resulted in the racial profiling and internment of Japanese in America, the 'war on terrorism' has resulted in the racial profiling and detainment of Arabs, Muslims, South Asians, and all people of color living in the U.S. today." As during the Iran hostage crisis two decades earlier, Yuri once again worked to galvanize Japanese American condemnation of discriminatory treatment of Arabs and Muslims.[14]

But more than merely defending civil liberties, Yuri's politics embody a revolutionary, anti-imperialist ideology. By subverting the very definition of terrorism, she hopes to contextualize the motives for, from her perspective, the U.S. government's fanatical targeting of an Osama bin Laden or a Saddam Hussein: "It's important that we all understand that the main terrorist and the main enemy of the world's people is the U.S. government. Racism has been a weakness of this country from the beginning. Throughout history, all people of color, and all people who don't see eye-to-eye with the U.S. government have been subjected to American terror." In the Bay Area, Yuri has been one of the most sought after speakers for the growing antiwar movement, one that Yuri believes has the potential to match that of the Vietnam era. The significance of this parallel would not be lost on historian Howard Zinn, who documented the crucial role of the American antiwar movement, in conjunction with the fierce fighting of the Vietnamese, in ending that war. Zinn relayed, for example, that President Richard Nixon, who at the height of the antiwar activities vowed that "under no circumstances will I be affected by [the antiwar protests,]" admitted a decade later: "I knew, however, that after all the protests and the Moratorium, American public opinion would be seriously divided by any military escalation of the war." Zinn noted, "It was a rare presidential admission of the power of public protest." To Yuri, building an antiwar movement requires more than public speaking; it requires organizing at the grassroots level. So in the Bay Area, she, along with 1960s revolutionary nationalists from the Black Panther Party, the American Indian Movement, and the Young Lords, among others, formulated radical responses to the "war on terrorism" through the short-lived People's United Front.[15]

The power of ordinary people to effect social change, experienced by Yuri many times over the past four decades, has strengthened her resolve to continue marching in demonstrations to free wrongly incarcerated prisoners; visiting political prisoner Marilyn Buck at FCI Dublin, about thirty minutes east of Oakland; writing her semiannual political prisoner update; attending political meetings; establishing new organizations; and informing people about a variety of political issues.

Despite illness, the death of loved ones, the incarceration of numerous comrades, and other difficulties, Yuri Kochiyama carries in her heart a love for people and concern for making this world a better place. It is this unwavering struggle for justice that is Yuri's legacy.

Notes

Introduction

1. Yuri Kochiyama, interview with author; Arthur Tobier, ed., *Fishmerchant's Daughter: Yuri Kochiyama, an Oral History,* vol. 1 (New York: Community Documentation Workshop, 1981), 7; Rea Tajiri and Pat Saunders, *Yuri Kochiyama: Passion for Justice* (video, 1993).

2. Tobier, *Fishmerchant's Daughter,* 6–7; Yuri Kochiyama, interview with author.

3. Yuri Kochiyama, interview with author; Tetsudan Kashima, "American Mistreatment of Internees during World War II: Enemy Alien Japanese," in *Japanese Americans: From Relocation to Redress,* ed. Roger Daniels, Sandra Taylor, and Harry Kitano (Seattle: University of Washington Press, 1991), 52–53; Paul Spickard, *Japanese Americans: The Formation and Transformations of an Ethnic Group* (New York: Twayne Publishers, 1996), 93–96.

4. Bob Kumamoto, "The Search for Spies: American Counterintelligence and the Japanese American Community, 1931–1942," *Amerasia Journal* 6 (1979): 45–75; Jacobus tenBroek, Edward Barnhart, and Floyd Matson, *Prejudice, War and the Constitution* (Berkeley and Los Angeles: University of California Press, 1954), 99–103; Michi Weglyn, *Years of Infamy: The Untold Story of America's Concentration Camps* (New York: Morrow Quill, 1976), 33–53; Roger Daniels, *Prisoners without Trial* (New York: Hill and Wang, 1993), 22–26.

5. Yuri Kochiyama, interview with author. Yuri's memories of the community's reactions to her father's arrest were confirmed by childhood friends Vivian (Martinez) Hardy, interview with author, January 26, 2000; and Norma (Benedetti) Brutti, interview with author, January 16, 2000.

6. Kenji Murase, "An 'Enemy Alien's' Mysterious Fate," *National Japanese American Historical Society* 9 (Winter 1997): 5; Peter Nakahara, interview with author, February 17, 1999; Elizabeth Nakahara, interview with author, February 27, 2000; Yuri Kochiyama, interview with author; entry on Kichisa-

buro Nomura in *Japan: An Illustrated Encyclopedia* (Tokyo: Kodansha, 1993), 1111–12; entry on Kichisaburo Nomura in *Current Biography* (New York: H. W. Wilson, 1941), 614–16.

7. The FBI files on Seiichi Nakahara were obtained under the Freedom of Information Act by Yuri Kochiyama. Memorandum, Special Agent in Charge, Los Angeles, August 27, 1941; Memorandum to Chief, Special Defense Unit, FBI, December 6, 1941; Los Angeles, 100:7067, 12/23/41; Memorandum, (name deleted), Los Angeles, n.d. Also see Yuji Ichioka, "Japanese Immigrant Nationalism: The Issei and the Sino-Japanese War, 1927–1941," *California History* (Fall 1990): 260–311; Yuji Ichioka, *The Issei: The World of the First Generation Japanese Immigrants, 1885–1924* (New York: Free Press, 1988), 156–61; Kumamoto, "The Search for Spies," 55–62.

8. Yuri Kochiyama, interview with author; Tobier, *Fishmerchant's Daughter*, 9.

9. Murase, "An 'Enemy Alien's' Mysterious Fate"; Peter Nakahara, interview with author, February 17, 1999; Yuri Kochiyama, interview with author.

10. FBI files indicate that Seiichi Nakahara had a hearing before the Alien Enemy Control Board on January 10, 1942, during which they discussed his involvement with various Japanese American organizations and his family's loyalty to America. The board recommended that Nakahara be paroled on a bond of $3,500 in the care of Attorney Ben A. Hill, and he was released from custody on January 20, 1942 (FBI report, Los Angeles, January 22, 1942; FBI report, Los Angeles, January 23, 1942; Department of Justice file 146:13:2:12:58, n.d.). Although the FBI files report that Seiichi Nakahara died of natural causes on January 22, 1942, most reports, including those of the family and the death certificate, indicate that he died on January 21, 1942 (certificate of death for Seiichi Nakahara, Certification of Vital Record, County of Los Angeles, Registrar-Recorder/County Clerk; FBI file, Los Angeles, January 22, 1942).

11. Yuri Kochiyama, interview with author; Elizabeth Nakahara, interview with author, February 27, 2000; Peter Nakahara, interview with author, February 19, 1999; death certificate for Seiichi Nakahara; FBI file, Los Angeles, January 22, 1942.

12. Diary by Yuri Kochiyama (Mary Nakahara), "The Bordered World," vol. 2, July 21, 1942, Japanese American National Museum.

13. Tajiri and Saunders, *Yuri Kochiyama: Passion for Justice* (video).

14. For a discussion of the significance of race and place in Yuri Kochiyama's political development, see Diane C. Fujino, "Race, Place, and Political Development," unpublished manuscript. On oppositional consciousness, see Jane Mansbridge and Aldon Morris, eds., *Oppositional Consciousness: The Subjective Roots of Social Protest* (Chicago: University of Chicago Press, 2001). Harlem had a much denser Black population than did midtown Manhattan; see Davis McEntire, *Residence and Race* (Berkeley and Los Angeles: University of California Press, 1960), 25.

15. Yuri Kochiyama, "The Role of Political Prisoners: Internationally and Here," speech, Columbia University, October 1, 1996.

16. Charles M. Payne, *I've Got the Light of Freedom: The Organizing Tradition and the Mississippi Freedom Struggle* (Berkeley and Los Angeles: University of California Press, 1995), 365.

17. Yuri has been the backbone of the support committee for David Wong, whose twenty-five-year-to-life sentence for killing another prisoner was based on flimsy evidence, claim Yuri and other supporters. Through the work of his defense committee, Wong became politically conscious. For a detailed account of Wong's case, see chapter 9.

18. The model minority image locates the cause of Asian American's relatively high educational and occupational success, at least relative to other minority groups, in their ability to work hard, delay gratification, and make personal sacrifices. The historical moment at which the image emerged—in two mainstream magazines in the mid-1960s, though certainly based on ideas from a couple of decades earlier—is important. The mid-1960s was a period in which the Black movement was becoming increasingly radical. The model minority logic promotes passivity and hard work as a pathway to upward mobility, while suppressing political dissent. The model minority logic has also been criticized for creating racial conflict between Asian Americans and other minority groups, hiding social problems within Asian America, and homogenizing the community. See William Petersen, "Success Story, Japanese-American Style," *New York Times Magazine,* January 9, 1966; "Success Story of One Minority Group in U.S.," *U.S. News and World Report,* December 26, 1966; Bob Suzuki, "Education and the Socialization of Asian Americans: A Revisionist Analysis of the 'Model Minority,' Thesis," *Amerasia Journal* 4:2 (1977): 23–25; Lucie Cheng and Philip Q. Yang, "The 'Model Minority' Deconstructed," in *Contemporary Asian America,* ed. Min Zhou and James Gatewood (New York: New York University Press, 2000).

19. While information from the documentary, *Yuri Kochiyama: Passion for Justice* by Rea Tajiri and Pat Saunders (1993), is contained in this book, I cannot at present discuss the unique contributions of this book in relation to the other two written publications. Her Japanese biography, *Yuri: The Life and Times of Yuri Kochiyama,* by journalist Mayumi Nakazawa (Tokyo: Bungenshugu, 1998), is written in Japanese and has received very little attention in the United States. Her memoir, *Passing It On,* ed. Marjorie Lee, Akemi Kochiyama-Sardinha, and Audee Kochiyama-Holman (Los Angeles: UCLA Asian American Studies Center, 2004), is just now being released as this book goes to press.

20. My Ph.D.-level training in clinical psychology positions me to create a psychologically framed biography. While I analyze motivations and psychological issues particularly with respect to Yuri's political development, I consciously chose not to make any psychoanalysis of her personality and "nonpolitical" life choices the primary impetus of this book. As described in this biography, the wide-reaching significance of Yuri's life rests with her political contributions, work that lies at the intersections of psychology, sociology, and history.

21. Sherna Berger Gluck and Daphne Patai, eds., *Women's Words: The Feminist Practice of Oral History* (New York: Routledge, 1991); Mary Maynard

and June Purvis, eds., *Researching Women's Lives from a Feminist Perspective* (Bristol, PA: Taylor and Francis, 1994); James Bennett, "Human Values in Oral History," *Oral History Review* 11 (1983): 1–15.

22. On oral history methodology, see Ronald J. Grele, ed., *Envelopes of Sound: The Art of Oral History* (New York: Praeger, 1991); David K. Dunaway and Willa K. Baum, eds., *Oral History: An Interdisciplinary Anthology*, 2nd ed. (Walnut Creek, CA: AltaMira, 1996); Gluck and Patai, *Women's Words*; Eva M. McMahan and Kim Lacy Rogers, eds., *Interactive Oral History Interviewing* (Hillsdale, NJ: Lawrence Erlbaum, 1994); Robert Pers and Alistair Thomson, eds., *The Oral History Reader* (London and New York: Routledge, 1998); Donald Ritchie, *Doing Oral History* (New York: Twayne Publishers, 1995); Kim Lacy Rogers, "Memory, Struggle, and Power: On Interviewing Political Activists," *Oral History Review* 15 (1987): 165–84.

23. Gary Y. Okihiro, "Oral History and the Writing of Ethnic History," in Dunaway and Baum, *Oral History*, 209.

24. Petersen, "Success Story, Japanese-American Style"; "Success Story of One Minority Group in U.S."; Suzuki, "Education and the Socialization of Asian Americans: A Revisionist Analysis of the 'Model Minority,' Thesis."

25. Robert F. Barsky, *Noam Chomsky: A Life of Dissent* (Cambridge, MA: MIT Press, 1997), 5.

26. Aldon Morris and Carol McClurg Mueller, eds., *Frontiers in Social Movement Theory* (New Haven, CT: Yale University Press, 1992); Mansbridge and Morris, *Oppositional Consciousness*; James M. Jasper, *The Art of Moral Protest: Culture, Biography, and Creativity in Social Movements* (Chicago: University of Chicago Press, 1997), 29–39; Donatella della Porta, "Life Histories in the Analysis of Social Movement Activists," in *Studying Collective Action*, ed. Mario Diani and Ron Eyerman (London: Sage, 1992), 168–93; Rogers, "Memory, Struggle, and Power"; Kim Lacy Rogers, *Righteous Lives: Narratives of the New Orleans Civil Rights Movement* (New York: New York University Press, 1993).

27. For useful overviews and critiques of social movements theories, see Doug McAdam, *Political Process and the Development of Black Insurgency, 1930–1970*, 2nd ed. (Chicago: University of Chicago Press, 1999), 5–59; Steven M. Buechler, *Social Movements in Advanced Capitalism: The Political Economy and Cultural Construction of Social Activism* (Oxford: Oxford University Press, 2000), 19–58.

28. Michael Omi and Howard Winant, *Racial Formation in the United States from the 1960s to the 1990s*, 2nd ed. (New York: Routledge, 1994), 9–50, 55, 99; Everett Hughes, ed., *Race and Culture*, vol. 1 of *The Collected Papers of Robert E. Park* (Glencoe, IL: Free Press, 1950); Robert Blauner, *Racial Oppression in America* (New York: Harper and Row, 1972), 2–110.

29. I thank Marilyn Buck and Matef Harmachis for helping me think through this issue.

30. Scholars use the term *social movements* to refer to, according to Marcy Darnovsky, Barbara Epstein, and Richard Flacks, "collective efforts by socially and politically subordinated people to challenge the conditions and assumptions of their lives." They go on: "collective action becomes a 'movement' when participants refuse to accept the boundaries of established institutional rules and routinized roles. Single instances of such popular defiance don't make a movement; the term refers to persistent, patterned, and widely distributed collective challenges to the status quo." See Marcy Darnovsky, Barbara Epstein, and Richard Flacks, eds., *Cultural Politics and Social Movements* (Philadelphia: Temple University Press, 1995), vii.

1. A Color-Blind Patriot in Prewar America

1. Tobier, *Fishmerchant's Daughter,* vol. 1, 10; Yuri Kochiyama, interview with author; Tajiri and Saunders, *Yuri Kochiyama: Passion for Justice* (video).

2. Yuri Kochiyama, "War-Time Experiences in Relation to Today," speech, Hunter College High School, New York, May 5, 1969; Yuri Kochiyama, "Fifty Years' Commemoration of Japanese American Internment," speech, Binghamton University, February 22, 1992; Daniels, *Prisoners without Trial,* 27–29.

3. Morton Grozdins, *Americans Betrayed: Politics and the Japanese Evacuation* (Chicago: University of Chicago Press, 1949), 19–61, 180–207; tenBroek, Barnhart, and Matson, *Prejudice, War and the Constitution,* 185–98.

4. Yuri Kochiyama, interview with author; Yuri Kochiyama, "Fifty Years' Commemoration of Japanese American Internment," speech; Peter Nakahara's army records indicate he attended UC Berkeley following his tenure at [Compton] junior college (Army of the United States, Separation Qualification Record, WD AGO form).

5. Peter Nakahara, interviews with author, February 17, 1999, and January 12, 2000; Army of the United States, Separation Qualification Record, WD AGO Form 100; Army of the United States, Honorable Discharge, WD AGO Form 53-55, December 6, 1945; Yuri Kochiyama, interview with author.

6. Yuri Kochiyama, interview with author; Jeanne Wakatsuki Houston, *Farewell to Manzanar* (New York: Bantam Books, 1974), 13–15; Lauren Kessler, *Stubborn Twig* (New York: Penguin Books, 1993), 207.

7. Yuri Kochiyama, interview with author.

8. Yuri Kochiyama, interview with author; Peter Nakahara, interview with author, February 17, 1999; Kanichi Kawasaki, "The Japanese Community of East San Pedro, Terminal Island, California" (master's thesis, University of Southern California, 1931). On residential segregation, see John Modell, *The Economics and Politics of Racial Accommodation: The Japanese of Los Angeles, 1900–1942* (Urbana: University of Illinois Press, 1977); Davis McEntire, *Residence and Race* (Berkeley and Los Angeles: University of California Press, 1960).

9. Yuri Kochiyama, interview with author; Yuri Kochiyama, "Strength and

Diversity: Japanese American Women and Civil Rights," speech, Gene Autry Western Heritage Museum, Los Angeles, April 23, 1994; Tobier, *Fishmerchant's Daughter*, 1–2; Kanichi Kawasaki, *The Japanese Community of East San Pedro, Terminal Island, California*; John Modell, *Economics and Politics of Racial Accommodation*, 70–71; Monica Miya (Miwako Oana), interview with author, January 17, 2000.

10. *Harbor Light*, San Pedro High School yearbook, San Pedro, California, summer 1939, courtesy of Norma (Benedetti) Brutti; Norma (Benedetti) Brutti, Autograph Book, 1933; Yuri Kochiyama, interview with author; Norma (Benedetti) Brutti, interview with author, January 16, 2000; Nan (Carlson) Grimm, interview with author, January 19, 2000; Vivian (Martinez) Hardy, interview with author, January 26, 2000; Monica Miya (Miwako Oana), interview with author, January 24, 2000; Yuriko (Endo) Yoshihara, letter to author, February 2000; Spickard, *Japanese Americans*, 81–82.

11. Monica Sone, *Nisei Daughter* (Seattle: University of Washington Press, 1953), 118–19; Yuri Kochiyama, interview with author.

12. Omi and Winant, *Racial Formation in the United States*, 117; Tobier, *Fishmerchant's Daughter*, 2–3; Yuri Kochiyama, interview with author.

13. Article by Teek Kondo and Mary Tama (Nakahara) Kondo in a family photo album compiled by Elizabeth Nakahara and Chiyo Nakahara, n.d. Their description of Seiichi Nakahara's history is generally supported by archival documents. See Certification of Vital Records, County of Los Angeles; Immigration Service record, located at Japanese American National Museum; Family Record Card, Records of U.S. Army Commands, Western Defense Command and Fourth Army, no. 0309, located at U.S. National Archives, Washington, D.C.; Yamato Ichihashi, *Japanese in the United States* (Palo Alto, CA: Stanford University Press, 1932), 80; *Japan: An Illustrated Encyclopedia* (Tokyo: Kondasha, 1993), 429, 643.

14. Seiichi Nakahara and Tsuma Nakahara, Immigration Service record, located at Japanese American National Museum; Ichioka, *The Issei*, 71–72; Yuri Kochiyama, interview with author.

15. Nakahara Family Record Card, Records of U.S. Army Commands, Western Defense Command and Fourth Army, no. 0309, located at U.S. National Archives, Washington, D.C.; Separation Qualification Record, Army of the United States, WD AGO form; Malcolm X with Alex Haley, *The Autobiography of Malcolm X* (New York: Grove Press, 1965), 2; *Our President Ho Chi Minh* (Hanoi: Foreign Languages Publication House, 1970), introduction; Mei Nakano, *Japanese American Women: Three Generations, 1890–1990* (Berkeley: Mina Press, 1990), 40–41; Linda Tamura, *The Hood River Issei: An Oral History of Japanese Settlers in Oregon's Hood River Valley* (Urbana: University of Illinois Press, 1993), 102–3; Yuri Kochiyama, interview with author.

16. Evelyn Nakano Glenn, *Issei, Nisei, War Bride* (Philadelphia: Temple University Press, 1986), 51, 68; Ichioka, *The Issei*, 40–56, 71–72, 164–67, 172–75; Nakano, *Japanese American Women*, 36, 40, 45–48, 104; Spickard, *Japanese*

Americans, 68; Jere Takahashi, *Nisei Sansei: Shifting Japanese American Identities and Politics* (Philadelphia: Temple University Press, 1997), 35; Tamura, *Hood River Issei,* 102.

17. Ichioka, *The Issei,* 164–69; Nakano, *Japanese American Women,* 41–48; Nakano Glenn, *Issei, Nisei, War Bride,* 68–75; Tamura, *Hood River Issei,* 98–102; Sylvia Yanagisako, *Transforming the Past: Tradition and Kinship among Japanese Americans* (Palo Alto, CA: Stanford University Press, 1985), 46; Seiichi Nakahara and Tsuma Nakahara, Immigration Service Record, located at Japanese American National Museum; FBI Files, Masaichi Nakahara (a.k.a. Seiichi Nakahara), 100-40117-16x, n.d., stamped September 19, 1942; Yuri Kochiyama, interview with author.

18. FBI Files, Masaichi Nakahara (a.k.a. Seiichi Nakahara), 100-40117-16x, n.d., stamped September 19, 1942; Monica Miya (Miwako Oana), interview with author, January 17, 2000; Peter Nakahara, interview with author, February 17, 1999; Nan (Carlson) Grimm, interview with author, January 19, 2000; Sumi (Seo) Seki, interview with author, February 13, 2000; Yuriko (Endo) Yoshihara, letter to author, February 2000; Tobier, *Fishmerchant's Daughter,* 3.

19. Yuri Kochiyama, interview with author; Nan (Carlson) Grimm, interview with author, January 19, 2000; Vivian (Martinez) Hardy, interview with author, January 26, 2000; Monica Miya (Miwako Oana), interview with author, January 17, 2000.

20. Vivian (Martinez) Hardy, interview with author, January 26, 2000; Yuriko (Endo) Yoshihara, letter to author, February 2000.

21. Yanagisako, *Transforming the Past,* 27–62; Judith Stacey, "Backward toward the Postmodern Family: Reflections on Gender, Kinship, and Class in the Silicon Valley," in *Rethinking the Family: Some Feminist Questions,* ed. Barrie Thorne with Marilyn Yalom (Boston: Northeastern University Press, 1992), 91–118; Nakano, *Japanese American Women,* 33–39; Akemi Kikumura, *Through Harsh Winters* (Novato, CA: Chandler and Sharp, 1995), 119–35; Harry Kitano, *Japanese Americans: The Evolution of a Subculture* (Englewood Cliffs, NJ: Prentice-Hall, 1976), 32–52; Yuri Kochiyama, interview with author.

22. Peter Nakahara, interview with author, January 12, 2000; Monica Miya (Miwako Oana), interview with author, January 17, 2000; Yuri Kochiyama, interview with author.

23. Monica Miya (Miwako Oana), interview with author, January 17, 2000; Norma (Benedetti) Brutti, interview with author, January 16, 2000; Nan (Carlson) Grimm, interview with author, January 19, 2000; Vivian (Martinez) Hardy, interview with author, January 26, 2000; Nakano, *Japanese American Women,* 105; Spickard, *Japanese Americans,* 69–73.

24. Peter Nakahara, interviews with author, February 17, 1999, and January 12, 2000; Elizabeth Nakahara, interview with author, February 27, 2000; Yuri Kochiyama, interview with author.

25. Yuri Kochiyama, interview with author; Peter Nakahara, interview with

author, February 17, 1999; Monica Miya (Miwako Oana), interview with author, January 17, 2000; Yuriko (Endo) Yoshihara, letter to author, February 2000.

26. Nan (Carlson) Grimm, interview with author, January 19, 2000; Yuri Kochiyama, interview with author; Monica Miya (Miwako Oana), interview with author, January 17, 2000; Peter Nakahara, interviews with author, February 17, 1999, and January 12, 2000; Sumi (Seo) Seki, interview with author, February 13, 2000; Yuriko (Endo) Yoshihara, letter to author, February 2000.

27. Tsuma Nakahara, Immigration Service Record, located at Japanese American National Museum; Yanagisako, *Transforming the Past,* 51–58; Spickard, *Japanese Americans,* 68–70; Peter Nakahara, interview with author, January 12, 2000.

28. Sumi (Seo) Seki, interview with author, February 13, 2000.

29. Peter Nakahara, interview with author, January 12, 2000.

30. Yuri Kochiyama, interview with author; Nan (Carlson) Grimm, interview with author, January 19, 2000; Vivian (Martinez) Hardy, interview with author, January 26, 2000; Monica Miya (Miwako Oana), interview with author, January 24, 2000.

31. Peter Nakahara, interviews with author, February 17, 1999, and January 12, 2000; Monica Miya (Miwako Oana), interviews with author, January 17 and 24, 2000; Yuri Kochiyama, interview with author; Spickard, *Japanese Americans,* 69.

32. Peter Nakahara, interview with author, February 17, 1999; Yuri Kochiyama, interview with author. Seiichi Nakahara's death certificate indicates that he had "chronic bronchial asthma" from 1925 and "old pulmonary tuberculosis" from 1928 (Certification of Vital Record, County of Los Angeles).

33. Yuri Kochiyama, interview with author; Elizabeth Nakahara, interview with author, February 27, 2000.

34. Nan (Carlson) Grimm, interview with author, January 19, 2000; Vivian (Martinez) Hardy, interview with author, January 26, 2000.

35. Yuri's traditional views on marriage are discussed in chapter 3.

36. Nan (Carlson) Grimm, interview with author, January 19, 2000; Nan (Carlson) Grimm, letter to Mary Kochiyama, February 22, 1994.

37. Yuriko (Endo) Yoshihara, letter to author, February 2000; Norma (Benedetti) Brutti, interview with author, January 16, 2000; Sumi (Seo) Seki, interview with author, February 13, 2000.

38. Peter Nakahara, interview with author, February 17, 1999; Nan (Carlson) Grimm, interview with author, January 19, 2000; Nan (Carlson) Grimm, letter to Mary Kochiyama, February 22, 1994.

39. Nan (Carlson) Grimm, interview with author, January 19, 2000; Yuriko (Endo) Yoshihara, letter to author, February 2000; Peter Nakahara, interview with author, February 17, 1999; Elizabeth Nakahara, interview with author, February 27, 2000; Sumi (Seo) Seki, interview with author, February 13, 2000; Yuri Kochiyama, interview with author.

40. Yuri Kochiyama, interview with author; Vivian (Martinez) Hardy, interview with author, January 26, 2000; Norma (Benedetti) Brutti, interview with author, January 16, 2000; Monica Miya (Miwako Oana), interviews with author, January 17 and 24, 2000; Peter Nakahara, interview with author, February 17, 1999.

41. Peter Nakahara, interview with author, February 17, 1999; Yuri Kochiyama, interview with author; Monica Miya (Miwako Oana), interview with author, January 17, 2000; Yuriko (Endo) Yoshihara, letter to author, February 2000.

42. Ichioka, *The Issei*, 156–64, 207–10, 226–37; Modell, *Economics and Politics of Racial Accommodation*, 100–102; FBI Files, Masaichi Nakahara (a.k.a. Seiichi Nakahara), 100-40117-16x, n.d., stamped September 19, 1942; Seiichi Nakahara, certificate of death, County of Los Angeles, Registrar-Recorder/County Clerk, 1942.

43. About 25 percent of Japanese in Los Angeles County in the early 1930s were Christians. See Brian Hayashi, *For the Sake of Our Japanese Brethren* (Palo Alto, CA: Stanford University Press, 1995), 2–4; Ichioka, *The Issei*, 16–19; Spickard, *Japanese Americans*, 54–56, 81–82; Yuri Kochiyama, interview with author.

44. Yuri Kochiyama, group letter to the Crusaders, May 7, 1944, courtesy of Dollie (Nagai) Fukawa.

45. Yuri Kochiyama, interview with author. On leveling inequalities and the year of jubilee, in the Bible, see Isaiah 61 and Luke 4; on serving others, see Matthew 25: 31–46 and Luke 9:13–17; on releasing captives, see Isaiah 61:1–2, Luke 4:18.

46. Yuri Kochiyama, interview with author. For the biblical reference, see Deuteronomy 5:9–10.

47. Yuri Kochiyama, letter to author, n.d.

48. Nan (Carlson) Grimm, interview with author, January 19, 2000; Betty Robinson, interview with author, February 6, 2000.

49. See the poems of Rudyard Kipling at www.poetryloverspage.com/poets/kipling/kipling_ind.html; Mary Nakahara Kochiyama, "Poem Embodies the Lasting Spirit of San Pedro," *San Pedro News-Pilot*, April 1, 1989; Yuri Kochiyama, scrapbook, 1942; Yuri Kochiyama, interview with author.

50. Yuri Kochiyama, interview with author.

51. Steve Marconi, "San Pedro's Favorite Daughter Given a Hero's Return," *San Pedro News-Pilot*, August 7, 1989; Yuri Kochiyama, interview with author; *Harbor Light*, San Pedro High school yearbook, San Pedro, California, summer 1939, courtesy of Norma (Benedetti) Brutti.

52. Yuri Kochiyama, interview with author; Tobier, *Fishmerchant's Daughter*, 4; Marconi, "San Pedro's Favorite Daughter Given a Hero's Return"; Tom Coulter, "'Welcome Home, Mary' Reunion Salutes San Pedro High School's 1939 Spirit Girl," *San Pedro News-Pilot*, June 7, 1984; Panovich quoted in Barbara Baird, "School Spirit," *Los Angeles Times*, August 10, 1989; San Pedro High School newspaper, *Fore 'N' Aft*, November 3, 1938, lists Mary Nakahara as editor of girls' sports.

53. Yuri Kochiyama, interview with author; Mary Nakahara Kochiyama, "Poem Embodies the Lasting Spirit of San Pedro."

54. Yuri Kochiyama, interview with author; Coulter, "'Welcome Home, Mary.'"

55. Coulter, "'Welcome Home, Mary.'" "Sportsman Prayer" plaque in Yuri's home; Yuri Kochiyama, interview with author.

56. Coulter, "'Welcome Home, Mary.'" Mary Nakahara's "Sunday School Teacher's" creed, written in 1939, cited in Mary Nakahara, group letter to the Crusaders, May 7, 1944, courtesy of Dollie (Nagai) Fukawa; Yuri Kochiyama, interview with author; Nakano, *Japanese American Women,* 111.

57. W. E. B. Du Bois, *The Souls of Black Folk* (1903; reprint, New York: Bantam Books, 1989), 3; Sone, *Nisei Daughter,* 22; Nakano, *Japanese American Women,* 105; Yuri Kochiyama, interview with author.

58. Spickard, *Japanese Americans,* 73–75; Nakano, *Japanese American Women,* 55–56, 114–15.

59. Yuri Kochiyama, interview with author.

60. Yuri Kochiyama, interview with author; Peter Nakahara, interview with author, January 12, 2000; Sumi (Seo) Seki, interview with author, February 13, 2000; Raymond Okamura, "Iva Ikuko Toguri: Victim of an American Fantasy," in *Counterpoint: Perspectives on Asian America,* ed. Emma Gee (Los Angeles: UCLA Asian American Studies Center, 1976), 86–96.

61. Nakano, *Japanese American Women,* 111; Takahashi, *Nisei Sansei,* 42–44; Paul Spickard, *Mixed Blood: Intermarriage and Ethnic Identity in Twentieth-Century America* (Madison: University of Wisconsin Press, 1989), 70, 279–80, 374–75; Yuri Kochiyama, interview with author; Peter Nakahara, interview with author, January 12, 2000; Monica Miya (Miwako Oana), interview with author, January 17, 2000; Sumi (Seo) Seki, interview with author, February 13, 2000.

62. Yuri Kochiyama, interview with author; Peter Nakahara, interview with author, January 12, 2000.

63. Nakano, *Japanese American Women,* 110–13; Spickard, *Japanese Americans,* 80; Takahashi, *Nisei Sansei,* 40–42; Dorothy Thomas with Charles Kikuchi and James Sakoda, *The Salvage* (Berkeley and Los Angeles: University of California Press, 1952), 72–142, 611; Yuri Kochiyama, interview with author; Yuri's educational history is confirmed by War Relocation Authority, Census Form 26, located at U.S. National Archives, Washington, D.C., courtesy of Brian Hayashi.

64. Tobier, *Fishmerchant's Daughter,* 5–6; Yuri Kochiyama, interview with author; Yuri's work history is confirmed by War Relocation Authority, Census Form 26, located at U.S. National Archives, Washington, D.C., courtesy of Brian Hayashi; Nakano Glenn, *Issei, Nisei, War Bride,* 29; Modell, *Economics and Politics of Racial Accommodation,* 129–31; Nakano, *Japanese American Women,* 117–21; Spickard, *Japanese Americans,* 85–88; Takahashi, *Nisei Sansei,* 36–38; Sone, *Nisei Daughter,* 121.

65. Yuri Kochiyama, "50th Anniversary of the Bombing of Pearl Harbor," speech, Hampshire College, December 5, 1991; Yuri Kochiyama, interview with author.

66. Yuri Kochiyama, interview with author.

2. Concentration Camps and a Growing Awareness of Race

1. Nakahara Family Record Card, Records of U.S. Army Commands, Western Defense Command and Fourth Army, no. 0309, located at U.S. National Archives, Washington, D.C., courtesy of Brian Hayashi; Diary by Yuri Kochiyama (Mary Nakahara), "The Bordered World," vol. 1, April 3, 1942, Japanese American National Museum; Yuri Kochiyama, interview with author; Daniels, *Prisoners without Trial,* 49–55.

2. Kanshi Stanley Yamashita, "Terminal Island: Ethnography of an Ethnic Community: Its Dissolution and Reorganization to a Non-spatial Community" (Ph.D. diss., University of California, Irvine, 1985), 139–47; Daniels, *Prisoners without Trial,* 50; Spickard, *Japanese Americans,* 104.

3. Taft quoted in Roger Daniels, *The Decision to Relocate the Japanese Americans* (Malabar, FL: Robert E. Krieger Publishing, 1990), 53; Daniels, *Prisoners without Trial,* 30–54, 129–30.

4. I consciously use terms such as *forced removal, uprooting,* or *dislocation* instead of the more common and government-sanctioned *evacuation,* which implies movement to protect people from temporary dangerous situations such as floods or earthquakes. The forced removal of Japanese Americans was not for their safety but rather was due to "racism, war hysteria, and the failure of political leadership," as determined by the Commission on Wartime Relocation and Internment of Civilians in 1983. I also consciously use the term *concentration camp* rather than the government-sanctioned, euphemistic *relocation center.* See Raymond Okumura, "The American Concentration Camps: A Cover-up through Euphemistic Terminology," *Journal of Ethnic Studies* 10 (1982): 95–108.

5. On the concentration camps, see Dorothy S. Thomas and Richard S. Nishimoto, *The Spoilage* (1946; reprint, Berkeley and Los Angeles: University of California Press, 1969); Thomas, *The Salvage;* tenBroek, Barnhart, and Matson, *Prejudice, War and the Constitution;* Grodzins, *Americans Betrayed;* Roger Daniels, *Concentration Camps USA: Japanese Americans and World War II* (New York: Holt, Rinehard and Winston, 1971); Weglyn, *Years of Infamy;* Daniels, *The Decision to Relocate the Japanese Americans;* Peter Irons, *Justice at War: The Story of the Japanese American Internment Cases* (New York: Oxford University Press, 1983); Daniels, Taylor, and Kitano, *Japanese Americans;* Daniels, *Prisoners without Trial.* For more, see Paul Spickard's bibliographic essay, *Japanese Americans,* 177–85.

6. Yuri Kochiyama, interview with author; Sumi (Seo) Seki, interview with author, February 13, 2000; Daniels, *Prisoners without Trial,* 55.

7. Yuri Kochiyama, scrapbook, 1942, courtesy of Yuri Kochiyama; Takahashi, *Nisei Sansei,* 85–92.

8. Nakahara Family Record Card, Records of U.S. Army Commands, Western Defense Command and Fourth Army, no. 0309, located at U.S. National Archives, Washington, D.C., courtesy of Brian Hayashi; Diary by Yuri Kochiyama (Mary Nakahara), "The Bordered World," 2 vols., 1942, Japanese American National Museum. There is one more entry in Yuri's diary after October 18; dated November 26, 1942, it simply stated, "Thanksgiving."

9. Kochiyama diary, vol. 1, April 3, 1942; Monica Miya (Miwako Oana), interview with author, January 24, 2000.

10. Kochiyama diary, vol. 1, April 3, 1942.

11. Kochiyama diary, vol. 1, April 3, 1942. On life in Santa Anita, see Anthony Lehman, *Birthright of Barbed Wire* (Los Angeles: Westernlore Press, 1970); Suzanne Marie Prows, "Santa Anita Assembly Center for the Japanese, Arcadia, California, 1942" (master's thesis, University of San Diego, 1988); Tsuchiyama, "A Preliminary Report on Japanese Evacuees at Santa Anita Assembly Center," n.d., Japanese American Evacuation and Resettlement Study, Bancroft Library, University of California, Berkeley, microfilm reel 016.

12. Kochiyama diary, vol. 1, April 4, 1942.

13. Kochiyama diary, vol. 1, April 4, 1942; Yuri Kochiyama, interview with author.

14. Yuri Kochiyama, interview with author; Sumi (Seo) Seki, interview with author, February 13, 2000; Dollie (Nagai) Fukawa, interview with author, February 14, 2000.

15. Spickard, *Japanese Americans,* 110–12; War Relocation Authority, Final Accountability Record, copy located at the Japanese American National Museum (original at the Japanese American Evacuation and Resettlement Study, Bancroft Library, University of California, Berkeley). Arthur's wife, Chiyo Nakahara, who was in the Jerome, Arkansas, concentration camp with the Nakaharas, declined an interview with the author.

16. Sumi (Seo) Seki, interview with author, February 13, 2000.

17. Rinko Shimasaki, letter to the Crusaders Sunday school class, Santa Anita Assembly Center, August 7, 1942, contained in Rinko Shimasaki's scrapbook, Japanese American National Museum, Los Angeles, CA; Yuri Kochiyama, interview with author.

18. Rinko Shimasaki, letter to the Crusaders, August 7, 1942; other materials from Shimasaki's scrapbook; Yuri Kochiyama, interview with author; Dollie (Nagai) Fukawa, interview with author, February 14, 2000.

19. Shimasaki's scrapbook (emphasis in the original); Yuri Kochiyama, interview with author.

20. Mary Nakahara (Yuri Kochiyama), "Nisei in Khaki," *Denson Tribune,* circa 1943, located at the Japanese American National Museum, Los Angeles, CA; Shimasaki's scrapbook.

21. On accommodationism, see Bill Hosokawa, *Quiet Americans* (New York: Morrow, 1969); Hosokawa, *JACL in Quest for Justice* (New York: Morrow, 1982); Mike Masaoka, with Bill Hosokawa, *They Call Me Moses Masaoka* (New York: Morrow, 1987). On criticism of JACL's accommodationist leadership, see Deborah Lim, "The Lim Report," unpublished report commissioned by the JACL but suppressed because of its findings critical of JACL's role in incarceration, 1989; the report was widely distributed via the Internet: see www.resisters.com or www.javoice.com; Paul Spickard, "The Nisei Assume Power: The Japanese American Citizens League, 1941–1942," *Pacific Historical Review* 52 (1983): 147–74. On wartime resistance, see Irons, *Justice at War*; Steven Okazaki, *Unfinished Business the Japanese American Internment Cases* (documentary, 1985); Arthur A. Hansen, "James Matsumoto Omura: An Interview," *Amerasia Journal* 13 (1986–87): 99–113; Arthur Hansen, interviews with Harry Ueno, George Fujii, James M. Omura, and Frank Emi, *Japanese American World War II Evacuation Oral History Project*, vol. 4 (Fullerton, CA: Oral History Program, California State University, 1991–94). On draft resistance, see endnote 54. On Manzanar and Poston "riots," see endnote 55. On resistance prior to World War II, see Edward D. Beechert, *Working in Hawaii: A Labor History* (Honolulu: University of Hawaii Press, 1985); Ichioka, *The Issei*; Chris Friday, *Organizing Asian American Labor: The Pacific Coast Canned-Salmon Industry, 1870–1942* (Philadelphia: Temple University Press, 1994).

22. Takahashi, *Nisei Sansei*, 53–65, 85–92; Daniels, *Prisoners without Trial*, 26–27; Spickard, *Japanese Americans*, 93–96; Sakamoto quoted in *Japanese American Courier*, April 10, 1942, cited in Takahashi, *Nisei Sansei*, 89.

23. Dollie (Nagai) Fukawa, interview with author, February 14, 2000.

24. Yuri Kochiyama, interview with author.

25. Peter Nakahara, interview with author, January 12, 2000; Yuri Kochiyama, interview with author.

26. Yuri Kochiyama, interview with author; Coulter, "'Welcome Home, Mary.'" It seems almost unbelievable that the Crusaders could write to 13,000 Nisei soldiers, which represented 40 percent of 33,000 Nisei soldiers in the entire U.S. military. Although it is possible that the Crusaders sent a total of 13,000 *letters*, with multiple letters going to the same soldier over the course of the war, Yuri consistently states that the Crusaders had the *names* of 13,000 soldiers. In either case, the size of the Crusader's letter-writing campaign was phenomenal.

27. Kochiyama diary, vol. 1, April 6, 1942; Sumi (Seo) Seki, interview with author, February 13, 2000; Yuri Kochiyama, interview with author.

28. Shimasaki's scrapbook.

29. Yuri Kochiyama, Sunday school teacher's creed, in her group letter to the Crusaders, May 7, 1944, emphasis in the original, courtesy of Dollie (Nagai) Fukawa; Yuri Kochiyama, interview with author.

30. Dollie (Nagai) Fukawa, interview with author, February 14, 2000; Yuri Kochiyama, interview with author.

31. Yuri Kochiyama, "Strength and Diversity" speech.

32. Kochiyama diary, vol. 1, June 4, 1942.

33. Yuri Kochiyama, interview with author.

34. Lehman, *Birthright of Barbed Wire*, 31; Kochiyama diary, vols. 1 and 2, April 30, 1942, May 6, 1942, May 13, 1942, September 8, 1942; Yuri Kochiyama, interview with author. Spickard cites the monthly pay as $12, $16, or $19 per month (*Japanese Americans*, 112).

35. Kochiyama diary, vol. 1, May 12, 13, and 17, 1942.

36. Kochiyama diary, vol. 2, August 4, 1942; Lehman, *Birthright of Barbed Wire*, 62–63; Prows, "Santa Anita Assembly Center for the Japanese, Arcadia, California, 1942," 220–21; FBI report of Santa Anita riot, Los Angeles, August 10, 1042, Japanese American Evacuation and Resettlement Study, Bancroft Library, University of California, Berkeley, microfilm reel 016.

37. Kochiyama diary, vol. 2, August 8, 1942.

38. Kochiyama diary, vol. 2, September 9, 1942.

39. Kochiyama diary, vol. 2, September 9, 1942.

40. Kochiyama diary, vol. 2, September 11, 1942.

41. Kochiyama diary, vol. 2, September 11, 1942.

42. Around 1944, Yuri wrote a play that described the diverse views and feelings of Japanese Americans about their internment. While the script shows an understanding of the outrage at being unjustly treated, bitterness, and demoralization on the part of some, the overarching perspective is one of assimilationism, Christian benevolence, and optimism. Each scenario ends with this view; for example, "The only way to be happy is to look at the brighter side . . . that we won't have to move out; we can't let Pop down. . . . But if the orders come, whatever the orders are, let's cooperate." The narrator makes this appeal: "We need Love. We need understanding. We need broad-mindedness. We need tolerance, and yet a strong grasp on righteousness. We need courage to forget past grievances, but grateful hearts to remember past kindnesses. . . . We need youth to vision, create and build, but maturity to meet the set-backs and disillusions that also come with the results of visions. We need God!" Certainly, Yuri was motivating and inspirational. She could also understand and integrate differing views, but at this point, her philosophy was one of optimistic accommodationism, rather than of political protest. See Mary Nakahara, "The Exit We Search," circa 1944, Japanese American Evacuation and Resettlement Study, Bancroft Library, University of California, Berkeley, microfilm reel 138.

43. War Relocation Authority, Final Accountability Record, copy located at the Japanese American National Museum; Family Record Card, Records of U.S. Army Commands, Western Defense Command and Fourth Army, no. 0309, located at U.S. National Archives, Washington, D.C.; Kochiyama diary, vol. 2, October 11, 1942; Lehman, *Birthright of Barbed Wire*, 71–76.

44. Linda Sue Parker, "Community versus Camp: Japanese American Relocation Centers at Rohwer and Jerome, Arkansas, 1942–1945" (master's thesis,

University of Oklahoma, 1974), 1–17, 49–72; Daniels, *Prisoners without Trial,* 67, 131; "Population of States, by Sex, Race, Urban-Rural Residence, and Age: 1790–1970," *Historical Statistics of the United States: Colonial Times to 1970* (Washington, DC: U.S. Bureau of the Census, 1975), 24.

45. Masayo Umezawa Duus, *Unlikely Liberators: The Men of the 100th and 442nd* (Honolulu: University of Hawaii Press, 1983), 76; Yuri Kochiyama, interview with author; War Relocation Authority, Notice of Assignment, Form WRA-21, located at U.S. National Archives, Washington, D.C.; War Relocation Authority, Termination Notice, Form WRA-114, located at U.S. National Archives, Washington, D.C.; Spickard, *Japanese Americans,* 112; Sucheng Chan, *Asian Americans: An Interpretive History* (Boston: Twayne, 1991), 127; Valerie J. Matsumoto, *Farming the Home Place* (Ithaca, NY: Cornell University Press, 1993), 125.

46. War Relocation Authority, Form 26, located at Japanese American National Museum; Spickard, *Japanese Americans,* 112; Tobier, *Fishmerchant's Daughter,* 13–14.

47. Yuri Kochiyama, "50th Anniversary of the Bombing of Pearl Harbor," speech, Hampshire College, December 5, 1991; Yuri Kochiyama, interview with author.

48. Yuri Kochiyama, interview with author.

49. Mary Tsukamoto and Elizabeth Pinkerton, *We the People: A Story of Internment in America* (Elk Grove, CA: Laguna Publishers, 1988); Yuri Kochiyama, interview with author; Yuri Kochiyama, "War-Time Experiences in Relation to Today," speech.

50. Kochiyamas, *Christmas Cheer,* 1960, 4, 11; Yuri Kochiyama, "War-Time Experiences in Relation to Today," speech; Kochiyama diary, vol. 2, July 18, 1942; Yuri Kochiyama, conversations with author.

51. Yuri Kochiyama, interview with author. On non-Japanese in the concentration camps, see Paul Spickard, "Injustice Compounded: Amerasians and Non-Japanese Americans in World War II Concentration Camps," *Journal of American Ethnic History* 5 (1986): 5–22.

52. Richard Drinnon, *Keeper of Concentration Camps: Dillion S. Myer and American Racism* (Berkeley and Los Angeles: University of California Press, 1987), 78–80; Weglyn, *Years of Infamy,* 134–51.

53. Daniels, *Prisoners without Trial,* 69–70; Spickard, *Japanese Americans,* 120; Yuri Kochiyama, interview with author. For a moving fictional account of one deemed disloyal, see John Okada, *No-no Boy* (1957; reprint, Seattle: University of Washington Press, 1981).

54. Yuri Kochiyama, interview with author. On draft resistance, see Douglas W. Nelson, *Heart Mountain: The History of an American Concentration Camp* (Madison: State Historical Society of Wisconsin, 1976), 150, also 116–49; Arthur A. Hansen, "James Matsumoto Omura: An Interview," *Amerasia Journal* 13 (1986–87): 99–113; Frank Emi, "Draft Resistance at the Heart Mountain

Concentration Camp and the Fair Play Committee," in *Frontiers of Asian American Studies,* ed. Gail Nomura, Russell Endo, Steve Sumida, and Russell Leong (Pullman: Washington State Press, 1989), 41–48; Emiko Omori, *Rabbit in the Moon* (film, 1999); Frank Abe, *Conscience and the Constitution* (documentary, 2000); Eric L. Muller, *Free to Die for Their Country: The Story of the Japanese American Draft Resisters of World War II* (Chicago: University of Chicago Press, 2001); William Minoru Hohri, *Resistance: Challenging America's Wartime Internment of Japanese-Americans* (Lomita, CA: Epistolarian, 2001); Mike Mackey, ed., *A Matter of Conscience: Essays on the World War II Heart Mountain Draft Resistance Movement* (Powell, WY: Western History Publications, 2002).

55. Yuri Kochiyama, interview with author; Tsukamoto and Pinkerton, *We the People,* 146–47. On the Manzanar and Poston "riots," see Arthur A. Hansen and David A. Hacker, "The Manzanar Riot: An Ethnic Perspective," *Amerasia Journal* 2 (1974): 112–57; Gary Y. Okihiro, "Japanese Resistance in America's Concentration Camps: A Re-evaluation," *Amerasia Journal* 2 (1973): 20–33; Sue Kunitoni Embrey, Arthur A. Hansen, and Betty Kulberg Mitson, *Manzanar Martyr: An Interview with Harry Ueno* (Anaheim, CA: Shumway Family History Services, 1986), 33–48, 57–63. *Kibei* refers to second-generation Japanese Americans who are born in the United States, raised in Japan, and usually return to the United States as young adults.

56. Thelma Chang, *"I Can Never Forget": Men of the 100th/442nd* (Honolulu: Sigi Productions, 1991), 112–13; Chester Tanaka, *Go for Broke: A Pictorial History of the Japanese American 100th Infantry Battalion and 442nd Regimental Combat Team* (Richmond, CA: Go for Broke, Inc., 1982), 23; Selective Service System, Special Groups, Special Monograph no. 10, vol. 1 (Washington, DC: U.S. Department of the Army), 142, cited in United States Congressional Commission, *Personal Justice Denied: Report of the Commission on Wartime Relocation and Internment of Civilians* (Washington, DC: Civil Liberties Public Education Fund and Seattle: University of Washington Press, 1997), 253; Chan, *Asian Americans,* 134; Spickard, *Japanese Americans,* 122; Mei Nakano, *Japanese American Women: Three Generations, 1890–1990* (Berkeley: Mina Press, 1990), 170.

57. Chang, *"I Can Never Forget,"* 24–60, 164–77; Duus, *Unlikely Liberators,* 155–219; Pierre Moulin, *U.S. Samurais in Bruyeres* (France, Peace and Freedom Trail, 1993), translated from *U.S. Samurais en Lorraine* (Vagney: Éditions Gérard Louis, 1988), 31–116; Tanaka, *Go for Broke,* 13–22, 75–105, 117; Jack K. Wakamatsu, *Silent Warriors: A Memoir of America's 442nd Regimental Combat Team* (New York: Vantage Press, 1995), 169–208; Tamotsu Shibutani, *The Derelicts of Company K: A Sociological Study of Demoralization* (Berkeley and Los Angeles: University of California Press, 1978); Daniels, *Prisoners without Trial,* 64. Also see Loni Ding's documentaries, *Nisei Soldier* and *Color of Honor*; the latter contains footage of Bill Kochiyama.

58. Chang, *"I Can Never Forget,"* 59; Spickard, *Japanese Americans,* 122; Tanaka, *Go for Broke,* 99.

59. Stanley L. Falk and Warren M. Tsuneishi, eds., *MIS in the War against Japan* (Vienna, VA: Japanese American Veterans Association of Washington, D.C., 1995), 3–8; Joseph D. Harrington, *Yankee Samurai: The Secret Role of Nisei in America's Pacific Victory* (Detroit: Pettigrew Enterprises, 1979), 199; Tad Ichinokuchi, ed., *John Aiso and the M.I.S.: Japanese-American Soldiers in the Military Intelligence Service, World War II* (Los Angeles: MIS Club of Southern California, 1988), 76–84; Clifford Uyeda and Barry Saiki, eds., *The Pacific War and Peace: Americans of Japanese Ancestry in Military Intelligence Service, 1941–1952* (San Francisco: Military Intelligence Service Association of Northern California and the National Japanese American Historical Society, 1991), 15–19, 34–48.

60. Yuri Kochiyama, interview with author; Daniels, *Prisoners without Trial,* 64, 82.

61. Mary Nakahara (Yuri Kochiyama), "Nisei in Khaki," November 5, 1943, and various issues, located at Japanese American National Museum.

62. Mary Nakahara (Yuri Kochiyama), "Nisei in Khaki," October 8, 1943, and another issue, circa 1943; Dollie (Nagai) Fukawa, interview with author, February 14, 2000.

63. Mary Nakahara (Yuri Kochiyama), "Nisei in Khaki," circa 1943.

64. Tsukamoto and Pinkerton, *We the People,* 179; Duus, *Unlikely Liberators,* 75. For an analysis of the use of women's bodies to buttress military morale and masculinity, see Cynthia Enloe, *Bananas, Beaches, and Bases: Making Feminist Sense of International Politics* (Berkeley and Los Angeles: University of California Press, 1990).

65. Tsukamoto and Pinkerton, *We the People*; Yuri Kochiyama, interview with author.

66. Yuri Kochiyama, interview with author.

67. Duus, *Unlikely Liberators,* 75–77.

68. Yuri Kochiyama, interview with author; Tsukamoto and Pinkerton, *We the People,* 182; Duus, *Unlikely Liberators,* 75.

69. Tsukamoto and Pinkerton, *We the People,* 173; Duus, *Unlikely Liberators,* 138.

3. New York, New Life

1. Tobier, *Fishmerchant's Daughter,* 18–19; Renee Tajima-Peña, transcripts from interview with Bill and Yuri Kochiyama for *My America . . . or Honk if You Love Buddha* (video, 1996); Duus, *Unlikely Liberators,* 140–41; Sumi (Seo) Seki, script of "This Is Your Life" program written to honor Mary (Nakahara) Kochiyama, 1958; Sumi (Seo) Seki, interview with author, February 13, 2000; Yuri Kochiyama, interview with author.

2. Yuri Kochiyama, interview with author; Yuri Kochiyama, various letters and envelopes addressed to author; Tajiri and Saunders, *Yuri Kochiyama: Passion for Justice* (video, 1993); Yuri Kochiyama, "Geronimo's 'Beautiful Friend,'" *Rafu Shimpo,* April 6, 1998.

3. War Relocation Authority, Citizen's Short-term Leave, WRA-133, located at the U.S. National Archives, Washington, D.C.; Yuri Kochiyama, interview with author; Tobier, *Fishmerchant's Daughter,* 19–20. In Tobier, *ogenie* was used to refer to bowing to show respect, but Yuri corrected this to *ojigi*.

4. Melvin H. Harter, director of United Service Organization, Japanese American Unit, letter to William C. Love, Leave Clearance Office, Jerome Relocation Center, April 17, 1944, U.S. National Archives, Washington, D.C.; Yuri Kochiyama, interview with author; War Relocation Authority, Application for Indefinite Leave, WRA-130; War Relocation Authority, Citizen's Indefinite Leave, WRA-137, U.S. National Archives, Washington, D.C., courtesy of Brian Hayashi.

5. Yuri Kochiyama, group letter to the Crusaders, May 7, 1944, courtesy of Dollie (Nagai) Fukawa. On critique of the nuclear family, see Thorne, *Rethinking the Family*; Frederick Engels, *The Origin of the Family, Private Property, and the State* (1884; reprint, New York: Pathfinder Press, 1972).

6. Yuri Kochiyama, interview with author.

7. Yuri Kochiyama, interview with author.

8. Kei Ishikawa, interview with author, January 17, 2000; Yuri Kochiyama, interview with author.

9. Yuri Kochiyama, interview with author.

10. Yuri Kochiyama, interview with author; Elizabeth Nakahara, interview with author, February 27, 2000; Daniels, *Prisoners without Trial,* 69–70; War Relocation Authority, Final Accountability Record, copy located at Japanese American National Museum; Kochiyamas, *Christmas Cheer,* 1963, 12.

11. War Relocation Authority, Final Accountability Record, copy located at Japanese American National Museum; Yuri Kochiyama, interview with author.

12. Tobier, *Fishmerchant's Daughter,* 21; Yuri Kochiyama, interview with author. On resettlement, see Valerie J. Matsumoto, *Farming the Home Place: A Japanese American Community in California, 1919–1982* (Ithaca, NY: Cornell University, 1993), 156–59; Tamura, *Hood River Issei,* 224–30; Sandra Taylor, *Jewel of the Desert: Japanese American Internment at Topaz* (Berkeley and Los Angeles: University of California Press, 1993), 174–77.

13. Tobier, *Fishmerchant's Daughter,* 21–22.

14. Tajiri and Saunders, *Yuri Kochiyama: Passion for Justice* (video).

15. Yuri Kochiyama, interview with Masumi Hayashi, November 4, 1997; script of "Mary (Nakahara) Kochiyama—This Is Your Life"; William Masayoshi Kochiyama, "Questionnaire: Japanese Americans in the United States," February 21, 1975, source unknown; Yuri Kochiyama, interview with author.

16. Yuri Kochiyama, interview with author; Monica Miya (Miwako Oana), interview with author, January 17, 2000.

17. In the prewar years, New York represented the largest Japanese American community east of the Mississippi, with 2,087 Japanese, 70 percent Issei, living in New York in 1940. Domestic work was among the top three forms of employment among the Issei. See War Agency Liquidation Unit, *People in Motion: The Postwar Adjustment of the Evacuated Japanese Americans* (Washington, DC: U.S. Department of Interior, 1947, and New York: AMS Press, 1975), 159–62; Nakano Glenn, *Issei, Nisei, War Bride*, 74; Ichioka, *The Issei*, 22–28; Kochiyamas, *Christmas Cheer*, 1966, 1; Kochiyama, "Questionnaire"; Tobier, *Fishmerchant's Daughter*, 24–26.

18. Yuri Kochiyama, interview with author.

19. Yuri Kochiyama, interview with author; Kochiyama, "Questionnaire."

20. Kochiyama, "Questionnaire"; Yuri Kochiyama, interview with author.

21. Nan (Grimm) Carlson, interview with author, January 19, 2000; Peter Nakahara, interview with author, February 17, 1999; Betty Robinson, interview with author, February 6, 2000; Yuriko (Endo) Yoshihara, letter to author, February 2000; Yuri Kochiyama, interview with author.

22. Yuri Kochiyama, interview with author.

23. Yanagisako, *Transforming the Past*, 77–78; Yuri Kochiyama, interview with author.

24. Yuri Kochiyama, interview with author; Tajiri and Saunders, *Yuri Kochiyama: Passion for Justice* (video); Tobier, *Fishmerchant's Daughter*, 26.

25. Yuri Kochiyama, interview with author.

26. Kochiyamas, *Christmas Cheer*, 1960, 1; Yuri Kochiyama, interview with author; McEntire, *Residence and Race*, 25.

27. Yuri Kochiyama, interview with author; Yanagisako, *Transforming the Past*, 63–94.

28. Yuri Kochiyama, interview with author.

29. Yuri Kochiyama, interview with author.

30. Yuri Kochiyama, interview with author; Audee Kochiyama-Holman, interview with author, September 27, 2000.

31. Audee Kochiyama-Holman, interview with author, September 27, 2000; Amado Cabezas, Tse Ming Tran, Brenda M. Lowe, Anna S. Wong, and Kathy Turner, "Empirical Study of Barriers to Upward Mobility for Asian Americans in the San Francisco Bay Area," in *Frontiers of Asian American Studies,* ed. Gail Nomura, Russell Endo, Stephen Sumida, and Russell Leong (Pullman: Washington State University Press, 1989), 85–96; Bob Suzuki, "Education and the Socialization of Asian Americans: A Revisionist Analysis of the 'Model Minority' Thesis," *Amerasia Journal* 4, no. 2 (1977): 23–51; Takahashi, *Nisei Sansei*, 118; Monica Miya (Miwako Oana), interview with author, January 24, 2000.

32. Dollie (Nagai) Fukawa, interview with author, February 14, 2000; Elizabeth Nakahara, interview with author, February 27, 2000.

33. Kochiyamas, *Christmas Cheer*, 1952, 2; 1955, 1; 1957, 1; 1959, 1.

34. One study found that Nisei married women had an average of 2.4 children (see Watanabe, 1977, 28, cited in Yanagisako, *Transforming the Past*, 63–64); Yuri Kochiyama, interview with author.

35. Betty Robinson, interview with author, February 6, 2000.

36. Yanagisako, *Transforming the Past*, 63–94, 107–30.

37. Yuri Kochiyama, interview with author; Yanagisako, *Transforming the Past*, 88–91, 115–18.

38. Kochiyamas, *Christmas Cheer*, 1954, 2; 1955, 2; 1960, 2; 1962, 2, 9; Elizabeth Nakahara, interview with author, February 27, 2000; Yuri Kochiyama, interview with author.

39. Elizabeth Nakahara, interview with author, February 27, 2000.

40. On domestic work, see Angela Y. Davis, *Women, Race and Class* (New York: Vintage Books, 1983), 222–44; Jacqueline Jones, *Labor of Love, Labor of Sorrow: Black Women, Work, and the Family from Slavery to the Present* (New York: Basic Books, 1985); Nakano Glenn, *Issei, Nisei, War Bride;* Mary Romero, *Maid in the USA* (New York: Routledge, 1992); Grace Chang, *Disposable Domestics: Immigrant Women Workers in the Global Economy* (Cambridge, MA: South End Press, 2000); Pierrette Hondagneu-Sotelo, *Doméstica: Immigrant Workers Cleaning and Caring in the Shadows of Affluence* (Berkeley and Los Angeles: University of California Press, 2001); Rhacel Salazar Parreñas, *Servants of Globalization: Women, Migration, and Domestic Work* (Palo Alto, CA: Stanford University Press, 2001).

41. Yuri Kochiyama, interview with author; Kochiyamas, *Christmas Cheer*, 1952, 3; 1956, 3; 1959, 3; 1962, 4.

42. Kochiyamas, *Christmas Cheer*, 1951, 3; 1952, 2; 1953, 3; 1955, 3; 1958, 3; 1959, 3; 1960, 3; 1962, 4, 5; 1964, 3, 4; Betty Robinson, interview with author, February 6, 2000; Yuri Kochiyama, interview with author.

43. Kochiyamas, *Christmas Cheer*, 1954, 2; 1955, 8; 1960, 2, 9; 1961, 2–3; 1962, 12; Yuri Kochiyama, interview with author; Yuri Kochiyama, conversation with author, March 11, 1999; Akemi Kochiyama-Ladson, conversation with author, March 11, 1999.

44. Kochiyamas, *Christmas Cheer*, 1960, 9; 1961, 3, 6; 1962, 4; 1963, 5; Audee Kochiyama-Holman, interview with author, September 27, 1998; Yuri Kochiyama, interview with author.

45. Yuri Kochiyama, interview with author.

46. Kochiyamas, *Christmas Cheer*, 1956, 8; 1958, 1, 4; 1959, 6; 1961, 3, 10; Kazu Iijima, interview with author, June 21, 1996; Genevieve Hall-Duncan, interview with author, January 17, 2000; Betty Robinson, interview with author, February 6, 2000; Yuri Kochiyama, interview with author.

47. War Agency Liquidation Unit, *People in Motion*, 166–86; Yuri Kochiyama, interview with author; Tobier, *Fishmerchant's Daughter*, 23; Kei Ishikawa, interview with author, January 17, 2000.

48. Kochiyamas, *Christmas Cheer*, 1962, 3; 1963, 3; Betty Robinson, interview with author, February 6, 2000; Yuri Kochiyama, interview with author.

49. Kochiyamas, *Christmas Cheer*, 1954, 6; 1960, 10; Dollie (Nagai) Fukawa, interview with author, February 14, 2000; Yuri Kochiyama, interview with author.

50. Yuri Kochiyama, interview with author.

51. Kochiyamas, *Christmas Cheer*, 1959, 3; 1960, 3; 1962, 3; Yuri Kochiyama, interview with author.

52. Kochiyamas, *Christmas Cheer*, 1961, 3, 5; 1962, 2; Yuri Kochiyama, interview with author.

53. Kochiyamas, *Christmas Cheer*, 1962, 1; 1963, 1, 10; Yuri Kochiyama, interview with author.

54. Kochiyamas, *Christmas Cheer*, 1962, 1; 1963, 1, 10; Yuri Kochiyama, interview with author; Dollie (Nagai) Fukawa, interview with author, February 14, 2000. In the Bible, Hebrews 13:2–5 contains a passage embodied in Yuri's practice: "Do not forget to entertain strangers, for by so doing some people have entertained angels without knowing it. Remember those in prison as if you were their fellow prisoners, and those who are mistreated as if you yourselves were suffering. . . . Keep your lives free from the love of money and be content with what you have, because God has said, 'Never will I leave you; never will I forsake you.'"

55. Kochiyamas, *Christmas Cheer*, 1956, 3; 1957, 3; 1960, 1, 3; 1961, 3; Yuri Kochiyama, interview with author; Jimmy Kochiyama, interview with author, November 29, 1998; Audee Kochiyama-Holman, interview with author, September 27, 1998.

56. Yuri Kochiyama, interview with author.

57. Yuri Kochiyama, interview with author; Betty Robinson, interview with author, February 6, 2000.

58. A copy of the entire collection of *Christmas Cheer*, save the first issue, which is missing from Yuri's collection, is in the possession of the author, courtesy of Yuri Kochiyama; Yuri Kochiyama, interview with author.

59. Kochiyamas, *Christmas Cheer*, 1955, 1; 1954, 2; 1956, 1; 1960, 1; 1961, 1; 1963, 1; Yuri Kochiyama, interview with author.

60. Yanagisako, *Transforming the Past*, 92; Kochiyamas, *Christmas Cheer*, 1954, 2; 1967, 1; Yuri Kochiyama, interview with author.

61. Kochiyamas, *Christmas Cheer*, 1951, 4, 6; 1955, 6; 1957, 2; 1958, 12; 1959, 3, 12; Yuri Kochiyama, interview with author.

62. Kochiyamas, *Christmas Cheer*, 1954, 2.

63. Kochiyamas, *Christmas Cheer*, 1953, 7; 1954, 2, 7; 1956, 2; 1957, 1, 7; 1958, 2, 12; 1961, 2; 1962, 7; 1963, 2, 8; 1965, 1, 8; 1967, 1; 1968, 1, 3; Yuri Kochiyama, interview with author.

64. Kochiyamas, *Christmas Cheer*, 1951, 1, 5, 8.

65. Yuri Kochiyama, interview with author; Tommy Kochiyama, interview with author, October 18, 1998.

66. Kochiyamas, *Christmas Cheer,* 1956, 6; 1960, 5; Yuri Kochiyama, interview with author; Yen Le Espirtu, *Asian American Panethnicity* (Philadelphia: Temple University Press, 1992), 19–52.

67. Kochiyamas, *Christmas Cheer,* 1960, 5; Yuri Kochiyama, interview with author.

68. Yuri Kochiyama, interview with author.

69. Kochiyamas, *Christmas Cheer,* 1953, 1, 3, 5.

70. Kochiyamas, *Christmas Cheer,* 1958, 7.

71. Kochiyamas, *Christmas Cheer,* 1951, 1, 3; 1952, 2, 3; 1953, 3; 1955, 3; 1956, 1, 3; 1958, 3, 7; 1963, 1, 3, 4, 5, 12; Elizabeth Nakahara, interview with author, February 27, 2000; Peter Nakahara, interview with author, February 17, 1999; Yuri Kochiyama, interview with author; Stanford University Law School Graduating Class, 1954; Takahashi, *Nisei Sansei,* 37–42, 114–16.

72. Ralph Edwards's *This Is Your Life* on NBC ranked among the top ten in television popularity ratings. In 1955, Rev. Kiyoshi Tanimoto spoke about the Hiroshima Maidens project on *This Is Your Life.* See Rodney Barker, *The Hiroshima Maidens: A Story of Courage, Compassion, and Survival* (New York: Viking, 1985), 3–12; script of "This Is Your Life" program written to honor Mary (Nakahara) Kochiyama, 1958; Kochiyamas, *Christmas Cheer,* 1958, 2, 8, 9; "'Mary Nakahara' This Is Your Life," *San Pedro News-Pilot,* August 4, 1958.

73. Baird, "School Spirit"; Marconi, "San Pedro's Favorite Daughter Given a Hero's Return"; Mary (Nakahara) Kochiyama, group thank-you letters, June 1984 and 1989; Norma (Benedetti) Brutti, interview with author, January 16, 2000; videotape of 1989 reunion to honor Yuri Kochiyama, courtesy of Norma (Benedetti) Brutti.

74. Barker, *Hiroshima Maidens;* Kochiyamas, *Christmas Cheer,* 1955, 5; 1956, 7.

75. Yuri Kochiyama, interview with author; Kochiyamas, *Christmas Cheer,* 1956, 7.

76. Kochiyamas, *Christmas Cheer,* 1955, 5; 1956, 7.

77. Barker, *Hiroshima Maidens,* 195; Kochiyamas, *Christmas Cheer,* 1959, 1.

4. Plunging into Civil Rights

1. Yuri Kochiyama, interview with author; Kochiyamas, *Christmas Cheer,* 1960, 1.

2. Kochiyamas, *Christmas Cheer,* 1960, 1, 10; 1961, 5; Tajiri and Saunders, *Yuri Kochiyama: Passion for Justice* (video, 1993).

3. Participant observations by author.

4. Eddie Kochiyama, interview with author, September 25, 1998; Yuri Kochiyama, interview with author; participant observations by author.

5. Yuri Kochiyama, interview with author; Audee Kochiyama-Holman, interview with author, September 27, 1998; participant observations by author.

6. Gilbert Osofsky, *Harlem: The Making of a Ghetto* (New York: Harper

and Row, 1963), 17–24, 71–80, 112–49; John Henrik Clarke, "Introduction," in *Harlem: A Community in Transition*, ed. John Henrik Clarke (1964; reprint, New York: Citadel Press, 1970), 4–11.

7. Clarke, "Introduction," in *Harlem*, 4–11; Richard B. Moore, "Africa Conscious Harlem," in Clarke, *Harlem*, 83–85; Theodore G. Vincent, *Black Power and the Garvey Movement* (Berkeley, CA: Ramparts Press, 1971), 13–30; Marcus Garvey Jr., "Garveyism: Some Reflections on Its Significance for Today," in *Marcus Garvey and the Vision of Africa*, ed. John Henrik Clarke (New York: Vintage Books, 1974), 375–87; John Henrik Clarke, "The Impact of Marcus Garvey on the Harlem Renaissance," in Clarke, *Marcus Garvey*, 180–88; Osofsky, *Harlem*, 179–87.

8. Fred Halstead, *Harlem Stirs* (New York: Marzani and Munsell, 1966), 21–37, 45–48, 101–4; Klytus Smith and Abiola Sinclair, *The Harlem Cultural/ Political Movements, 1960–1970* (New York: Gumbs and Thomas, 1995), 1–4. Yuri Kochiyama's prominence in the Harlem political movement is noted by her inclusion in the latter book (p. 66).

9. Clayborne Carson, David J. Garrow, Gerald Gill, Vincent Harding, and Darlene Clark Hine, eds., *The Eyes on the Prize Civil Rights Reader* (New York: Penguin Books, 1991), 45–64, 97–106; Kochiyamas, *Christmas Cheer*, 1957, 12; 1958, 1; Yuri Kochiyama, interview with author.

10. Kochiyamas, *Christmas Cheer*, 1961, 1, 3, 5, 10; 1962, 3. On James Peck, see James Peck, *Freedom Ride* (New York: Simon and Schuster, 1962); Henry Hampton and Steve Fayer, *Voices of Freedom: An Oral History of the Civil Rights Movement from the 1950s through the 1980s* (New York: Bantam Books, 1990), 74, 77–78; Juan Williams, *Eyes on the Prize: America's Civil Rights Years, 1954–1965* (New York: Penguin Books, 1987), 148–49.

11. Yuri Kochiyama, interview with author; Kochiyamas, *Christmas Cheer*, 1963, 5.

12. August Meier and Elliott Rudwick, *CORE: A Study in the Civil Rights Movement, 1942–1968* (New York: Oxford University Press, 1973), 4, 135–44; Aldon D. Morris, *The Origins of the Civil Rights Movement: Black Communities Organizing for Change* (New York: Free Press, 1984), 231–36; Williams, *Eyes on the Prize*, 148–49; Kochiyamas, *Christmas Cheer*, 1961, 3, 5.

13. Meier and Rudwick, *CORE*, 3–11; August Meier, Elliott Rudwick, and Francis L. Broderick, eds., *Black Protest Thought in the Twentieth Century* (Indianapolis: Bobbs-Merrill, 1971), 239–43; Morris, *Origins of the Civil Rights Movement*, 128–30.

14. Meier and Rudwick, *CORE*, 130–31, 199–210, 304; Morris, *Origins of the Civil Rights Movement*, 130–38, 230–31.

15. Meier and Rudwick, *CORE*, 10; James M. Washington, *A Testament of Hope: The Essential Writings of Martin Luther King, Jr.* (San Francisco: Harper and Row, 1986), 7–8; John J. Ansbro, *Martin Luther King, Jr.: The Making of a Mind* (Maryknoll, NY: Orbis Books, 1982), 231–34.

16. Homer Bigart, "Near-Riot Flares in Race Protest at Project Here," *New York Times,* August 1, 1963; Peter Kirss, "200 Racial Pickets Seized at Building Projects Here," *New York Times,* July 23, 1963; Tajiri and Saunders, *Yuri Kochiyama: Passion for Justice* (video, 1993); Arthur Tobier, ed., *Fishmerchant's Daughter: Yuri Kochiyama, an Oral History,* vol. 2 (New York: Community Documentation Workshop, 1982), 1; Yuri Kochiyama, interview with author.

17. Bigart, "Near-Riot Flares"; Kirss, "200 Racial Pickets Seized"; Yuri Kochiyama, interview with author; FBI file, New York, 100-155496, January 16, 1968.

18. Yuri Kochiyama, interview with author; Takahashi, *Nisei Sansei,* 89–92.

19. Martin Luther King Jr., *Why We Can't Wait* (New York: New American Library, 1963), 54; Martin Luther King Jr., "Letter from Birmingham City Jail," in Carson et al., *Eyes on the Prize Civil Rights Reader,* 154; Williams, *Eyes on the Prize,* 148–49, 179; Kochiyamas, *Christmas Cheer,* 1963, 1, 8, 12.

20. King, *Why We Can't Wait,* 54; Morris, *Origins of the Civil Rights Movement,* 250–74; Williams, *Eyes on the Prize,* 179–95.

21. Kochiyamas, *Christmas Cheer,* 1963, 1, 8, 12; Hampton and Fayer, *Voices of Freedom,* 171–72; Williams, *Eyes on the Prize,* 182.

22. Bill Epton, interview with author, February 7, 2000; Kochiyamas, *North Star,* 1966, 3, 7, 8. For the origins of the second family newsletter, the *North Star,* see chapter 6.

23. Bill Epton, interview with author, February 7, 2000; Yuri Kochiyama, interview with author; Constance Mackey, quoted in Tajiri and Saunders, *Yuri Kochiyama: A Passion for Justice* (video).

24. *Brown v. Board of Education,* cited in Carson et al., *Eyes on the Prize Civil Rights Reader,* 72; Yuri Kochiyama, interview with author.

25. Luther Whitfield Seabrook, "Parent Advocacy for Educational Reform: A Case Study of the Harlem Parents Committee" (Ph.D diss., University of Massachusetts, 1978), 20–21, 65; Yuri Kochiyama, interview with author.

26. Tajiri and Saunders, *Yuri Kochiyama: Passion for Justice* (video); Halstead, *Harlem Stirs,* 104; Seabrook, "Parent Advocacy for Educational Reform," 85–90.

27. Seabrook, "Parent Advocacy for Educational Reform," 103–5; Yuri Kochiyama, interview with author.

28. Seabrook, "Parent Advocacy for Educational Reform," 68–72; Kochiyamas, *Christmas Cheer,* 1963, 3; 1964, 1, 5, 12; Yuri Kochiyama, interview with author; Tobier, *Fishmerchant's Daughter,* vol. 2, 6. Note that in her documentary video and elsewhere, Yuri recalled that she, Bill, and "our three older children" attended the Freedom School, but Eddie and Jimmy also remember attending the Freedom School (Kochiyamas, *Christmas Cheer,* 1964, 5; Jimmy Kochiyama, interview with author, November 29, 1998).

29. Du Bois, *The Souls of Black Folk,* 1–9, 43–52, 94–132; Henry Louis Gates Jr., introduction to *The Souls of Black Folk,* xxii; Tajiri and Saunders, *Yuri Kochiyama: Passion for Justice* (video). For an introduction to the study

of racism, see Martin Blumer and John Solomos, eds., *Racism* (Oxford: Oxford University Press, 1999).

30. Betty Robinson, interview with author, February 6, 2000.

31. Monica Miya (Miwako Oana), interview with author, January 17, 2000; Yuri Kochiyama, interview with author; Billy Kochiyama, *Christmas Cheer,* 1963, 4.

32. Audee Kochiyama-Holman, interview with author, September 27, 1998; Tommy Kochiyama, conversation with author, March 7, 1999; Yuri Kochiyama, interview with author.

33. Yuri Kochiyama, interview with author; Eddie Kochiyama, interview with author, September 25, 1998; Audee Kochiyama-Holman, interview with author, September 27, 1998.

34. Yuri Kochiyama, interview with author; Billy Kochiyama, *Christmas Cheer,* 1965, 6; Audee Kochiyama-Holman, interview with author, September 27, 1998.

35. Payne, *I've Got the Light of Freedom,* 118–31; Carson et al., *Eyes on the Prize Civil Rights Reader,* 167–68; John Dittmer, *Local People: The Struggle for Civil Rights in Mississippi* (Champaign: University of Illinois Press, 1994), 246–52, 268–83; Hampton and Fayer, *Voices of Freedom,* 188–96; Kochiyamas, *Christmas Cheer,* 1968, 1; Yuri Kochiyama, interview with author; Audee Kochiyama-Holman, interview with author, September 27, 1998.

36. Lorrie (Aichi) Kochiyama, *Christmas Cheer,* 1964, 4; 1966, 7.

37. Eddie Kochiyama, interview with author, September 25, 1998; Eddie Kochiyama, "A Son Reflects on His Parents," *Hawaii Herald,* March 19, 1993; Yuri Kochiyama, interview with author.

38. "Chickens Come Home to Roost," *Asian Americans for Action Newsletter,* October 1970, 2; Eddie Kochiyama, interview with author, September 25, 1998; Eddie Kochiyama, letter to author, March 5, 1999; Jimmy Kochiyama, interview with author, November 29, 1998; Tommy Kochiyama, interview with author, October 18, 1998.

39. Tommy Kochiyama, interview with author, October 18, 1998; Jimmy Kochiyama, interview with author, November 29, 1998; Yuri Kochiyama, interview with author.

40. Tommy Kochiyama, interview with author, October 18, 1998; Jimmy Kochiyama, interview with author, November 29, 1998.

41. Kochiyamas, *Christmas Cheer,* 1963, 2, 11; 1964, 3–4; Yuri Kochiyama, interview with author; Tajiri and Saunders, *Yuri Kochiyama: Passion for Justice* (video).

42. Yuri Kochiyama, interview with author; Norma (Benedetti) Brutti, interview with author, January 16, 2000.

43. Kochiyamas, *Christmas Cheer,* 1968, 2.

44. Mary Nakahara (Yuri Kochiyama), "Poem Embodies the Lasting Spirit of San Pedro."

5. Meeting Malcolm X

1. The correct date of this meeting comes from a letter Yuri wrote to Malcolm X, dated October 17, 1963: "Then, almost like a dream-come-true, I did actually get to meet you; exchange a few words with you; and shake your hands. I would not expect you to remember that fleeting moment, but it was in the Brooklyn Court-house just yesterday morning, October 16." In various materials, including published works, September 16, 1963, sometimes appears as their meeting date because for years Yuri believed September 16 was the correct date until she reread her October 17, 1963, letter to Malcolm X; Yuri Kochiyama, interview with author; Malcolm X, *The Autobiography of Malcolm X*, 292.

2. A. Peter Bailey, interview with author, March 3, 2000; C. Eric Lincoln, *The Black Muslims in America* (Boston: Beacon Press, 1961), 26, 75–76, 87–90, 187–89; Louis E. Lomax, *When the Word Is Given* . . . (Cleveland: World Publishing Company, 1963), 54–55: Marc Gallicchio, *The African American Encounter with Japan and China: Black Internationalism in Asia, 1895–1945* (Chapel Hill: University of North Carolina Press, 2000). I thank Mumia Abu-Jamal for reminding me of the Nation of Islam's views of Japan and Asia.

3. Yuri Kochiyama, interview with author; Yuri Kochiyama, "Reflections of History: Malcolm in Context," speech, San Francisco, May 27, 1993.

4. Yuri Kochiyama, "Reflections of History: Malcolm in Context," speech; Mary Kochiyama, letter to the editor [on Malcolm X], *New York Nichibei*, March 11, 1965; Yuri Kochiyama, interview with author.

5. "Mrs. Mary Kochiyama & family," letter to Malcolm X, October 17, 1963; Yuri Kochiyama, interview with author.

6. Sonia Sanchez, quoted in "The Time Has Come, 1964–66," *Eyes on the Prize, Series II* (video, 1986); A. Peter Bailey, interview with author, February 25, 2000; William Sales, *From Civil Rights to Black Liberation: Malcolm X and the Organization of Afro-American Unity* (Boston: South End Press, 1994), 119. This ability to name the unnamed was part of the significance of Du Bois in his classic, *The Souls of Black Folk,* about which Henry Louis Gates Jr. remarked, "These passages . . . attest to Du Bois's uncanny capacity to name the collective cultural text of the African-American"(xxv).

7. A. Peter Bailey, interview with author, February 25, 2000; Yuri Kochiyama, interview with author; Yuri Kochiyama, letter to Malcolm X, June 8, 1964.

8. Malcolm X, *Autobiography,* 307–9; Karl Evanzz, *The Judas Factor: The Plot to Kill Malcolm X* (New York: Thunder's Mouth Press, 1992), 161–66, 170–71, 264; Clayborne Carson, *Malcolm X: The FBI File* (New York: Carroll and Graf, 1991), 245–48.

9. Breitman, *Malcolm X Speaks* (New York: Grove Press, 1965), 20–22. For more on the NOI purge of Malcolm X, see Benjamin Karim with Peter Skutches and David Gallen, *Remembering Malcolm: The Story of Malcolm X from Inside the Muslim Mosque by His Assistant Minister Benjamin Karim* (New York: Car-

roll and Graf, 1992); Evanzz, *The Judas Factor*; Carson, *Malcolm X*; Malcolm X, *Autobiography*; George Breitman, *The Last Year of Malcolm X: The Evolution of a Revolutionary* (New York: Schocken Books, 1967).

10. Yuri Kochiyama, letter to the editor of the *Amsterdam News*, copy of original letter dated June 14, 1964; Yuri Kochiyama, interviews with author; Kochiyamas, *Christmas Cheer*, 1964, 5; Yuri Kochiyama, speeches.

11. Yuri previously believed the reception was on June 14, 1964. However, in a letter to the editor of the *Amsterdam News*, dated June 14, 1964, she mentioned that the date of Malcolm X's visit was Saturday, June 6. Yuri Kochiyama, interview with author.

12. Yuri Kochiyama, interview with author. On how Black internationalists mistakenly elevated Japan as a symbol of triumph over global White supremacy, see Gallicchio, *The African American Encounter with Japan and China*.

13. Yuri Kochiyama, interview with author; Yuri Kochiyama, "Reflection of History: Malcolm in Context," speech.

14. Malcolm X, postcards to "Mr. & Mrs. Wm Kochiyama & Family," 1964, in Yuri Kochiyama's scrapbook; Yuri Kochiyama, interview with author; Mae Mallory, interview with author, February 23, 2000.

15. Billy Kochiyama, letter to his parents, postmarked July 16, 1965, emphasis in the original; Yuri Kochiyama, interview with author; Audee Kochiyama, K-kids column, *Christmas Cheer*, 1964, 5.

16. The full text of the memorandum Malcolm circulated to the OAU delegates is in Breitman, *Malcolm X Speaks*, 72–87, 84–86; Carson, *Malcolm X*, 304–7.

17. William Sales concurs: "It is important to recognize in Malcolm X's political thought that ideas which flowered in subsequent periods were present in some manner and strength from the beginning. The periods in the development of his thinking are not set off so much by the emergence of new ideas as by the redefinition and changing emphasis placed on ideas already present (of course, some ideas of earlier periods were subsequently discarded)." See Sales, *From Civil Rights to Black Liberation*, 60; Louis DeCaro, *On the Side of My People: A Religious Life of Malcolm X* (New York: New York University Press, 1996), 221–22.

18. Theodore Draper, *The Rediscovery of Black Nationalism* (New York: Viking Press, 1969), 91; Breitman, *The Last Year*, 32–33.

19. Malcom X, *Autobiography*, 334; Breitman, *The Last Year*, 32; Breitman, *Malcolm X Speaks*, 58–59. Although Malcolm no longer made sweeping anti-White indictments, he remained suspicious of the motives of the majority of White Americans raised in a deeply racist society, asserted Malcolm associate Herman Ferguson. If American Whites could adopt Islam, Malcolm believed they might learn to practice the antiracist humanity it espoused. But added Ferguson, "Malcolm doubted most White Americans would adopt Islam or shed their racism" (Herman Ferguson, letter to author, February 14, 1999).

20. Breitman, *The Last Year*, 64–65; Breitman, *Malcolm X Speaks*, 197; Sales,

From Civil Rights to Black Liberation, 53–94, 99–109; Muhammad Ahmad, interview with author, January 30, 2000.

21. A. Peter Bailey, conversation with author, July 24, 2000; Breitman, *The Last Year,* 57; James Campbell, interview with author, January 25, 2000.

22. Yuri Kochiyama, "Malcolm, the Person—Malcolm X, the Film," speech, February 5, 1993, Hunter College, New York City.

23. The Liberation School, which met throughout the entire period of the Organization of Afro-American Unity's (OAAU) existence, held Saturday morning classes at the Hotel Theresa, with separate classes for children and for adults (*Backlash,* September 28, 1964, October 19, 1964; Sales, *From Civil Rights to Black Liberation,* 121).

24. James Campbell, interview with author, January 25, 2000; Sales, *From Civil Rights to Black Liberation,* 112; *Backlash,* September 28, 1964; Yuri Kochiyama, interview with author; Yuri Kochiyama, class notes from the OAAU Liberation School, December 5, 1964. Information on the Liberation School classes comes from Yuri Kochiyama's handwritten notes, a complete copy of which is in the author's possession.

25. James Campbell was charged with running the Liberation School, according to Campbell, Yuri, and William Sales. By contrast, Herman Ferguson, who was in exile when Sales conducted interviews for his OAAU book, recalled that it was he, as chair of OAAU's education committee, who developed the idea of the school. According to Ferguson, Campbell joined the OAAU after the Liberation School began and instead originated the leadership training program, which was connected with the Liberation School (James Campbell, interview with author, January 25, 2000; Yuri Kochiyama, interview with author; Sales, *From Civil Rights to Black Liberation,* 120–21; Herman Ferguson, letter to author, February 14, 1999; Herman Ferguson, conversation with author, February 14, 1999).

26. James Campbell, interview with author, January 25, 2000; A. Peter Bailey, interview with author, March 3, 2000; Yuri Kochiyama, interview with author.

27. Yuri's lecture notes show that she attended every Saturday from December 5, 1964, until April 3, 1965, except for three classes in late December and early January. It is unclear whether she missed those classes or if classes were canceled during the holidays. Yuri Kochiyama, interview with author; Yuri Kochiyama, class notes, OAAU Liberation School.

28. Yuri Kochiyama, class notes from the OAAU Liberation School, December 12, 1964. Also see Fannie Lou Hamer, "To Praise Our Bridges," in Carson et al., *Eyes on the Prize Civil Rights Reader,* 176–79; Payne, *I've Got the Light of Freedom,* 227–28. The tape of Hamer's narration of her prison beating might well have come from her testimony before the Credentials Committee in an effort to seat the Mississippi Freedom Democratic Party at the 1964 Democratic National Convention. See Clayborne Carson, *In Struggle: SNCC and the Black Awakening of the 1960s* (Cambridge, MA: Harvard University Press, 1981), 125.

29. It is recognized that the United States was not simple born racist, as a con-

genital deformity implies. As George Fredrickson argues, "It became so gradually as the result of a series of crimes against black humanity that stemmed primarily from selfishness, greed, and the pursuit of privilege"; *The Arrogance of Race: Historical Perspectives on Slavery, Racism, and Social Inequality* (Hanover, NH: Wesleyan University Press, 1988), 205.

30. Yuri Kochiyama, class notes from the OAAU Liberation School, March 13, 1965; James Campbell, interview with author, January 25, 2000; Frantz Fanon, *The Wretched of the Earth* (New York: Grove Press, 1961); Kwame Nkrumah, *Consciencism* (New York: Monthly Review Press, 1964); Herbert Aptheker, *American Negro Slave Revolts* (New York: International Publishers, 1963). On the development of racism in the context of slavery, colonialism, imperialism, and capitalism, see Eric Williams, *Capitalism and Slavery* (1964; reprinted London: André Deutsch, 1988); Fredrickson, *The Arrogance of Race*; Bulmer and Solomos, *Racism*; Tomás Almaguer, *Racial Fault Lines: The Historical Origins of White Supremacy in California* (Berkeley and Los Angeles: University of California Press, 1994); Winthrop Jordan, *The White Man's Burden: Historical Origins of Racism in the United States* (London: Oxford University Press, 1974); W. E. B. Du Bois, *The World and Africa* (1946; reprint, New York: International Publishers, 1990); Howard Winant, *The World Is a Ghetto* (New York: Basic Books, 2001); Robert Blauner, *Racial Oppression in America* (New York: Harper and Row, 1972); Lerone Bennett Jr., *The Shaping of Black America* (New York: Penguin Books, 1969); Lucie Cheng and Edna Bonacich, eds., *Labor Immigration under Capitalism: Asian Workers in the United States Before World War II* (Berkeley and Los Angeles: University of California Press, 1984); Audrey Smedley, *Race in North America: Origin and Evolution of a Worldview*, 2nd ed. (Boulder, CO: Westview Press, 1990).

31. James Shabazz, "The Economics of Morality," *OAAU Blacklash*, September 28, 1964, 3, 5, emphasis in original.

32. Malcolm X, "Message to the Grass Roots," in *Malcolm X Speaks*, 7–8; Timothy Tyson, *Radio Free Dixie: Robert F. Williams and the Roots of Black Power* (Chapel Hill: University of North Carolina Press, 1999), 214. Although I contrast the general ideology of the Civil Rights Movement, symbolized by King, and Black liberation movement, symbolized by Malcolm X, it is recognized that many civil rights activists, rank-and-file members as well as some leaders, protected themselves with guns, even as they advocated nonviolence. Other civil rights activists and organizations, notably SNCC, moved from a position of philosophical nonviolence to one of self-defense.

33. Malcolm X, "There's a Worldwide Revolution Going On," in *Malcolm X: The Last Speeches*, ed. Bruce Perry (New York: Pathfinder Press, 1989), 148–49.

34. Breitman, *Malcolm X Speaks*, 42, 138–39; Fanon, *Wretched of the Earth*, 37, 94; Tyson, *Radio Free Dixie*, 88–89.

35. My appreciation to Douglas Daniels for emphasizing this point.

36. Meier and Rudwick, *CORE*, 199–210, 304; Draper, *The Rediscovery*

of Black Nationalism, 132. For an analysis of the development of Yuri's radical politics, see Diane C. Fujino, "Black Liberation Movement and the Making of Japanese American Radicals," in *AFRO/ASIA: Revolutionary Political and Cultural Connections between African and Asian Americans,* ed. Fred Ho and Bill V. Mullen (Durham, NC: Duke University Press, forthcoming).

37. "The Time Has Come, 1964–66," *Eyes on the Prize, Series II* (video, 1986).

38. Ossie Davis, "Our Shining Black Prince," in Clarke, *Malcolm X,* xii; Davis, "Why I Eulogized Malcolm X," in Clarke, *Malcolm X,* 128. Davis's words resonate with theories of masculinities and the constant need for men to prove their manhood, especially for the "other," such as men of color, who have been excluded from hegemonic masculinity. See Michael Kimmel, *Manhood in America: A Cultural History* (New York: Free Press, 1996); R. W. Connell, *Masculinities* (Berkeley and Los Angeles: University of California Press, 1995).

39. See Cheikh Anta Diop, *Precolonial Black Africa* (Brooklyn, NY: Lawrence Hill Books, 1987); W. E. B. Du Bois, *Black Reconstruction in America, 1860–1880* (1935; reprinted, New York: Touchstone, 1995); Vincent Bakpetu Thompson, *Africa and Unity: The Evolution of Pan-Africanism* (New York: Humanities Press, 1969).

40. Malcolm X, "There's a World Wide Revolution Going On," 148.

41. John K. Jessup, "An Urgent New Reach to Be Equal," *Life,* June 3, 1966; Russell Sackett, "Plotting a War on 'Whitey,'" *Life,* June 10, 1966; Yuri Kochiyama, interview with author.

42. Yuri Kochiyama, interview with author. Malcolm said in his "Message to the Grassroots" speech: "Of all our studies, history is best qualified to reward our research. And when you see you've got problems, all you have to do is examine the historic method used all over the world by others who have problems similar to yours. Once you see how they got theirs straight, then you know how you can get yours straight" (Breitman, *Malcolm X Speaks,* 8).

43. Yuri Kochiyama, speech, Malcolm X Commemoration Committee program, "Who Really Killed Malcolm X" (video, February 20, 1994). These events are verified in Karim, *Remembering Malcolm,* 189–91; Michael Friedly, *Malcolm X: The Assassination* (New York: Carroll and Graf, 1992), 18–19; Peter Goldman, *The Death and Life of Malcolm X,* 2nd ed. (Champaign: University of Illinois Press, 1973), 271–78.

44. Yuri Kochiyama, speech, "Who Really Killed Malcolm X" (video, February 20, 1994); "The Violent End of the Man Called Malcolm X," *Life,* March 5, 1965, 26.

45. Yuri Kochiyama, letter to the editor, *New York Nichibei,* March 11, 1965.

46. Yuri Kochiyama, "Malcolm X: An Internationalist by International Demand," speech, University of Connecticut, February 25, 1997; Ei Nagata, *Kokujin wa Hangyakusuru* (Tokyo: San'ichi Shobo, 1966; subject is Malcolm X). Since the time of Yuri's speech, a fourth country, the United States in January 1999, has is-

sued a Malcolm X stamp. Although many would interpret this as signaling endorsement of Malcolm X, many of Malcolm's associates view this as an effort by the U.S. government to co-opt Malcolm's image, even as they oppose his political vision.

47. Malcolm X Commemoration Committee letterhead.

48. The *North Star*, 1965, 1. Because Yuri is so collective she does not like to identify her individual contributions, but given her interactions with Malcolm, she probably wrote this article. Note also that *North Star* was the name of a newspaper edited by Frederick Douglass and Martin R. Delany. See Clarke, *Marcus Garvey and the Vision of Africa*, xxv.

6. Transformation of a Revolutionary Nationalist

1. Max Stanford, "Revolutionary Action Movement: A Case Study of an Urban Revolutionary Movement in Western Capitalist Society" (master's thesis, Atlanta University, 1986), 2, 74–109, 125–26; William W. Sales, *From Civil Rights to Black Liberation,* 106, 179. RAM consciously built on the self-defense tactics of the Pan-Africanist and Marxist African Blood Brotherhood, founded in the late 1910s by Cyril V. Briggs. On the African Blood Brotherhood, see Theman Ray Taylor, "Cyril Briggs and the African Blood Brotherhood: Another Radical View of Race and Class during the 1920s" (Ph.D. diss., University of California, Santa Barbara, 1981); Draper, *Rediscovery of Black Nationalism,* 59–61; Wilson J. Moses, *The Golden Age of Black Nationalism, 1850–1925* (Oxford: Oxford University Press, 1987), 90; Imari Obadele, *Foundations of the Black Nation* (Detroit: House of Songhay, 1975), viii, x; Theodore G. Vincent, *Black Power and the Garvey Movement* (Berkeley, CA: Ramparts Press, 1971), 74–87.

2. Yuri Kochiyama, interview with author.

3. There were at least three Black Panther Party formations: Lowndes County Freedom Organization, founded in Alabama in 1965; the RAM Black Panther Party, founded in Harlem in August 1966; and the most famous Black Panther Party, founded in Oakland in October 1966. Clayborne Carson, *In Struggle: SNCC and the Black Awakening of the 1960s* (Cambridge, MA: Harvard University Press, 1981), 162–66; Philip S. Foner, ed., *The Black Panthers Speak* (Philadelphia: J. B. Lippincott, 1970), xv, 2–4; Stanford, "Revolutionary Action Movement," 120–21; Muhammad Ahmad (Max Stanford), interview with author, January 30, 2000; Kochiyama, "The Power of Positive Thinking," *North Star,* December 1966, 1, 8; *The Muhammad Ahmad (Max Stanford) Story* leaflet (Afro-American Historical Association of the Niagara Frontier; Buffalo, NY, 1972, microfilm); A. Peter Bailey, interview with author, February 25, 2000; James Campbell, interview with author, January 25, 2000; Yuri Kochiyama, interview with author.

4. Muhammad Ahmad, *Toward Black Liberation, Part I* (Cleveland: Legacy Communications, n.d.); Yuri Kochiyama, interview with author; participant observation by author.

5. Stanford asserted that Robert F. Williams agreed to serve as RAM's international chair and that RAM and Malcolm X's OAAU were ideologically and structurally linked, "The OAAU was to be the broad front organization and RAM the underground Black Liberation Front of the U.S.A." ("Revolutionary Action Movement," 103–7); this has not been verified from other sources. On the Kissing Case, see Tyson, *Radio Free Dixie*, 90–136; Conrad J. Lynn, *There Is a Fountain: The Autobiography of Conrad Lynn* (Brooklyn, NY: Lawrence Hill Books, 1993). On the Southern taboo against interracial sexual contact and its promotion of White hegemonic masculinity, patriarchy, and White supremacy, see Jacqueline Dowd Hall, "'The Mind That Burns in Each Body': Women, Rape, and Racial Violence," in *Powers of Desire: The Politics of Sexuality,* ed. Ann Snitow, Christine Stansell, and Sharon Thompson (New York: Monthly Review Press, 1983), 328–49; Angela Davis, "Rape, Racism and the Myth of the Black Rapist," in *Women, Race, and Class,* 172–201; Abby L. Ferber, "Constructing Whiteness," in *Racism,* ed. Bulmer and Solomos, 213–23.

6. On Robert F. Williams, see Williams's autobiographical account, *Negroes with Guns* (1962; reprinted, Chicago: Third World Press, 1973); Truman Nelson's Leftist pamphlet, "People with Strength: The Story of Monroe, NC" (n.d.); Tyson's scholarly biography, *Radio Free Dixie*. For Julian Mayfield's eyewitness account of a 1957 Klan motorcade targeting the Monroe NAACP vice president's home, see James Forman, *The Making of Black Revolutionaries* (Seattle: Open Hand Publishing, 1985), 167.

7. In the latter case, a White hotel guest kicked the maid down a flight of stairs because she was making too much noise and disturbing his sleep. In the former case, the defense used sexualized, racist arguments that enabled the jury, despite witnesses to the defendant's guilt, to render a not guilty verdict. The defense attorney said: "Judge, Your Honor, and ladies and gentlemen of the jury, you see this man. This is his wife. This woman, this white woman, is the pure flower of life. She is one of God's lovely creatures, a pure flower. And do you think this man would have left this pure flower for that? . . . Judge, Your Honor, this man is not guilty of any crime. He was just drinking and having a little fun." See Forman, *Making of Black Revolutionaries,* 176–78; Williams, *Negroes with Guns,* 61–64.

8. Forman, *Making of Black Revolutionaries,* 176–78; Williams, *Negroes with Guns,* 61–64.

9. The national NAACP was forced to officially reaffirm the right to self-defense later that year. The preamble to the resolution of the fiftieth convention of the NAACP, New York City, July 1959, states: "we do not deny, but reaffirm, the right of an individual and collective self-defense against unlawful assaults." Williams, *Negroes with Guns,* 40; Forman, *Making of Black Revolutionaries,* 177–78; Jackson, Mississippi, *State-Times,* May 6, 1959, and *New York Times,* May 7, 1959, cited in Tyson, *Radio Free Dixie,* 149–50. For background on the clash between Williams and the NAACP national leadership, see Tyson, *Radio Free Dixie,* 149–65.

10. Williams's Harlem base included attorney Conrad Lynn, Malcolm X, former Communist Party member and longtime nationalist "Queen Mother" Audley Moore, Julian Mayfield, Mae Mallory, and the Socialist Workers Party. Some Harlem supporters demonstrated their belief in armed self-defense by supplying guns, including two machine guns, to Monroe activists. See Tyson, *Radio Free Dixie*, 112, 203–6; Robert Sherill, "We Also Want Four Hundred Billion Dollars Back Pay," *Esquire*, January 1969.

11. Apparently, the attempted rape victim's brothers had wanted to blow up the defendant's house, and several NAACP women wanted to machine-gun the defendant's house. Williams informed national NAACP leader Roy Wilkins by telephone: "For your information, I told them that this matter would be handled through the law. . . . We would be as bad as the white people if we resorted to violence." See Robert F. Williams, interview with Thomas Mosby, 1970, transcript, Ralph J. Bunche Oral History Collection, Moorland-Spingarn Research Center, Howard University, Washington, DC; "Telephone conversation between Mr. Wilkins in New York and Mr. Robert Williams in Monroe, North Carolina, May 6, 1959, at 11:04 a.m.," box A333, group 3, NAACP Papers, 3; both quoted in Tyson, *Radio Free Dixie*, 147–48, 279.

12. Tyson, *Radio Free Dixie*, 149–52; Williams, *Negroes with Guns*, 40; Robert F. Williams, "The Resistant Spirit: Why Do I Speak from Exile?" in Revolutionary Action Movement, *Black America*, 1965, 11, Social Protest Collection, Bancroft Library, University of California, Berkeley, box 18, folder 21.

13. For a vivid eyewitness account of this incident, see Forman, *Making of a Black Revolutionary*, 186–98; also Williams, *Negroes with Guns*, 78–84; Tyson, *Radio Free Dixie*, 262–91. On CORE, see Inge Powell Bell, *CORE and the Strategy of Nonviolence* (New York: Random House, 1968), 57; Meier and Rudwick, *CORE*, 263–64.

14. Julian Mayfield, "The Monroe Kidnapping," *West Indian Gazette and Afro-Asian Carribean News*, reprinted in Revolutionary Action Movement, *Black America*, 1965, 3–9, Social Protest Collection, Bancroft Library, University of California, Berkeley, box 18, folder 21; Forman, *Making of Black Revolutionaries*, 158–59, 206–7; John H. Clarke, "Introduction," in Williams, *Negroes with Guns*, 4–5; Tyson, *Radio Free Dixie*, 276–83; Williams, *Negroes with Guns*, 75–90, 104; Robert F. Williams, interview with Mosley, 1970, cited in Tyson, *Radio Free Dixie*, 279; Ahmad, *Toward Black Liberation, Part I*, 43–44.

15. Kochiyama, interview with author; Tyson, *Radio Free Dixie*, 282–85; Mabel Williams, "Self Respect, Self Defense, and Self Determination," speech, March 14, 2004, Oakland, CA (see www.freedomarchives.org).

16. Cruse, *The Crisis of the Black Intellectual*, 356–59; Tyson, *Radio Free Dixie*, 223–32; LeRoi Jones, "Cuba Libre," *Home* (Hopewell, NJ: Ecco Press, 1961), 11–62.

17. Mae Mallory, transcript, 1970, Ralph J. Bunche Oral History Collection,

Moorland-Spingarn Research Center, Howard University, Washington, D.C., cited in Tyson, *Radio Free Dixie*, 190; see also 189–90, 203–6.

18. Forman, *Making of Black Revolutionaries*, 189–90.

19. Yuri Kochiyama, interview with author; "Protest the Ban," the *Crusader*, October 1967, 16; press release for Mallory fund-raiser, circa January 1965; invitation to fund-raiser, January 19, 1965; Yuri Kochiyama, letter to LeRoi Jones, January 17, 1965; Yuri Kochiyama, Mallory fund-raiser, handwritten notes; Forman, *Making of Black Revolutionaries*, 206–7; Williams, *Negroes with Guns*, 93–94, 104–5.

20. Cruse, *Crisis of the Negro Intellectual*, 355–64, 535–36; Tobier, *Fishmerchant's Daughter*, vol. 1, 7–8.

21. Segregated spaces, especially when controlled by group members, have been found to foster the development of an oppositional political consciousness; see Aldon Morris and Naomi Braine, "Social Movements and Oppositional Consciousness," in *Oppositional Consciousness: The Subjective Roots of Social Protest*, ed. Jane Mansbridge and Aldon Morris (Chicago: University of Chicago Press, 2001), 20–37; Sharon Groch, "Free Spaces: Creating Oppositional Consciousness in the Disability Rights Movement," in Mansbridge and Morris, *Oppositional Consciousness*, 65–98.

22. Indeed, Yuri had a caustic social critic as a teacher, who concluded: "Negroes are given to spontaneous and emotional activist outbursts. Due to their American conditioning, they are neither theoretical nor analytical; their civil rights practices reveal that they are pragmatists par excellence." Cruse, *Crisis of the Negro Intellectual*, 388; also 355–58, 538–39; Tobier, *Fishmerchant's Daughter*, vol. 2, 7–8; Harold Cruse, *Rebellion or Revolution?* (New York: William Morrow, 1968).

23. Yuri Kochiyama, interview with author; Tobier, *Fishmerchant's Daughter*, vol. 2, 8–9; Herman Ferguson, conversation with author, March 23, 1999; photo of Duncan in *North Star*, 1966, 2, 8.

24. When formed and in the 1970s, RNA documents referred to the organization as the Republic of New Africa. By the 1990s, organizational documents used the spelling "Afrika." Because most of the biography makes reference to Yuri's involvement in the early years of RNA, the spelling "Africa" will be used throughout.

25. The agent's name has since been made public. Yuri Kochiyama, interview with author; Herman Ferguson, conversation with author, March 23, 1999; Family and Friends of Dr. Mutulu Shakur, "Despite Evidence Judge Haight Reserves Decision," *DMS Drumbeat*, July–September 1998, 1.

26. FBI files, New York 157-1258, October 4, 1966; FBI files, New York 100-155496, November 22, 1966; Yuri Kochiyama, interview with author.

27. Eddie Kochiyama, interview with author, September 25, 1998; Ward Churchill and Jim Vander Wall, *Agents of Repression: The FBI's Secret Wars against the Black Panther Party and the American Indian Movement*, 2nd ed.

(Boston: South End Press, 2002), xv, 59; Yuri Kochiyama, FBI file, New York, January 16, 1968.

28. Churchill and Vander Wall, *Agents of Repression*; Ward Churchill and Jim Vander Wall, *The COINTELPRO Papers: Documents from the FBI's Secret Wars against Domestic Dissent* (Boston: South End Press, 1990); Nelson Blackstock, *COINTELPRO: The FBI's Secret War on Political Freedom* (New York: Pathfinder, 1975); James Kirkpatrick Davis, *Assault on the Left: The FBI and the Sixties Antiwar Movement* (Westport, CT: Praeger, 1997); H. Wesley Wearingen, *FBI Secrets: An Agent's Exposé* (Boston: South End Press, 1995); Mae Mallory, interview with author, February 23, 2000.

29. Yuri Kochiyama, interview with author; Muhammad Ahmad, interview with author, January 30, 2000; Wayne Lum, interview with author, July 3, 2000; Mae Mallory, interview with author, February 23, 2000; Ahmed Obafemi, interview with author, February 7, 2000.

30. Yuri Kochiyama, interview with author.

31. Yuri Kochiyama, interview with author. APP formed when various revolutionary nationalists meeting at the Black Power Conference in Philadelphia in August 1968 decided to merge into a single organization. After Robert Williams's resignation, Max Stanford became party chair. While APP's ten-point program resembled that of Oakland Black Panther Party, APP sought the establishment of an autonomous Black nation, whereas the Panthers made its demands of the U.S. government, which APP considered an integrationist strategy. As a legal, aboveground organization, APP also distinguished itself from RAM's clandestine activities. [Note: Despite the similarity in name, the APP is not the All-African People's Revolutionary Party (A-APRP), of which Kwame Ture (Stokely Carmichael) was a leader.] See APP leaflet, August 7, 1971; APP, "On the All-African People's Party (APP)," n.d.; APP Ten-Point Program; all on microfilm (Afro-American Historical Association of the Niagara Frontier, Buffalo, NY).

32. David Lorens, "Black Separatism in Perspective: Movement Reflects Failure of Integration," *Ebony,* September 1968, 93; Sherrill, "We Also Want Four Hundred Billion Dollars Back Pay," 73–74; Stanford, "Revolutionary Action Movement," 131–32; Ukali, "Republic of New Afrika: 31 Years of Struggle for Nationhood," *Nation Time: The Voice of the New Afrikan Liberation Front,* Spring 1999, 3, 10.

33. Ahmed Obafemi, interview with author, February 7, 2000; Yuri Kochiyama, interview with author.

34. RNA, New African Creed, n.d.; David Deutschmann, ed., *Che Guevara and the Cuban Revolution: Writings and Speeches of Che Guevara* (Sydney, Australia: Pathfinder, 1987), 246–61.

35. To this day, many older friends call her "Mary," which seems acceptable to Yuri. Yuri Kochiyama, interview with author; participant observation by author.

36. Information comes from Yuri Kochiyama's notes from RNA classes on nation building, revolutionary first aid, and gun control (copy is in possession of

author); Yuri Kochiyama, interview with author; Bolanile Akinwole, interview with author, February 21, 2000; Robert Sherrill, "We Also Want Four Hundred Billion Dollars Back Pay," 73, 75; Obadele, *Foundations of the Black Nation*, 74, 80.

37. Yuri Kochiyama, interview with author.

38. Yuri Kochiyama, interview with author.

39. Bolanile Akinwole, interview with author, February 21, 2000; Yuri Kochiyama, interview with author; Ahmed Obafemi, interview with author, February 7, 2000.

40. Ahmed Obafemi, interview with author, February 7, 2000; participant observation by author; Yuri Kochiyama, interview with author.

41. Ahmed Obafemi, interview with author, February 7, 2000; Bibi Angola, interview with author, December 6, 1999; Muhammad Ahmad, interview with author, January 30, 2000. According to Yuri, she did not see Malcolm X patronize Thomford's Ice Cream Parlor, as indicated by Sales (*From Civil Rights to Black Liberation*, 58).

42. Ahmed Obafemi, interview with author, February 7, 2000; Mutulu Shakur, interview with author, October 19, 1998.

43. Bolanile Akinwole, interview with author, February 21, 2000; Ahmed Obafemi, interview with author, February 7, 2000; Renee Tajima, "Site-Seeing through Asian America," in *Mapping Multiculturalism,* ed. Avery Gordon and Chris Newfield (Minneapolis: University of Minnesota Press, 1996), 276.

44. Participant observations by author.

45. A copy of the complete collection of *Christmas Cheer* (except the first issue) and *North Star* is in the author's possession, courtesy of Yuri Kochiyama.

46. Bill Kochiyama and Richie Perez, quoted in Tajiri and Saunders, *Yuri Kochiyama: A Passion for Justice* (video, 1993); Muhammad Ahmad, interview with author, January 30, 2000; Nyisha Shakur, interview with author, October 15, 1998; Herman Ferguson, interview with author, June 19, 1996; Mutulu Shakur, interview with author, October 19, 1998.

47. Gibson quoted in Tyson, *Radio Free Dixie,* 297; see also, 82–87, 114–15, 206–7, 244–60, 284–85; Cruse, *Crisis of the Negro Intellectual,* 359; Williams, *Negroes with Guns,* 117, 120.

48. Cruse, *Crisis of the Negro Intellectual,* 246, 359, 382–401, 564; Tyson, *Radio Free Dixie,* 150–64, 289; Omi and Winant, *Racial Formation in the United States,* 14–23.

49. Henry Adams quoted in John H. Bracey Jr., August Meier, and Elliott Rudwick, *Black Nationalism in America* (Indianapolis: Bobbs-Merrill, 1970), 163–64; Elijah Muhammad, *Message to the Blackman in America* (Chicago: Muhammad Mosque No. 2, 1965), 162, cited in Draper, *Rediscovery of Black Nationalism,* 83; Yuri Kochiyama, interview with author.

50. Tyson, *Radio Free Dixie,* 206–7; Sherrill, "We Also Want Four Hundred Billion Dollars in Back Pay," 73, 75; Breitman, *Last Year of Malcolm X,* 26–39.

51. Max Stanford wrote that RAM's objective was to build an independent

socialist Black nation in the South. I recognize that various forms of socialism exist, including but not limited to democratic socialism, African socialism, and revolutionary socialism. I also recognize that according to Marx, socialism is a transitional stage between capitalism and communism. My point here is that in contrast to the frequent polarization of nationalism and socialism, revolutionary nationalism usually involves some form of socialism. RNA Declaration of Independence; RNA "Political Statement," n.d.; Stanford, "Revolutionary Action Movement," 2, 146–54; Draper, *Rediscovery of Black Nationalism*, 100–17; V. I. Lenin, *The State and Revolution* (Peking: Foreign Language Press, 1973), 109–22.

52. The Black Panther Party and All-African People's Revolutionary Party fall into the scientific socialist camp of revolutionary nationalism. Foner, *Black Panthers Speak*, xv–xvi, xix; Huey Newton, "Huey Newton Talks to the Movement about the Black Panther Party, Cultural Nationalism, SNCC, Liberals and White Revolutionaries," *Black Panthers Speak*, 50–51; Gene Marine, *The Black Panthers* (New York: Signet, 1969), 40; Huey Newton, *Revolutionary Suicide* (New York: Ballantine, 1973), 123; Kwame Nkrumah, *Handbook of Revolutionary Warfare* (London: Panaf Books, 1968), 28–29, 56–57.

53. RNA, "Political Statement," n.d.; Huey Newton, "Huey Newton Talks to the Movement," 50–52; Linda Harrison, "On Cultural Nationalism," *Black Panther*, February 2, 1969, reprinted in *Black Panthers Speak*, 151–54; Stanford, "Revolutionary Action Movement," 152; Amilcar Cabral, *Return to the Source* (New York: Monthly Review Press, 1973), 39–44.

54. Nkrumah, *Handbook of Revolutionary Warfare*, 24–30, 43–46; Leon Trotsky, *Revolution Betrayed* (1937; reprint, New York: Merit Publishers, 1965), 291–308; Leon Trotsky, *The Third International after Lenin* (New York: Pathfinder Press, 1970), 24–73; Yuri Kochiyama, interview with author.

55. For a history of Black nationalism, see Bracey, Meier, and Rudwick, *Black Nationalism in America*; Moses, *Golden Age of Black Nationalism*; Draper, *Rediscovery of Black Nationalism*; Obadele, *Foundations of the Black Nation*.

56. Michael Lowy, "Marxists and the National Question," *New Left Review* 96 (1976): 81–100; Cedric J. Robinson, *Black Marxism: The Making of the Black Radical Tradition* (London: Zed Press, 1983), 77–81; V. I. Lenin, "The Right of Nations to Self-Determination," in *Collected Works*, vol. 20 (Moscow: Foreign Languages, 1914), 397. On imperialism, see V. I. Lenin, *Imperialism: The Highest Stage of Capitalism* (1917; reprint, Moscow: Progressive Publishers, 1975).

57. V. I. Lenin, "The Right of Nations to Self-Determination," *Selections from V. I. Lenin and J. V. Stalin on National Colonial Question* (Calcutta: Calcutta Book House, 1970), 13–31; Lowy, "Marxists and the National Question," 83.

58. Cruse, *Rebellion or Revolution?* 74–76, 232; Stokely Carmichael and Charles V. Hamilton, *Black Power: The Politics of Liberation in America* (New York: Vintage Books, 1967), 3–32; Robert Blauner, *Racial Oppression in America* (New York: Harper and Row, 1972), 54; Yuri Kochiyama, interview with author.

Robin D. G. Kelley contends that rather than focusing primarily on whether activists, especially radicals who set lofty aims, reached their goals, the ideas and imaginations of activists, in this case about the land question, contain political and analytic importance. See Kelley, *Freedom Dreams: The Black Radical Imagination* (Boston: Beacon Press, 2002), especially 13–35.

59. Nkrumah, *Handbook of Revolutionary Warfare*, 28–29, 56–57; Vincent, *Black Power and the Garvey Movement*, 21–23; All-African People's Revolutionary Party, "500 Years of Resistance" (leaflet, 1992); Yuri Kochiyama, interview with author; Howard Zinn, *A People's History of the United States, 1492–Present* (New York: Harper Perennial, 1995), 136–46; Obadele, *Foundations of the Black Nation, 7.*

60. Tom Boot, "Revolutionary Integration: Yesterday and Today," *Freedom Socialist,* Spring 1983, 1, 4–8; Smedley, *Race in North America,* 14–35; Spickard, "Illogic of American Race Categories," in *Racially Mixed People in America,* 12–23. According to Stalin: "A nation is a historically constituted, stable community of people, formed on the basis of a common language, territory, economic life, and psychological make-up manifested in a common culture. . . . It is only when all these characteristics are present together that we have a nation." See Joseph Stalin, "Marxism and the National Question," in *Works,* vol. 2 (Moscow: Foreign Languages, 1953), 307–8. This definition has been criticized as a rigid, mechanical application of Lenin's ideas of national self-determination. See Robinson, *Black Marxism,* 79; Lowy, "Marxists and the National Question," 95.

61. Obadele, *Foundations of the Black Nation,* 77–78; Imari Obadele, *Free the Land* (Washington, DC: House of Songhay, 1984), 9; Muhjah Shakur, "Plebiscite, Land before Independence, Economic Development, and Self-Determination," *New Afrikan Journal* 4 (April–May 1998): 15–17; Foner, *Black Panthers Speak,* 2–4, 70–73; George Breitman, "Freedom Now: The New Stage in the Struggle for Negro Emancipation," *International Socialist Review* 24 (1963): 106.

62. Kochiyamas, "Rob Williams Comes Home," *North Star,* 1969, 1, 8; Yuri Kochiyama, interview with author; Stanford, "Revolutionary Action Movement," 134; Clarke, "Introduction," in Williams, *Negroes with Guns,* 5–6.

63. Herman Ferguson, interview with author, June 19, 1996.

64. Stanford, "Revolutionary Action Movement," 99, 134–35; Obadele, *Foundations of the Black Nation,* 109; Imari Obadele, *War in America: The Malcolm X Doctrine* (Chicago: Ujamaa Distributors, 1977), 15–16.

65. Grace Lee Boggs, *Living for Change: An Autobiography* (Minneapolis: University of Minnesota Press, 1998), 136–37; James Boggs, *Racism and the Class Struggle* (New York: Modern Reader, 1970), 39–50; Malcolm X, "Message to the Grassroots," 9; Michael Eric Dyson, "Inventing and Interpreting Malcolm X," in *The Seductions of Biography,* ed. Mary Rhiel and David Suchoff (New York, Routledge, 1996), 51; A. Peter Bailey, conversation with author, July 24, 2000; Herman Ferguson, letter to author, February 14, 1999.

66. Bolanile Akinwole, interview with author, February 21, 2000; Yuri

Kochiyama, interview with author. For RNA's plans, see Obadele, *Foundations of the Black Nation*; Sherrill, "We Also Want Four Hundred Billion Dollars Back Pay."

67. Kochiyamas, "'Black Power': SNCC's New Battle Cry!" *North Star*, 1966, 1; Mary Kochiyama, "The Black Struggle and Political Prisoners," *Asian Americans for Action* newsletter, February 1970, 5. For more on Carmichael's views on Black Power, see Carmichael and Hamilton, *Black Power*.

7. Political Prisoners and the Heartbeat of Struggle

1. Although its masthead identifies the *North Star* as "the Kochiyama Family's Annual News-sheet"—a sentiment reflecting Yuri's collective orientation— Yuri, the primary participant in the militant Black movement, was the main mover and shaker behind the newsletter. Upon inquiry, Yuri did explain that after they started this second newsletter, Bill took on more responsibility for *Christmas Cheer* while she concentrated on *North Star*.

2. Kochiyama, *North Star*, December 1967, articles throughout; J. Edgar Hoover, "Counterintelligence Program, Black Nationalist-Hate Groups, Internal Security," memo dated August 25, 1967, reprinted in Ward Churchill and Jim Vander Wall, *COINTELPRO Papers*, 92–93. The *North Star* contained information on Huey Newton's arrest and the Free Huey campaign (1967, 2; 1968, 1); also see Huey P. Newton's autobiography *Revolutionary Suicide*.

3. Only two of the four FBI-identified "most radical and violence-prone" Black nationalist groups could be considered radical and Black nationalist—RAM and SNCC. The Nation of Islam was nationalist but hardly ideologically radical, and the Southern Christian Leadership Conference was neither nationalist nor radical. J. Edgar Hoover, "Counterintelligence Program, Black Nationalist-Hate Groups, Racial Intelligence," FBI memo dated March 4, 1968, reprinted in Churchill and Vander Wall, *COINTELPRO Papers*, 108–11; Churchill and Vander Wall, *Agents of Repression*, 45–47; "The Muhammad Ahmad (Max Stanford) Story" (leaflet, microfilm, Afro-American Historical Association of the Niagara Frontier; Buffalo, NY); Tyson, *Radio Free Dixie*, 161–62; Yuri Kochiyama, interview with author.

4. Yuri believes that their grassroots campaign helped get charges dropped or reduced for fifteen of the defendants. But, Ferguson and Harris were found guilty based on the testimony of undercover Black police detective Edward Lee Howlette and sought refuge in Guyana to avoid three-and-a-half-to-seven-year sentences. Max Stanford was arrested in 1972. Mike McAlary, "Only DA Santucci Could Swallow This Mouthful," *Daily News*, April 5, 1980; Stewart Ain and Don Gentile, "An Exile Who Ran Asks to Return," *Daily News*, December 28, 1988; Curtis Rist, "After 19 Years, Black Militant Seeks New Trial," *Newsday*, April 9, 1990; *Can't Jail the Spirit: Political Prisoners in the US*, 4th ed. (Chicago: Editorial El Coquí, 1992), 60–61; Freedom for Herman Ferguson Committee, "Herman

Benjamin Ferguson: Speech at Sentencing on Bail Jumping Charge," June 28, 1990; "Ferguson to Be Sentenced on Bail Jumping Rap," *Amsterdam News,* June 23, 1990; "Max Stanford (Muhammad Ahmad) Arrested at C.A.P.," *The Black Scholar,* press release in microfilm, circa 1972 (Afro-American Historical Association of the Niagara Frontier; Buffalo, NY); Kochiyama, "Support the Seventeen," *North Star,* 1967, 3.

5. Hoover, "Counterintelligence Program, Black Nationalist-Hate Groups, Internal Security," August 25, 1967; Hoover, "Counterintelligence Program, Black Nationalist-Hate Groups, Racial Intelligence," FBI memo dated March 4, 1968, emphasis in the original.

6. Churchill and Vander Wall, *Agents of Repression,* 1–38; Churchill and Vander Wall, *COINTELPRO Papers.*

7. *New York Times,* September 8, 1968, cited in Carson et al., *Eyes on the Prize,* 529; Hoover, "Counterintelligence Program, Black Nationalist-Hate Groups, Racial Intelligence"; J. Edgar Hoover, chairman, *Special Report of Interagency Committee on Intelligence* (Ad Hoc), June 25, 1970, cited in Noam Chomsky, "Introduction," in Blackstock, *COINTELPRO,* 17; Foner, *Black Panthers Speak,* xiv; Marine, *Black Panthers,* 23, 61–66.

8. On FBI and police repression of the BPP, see Churchill and Vander Wall, *Agents of Repression;* Churchill and Vander Wall, *COINTELPRO Papers.* On Geronimo ji Jaga (Pratt), see Jack Olsen, *Last Man Standing: The Tragedy and Triumph of Geronimo Pratt* (New York: Doubleday, 2000); Ward Churchill, "A Person Who Struggles for Liberation: An Interview with Geronimo Pratt," in *Cages of Steel: The Politics of Imprisonment in the United States,* ed. Ward Churchill and J. J. Vander Wall (Washington, DC: Maisonneuve Press, 1992), 203–23; Geronimo ji Jaga, letter to Yuri Kochiyama, August 21, 1991; Geronimo ji Jaga (Pratt), conversation with author, February 1998; Edward J. Boyer, "Pratt Strides into Freedom," *Los Angeles Times,* June 11, 1997; Yuri Kochiyama, interview with author; Yuri Kochiyama, "Welcome Home for Geronimo Pratt," speech, Brooklyn, NY, July 11, 1997.

9. On Panther 21, see Peter L. Zimroth, *Perversions of Justice: The Prosecution and Acquittal of the Panther 21* (New York: Viking Press, 1974); Dhoruba bin Wahad, "Speaking Truth to Power: Political Prisoners in the United States," in *Criminal Injustice,* ed. Elihu Rosenblatt (Boston: South End Press, 1996), 270–71, 278; Churchill and Vander Wall, *COINTELPRO Papers,* 147–48, 361–62; The Committee to Defend the Panther 21, "The Black Panther Party and the Case of the New York 21," pamphlet, 1970.

10. Nyisha Shakur, interview with author, October 15, 1998; Ahmed Obafemi, interview with author, February 7, 2000; Bibi Angola, interview with author, December 6, 1998; Mutulu Shakur, interview with author, October 19, 1998; Yuri Kochiyama, interview with author.

11. Yuri Kochiyama, interview with author; Yuri Kochiyama, résumé; various leaflets of political prisoner cases.

12. Yuri Kochiyama, "Statement for the Subpoenees for the Forum on Political Repression," speech, St. Mark's Church, New York, February 6, 1975; Tobier, *Fishmerchant's Daughter,* vol. 1, 16–17. The Japanese Americans were not incarcerated for any criminal act—and never received a trial or hearing—but were rounded up solely on the basis of their ethnicity. Thus, they can be considered political prisoners, under a broad definition, even though the vast majority were not imprisoned for their resistance to oppression. A few Japanese Americans, those tried and convicted for refusing to obey evacuation or draft orders, can be considered political prisoners by the narrow definition of the term; that is, being targeted for imprisonment because their political actions, beliefs, or associations threatened the established order.

13. Assata Shakur, *Assata: An Autobiography* (Chicago: Lawrence Hill Books, 1987), 49–51.

14. Yuri Kochiyama, "The Black Struggle and Political Prisoners," 1, 5, 6; Yuri Kochiyama, "A Generation of Struggle," speech, November 21, 1986; Yuri Kochiyama, interview with author; the Jericho movement, mission statement, www.thejerichomovement.com.

15. Karen Wald and Ward Churchill, "Remembering the Real Dragon: An Interview with George Jackson," in Churchill and Vander Wall, *Cages of Steel,* 174–93; Churchill and Vander Wall, *Agents of Repression,* 94–99; also see George Jackson, *Soledad Brother: The Prison Letters of George Jackson* (New York: Bantam, 1970); Angela Y. Davis, *If They Come in the Morning: Voices of Resistance* (New York: Third Press, 1971); Angela Y. Davis, *An Autobiography* (New York: International Publishers, 1974).

16. Jericho movement, mission statement, www.thejerichomovement.com; Yuri Kochiyama, interview with author.

17. United Nations General Assembly Resolution 1514, "Declaration of the Granting of Independence to Colonial Countries and Peoples," December 12, 1960; United Nations General Assembly Resolution 2621, "Programme of Action for the Full Implementation of the Declaration on the Granting of Independence to Colonial Countries and Peoples," October 12, 1970; United Nations General Assembly Resolution 3103, "Basic Principles of the Legal Status of the Combatants Struggling against Colonial and Alien Domination and Racist Regimes," December 12, 1973; United Nations General Assembly Resolution 32/122, "Protection of Persons Detained or Imprisoned as a Result of Their Struggle against Apartheid, Racism and Racial Discrimination, Colonialism, Aggression and Foreign Occupation and for Self-Determination, Independence and Social Progress for Their People," December 16, 1977.

18. Yuri Kochiyama, conversations with author, August 2001; participant observation at Jericho meeting, Oakland, August 2001.

19. On the politics of imprisonment, see Ruth Wilson Gilmore, "Globalisation and US Prison Growth: From Military Keynesianism to Post-Keynesian Militarism," *Race and Class* 40 (October 1998–May 1999): 171–88; Avery F.

Gordon, "Globalism and the Prison Industrial Complex: An Interview with Angela Davis," *Race and Class* 40 (October 1998–May 1999): 145–57; Special issue on prisons, *Monthly Review* 53 (July–August 2001); Elihu Rosenblatt, *Criminal Injustice*; Marc Mauer, *Race to Incarcerate* (New York: New Press, 1999); Marc Mauer, *Invisible Punishment: The Collateral Consequences of Mass Imprisonment* (New York: New Press, 2002); Daniel Burton-Rose, with Dan Pens and Paul Wright, eds., *The Celling of America: An Inside Look at the US Prison Industry* (Monroe, ME: Common Courage Press, 1998); Churchill and Vander Wall, *Cages of Steel*; Chinosole, ed., *Schooling the Generations in the Politics of Prison* (Berkeley, CA: New Earth Publications, 1996); Eve Goldberg and Linda Evans, "The Prison Industrial Complex and the Global Economy," *Turning the Tide*, summer 1998, www.prisonactivist.org.

20. Susie Day, "Cruel but Not Unusual: The Punishment of Women in US Prisons: An Interview with Marilyn Buck and Laura Whitehorn," *Monthly Review* 53 (July–August 2001): 42–55; Elihu Rosenblatt, "In Critical Condition: Abuse, Neglect, and Poor Health Care in US Prisons" and "The Prison Discipline Study: Exposing the Myth of Humane Imprisonment in the United States," in Rosenblatt, *Criminal Injustice*, 84–99; *Can't Jail the Spirit*, 20–21; Churchill, introduction, Churchill and Vander Wall, *Cages of Steel*, 1, 16; Fay Dowker and Glenn Good, "From Alcatraz to Marion to Florence: Control Unit Prisons in the United States," in Churchill and Vander Wall, *Cages of Steel*, 131–51; Bill Dunne, "The US Prison at Marion, Illinois: An Instrument of Oppression," in Churchill and Vander Wall, *Cages of Steel*, 38–82; Mary O'Melveny, "Portrait of a U.S. Political Prison: The Lexington High Security Unit for Women," in Churchill and Vander Wall, *Cages of Steel*, 112–22; Mike Ryan, "Solitude as Counterinsurgency: The US Isolation Model of Political Incarceration," in Churchill and Vander Wall, *Cages of Steel*, 83–109; Rosenblatt, *Criminal Injustice*, 252.

21. Susie Day, "Cruel but Not Unusual," 52; Churchill, introduction, Churchill and Vander Wall, *Cages of Steel*, 16; Yuri Kochiyama, "The Role of Political Prisoners: Internationally and Here," speech, Columbia University, October 1, 1996. On Laura Whitehorn, see Sonia de Vries and Rhonda Collins, *Out: The Making of a Revolutionary* (documentary, 2000).

22. Yuri Kochiyama, interview with author; Yuri Kochiyama, "A Generation of Struggle," speech, November 21, 1986, New York.

23. Yuri Kochiyama, interview with author.

24. Yuri Kochiyama, interview with author.

25. Gustavo Gutiérrez, *A Theology of Liberation: History, Politics, and Salvation* (1971; reprint, Maryknoll, NY: Orbis Books, 1988); Philip Berryman, *Liberation Theology* (Philadelphia: Temple University Press, 1987); Sékou Turé, quoted in All-African People's Revolutionary Party, *African Liberation Day* newspaper, 1994, 1; Yuri Kochiyama, interview with author.

26. A former Panther, Bukhari would herself become a political prisoner and manage a daring escape from the Virginia Correctional Prison in Goochland in

1976. In the late 1990s, Bukhari headed the New York Mumia Coalition and the Jericho movement for political prisoners and was vice president of the RNA. Yuri was on her way to visit political prisoner Marilyn Buck when she learned of Bukhari's death in August 2003. Yuri Kochiyama, interview with author; Yuri Kochiyama, conversation with author, August 24, 2003.

27. Eddie Kochiyama, interview with author, September 25, 1998; Audee Kochiyama-Holman, interview with author, September 27, 1998.

28. Eddie Kochiyama, interview with author, September 25, 1998; Yuri Kochiyama, interview with author. Bibi Angola's memories coincide with Eddie's description of Yuri's weekly schedule (interview with author, December 6, 1998).

29. Jimmy Kochiyama, interview with author, November 29, 1998; Eddie Kochiyama, interview with author, September 27, 1998; Yuri Kochiyama, interview with author.

30. Nyisha Shakur, interview with author, October 15, 1998.

31. Nyisha Shakur, interview with author, October 15, 1998; Herman Ferguson, interview with author, June 9, 1996.

32. Yuri Kochiyama, interview with author; Estella Habal, "How I Became a Revolutionary," in *Legacy to Liberation: The Politics and Culture of Revolutionary Asian Pacific America,* ed. Fred Ho (San Francisco: AK Press, 2000), 197–209; Fred Ho, conversations with author, circa 1999; David Monkawa, conversation with author, December 5, 1996.

33. Yuri Kochiyama, "Mothers and Daughters," *AWU Journal,* circa 1984; Yuri Kochiyama, *Discover Your Mission: Selected Speeches and Writings by Yuri Kochiyama* (Los Angeles: UCLA Asian American Studies Center Reading Room/ Library, 1998), 33; Audee Kochiyama-Holman, letter to author, March 2, 1999; Eddie Kochiyama, interview with author, September 25, 1998.

34. Audee Kochiyama-Holman, interview with author, October 25, 1998; Yuri Kochiyama, interview with author.

35. Yuri Kochiyama, letter to author, December 27, 1998; Yuri Kochiyama, interview with author; Greg Morozumi, interview with author, October 12, 1998; Nyisha Shakur, interview with author, October 15, 1998.

36. Eddie Kochiyama, interview with author, September 25, 1998.

37. Audee Kochiyama-Holman, interview with author, September 27, 1998; Bibi Angola, interview with author, December 6, 1998; Yuri Kochiyama, interview with author; Nyisha Shakur, interview with author, October 15, 1998.

38. Audee Kochiyama-Holman, interview with author, September 27, 1998.

39. Kazu Iijima, interview with author, June 21, 1996; "Rally 'Round Projected Asian Community Center!" *Asian Americans for Action* newsletter, April–June 1972, 12; Bill Kochiyama, "Accent Is on Harmony at Official Opening of Asian Center," *Asian Americans for Action* newsletter, December 1972–January 1973, 5; William Wei, *The Asian American Movement* (Philadelphia: Temple University Press, 1993), 29.

40. Bill Kochiyama in Tajiri and Saunders, *Yuri Kochiyama: Passion for Justice*

(video, 1993); Kazu Iijima, interview with author, June 21, 1996; Yuri Kochiyama, interview with author.

41. Bibi Angola, interview with author, December 6, 1998; Audee Kochiyama-Holman, interview with author, September 27, 1998.

42. Eddie Kochiyama, "A Son Reflects on His Parents," *Hawaii Herald,* March 19, 1993; Tommy Kochiyama, letter to author, February 24, 1999; Greg Morozumi, interview with author, October 12, 1998; Nyisha Shakur, interview with author, October 15, 1998.

43. Audee Kochiyama-Holman, interview with author, October 25, 1998; Yuri Kochiyama, interview with author; funeral program for Billy Kochiyama, October 1975.

44. Funeral program for Billy Kochiyama, October 1975; Audee Kochiyama-Holman, interview with author, September 27 and October 25, 1998; Eddie Kochiyama, interview with author, September 25, 1998; Yuri Kochiyama, interview with author.

45. Eddie Kochiyama, interview with author, September 25, 1998; Tommy Kochiyama, interview with author, October 18, 1998; Yuri Kochiyama, interview with author.

46. Audee Kochiyama-Holman, interview with author, October 25, 1998.

47. Funeral program for Billy Kochiyama, October 1975.

48. Kazu Iijima, interview with author, June 21, 1996; Audee Kochiyama-Holman, interview with author, September 27, 1998; Yuri Kochiyama, interview with author.

49. Yuri Kochiyama, letter to author, January 15, 1996; funeral program for Billy Kochiyama, October 1975. It is possible that Bill also shared these words, written in Billy's funeral program. But conversations with family members suggest that this view was primarily Yuri's.

50. Bibi Angola, interview with author, December 6, 1998; Yuri Kochiyama, interview with author.

51. Juan Carlos Perez, "Lolita Lebron: Sigue Palante," *Latina,* January 1998, 28; Lolita Lebron, letter to Yuri Kochiyama, November 11, 1975; Yuri Kochiyama, interview with author.

52. Edwin Melendez and Edgardo Melendez, *Colonial Dilemma: Critical Perspectives on Contemporary Puerto Rico* (Boston: South End Press, 1993); Ronald Fernandez, *Prisoners of Colonialism: The Struggle for Justice in Puerto Rico* (Monroe, ME: Common Courage Press, 1994); Angela Davis, *Women, Race and Class,* 219; Deborah Santana, testimony, *USA on Trial: The International Tribunal on Indigenous Peoples and Oppressed Nations in the United States* (Chicago: Editorial El Coquí, 1996), 100–108.

53. Lolita Lebron, "To Love Me Is to Love My Country," pamphlet produced by the Committee to Free the Five Nationalists, circa 1975.

54. Rafael Cancel Miranda, panel discussion at *The Double Life of Ernesto Gomez Gomez* video showing, Critical Resistance conference, Berkeley, CA, Sep-

tember 25, 1998; Rafael Cancel Miranda, conversation with author, November 1, 1998; Lebron, "To Love Me Is to Love My Country"; Tajiri and Saunders, *Yuri Kochiyama: Passion for Justice* (video, 1993); Fernandez, *Prisoners of Colonialism*, 206–7; Jan Susler, "Unreconstructed Revolutionaries: Today's Puerto Rican Political Prisoners/Prisoners of War," in *The Puerto Rican Movement: Voices from the Diaspora,* ed. Andrés Torres and José E. Velázquez (Philadelphia: Temple University Press, 1998), 147, 356.

55. Yuri Kochiyama, interview with author; Anne L. Fuller, Federal Reformatory for Women, Alderson, WV, letter to Yuri Kochiyama authorizing prison visits with Lolita Lebron, September 29, 1975.

56. Juan Gonzalez, "Young Lords Party," Ethnic Studies Interim Conference, *Hawaii Pono Journal,* 1971, 48–52; Iris Morales, "¡Palante, Siempre Palante! The Young Lords," in Torres and Velázquez, *Puerto Rican Movement,* 213–14; Young Lords Party and Michael Abramson, *Palante: Young Lords Party* (New York: McGraw-Hill, 1971).

57. James Early, "An African American-Puerto Rican Connection," in Torres and Velázquez, *Puerto Rican Movement,* 316–17; Jan Susler, "Unconstructed Revolutionaries," 145; Fernandez, *Prisoners of Colonialism,* 205–18, 227–35, 242–52; Yuri Kochiyama, interview with author.

58. Mary Breasted, "30 in Puerto Rican Group Held in Liberty I. Protest," *New York Times,* October 26, 1977; "Puerto Rican Demonstration: Statue of Liberty Takeover," *San Francisco Chronicle,* October 26, 1977; Richie Perez in Tajiri and Saunders, *Yuri Kochiyama: Passion for Justice* (video, 1993); Fernandez, *Prisoners of Colonialism,* 198.

59. Yuri Kochiyama, interview with author; Yuri Kochiyama, guest lecture, Asian American Social Movement course, University of California, Santa Barbara, April 30, 1996. On October 26, 1977, the *New York Times* and *San Francisco Chronicle* reported thirty protesters. But the next day, the *New York Times* reported twenty-nine protesters, seventeen men and twelve women, which matches Yuri's firm recollection.

60. Yuri Kochiyama, interview with author; brief article, *New York Times,* October 27, 1977; Jo Freeman, *The Politics of Women's Liberation: A Case Study of an Emerging Social Movement and Its Relation to the Policy Process* (New York: Longman, 1975); Sara Evans, *Personal Politics: The Roots of Women's Liberation in the Civil Rights Movement and the New Left* (New York: Vintage Books, 1979), 212–32; Steven Buechler, *Women's Movement in the United States* (New Brunswick, NJ: Rutgers University Press, 1990), 66.

61. Yuri Kochiyama, interview with author; Fernandez, *Prisoners of Colonialism,* 197–99; Perez, "Lolita Lebron: Sigue Palante," 28. The image of the Puerto Rican flag on the Statue of Liberty is on the cover of *The Puerto Rican Movement* by Torres and Velázquez.

62. Jerry Schmetterer and Stuart Marques, "Top FALN Bomber Morales Seized," *New York Daily News,* May 28, 1983; Jack Anderson, "Mexico Set

to Free Terrorist Chief Morales," *New York Post,* May 23, 1984; Murray Weiss and Michael Shain, "Mexico Frees Terrorist Bomber," *New York Post,* June 28, 1988; "US Assails Mexico for Releasing Militant," *New York Times,* June 28, 1988; Douglas Montero, "Puerto Rican Bomber Asks for Amnesty," *New York Post,* December 7, 1997; Yuri Kochiyama, "Statement for the Subpoenees for the Forum on Political Repression," speech, St. Mark's Church, New York, February 6, 1975; Yuri Kochiyama, "A Generation of Struggle," speech, November 21, 1986, New York; Guillermo Morales, letters to Yuri Kochiyama, January 11, 1984, January 14, 1985, April 1, 1985, January 15, 1987, October 15, 1997; Dylcia Pagán, interview with author, October 6, 1998.

63. Shakur, *Assata: An Autobiography;* Lennox S. Hinds, foreword, *Assata: An Autobiography,* viii–xii; Lennox S. Hinds, *Illusions of Justice: Human Rights Violations in the United States* (Iowa City: School of Social Work, University of Iowa, 1978), 254–57; Churchill and Vander Wall, *COINTELPRO Papers,* 308; M. Annette Jaimes, "Self-Portrait of a Black Liberationist: An Appraisal of Assata Shakur's Autobiography," in Churchill and Vander Wall, *Cages of Steel,* 240–43; Frank McKeown and Henry Lee, "Black Rebel, Trooper Die in Shootout," *New York Daily News,* May 3, 1973; John T. McQuiston, "Fugitive Murderer Reported in Cuba," *New York Times,* October 12, 1987; Cheryll Y. Greene, "Word from a Sister in Exile," *Essence,* February 1988; Evelyn C. White, "Prisoner in Paradise," *Essence,* June 1997; Assata Shakur, "Open Letter from Assata Shakur," March 31, 1998; Yuri Kochiyama, "A Generation of Struggle," speech, November 21, 1986, New York. On Acoli, see biography of Sundiata Acoli, in *Can't Jail the Spirit,* 44–46; "Sundiata's Freedom Is Your Freedom," *Crossroad: A New Afrikan Captured Combatant Newsletter,* spring 1992, 5–8.

64. Yuri Kochiyama, interview with author; Bethany Leal, conversation with author, circa October 1997.

65. Jan Susler, "Unreconstructed Revolutionaries," 146–49; Fernandez, *Prisoners of Colonialism,* 146–263; Gary Weimberg and Cathy Ryan, *The Double Life of Ernesto Gomez Gomez* (video, 1999); Dylcia Pagán, interview with author, October 6, 1998; Hector Tobar, "Puerto Ricans Hail Activists as Patriots," *Los Angeles Times,* September 12, 1999; Nora Wallace, "Liberated by Clemency, Imprisoned by Its Terms," *Santa Barbara News-Press,* September 11, 1999; Mireya Navarro, "Puerto Ricans Protest Navy Firing Range on Vieques," *New York Times,* July 9, 1999; editorial, "The 'War' Over Vieques," *Toledo Blade,* November 18, 1999; Diane Fujino, "Dancing to Victory: The Release of the Puerto Rican Political Prisoners," *Shades of Power,* Fall 1999, 5–6.

66. Mtayari Shabaka Sundiata, letter to Yuri Kochiyama, April 27, 1975; Yuri Kochiyama, "Remembering Mtayari Shabaka Sundiata," *Nation Time: The Voice of the New Afrikan Liberation Front,* Fall 1998, 20; Dylcia Pagán, interview with author, October 6, 1998.

8. Asian Americans and the Rise of a New Movement

1. On the Asian American Movement of 1960s and 1970s, see Asian Women's Journal, *Asian Women* (Berkeley: University of California, 1971); Amy Tachiki, Eddie Wong, Franklin Odo, and Buck Wong, eds., *Roots: An Asian American Reader* (Los Angeles: UCLA Asian American Studies Center, 1971); Emma Gee, ed., *Counterpoint: Perspectives on Asian America* (Los Angeles: UCLA Asian American Studies Center, 1976); Susie Ling, "The Mountain Movers: Asian American Women's Movement, Los Angeles, 1968–1976" (master's thesis, UCLA, 1984); special issue on the San Francisco State Strike, *Amerasia Journal* 15 (1989); Karen Umemoto, "Asian American Students in the San Francisco State College Strike, 1964–1968" (master's thesis, UCLA, 1989); William Wei, *The Asian American Movement* (Philadelphia: Temple University Press, 1993); Craig Scharlin and Lilia V. Villanueva, *Philip Vera Cruz: A Personal History of Filipino Immigrants and the Farmworkers Movement* (Seattle: University of Washington Press, 2000); Fred Ho, ed., *Legacy to Liberation*; Steve Louie and Glenn Omatsu, eds., *Asian Americans: The Movement and the Moment* (Los Angeles: UCLA Asian American Studies Center, 2001); Harvey C. Dong, "The Origins and Trajectory of Asian American Political Activism in the San Francisco Bay Area, 1968–1978" (Ph.D. diss., UC Berkeley, 2002). For critical reviews of William Wei's book, see Steve Louie, *Amerasia Journal* 19 (1993): 155–59; Harvey Dong, *Hitting Critical Mass: A Journal of Asian American Cultural Criticism* 3 (1996); for more favorable reviews, see Clarence Y. H. Lo, *Contemporary Sociology* 24 (1995): 344–45; K. Scott Wong, *International Migration Review* 29 (1995): 1069–70. Also see Asian American documents collected by Steve Louie and housed at UCLA, and bibliographies compiled for *Amerasia Journal* containing hundreds of articles from academic journals and newspapers on "contemporary politics and social movement" since the journal began indexing articles by subject in 1986.

2. The Gulf of Tonkin signaled the official involvement of U.S. troops in Vietnam. President Lyndon Johnson and Secretary of Defense Robert McNamara told the American public that the North Vietnamese had attacked American destroyers in the Gulf of Tonkin. Since then, researchers have uncovered evidence that the attack was fictitious. But the U.S. Congress, with unanimous support in the House and only two dissenting votes in the Senate, had already authorized the president to take military action in Southeast Asia as he saw fit, to initiate conflict without a formal declaration of war by Congress. The government immediately deployed American troops into Vietnam and began bombing North Vietnam. On the Vietnam War and the American antiwar movement, see George Herring, *America's Longest War: The United States and Vietnam, 1950–1975* (New York: Wiley, 1979); Marvin E. Gettleman, ed., *Vietnam and America: A Documented History* (New York: Grove Press, 1985); Charles DeBenedetti, *An American Ordeal: The Antiwar Movement of the Vietnam Era* (Syracuse, NY:

Syracuse University Press, 1990); Melvin Small and William Hoover, *Give Peace a Chance: Exploring the Vietnam Antiwar Movement* (Syracuse, NY: Syracuse University Press, 1992); Nancy Zaroulis and Gerald Sullivan, *Who Spoke Up? American Protest against the War in Vietnam, 1963–75* (New York: Doubleday, 1984); Edward Morgan, *The 60s Experience: Hard Lessons about Modern America* (Philadelphia: Temple University Press, 1991); Davis, *Assault on the Left*; Zinn, *People's History*.

3. Zaroulis and Sullivan, *Who Spoke Up?* 76; DeBenedetti, *American Ordeal*, 4–5, 111–22; Gettleman, *Vietnam and America*, 296–300; *Asian Americans for Action* newsletters, October 1969, 1; special issue, "US Imperialism and Pacific Rim," n.d.; March–April 1971, entire issue; June–August 1975, 13–14; Asian Coalition, "Asian Coalition: On White Antiwar Movement," *Gidra*, March 1973, 20; Zinn, *People's History*, 475; Rodolfo Acuña, *Occupied America: A History of Chicanos*, 3rd ed. (New York: HarperCollins, 1988), 345–49.

4. *Gidra*, December 1969, 2, 4, 11; June–July 1970, 7, 18–20; Yuri Kochiyama, speech for the Vietnam Moratorium, Reclamation Site number 1, New York City, October 15, 1969.

5. Kazu's son, Chris Iijima, initiated the idea of a pan-Asian, rather than a Japanese-specific, formation. On Asian American panethnicity, see Yen Le Espiritu, *Asian American Panethnicity: Bridging Institutions and Identities* (Philadelphia: Temple University Press, 1992).

6. The rationale for this decision, Karl Yoneda contends, is that Earl Browder, Communist Party USA general secretary, believed that "the best place for any Japanese fifth columnist to hide is within the Communist Party ranks and consequently no Japanese American should be kept in the Party while the war against Japan in going on." Although always numerically small, the Japanese American Left had grown to such an extent that by the 1930s, 1 in 650 Japanese Americans were in the CPUSA, compared to 1 in 5,000 for the general population. However, Browder-initiated party policies and intense state repression, including deportations of foreign-born Communists, spelled the virtual collapse of the Japanese American Left by the early 1940s as well as the temporary termination of the party itself by the mid-1940s. See Karl Yoneda, *Ganbatte: Sixty-Year Struggle of a Kibei Worker* (Los Angeles: UCLA Asian American Studies Center, 1983); James Oda, *Heroic Struggles of Japanese Americans* (North Hollywood, CA: KNI, 1980); Scott Kurashige, "Transforming Los Angeles: Black and Japanese American Struggles for Racial Equality in the 20th Century" (Ph.D. diss., UCLA, 2000), chapter 6; William Z. Foster, *History of the Communist Party of the United States* (New York: Greenwood Press, 1968), 391–93, 422–38.

7. Sakae Ishihara stated that the all-Nisei Young Democrats in Los Angeles wrote to congressional representatives and city council officials urging them to oppose the forced removal of Japanese Americans (interview with author, June 17, 2003).

8. Information on Asian Americans for Action comes from Kazu Iijima,

"Brief History of AAA and the NY Asian Movement," speech, n.d.; Kazu Iijima, letter to author, February 4, 1999; Glenn Omatsu, "Always a Rebel: An Interview with Kazu Iijima," *Amerasia Journal* 13 (1986–87): 83–84, 89, 91–94; *Asian Americans for Action* newsletters, December 1969, 1; October 1970, 1; February–March 1972, 3; Merilynne Hamano, "The New York Asian Movement," *Gidra*, July 1973, 20–22; Tajiri and Saunders, *Yuri Kochiyama: Passion for Justice* (video, 1993); Wei, *The Asian American Movement*, 25–29.

9. Yuri Kochiyama, interview with author; Kazu Iijima, interview with author, June 21, 1996.

10. Yuri Kochiyama, interview with author; Kazu Iijima, interview with author, June 21, 1996.

11. A photocopied set of *Asian Americans for Action* newsletters is in the possession of the author, courtesy of Kazu Iijima, photocopied by Kofi Taha; Yuri Kochiyama, interview with author.

12. Greg Morozumi, interview with author, October 12, 1998; Richard Aoki, interview with author, November 17, 1999; David Monkawa, conversation with author, December 5, 1996; Nick Nagatani, interview with author, November 17, 1999; Nobuko Miyamoto, interview with Eric Nakamura, *Giant Robot*, 1998, 73; Victor Shibata, interview with author, November 17, 1999; Martin Wong, interview with Lee Lew-Lee, *Giant Robot*, 1998, 67; Steve Yip, interview with author, July 3, 2000.

13. Steve Yip, interview with author, July 3, 2000; Steve Yip, "Thinking about Yuri and the Days Back Then, or More Accurately, There Was Something about Mary," birthday tribute, May 26, 2000; Yuri Kochiyama, "Who Is Rob Williams, and What Is His Relationship to Asians?" *Asian Americans for Action* newsletter, October 1969, 4, 8.

14. Collection of *AAA* newsletters.

15. Yuri Kochiyama, "March on Washington Message," speech, Washington, DC, August 28, 1993; Yuri Kochiyama, guest lecture, Asian American Social Movement class, University of California, Santa Barbara, April 30, 1996. The Los Angeles organization to which Yuri referred is the Van Troi Anti-Imperialist Youth Brigade, which opposed U.S. and Japanese imperialism and corporate interests in Southeast Asia ("Statement from the Van Troi Anti-Imperialist Youth Brigade," *Gidra*, September 1972, 4).

16. Yuri Kochiyama, "What Is Vietnam?" speech, City College of New York, 1969; Eisenhower's speech is reported in W. H. Lawrence, "Indo-China Is Cited," *New York Times*, August 5, 1953; also see Zinn, *People's History*, 462, 465–66.

17. Yuri Kochiyama's speeches: "Imperialism and the Pacific Rim," Union Square, New York, November 14, 1969; "Hiroshima and Nagasaki/Yesterday and Today," Asian American Caucus for Disarmament-Hiroshima/Nagasaki Commemoration, Japanese American Christian Church, New York, August 5, 1984; "Hiroshima Observance," Duffy Square, August 6, 1971; and other Hiroshima–Nagasaki Week speeches in author's possession.

18. Yuri Kochiyama, untitled speech, U.S. Mission to the United Nations, August 6, 1969; Yuri Kochiyama, "US-Japan Security Treaty," *Asian Americans for Action* newsletter, 1970, 1–3; Waldo Bello, "From American Lake to a People's Pacific," in *Let the Good Times Roll: Prostitution and the US Military in Asia,* ed. Saundra Pollock Sturdevant and Brenda Stoltzfus (New York: New Press, 1992), 4–5, 14–16; Saundra Sturdevant, "Okinawa Then and Now," in Sturdevant and Stoltzfus, *Let the Good Times Roll,* 244–48; "Military Violence and Women in Okinawa," NGO Forum on Women, Beijing, 1995, 5–6, 10.

19. *Asian Americans for Action* newsletter articles: Mary [Yuri] Kochiyama, "Hiroshima-Nagasaki Week: Speech by Mrs. Mary Kochiyama at Central Park Rally," October 1969, 3–4; editorial, "Hiroshima Day," July 1969, 1; "US-Japan Security Treaty," 1970, 7–11, 17; "Okinawa Reversion and the Question of Tiao Yu Tai," "Sato Gets It at Home and in Washington," and "Notes on a Talk Session with Makoto Odo, Chairman of Beheiren," December 1969, 2, 7; Tetsu Iwasaki, "Mass Struggle against Reversion of Okinawa—May 15th to Permanent Struggle," April–June 1972, 10; editorial, "May 15th—Reversion of Okinawa Is It True" and "Japan Congress against A and H Bombs Statement on 'Why We Oppose the Okinawa Reversion Agreement,'" February–March 1972, 4. Also, Okinawa Prefecture Council against Atomic Hydrogen Bombs, "Okinawa White Paper," circa 1969.

20. Yuri Kochiyama's speeches: untitled, Hiroshima–Nagasaki Week observance, Central Park Mall, New York, August 8, 1970; "Redress of Japan's War Crimes against Korean Women in World War II," United Nations and march to Japanese Consulate, June 16, 1994; "Rally against Revival of Japanese Militarism," Ralph Bunche Park, United Nations, July 7, 1997; and other speeches in author's possession.

21. On Asian American participation in the ethnic studies strikes at San Francisco State College and UC Berkeley, see Karen Umemoto, "'On Strike!' San Francisco State College Strike, 1968–69: The Role of Asian American Students," *Amerasia Journal* 15 (1989): 3–4, 35–37; Umemoto, "Asian American Students in the San Francisco State College Strike, 1964–1968"; Dong, "Origins and Trajectory of Asian American Political Activism in the San Francisco Bay Area, 1968–1978." On the San Francisco State–UC Berkeley Strike, see William Barlow and Peter Shapiro, *An End to Silence: The San Francisco State College Student Movement of the 60s* (New York: Pegasus, 1971); Dikran Karagueuzian, *Blow It Up! The Black Student Revolt at San Francisco State College and the Emergence of Dr. Hayakawa* (Boston: Gambit, 1971); Robert Smith, Richard Axen, and DeVere Pentony, *By Any Means Necessary: The Revolutionary Struggle at San Francisco State* (San Francisco: Jossey-Bass, 1970); Jason Ferreira, "All Power to the People: A Comparative History of Third World Radicalism in San Francisco, 1968–1974" (Ph.D. diss., University of California, Berkeley, 2003); Stacy Ann Cook, "Power and Resistance: Berkeley's Third World Liberation Front Strikes" (Ed.D. diss., University of San Francisco, 2001); Irum Shiekh, Casey Peek, Vina

Na, and Francisco Nieto, *On Strike: Ethnic Studies 1969–1999* (documentary, circa 1999).

22. "The Asian Students Declaration of Principles," December 1973; Boreysa Tep, Richard K. Wong, and Jean Yonemura, "Asian Studies Manifesto," Asian Student Committee of City College, New York, 1973, in Ho, *Legacy to Liberation*, 408–11; Wei, *The Asian American Movement*, 133–34; R. Takashi Yanagida, "Asian Students vs. the Administration: The Confrontation at CCNY," *Bridge*, 1972, 1, 11–12; Yuri Kochiyama, "For CCNY Asian Studies Rally," May 9, 1974.

23. Yuri Kochiyama, interview with author; Denny Chin, "CCNY Professor Lauds Malcolm X," *Daily Princetonian*, February 22, 1973.

24. "Rally 'Round Projected Asian Community Center!"; *Asian Americans for Action* newsletter, April–June 1972, 12; Bill Kochiyama, "Accent Is on Harmony at Official Opening of Asian Center," *Asian Americans for Action* newsletter, December 1972–January 1973, 5; Iijima, "Brief History of AAA and of the NY Asian Movement"; Wei, *Asian American Movement*, 29.

25. Tommy Kochiyama, interview with author, October 18, 1998; Tommy Kochiyama, letter to author, February 24, 1999; Yuri Kochiyama, letter to author, January 2, 1999; Eddie Kochiyama, interview with author, September 25, 1998; Audee Kochiyama-Holman, letter to author, March 2, 1999; Jimmy Kochiyama, conversation with author, March 3, 1999.

26. Tommy Kochiyama, interview with author, October 18, 1998; Tommy Kochiyama, letter to author, February 24, 1999; Yuri Kochiyama, interview with author.

27. Tommy Kochiyama, interview with author, October 18, 1998.

28. Eddie Kochiyama, interview with author, September 25, 1998; *Asian Americans for Action* newsletter, January–February 1971, 2; "Chickens Come Home to Roost," *Asian Americans for Action* newsletter, October 1970, 2; Jimmy Kochiyama, interview with author, November 29, 1998; Tommy Kochiyama, interview with author, October 18, 1998; Nick Nagatani, interview with author, November 17, 1999.

29. Jimmy Kochiyama, interview with author, November 29, 1998; Tommy Kochiyama, interview with author, October 18, 1998; Sheri Miyashiro, "Yellow Brotherhood," *Gidra*, 1990, 122–23; Nick Nagatani and Victor Shibata, guest lecturer, Asian American Social Movements, UC Santa Barbara, November 17, 1999; Victor Shibata, interview with author, November 17, 1999; Mary Uyematsu, "Yellow Brotherhood," *Gidra*, November 1973; Evelyn Yoshimura, "Basketball and a Whole Lot More," *Rafu Shimpo*, October 21, 1995.

30. Jimmy Kochiyama, interview with author, November 29, 1998; Tommy Kochiyama, interview with author, October 18, 1998; Audee Kochiyama-Holman, letter to author, March 2, 1999; Eddie Kochiyama, interview with author, September 25, 1998; Victor Shibata, interview with author, November 19, 1999; Nick Nagatani, interview with author, November 19, 1999.

31. Yuri Kochiyama, interview with author.

32. Yuri Kochiyama, interview with author; participant observation by author.

33. Tajima-Peña, *My America . . . Or Honk If You Love Buddha* (film, 1998); Renee Tajima, "Site-Seeing through Asian America," in *Mapping Multiculturalism,* ed. Avery Gordon and Chris Newfield (Minneapolis: University of Minnesota Press, 1996), 278; Bibi Angola, conversation with author, November 25, 1998.

34. Nyisha Shakur, interview with author, October 15, 1998; Yuri Kochiyama, interview with author.

35. Greg Morozumi, interview with author, October 12, 1998.

36. Shakur, *Assata: An Autobiography,* 181; Yuri Kochiyama, interview with author.

37. Mutulu Shakur, interview with author, October 19, 1998.

38. Note that both Kazu Iijima and Yuri Kochiyama stated that there was no internal dissension when the youth—mostly Chinese but also several Japanese, including Iijima's son Chris—left to help form I Wor Kuen, as implied by Wei (*The Asian American Movement,* 27–29). Instead, the older Nisei members of AAA encouraged the youth to form their own organizations, and IWK and AAA mutually supported each other's work (Kazu Iijima, interview with author, June 21, 1996; Kazu Iijima, letter to author, February 4, 1999; Yuri Kochiyama, interview with author; various issues of *AAA* newsletter).

39. Nyisha Shakur, interview with author, October 15, 1998; participant observation by author.

40. Mao Tse-tung, "Combat Liberalism," *Selected Works* (Peking: Foreign Language Press, 1971); Yuri Kochiyama, interview with author; participant observation by author.

41. Yuri Kochiyama, interview with author; Diane C. Fujino, "Revolution's from the Heart: The Making of an Asian American Woman Activist, Yuri Kochiyama," in *Dragon Ladies: Asian American Feminists Breathe Fire,* ed. Sonia Shah (Boston: South End Press, 1997), 177–78.

42. On liberal and radical feminism, see Alison M. Jagger, *Feminist Politics and Human Nature* (Totowa, NJ: Rowman and Littlefield, 1983); Steven Buechler, *Women's Movements in the United States* (New Brunswick, NJ: Rutgers University Press, 1990), 85–129; Betty Friedan, *The Feminine Mystique* (New York: Dell, 1963); Mary Daly, *Gyn/Ecology: The Metaethics of Radical Feminism* (Boston: Beacon Press, 1978); Ti-Grace Atkinson, *Amazon Odyssey* (New York: Link Books, 1974), 11, cited in Verta Taylor and Nancy E. Whittier, "Collective Identity in Social Movement Communities: Lesbian Feminist Mobilization," in *Frontiers in Social Movement Theory,* ed. Aldon D. Morris and Carol McClurg Mueller (New Haven, CT: Yale University Press, 1992), 115. On critiques, see bell hooks, *Feminist Theory: From Margin to Center* (Boston: South End Press, 1984), 18; Davis, *Women, Culture and Politics,* 3–34; Patricia Hill Collins, *Black Feminist Thought* (New York: Routledge, 1990), 48–49; Sucheng

Chan, *Asian Americans: An Interpretative History* (Boston: Twayne, 1991), 103–9; Maria Mies, *Patriarchy and Accumulation on a World Scale* (London: Zed, 1986); Barrie Thorne and Marilyn Yalom, eds., *Rethinking the Family: Some Feminist Questions* (Boston: Northeastern University Press, 1992).

43. Combahee River Collective, "A Black Feminist Statement" in *This Bridge Called My Back: Writings by Radical Women of Color,* ed. Cherríe Moraga and Gloria Anzaldúa (New York: Kitchen Table Press, 1981), 211–13. On revolutionary feminism among women of color, see also Asian Women United of California, *Making Waves: An Anthology of Writings by and about Asian American Women* (Boston: Beacon Press, 1989); Asian Women's Journal, *Asian Women* (University of California, Berkeley, 1971); Toni Cade, ed., *The Black Woman: An Anthology* (New York: Penguin Books, 1970); Collins, *Black Feminist Thought*; Martha Cotera, *The Chicana Feminist* (Austin, TX: Information Systems Development, 1977); Davis, *Women, Race and Class*; Davis, *Women, Culture and Politics*. On socialist feminism, see Jagger, *Feminist Politics and Human Nature*; Gloria Martin, *Socialist Feminism: The First Decade, 1966–76* (Seattle, WA: Freedom Socialist Publications, 1978); Engels, *The Origin of the Family, Private Property, and the State*.

44. Yuri Kochiyama, interview with author.

45. Questionnaire, Japanese Americans in the United States: William Masayoshi Kochiyama, February 21, 1975; FBI file on Yuri Kochiyama, New York 100-155496, January 17, 1968; Yuri Kochiyama, interview with author.

46. Yuri Kochiyama, interview with author, July 2, 2000; Nyisha Shakur, interview with author.

47. Yuri Kochiyama, interview with author; Audee Kochiyama-Holman, interview with author, September 27, 1998; Eddie Kochiyama, interview with author, September 25, 1998; Herman Ferguson, interview with author, June 19, 1996; Kazu Iijima, interview with author, June 21, 1996.

48. On the redress movement, see Mitchell T. Maki, Harry H. L. Kitano, and S. Megan Berthold, *Achieving the Impossible Dream* (Urbana: University of Illinois Press, 1999); Takezawa, *Breaking the Silence*; William Minoru Hohri, *Repairing America: An Account of the Movement for Japanese-American Redress* (Pullman: Washington State University Press, 1988); United States Congressional Commission, *Personal Justice Denied: Report of the Commission on Wartime Relocation and Internment of Civilians* (Washington, DC: Civil Liberties Public Education Fund and Seattle: University of Washington Press, 1997); Glen Ikuo Kitayama, "Japanese Americans and the Movement for Redress: A Case Study of Grassroots Activism in the Los Angeles Chapter of the National Coalition for Redress/Reparations" (master's thesis, University of California, Los Angeles, 1993).

49. Kitayama, "Japanese Americans and the Movement for Redress," 11, 28–29; Nisei Progressive platform in Tim Carpenter, "Nisei Progressives: A Link in the Chain of Democratic Social Movements of Twentieth-Century America"

(master's project, California State University, Fullerton, 1998), 30–34; Sak Ishihara, interview with author, June 17, 2003; Kochiyamas, "Editorial: Christmas . . . 10 Years Ago," *Christmas Cheer,* 1951, 2.

50. Raymond Okamura, "Background and History of the Repeal Campaign," *Amerasia Journal* 2 (1974): 74–94; "Infamous Concentration Camp Bill: Title II-Emergency Detention Act," *Asian Americans for Action* newsletter, October 1970, 8; American Committee for Protection of Foreign Born, "Concentration Camps USA, It Has Happened Here, It Could Happen Again . . . to You: The Story of Mrs. Mary Kochiyama," n.d.; Hohri, *Repairing America,* 29–35, 225–26; Kitayama, "Japanese Americans and the Movement for Redress," 21–27; Maki, Kitano, and Berthold, *Achieving the Impossible Dream,* 6, 61–62, 72; Weglyn, *Years of Infamy*; Yuri Kochiyama, interview with author.

51. After the captors released all the Black and most of the female hostages, 52 U.S. hostages remained. "Concerned Japanese Americans: Who We Are," *CJA Update,* January 1983, 1; Leslee Inaba-Wong, interview with author, July 16, 2000; Leslee Inaba-Wong, letters to author, December 1997 and July 2000; Yuri Kochiyama, interviews with author; Leslie T. Hatamiya, *Righting a Wrong: Japanese Americans and the Passage of the Civil Liberties Act of 1988* (Stanford, CA: Stanford University Press, 1993), xi; Hayakawa, cited in Maki, Kitano, and Berthold, *Achieving the Impossible Dream,* 76, 156. On the hostage crisis, see "Teheran Students Seize US Embassy and Hold Hostages," *New York Times,* November 5, 1979; John Kiener, "Iran's Civil Government Out; Hostages Face Death Threat; Oil Exports Believed Halted," *New York Times,* November 7, 1979; Bernard Gwertzman, "Alive, Well and Free," *New York Times,* January 21, 1981; Craig L. Gordon, "US-Iranian Relations and the Hostage Crisis" (downloaded from magic.hofstra.edu/~cgordon1/iranhostage.html); Jonathan Kwitny, *Endless Enemies* (New York: Congdon and Weed, 1984), 179–98.

52. At the first CWRIC hearing in Washington, DC, on July 16, 1981, Sasha Hohri's testimony included an entreaty to add New York as a hearing site; United States Congressional Commission, *Personal Justice Denied,* 1; "Concerned Japanese Americans: Who We Are," *CJA Update,* January 1983, 1, 3; Coalition for a New York Hearing, agenda, September 9, 1981; Leslee Inaba-Wong, document on Japanese American redress and reparation, July 30, 2000; Gwertzman, "Alive, Well and Free"; John Kifner, "Teheran Captors Called Out Insults as the 52 Leave," *New York Times,* January 21, 1981.

53. Leslee Inaba-Wong, interview with author, July 16, 2000; Yuri Kochiyama, interview with author.

54. ECJAR leaflet, circa 1981; ECJAR press release, circa 1981; Leslee Inaba-Wong, document on Japanese American redress and reparation, July 30, 2000.

55. Bill Kochiyama, ECJAR media committee reports, October 8, October 22, November 6, and November 13, 1981; ECJAR leaflet, circa 1981; Leslee Inaba-Wong, document on Japanese American redress and reparation, July 30, 2000; Bill and Yuri Kochiyama, press release, November 7, 1981.

56. Moritsugu "Mo" Nishida, interviewed by Fred Ho, in Ho, *Legacy to Liberation*, 313; Leslee Inaba-Wong, document on Japanese American redress and reparation, July 30, 2000; Leslee Inaba-Wong, interview with author, July 16, 2000; Wayne Lum, conversation with author, September 1999; Steve Yip, conversation with author, September 1999; Yuri Kochiyama, interview with author.

57. Bill Kochiyama, ECJAR media committee reports, October 8 and November 6, 1981; Hohri, *Repairing America*, 44–57; Kitayama, "Japanese Americans and the Movement for Redress," 28–38; Yuri Kochiyama, interview with author; Leslee Inaba-Wong, interview with author, July 16, 2000.

58. Sasha Hohri, letter to Angus McBeth of CWRIC, November 9, 1981; agenda for New York CWRIC public hearing, November 23, 1981; Yuri Kochiyama, interview with author.

59. Leslee Inaba-Wong, interview with author, July 16, 2000; Yuri Kochiyama, interview with author.

60. Bill Kochiyama, testimony at CWRIC hearing, November 23, 1981; Greg Morozumi, interview with author, October 12, 1998; Leslee Inaba-Wong, interview with author, July 16, 2000; agenda for New York CWRIC public hearing, November 23, 1981. For a summary of the New York testimonies, see Hohri, *Repairing America*, 171–83; also CWRIC, *Personal Justice Denied*.

61. Agenda for Washington, DC, CWRIC public hearing, July 16, 1981; Yuri Kochiyama's testimony in Rockwell Chin, "The Long Road: Japanese Americans Move on Redress," *Bridge*, Winter 1981–82, 11–12; Sasha Hohri, testimony, CWRIC hearing, July 16, 1981; Hohri, *Repairing America*, 171–83; Maki, Kitano, and Berthold, *Achieving the Impossible Dream*, 99, 114–16; Spickard, *Japanese Americans*, 154.

62. CWRIC, *Personal Justice Denied*, 18.

63. United States Congressional Commission, *Personal Justice Denied*, 1. On JACL's redress efforts, see Hatamiya, *Righting a Wrong*; Takezawa, *Breaking the Silence*.

64. On NCJAR, see Hohri, *Repairing America*; Takezawa, *Breaking the Silence*.

65. On NCRR, see Kitayama, "Japanese Americans and the Movement for Redress"; also, Kochiyama, "CJA Statement," speech, February 22, 1981; "Concerned Japanese Americans: Who We Are," *CJA Update*, January 1983, 1, 3; Hatamiya, *Righting a Wrong*, 164.

66. The first Day of Remembrance program, sponsored in 1978 by the Seattle JACL and the brainchild of Frank Chin and Frank Abe, was a dramatic reenactment of the local community's displacement to the Puyallup Fairgrounds assembly center. Takezawa, *Breaking the Silence*, 42–45; Kochiyama, "CJA Statement," speech, February 22, 1981; Inaba-Wong, "Chronology of the Day of Remembrance Programs Held in New York," n.d.; programs for the New York Day of Remembrance events; Kitayama, *The Movement for Redress*, 79–83; Maki, Kitano, and Berthold, *Achieving the Impossible Dream*, 172–73;

Monkawa, guest lecturer, Japanese American history class, UC Santa Barbara, June 1, 1995.

67. Hatamiya, *Righting a Wrong*, 90, 147–48; Kitayama, "Japanese Americans and the Movement for Redress," 83–84, 88, 90; Maki, Kitano, and Berthold, *Achieving the Impossible Dream*, 189–97; Takezawa, *Breaking the Silence*, 56.

68. At the urging of the U.S. government, more than two thousand Japanese from Latin America, 80 percent from Peru, had been literally kidnapped off the streets and transported to U.S. concentration camps. In June 1998, a settlement was reached on a class action suit, offering an official apology but reparations of only five thousand dollars, one-quarter of the amount awarded to Japanese Americans ten years earlier and only as long as funds were available from the Civil Liberties Act. While more than six hundred Japanese Latin Americans applied for redress, others rejected this offer and have filed individual lawsuits against the United States. On Japanese Latin Americans, see Weglyn, *Years of Infamy*, 56–66; Takeshi Nakayama, "Bittersweet Victory: Nikkei Latin Americans Are Disappointed $5,000 Settlement Is One-Quarter Amount Given to JA Internees," *Rafu Shimpo*, June 15, 1998; National Coalition for Redress/Reparations, "Settlement Offers Japanese Latin Americans Choice," *Rafu Shimpo*, July 16, 1998. On funding appropriations and other struggles, see Maki, Kitano, and Berthold, *Achieving the Impossible Dream*, 217–25; Hatamiya, *Righting a Wrong*, 181–88; Daniels, *Prisoners without Trial*, 104–5.

69. "A New York Community Redress Celebration," program, November 4, 1988; Day of Remembrance program, New York, March 6, 1993; "Fighting Spirit Awards" presented to Yuri Kochiyama and the late Bill Kochiyama by NCRR, Los Angeles, 1996.

70. Eddie Kochiyama, interview with author, September 25, 1998; Eddie Kochiyama, letter to author, March 5, 1999; Don Broderick, "Mom and Daughter Struck by Taxi on Sidewalk," *New York Post*, November 20, 1989; "Aichi Kochiyama Is Mourned, Daughter Akemi Is Recovering," *New York Nichibei*, November 23, 1989; *New York Yomiuri*, a Japan-based newspaper, covered the story on November 23, 1989.

71. Eddie Kochiyama, "Eulogy for Aichi," *Gidra*, 1990, 116; Yuri Kochiyama, interview; Victor Shibata, interview with author, November 17, 1999.

72. Eddie Kochiyama, "Eulogy for Aichi"; Audee Kochiyama-Holman, interview with author, October 27, 1998.

73. Greg Morozumi, interview with author, October 12, 1998; Audee Kochiyama-Holman, interviews with author, September 27 and October 25, 1998.

74. Eddie Kochiyama, interview with author, September 25, 1998; Audee Kochiyama-Holman, interview with author, October 25, 1998; Yuri Kochiyama, interview with author; Genevieve Hall-Duncan, interview with author, January 17, 2000; Sasha Hohri, "Aichi," *Gidra*, 1990, 117.

75. Renee Tajima, "Site-Seeing through Asian America," 275; Renee Tajima-

Peña, *My America . . . or Honk If You Love Buddha* (film, 1998); Yuri Kochiyama, interview with author.

9. The Most Incessant Activist

1. David W. Chen, "An Inmate's Family of Strangers," *New York Times,* March 28, 1999; David Wong Support Committee (DWSC), "Free David Wong," leaflet; Yuri Kochiyama, interview with author.

2. Yuri Kochiyama, interview with author; DWSC, "Free David Wong" leaflet.

3. Chen, "Inmate's Family of Strangers"; DWSC, "David Wong Needs Your Support," "Free David Wong," and "David Wong Legal Fact Sheet," leaflets; David Wong, letter to Yuri Kochiyama, February 15, 1987; Yuri Kochiyama, interview with author.

4. Allan Parachini, "Murder Case of an Asian Cause Celebre," *Los Angeles Times,* April 30, 1979; "Free Chol Soo Lee," *Activist,* August–December 1978, 4; Chol Soo Lee defense committees, various leaflets; Chen, "Inmate's Family of Strangers"; DWSC, "Free David Wong," leaflet.

5. K. W. Lee, "Lost in a Strange Culture," *Sacramento Union,* January 29, 1978; K. W. Lee, "Alice-in-Chinatown Murder Case," *Sacramento Union,* January 30, 1978; Derrick E. Lim, "Learning from the Past: A Retrospective Look at the Chol Soo Lee Movement" (master's thesis, UCLA, 1985), 32–33, 41–51, 79–98; Yuri Kochiyama, "The Case of Chol Soo Lee . . . and the American Judicial System," *Ethnic Woman* 1 (1980); "Chol Soo Lee Retrial Now in Defense," *New York Nichibei,* August 26, 1982; "Chol Soo Lee Found Not Guilty," *New York Nichibei,* September 16, 1982; Susan Sward, "'True Believer' Figure Hurt," *San Francisco Chronicle,* September 24, 1991; New York Independent Committee to Free Chol Soo Lee, various leaflets. The movie *True Believers* portrays Lee's case, but takes literary liberty in attributing the primary investigative work to a white lawyer, rather than a Korean American journalist.

6. Wayne Lum, interview with author, July 3, 2000; Yuri Kochiyama, interview with author.

7. Yuri Kochiyama, "November 6 Fundraiser Supports David Wong," *New York Nichibei,* October 29, 1992; "'Bridging Gaps' for David Wong," *Asian New Yorker,* April 1994; DWSC, "David Wong Needs Your Support," "Free David Wong," and "David Wong Legal Fact Sheet," leaflets; DWSC, "Meeting with Michael Deutsch, William Kunstler, and Liz Fink," memo, January 6, 1994; agendas of different DWSC meetings; Chen, *New York Times,* March 28, 1999; Yuri Kochiyama, interview with author; participant observation by author; Wayne Lum, interview with author, July 3, 2000; Emily Woo-Yamasaki, interview with author, December 1995.

8. DWSC, "Free David Wong" leaflet; DWSC, agenda, January 22, 1994; Steering Committee Statement: Roles and Responsibilities and Structure, August 18,

1994; Wayne Lum, interview with author, July 3, 2000; Steve Yip, interview with author, July 3, 2000.

9. Wayne Lum, "Supporting US Political Prisoners: Incarceration Under US Capitalism," in Ho, *Legacy to Liberation,* 77–78; Yuri Kochiyama, interview with author.

10. Maggie Ho, quoted in Chen, "Inmate's Family of Strangers"; Wayne Lum, interview with author, July 3, 2000.

11. Excerpts from the Verdict of the International Tribunal on Political Prisoners and Prisoners of War in the United States, in Churchill and Vander Wall, *Cages of Steel,* 403–13; www.thejerichomovement.com; Yu Kikumura, "The Declaration for the Struggle," letter, December 16, 1990; Audee Kochiyama, conversation with author, May 2002; Yuri Kochiyama, conversation with author, May 2002.

12. Robert Hanley, "Suspected Terrorist Convicted in Bomb Case," *New York Times,* November 30, 1988; Yuri Kochiyama, interview with author.

13. Hanley, "Suspected Terrorist Convicted in Bomb Case"; Robert Hanley, "Defendant Gets 30 Years in Jail in Bombing Plot," *New York Times,* February 8, 1989; Richard Esposito and Scott Ladd, "Kikumura in Prison: 'This Is My World,'" *Newsday,* February 24, 1989; Yu Kikumura, "My Brief Biography," open letter, July 26, 1992; Yu Kikumura, "Part I: The Explanation of My Trial," July 26, 1992. Upon appeal, Kikumura's sentence was reduced to twenty-two years and ten months.

14. Yu Kikumura Support Committee (YKSC), "Fact Sheet on the Yu Kikumura Case," circa 1994; Yuri Kochiyama, interview with author.

15. Erica Thompson and Jan Susler, "Supermax Prisons: High-Tech Dungeons and Modern-Day Torture," in *Criminal Injustice: Confronting the Prison Crisis,* ed. Elihu Rosenbaltt (Boston: South End Press, 1996), 305; Amnesty International, "Allegations of Ill-treatment in Marion Prison, IL, USA" (London: Amnesty International, 1987), 15; Bill Dunne, "The U.S. Prison at Marion, Illinois: An Instrument of Oppression," in Churchill and Vander Wall, *Cages of Steel,* 62; Ray Luc Levasseur, "From USP Marion to ADX Florence (And Back Again)," in *The Celling of America,* ed. Daniel Burton-Rose (Monroe, ME: Common Courage Press, 1998), 200–5; S. Michael Yasutake, interview with author, September 2000; Yuri Kochiyama, interview with author; Wayne Lum, interview with author, July 3, 2000; Kikumura, *Can't Jail the Spirit,* 203–6.

16. YKSC, letter to "Political Prisoner Support Groups and Supporters," July 18, 1994; form letter to Warden Michael B. Cooksey protesting the confiscation of Kikumura's materials, July 18, 1994; YKSC, letter to "All Friends and Supporters," August 19, 1994; YKSC, letter to "Dear Friend," September 8, 1995; Kikumura, *Can't Jail the Spirit,* 203–6; Yuri Kochiyama, interview with author.

17. Yu Kikumura, letter to "Dear Comrade," September 3, 2001; S. Michael Yasutake, interview with author, September 2000.

18. *Yu Kikumura v. United States of America,* May 31, 2001; Yu Kikumura,

letter to "Dear Comrade," September 3, 2001; YKSC, "Fact Sheet on the Yu Kikumura Case," circa 1994.

19. Eddie Kochiyama, interview with author, September 25, 1998.

20. "Statement from the Kochiyama Children and Grandchildren," Bill Kochiyama's memorial, October 30, 1993; Abiola Sinclair, "Bill Kochiyama, Human Rights Activist, Dead at 72," *New York Amsterdam News,* November 6, 1993; "Longtime Activist Bill Kochiyama Dead at 72," *Asian New Yorker,* November 1993.

21. Yuri Kochiyama, "Bill Kochiyama—Who Was He?" statement at Bill Kochiyama's memorial, October 30, 1993; Kazu Iijima, interview with author, June 21, 1996; Kwame Ture, letter to Yuri Kochiyama, November 15, 1993. Exactly five years after writing this letter, on November 15, 1998, Kwame Ture died in Guinea, Africa.

22. Edward Lin, "Bill Kochiyama, 72, a Gentle Fighter for People of Color," copy of newspaper article, source unknown, courtesy of Yuri Kochiyama; East Coast Asian Student Union, "A Dedication/Candlelight Vigil to William Masayoshi Kochiyama," program, February 26, 1994; Yuri Kochiyama, letter to her family, February 15, 1994; Karleen Chinen, "'Aloha' to Bill Kochiyama," *Hawaii Herald,* November 5, 1993; Wendy Lin, "Bill Kochiyama, WWII Vet, Civil-Rights Activist, at 72," obituary, *Newsday,* October 26, 1993; Sinclair, "Bill Kochiyama"; "Community Activist William Kochiyama Dies," *San Francisco Hokkubei Mainichi,* October 27, 1993; "Longtime Activist Bill Kochiyama Dead at 72," *Asian New Yorker,* November 1993; "William Kochiyama, Activist in Asian American Comm., Dies," *New York Nichibei Times,* October 27, 1993.

23. Eddie Kochiyama, interview with author, September 25, 1998; Audee Kochiyama-Holman, interview with author, September 27, 1998.

24. Elizabeth Nakahara, interview with author, February 27, 2000.

25. Wayne Lum, interview with author, July 3, 2000; Elizabeth Nakahara, interview with author, February 27, 2000; Steve Yip, interview with author, July 3, 2000.

26. Audee Kochiyama-Holman, interview with author, September 27, 1998.

27. Eddie Kochiyama, interview with author, September 25, 1998; Eddie Kochiyama, letter to author, March 30, 1999; Eddie Kochiyama, letter to Yuri, February 23, 1994; International Emergency Committee to Defend the Life of Dr. Abimael Guzmán (IEC), "The International Campaign to Defend the Life of Dr. Abimael Guzman," booklet, September 1993, 4; Steve Yip, interview with author, July 3, 2000; Steve Yip, letter to author, July 31, 2000; Yuri Kochiyama, interview with author, July 31, 2000; Greg Morozumi, interview with author, October 12, 1998.

28. Yuri Kochiyama, letter to her family, February 15, 1994; Eddie Kochiyama, letter to Yuri, February 23, 1994.

29. Richard Clutterbuck, *Drugs, Crime and Corruption* (New York: New York University Press, 1995), 28–36; Peter A. Stern, *Sendero Luminoso: An*

Annotated Bibliography of the Shining Path Guerrilla Movement, 1980–1993 (New Mexico: SALALM, 1995), xvi–xvii; Yuri Kochiyama, "Eyewitness in Peru: A Learning Experience of People in Struggle," speech, St. Mary's Episcopal Church, New York, April 23, 1993; IEC, booklet, September 1993, 6, 22–23; Erlinder and Weinglass, quoted in IEC, booklet, September 1993, 23.

30. IEC, booklet, September 1993, 6; Weinglass, quoted in IEC, booklet, September 1993, 6.

31. Yuri Kochiyama, "Eyewitness in Peru" Yuri Kochiyama, interview with author; Phil Farnham of the Revolutionary Communist Party, letter, August 1992. On the Shining Path, see David Scott Palmer, ed., *Shining Path of Peru* (New York: St. Martin's Press, 1992); Michael L. Smith, "Taking the High Ground: Shining Path and the Andes," in Palmer, *Shining Path of Peru*, 23–24; Cynthia McClintock, *Revolutionary Movements in Latin America: El Salvador's FMLN and Peru's Shining Path* (Washington, DC: United States Institute of Peace Press, 1998); Cynthia McClintock, "Peru's Sendero Luminoso Rebellion: Origins and Trajectory," in *Power and Popular Protest,* ed. Susan Eckstein (Berkeley and Los Angeles: University of California Press, 1989), 61–101; Martin Koppel, "Peru's Shining Path: Anatomy of a Reactionary Sect" (pamphlet, New York: Pathfinder, 1993); Heriberto Ocasio, "Why the People's War in Peru Is Justified and Why It Is the Road to Liberation," speech, May 1995, obtained from www.csrp.org; Committee to Support the Revolution in Peru, Fact Sheet number 3, "Why Peru's People Need a Revolution," from www.csrp.org; "Peru: The Road of Liberation," *Revolutionary Worker,* February 9, 1997; Stern, *Sendero Luminoso.* On conditions in Peru, see Orin Starn, Carlos Ivan Degregori, and Robin Kirk, ed., *The Peru Reader* (Durham, NC: Duke University Press, 1995); Michael Reid, *Peru: Paths to Poverty* (London: Latin American Bureau, 1985); James D. Rudolph, *Peru: The Evolution of a Crisis* (Westport, CT: Praeger, 1992).

32. In a speech on Peru, Yuri read from the U.S. Declaration of Independence: "Whenever any form of government becomes destructive of these ends [i.e., life, liberty, and the pursuit of happiness], it is the right of the people to alter or abolish it, and to institute new government, laying its foundation on such principles and organizing its powers in such form, as to them shall seem most likely to effect their safety and happiness." Yuri Kochiyama, "Eyewitness in Peru"; Yuri Kochiyama, letter to "PP/POWs in the U.S.," May 2, 1993; Yuri Kochiyama, interview with author. When asked about Sendero's indiscriminate use of violence, Yuri's answer was equally vague.

33. IEC, booklet, September 1993, 22–26; IEC, "4th IEC Delegation to Peru Completes Successful Mission" and "Findings of the 4th Delegation," *Emergency Bulletin* 28, April 9, 1993; Yuri Kochiyama, interview with author.

34. Yuri Kochiyama, "The IEC's Tour of Philippines and Japan: Why?" speech, New York University Law School, April 13, 1994; Yuri Kochiyama, "Eyewitness

in Peru"; IEC, "4th IEC Delegation to Peru Completes Successful Mission" and "Findings of the 4th Delegation"; Reid, *Peru: Paths to Poverty,* 99.

35. IEC, "Defend the Life of Abimael Guzmán," *VOICE,* January 12, 1993, 19; IEC, leaflet, circa late 1994; Phil Farnham, letter to London and San Francisco IEC, February 8, 1994; Steve Yip, interview with author, July 3, 2000.

36. Amado Guerrero, *Philippine Society and Revolution* (1970; reprint, Hayward, CA: Philippine Information Network Service, 1996), 6, 55–97; Jose Maria Sison, *The Philippine Revolution: The Leader's View* (New York: Crane Russak, 1989), 21–23, 76–81, 173–74; Jose Maria Sison, "The Peruvian and Philippine Revolutions," speech, IEC Founding Conference, Germany, February 27–28, 1993; BAYAN, leaflet, circa 1994; "Peru: The Road of Liberation," *Revolutionary Worker,* February 9, 1997; Yuri Kochiyama, "The IEC's Tour of Philippines and Japan: Why?" speech; "Yuri Kochiyama: With Justice in Her Heart," *Revolutionary Worker,* December 13, 1998, 15; Yuri Kochiyama, letter to her family, February 15, 1994.

37. Yuri Kochiyama, letter to "PP/POWs in the U.S.," May 2, 1993.

38. "Yuri Kochiyama: With Justice in Her Heart," reprinted in Fred Ho, *Legacy to Liberation,* 276. On Abu-Jamal's essays and commentaries, see his three books—*Live from Death Row* (Reading, MA: Addison-Wesley, 1995); *Death Blossoms: Reflections from a Prisoner of Conscience* (Farmington, PA: Plough Publishing House, 1997); *All Things Censored* (New York: Seven Stories Press, 2000)—and at www.mumia.org and www.prisonradio.org/mumia.

39. On MOVE, see Margot Harry, *"Attention, MOVE! This Is America!"* (Chicago: Banner Press, 1987); Martin Smith, *The Bombing of West Philly* (documentary, 1987); Benjamin Garry and Ryan McKenna, *MOVE* (documentary, 2003); Move, "25 Years on the MOVE," 1996, pamphlet; biographies of MOVE 9 and Mumia Abu-Jamal in *Can't Jail the Spirit,* 41–43, 47–71.

40. On Abu-Jamal, see Terry Bisson, *On a Move: The Story of Mumia Abu-Jamal* (Canada: Litmus Books, 2001); Mumia Abu-Jamal, *We Want Freedom: A Life in the Black Panther Party* (Cambridge, MA: South End Press, 2004); S. E. Anderson and Tony Medina, eds., *In Defense of Mumia* (New York: Writers and Readers Publishing, 1996). On Abu-Jamal's case, see Leonard Weinglass, *Race for Justice* (Monroe, ME: Common Courage Press, 1995); Daniel R. Williams, *Executing Justice: An Inside Account of the Case of Mumia Abu-Jamal* (New York: St. Martin's Press, 2001); John Edington, *A Date with Death* (video, 1995); C. Clark Kissinger, "Justice Denied: Analysis of the Pennsylvania Supreme Court Decision on Mumia Abu-Jamal," pamphlet, November 5, 1998; www.mumia.org; www.freemumia.org; www.mumia2000.org; www.refuseandresist.org; www.fremumia.com.

41. "Yuri Kochiyama: With Justice in Her Heart"; Don Terry, "Black Journalist Granted Stay of Execution by the Judge Who Sentences Him," *New York Times,* August 8, 1995; Kissinger, "Justice Denied."

42. In late 1998, the Pennsylvania Supreme Court, composed largely of judges endorsed by the Fraternal Order of Police, denied Abu-Jamal's appeal for a new trial, and Gov. Tom Ridge reinstated the death warrant against Abu-Jamal. See Mumia Abu-Jamal, "A Statement from Death Row," e-mail, October 31, 1998, at www.refuseandresist.org/mumia/1998/103198mumia.html; Kissinger, "Justice Denied"; various e-mails regarding "Mumia Abu-Jamal's appeal denied" and "demonstrations"; International People's Tribunal for Justice for Mumia Abu-Jamal, program, December 6, 1997, and different leaflets; Shelley Ettinger, "People's Tribunal Verdict: Free Mumia," *Workers World,* December 18, 1997, 1, 6–7.

43. Asians for Mumia, brochure, circa 1999; Candy Kit Har Chan, "APAs March for Mumia," *Asian Week,* August 11, 1995; Wayne Lum, interview with author, July 3, 2000; Wayne Lum, "Supporting US Political Prisoners," 79; Diane C. Fujino, "Yuri Kochiyama: Unending Dedication to Political Prisoners," *Rafu Shimpo,* April 2, 1998.

44. Tajiri and Saunders, *Yuri Kochiyama: A Passion for Justice* (video, 1993); Yuri Kochiyama, *Passing It On*; Nakazawa, *Yuri*; Malcolm Kao, "Center Acquires Yuri Kochiyama Collection," *Crosscurrents,* newsmagazine of the UCLA Asian American Studies Center, spring–summer 1998, 3; Don Nakanishi, "Yuri Kochiyama Donates Archives to UCLA," e-mail, June 4, 1998; Marjorie Lee, conversations with author, spring 1998; Russell Leong, conversation with author, fall 1998; Yuri Kochiyama, interview with author; Audee Kochiyama-Holman, conversation with author, August 14, 2001; Greg Morozumi, conversation with author, March 29, 1999; participant observation by author.

45. The majority of Yuri's speeches were obtained from the Yuri Kochiyama collection at UCLA, courtesy of Marjorie Lee of UCLA's Asian American Studies Reading Room; others, particularly speeches from the 1960s and 1970s, were obtained from Yuri Kochiyama; participant observations by author; Yuri Kochiyama, interview with author.

46. Yuri has given this speech on numerous occasions, including Oberlin College, February 17, 1995; the Museum of Tolerance in Los Angeles, February 26, 1995, organized by UCLA's Asian American organizations; Purdue University, April 18, 1995; University of Oregon, May 17, 1995; Harvard University, February 17, 1996; Columbia University, February 27, 1997; Brecht Forum in New York, June 18, 1997. A condensed version was published in *Shades of Power: Newsletter of the Institute for Multi-Racial Justice,* spring 1998. On Asian-African political connections, see Vijay Prashad, *Everybody Was Kung Fu Fighting: Afro-Asian Connections and the Myth of Cultural Purity* (Boston: Beacon Press, 2001); Gary Okihiro, *Margins and Mainstreams: Asians in American History and Culture* (Seattle: University of Washington Press, 1994), 38–39; Ho and Mullen, *AFRO/ASIA*; Kelley, *Freedom Dreams,* 60–109; Gallicchio, *The African American Encounter with Japan and China*; "The Afro-Asian Century," ed. Andrew F. Jones and Nikhil Pal Singh, special issue, *positions: east asia cultural*

critiques 11 (2003). On Sen Katayama and Claude McKay, see Hyman Kublin, *Asian Revolutionary: The Life of Sen Katayama* (Princeton, NJ: Princeton University Press, 1964); Karl G. Yoneda, "The Heritage of Sen Katayama," *Political Affairs,* 1975, reprinted as pamphlet; Karl G. Yoneda, *Ganbatte: Sixty-Year Struggle of a Kibei Worker* (Los Angeles: UCLA Asian American Studies Center, 1983), 15, 66, 214; Mark Naison, *Communists in Harlem during the Depression* (New York: Grove Press, 1983), 171, 271.

47. *Discover Your Mission: Selected Speeches and Writings of Yuri Kochiyama* (Los Angeles: UCLA Asian American Studies Center Reading Room/ Library, 1998).

48. Fujino, "Yuri Kochiyama: Unending Dedication to Political Prisoners"; Akemi Kochiyama-Ladson, "An Activist Life: 15 Minutes with Yuri Kochiyama," *A. Magazine,* 33–34; participant observations by author.

49. Yuri Kochiyama, interview with author, echoing statements she made in Tajiri and Saunders, *Yuri Kochiyama: A Passion for Justice* (video, 1993) and "Because Movement Work Is Contagious: Reflections of Yuri Kochiyama as told to Sasha Hohri," *Gidra,* 1990, 6, 10.

Epilogue

1. For a geographic analysis of Yuri's development, see Fujino, "Race, Place, and Political Development."

2. Yuri Kochiyama, conversations with author; Audee Kochiyama-Holman, conversations with author, 1997–98; participant observations by author.

3. Yuri Kochiyama, letter to author, April 26, 1999; Yuri Kochiyama, conversations with author, spring–fall 1999; Audee Kochiyama-Holman, conversations with author, spring–fall 1999; Greg Morozumi, conversation with author, November 1999.

4. Audee Kochiyama-Holman, conversations with author, June 16 and July 9, 1999; Yuri Kochiyama, conversation with author, August 3, 2000; Man-Chui Leung, conversation with author, April 1999.

5. Audee Kochiyama-Holman, conversation with author, September 7, 1999; Yuri Kochiyama, conversations with author, fall 2000; Yuri Kochiyama, group letter to friends, September 19, 1999, courtesy of Mo Nishida; Laura Whitehorn, conversation with author, September 1999; Hector Tobar, "Puerto Ricans Hail Activists as Patriots," *Los Angeles Times,* September 12, 1999.

6. Audee Kochiyama-Holman, conversations with author, 1999–2000; Greg Morozumi, conversation with author, November 1999; Wayne Lum, conversation with author, late 1999; Yuri Kochiyama, conversations with author; participant observations by author.

7. Yuri Kochiyama, conversations with author; participant observations by author.

8. Yuri Kochiyama, conversations with author; participant observations by author; Audee Kochiyama-Holman, conversations with author, 1999–2000.

9. In New York, Yuri's adult grandchildren have two children each: Audee's son, Zulu, and his wife, Masai (Glushanok), have Kai and Kenji, and Aichi's daughter, Akemi, and her husband, Marc Sardinha, have Leilani and Malia.

10. Peter Nakahara passed away on November 28, 2003; funeral program for Peter Nakahara; Elizabeth Nakahara, note to author, January 7, 2004.

11. Audee Kochiyama-Holman, conversations with author; Yuri Kochiyama, group letter, June 2000; Elizabeth Nakahara, conversation with author, June 2000; Yuri Kochiyama, conversations with author; participant observations by author.

12. Various leaflets; Linda Evans, conversations with author, 2000–2001; Richard Aoki, conversations with author, 2001–2004; Wayne Lum, conversation with author, May 2001; Yuri Kochiyama, conversations with author; participant observations by author.

13. David Wong Support Committee, "Free David Wong," leaflet, circa 2001; Kochiyama, note to author, May 5, 2000; Yuri Kochiyama, conversations with author. On Wen Ho Lee, see Wen Ho Lee, with Helen Zia, *My Country versus Me: The First-Hand Account by the Los Alamos Scientist Who Was Falsely Accused of Being a Spy* (New York: Hyperion, 2001); Helen Zia, *Asian American Dreams: The Emergence of an American People* (New York: Farrar, Straus and Giroux, 2000), 309; Frank H. Wu, *Yellow: Race in America beyond Black and White* (New York: Basic Books, 2002), 176–90; George Koo, "Deutsch Is Sorry; Lee Is in Jail," *San Francisco Examiner*, February 8, 2000; Clarence Page, "Lee Case Shows Fear Is the Worst Enemy," *Riverside Press-Enterprise*, September 14, 2000; Walter Pincus, "Lee Disputes Classification of Weapons Data," *Washington Post*, April 20, 2000; Robert Sheer, "Case against Lee Is Flying Out Window," *Los Angeles Times*, April 18, 2000; Ling-Chi Wang, keynote address at Asian American Faculty and Staff Association banquet, University of California at Santa Barbara, May 21, 2002.

14. Josina Morita, interview with Yuri Kochiyama, *War Times*, August 2002, 5; Not In Our Name campaign, letter to Japanese American community, September 16, 2002, endorsed by Yuri Kochiyama; Yuri Kochiyama, conversations with author, 2001–2; Richard Aoki, conversations with author, 2001–2002.

15. Yuri Kochiyama, "Truth and Resistance about the 'War on Terrorism,'" speech, University of California, Santa Barbara, May 22, 2002; Josina Morita, interview with Yuri Kochiyama, *War Times*, August 2002, 5; Yuri Kochiyama, conversations with author, 2001–2004; Richard Aoki, conversations with author, 2001–2004; Warrior Woman, conversation with author, November 2002; Zinn, *People's History*, 489–92.

Index

Abe, Frank, 367n.66
Abu-Jamal, Mumia, 282, 291, 296–300, 373n.42
accommodationism: Japanese American adoption of, 46–47, 325n.21
Acoli, Sundiata (Clark Squire), 231
Adams, Henry, 187
Adkins, Homer, 57
Afoh, Kwame, 294
Africa, Ramona, 297
African: defined, xxxiii
African-American: defined, xxxiii
African-Asian interaction: Kochiyama's focus on, 301–3
African Blood Brotherhood, 343n.1
Ahmad, Muhammad (Max Stanford), 181, 185, 196, 348n.51; Black nationalism and, 147, 170, 177, 347n.31; FBI investigation of, 199–200; meeting with Kochiyama, 163–64; Revolutionary Action Movement and, 162–64
Akamatsu, Rev. Alfred, 79–80
Akinwole, Bolanile, 181, 183, 196–97
Alien Enemy Control Board, 314n.10

Alien Land Laws, 25
Alito, Samuel, 282
All-African People's Party (APP), 176–77, 194, 347n.31
All-African People's Revolutionary Party (A–APRP), 347n.31, 349n.52
All Power to the People (documentary), 300
American Civil Liberties Union (ACLU): lack of support for Japanese Americans, 2–3
American Friends Service Committee, 3, 108
American Legion: anti-Japanese attitudes of, 2
American Negro Slave Revolts (Apthekar), 151
Amnesty International, 283
Ampo, Felicimo, 29–30
Angola, Bibi, 219, 224, 251, 355n.28
antiwar movement: growth of, 234–38; Kochiyama's involvement with, 130, 142, 241–42, 310–11. *See also* Vietnam War: opposition to
Anzai, Gus, 111

377

Diane C. Fujino is associate professor of Asian American studies at the University of California, Santa Barbara.